RICKY ROUSE HAS A GUN
离老鼠有枪

First published in 2014
by SelfMadeHero
139–141 Pancras Road
London NW1 1UN
www.selfmadehero.com

Created and Written by: Jörg Tittel
Illustrated by: John Aggs
Cover Art by: William "xiaobaosg" Chua
Cover Design by: Jeff Willis
Chinese Translation by: Haina Jin

© 2014 Fengxian Amusements Limited

Publishing Assistant: Guillaume Rater
Editorial and Production Manager: Lizzie Kaye
Sales and Marketing Manager: Sam Humphrey
Publishing Director: Emma Hayley
With thanks to: Dan Lockwood

A CIP record for this book is available from the British Library

ISBN: 978-1-906838-82-9

10 9 8 7 6 5 4 3 2 1

Printed and bound in China

RICKY ROUSE HAS A GUN
离老鼠有枪

JÖRG TITTEL   JOHN AGGS

文字   绘画

FOREWORD
前言

I've never liked Mickey Mouse. Actually, I should qualify that – I've never liked the Mickey Mouse I grew up with in the 1970s. When I was much older, I found out that the early Mickey – the character that debuted in the 1928 cartoon *Steamboat Willie* and early cartoon talkies of the 1930s and '40s – was a different animal. The early Mickey was a working-class trickster with an anti-authoritarian streak. But by the time I tuned in, Mickey had settled down into the blandly friendly and utterly anodyne character that he is today. I can't say that I hated him. He wasn't interesting enough to hate. But the fact that so many Americans found Mickey compelling simply mystified me. I could not understand how anyone would prefer boring, conformist Mickey to the wily and subversive Bugs Bunny, or the dimwitted but delightfully self-destructive Daffy Duck.

I'm not alone in disliking Mickey Mouse. In particular, within the fraternity of cartoonists, many have reviled Mickey as a crushing bore and corporate shill. Back in 1955, *Mad Magazine* did a feature called "Mickey Rodent", in which a malevolent (and much more interesting) version of Mickey plots to jail the more popular "Darnold" Duck. Ed "Big Daddy" Roth, one of the grandfathers of the 1960s Kustom Kulture movement of automobile hot-rodders, launched a cartoon character named "Rat Fink" as an antihero reflection of Mickey Mouse. And more recently, Mickey has appeared in both *The Simpsons Movie*, where Bart puts a black bra on his head to imitate Mickey's ears and exclaims "I'm the mascot of an evil corporation!", and in an episode of *South Park*, where Mickey is depicted as the money-crazed, foul-mouthed CEO of The Walt Disney Company.

Perhaps the most wide-ranging attack on the banality of Mickey Mouse was launched in 1971 by a group of underground cartoonists calling themselves the "Air Pirates". In a comic titled "Air Pirates Funnies", the cartoonists depicted Mickey and Minnie Mouse having sex and using drugs. In return, Disney sued the Air Pirates for copyright infringement – and won.

The ruling against the Air Pirates was a horrible mistake, both legally and in terms of what's good for our culture. But over the years the law has evolved. In the United States at least, it has become increasingly clear in the decades since the Air Pirates lawsuit that parodies – which are surely what the Air Pirates Funnies were – are protected by the First Amendment against copyright lawsuits that aim to suppress them. So if the Air Pirate Funnies case were litigated again now, Disney would very likely lose and be obliged to stand by as Mickey finally receives the kicking he deserves. But that hasn't happened yet. Well — I'll amend that. It's starting to happen, and this comic book is part of that.

The story of *Ricky Rouse Has a Gun* is mostly about one man's quest to deal with the personal emotional fallout of war, to re-establish his relationship with his young daughter, and to find love after the failure of his marriage. But *Ricky Rouse* is also about the meaning of Mickey Mouse as refracted through the lens of a very different culture from the one in which he originated. In the comic, a mouse that looks at least something like Mickey is employed as the official mascot for a Chinese theme park that looks a lot like the Disney theme parks. In this respect, *Ricky Rouse* touches on the Chinese practice of shanzhai, in which foreign cultural icons are imitated but also indigenized — for example, fake Apple iPhones sold as "hiphones", fake KFC restaurants billed as "KFG", and Adidas sneakers masquerading as Adidas. Shanzhai involves a lot of intellectual property violations, but it's not simply that. It's also a form of cultural expression in China that enjoys great popularity and growing acceptability. And it's a vehicle for the assertion of Chinese nationalism and resistance to the ubiquity of foreign culture.

Shanzhai appropriates foreign culture by copying it. But it also demonstrates the ingenuity of the Chinese people, and more than a bit of nose-thumbing at the foreign brands that dominate the Chinese market. You can see this in *Ricky Rouse*, for example, in the scene in which the owner of the Chinese Disney knock-off amusement park, Hucheng, introduces the protagonist, Richard Rouse, to his namesake, Ricky Rouse — a giant costume of a mouse that bears a more than passing resemblance to Disney's famous rodent. Hucheng wants to hire Richard to dress up in the Ricky Rouse mascot costume. Richard isn't initially enthused:

> **Hucheng:** Richard, meet Ricky. Ricky Rouse.
> **Rouse:** You mean Ricky . . . Mouse?
> **Hucheng:** No, it's Rouse. Ricky Rouse. Like you.
> **Rouse:** That's uh, I'm very flattered, but people will ask. I mean, what's a "Rouse"?
> **Hucheng:** What is a Parker? It is his family name. Like John Smith, or Peter Parker. Also, this way we don't confuse people.
> **Rouse:** With all due respect, he's still a bit of a... rip off, don't you think?
> **Hucheng:** Rip off?! I tell you what is a rip off! For Hollywood to make and remake the same movie ten times every year. Remake here, sequel there, like the public has amnesia. Charging five dollars more each time just for 3D. That is a rip off. That is piracy. That is a crime. This is Ricky Rouse. Built on the past, designed for the future. A Chinese original. And don't let anyone tell you different.

This scene portrays something true about the Chinese practice of shanzhai – while Ricky Rouse is recognizably an imitation of Mickey Mouse, Hucheng insists that he's distinctively Chinese. Shanzhai represents a refusal of some Chinese to simply be assimilated by Western culture. But the refusal doesn't come as a rejection of Western culture. Rather, it comes as an embrace. One so tight that it insists not just on beholding the icon, but on the power to absorb, transform, and *own* it.

Western owners of intellectual property view this very simply – it's theft. But the matter is not that simple. The Disney Company wants to control some part of our culture. That's their business. And they've succeeded: even if you don't choose to see Disney's movies (many of which, including *Cinderella*, *The Little Mermaid*, *Pinocchio*, *Snow White*, *Sleeping Beauty*, and *The Jungle Book*, are based on stories that are in the public domain), the ways in which their iconic creations shape the culture means that every American – and now every Chinese person – must either reckon with the meaning of Mickey Mouse or risk cultural illiteracy. In short, Mickey Mouse is a contributor to our culture (maybe not a very good one) – but he's also an imposition. None of us asked The Walt Disney Company for Mickey Mouse. Nor did we ask to have the values he represents pushed upon us for Disney's benefit. One can see the same tension in America in feminist resistance to the impossible anatomy of the Disney "princesses" (huge eyes, narrow chins, tiny waists and feet, etc.). In this case, feminism gives us a lens that allows us easily to see that the Disney princesses aren't just property, but ideology, and a toxic ideology at that. The Chinese reaction to Western cultural icons like Mickey Mouse is not the same as this – it's more embrace and co-optation than rejection – but it shares the underlying feature of resistance to cultural domination. And in a very odd way, that is also a theme of *Ricky Rouse*.

I refer to the bloody ending of the comic. I'm not going to ruin it for you, but I will say that a lot of what drives *Ricky Rouse* is the tension between Westerners who expect China to simply take what we give them and be grateful, and Chinese entrepreneurs who have very different ideas about who owns culture and what can be done with it. This isn't to say that one side is right, and the other wrong. Both have valid claims, and both also fail to see the limits of those claims. I'm being oblique so as not to give away the plot, but when you reach the end, I hope you'll see what I mean.

In any event, *Ricky Rouse* is a great read. Enjoy the action. And also the parable.

Chris Sprigman is a professor at the New York University School of Law, and Co-Director of the Engelberg Center on Innovation Law and Policy. With Kal Raustiala, he co-authored *The Knockoff Economy: How Imitation Sparks Innovation* (Oxford University Press).

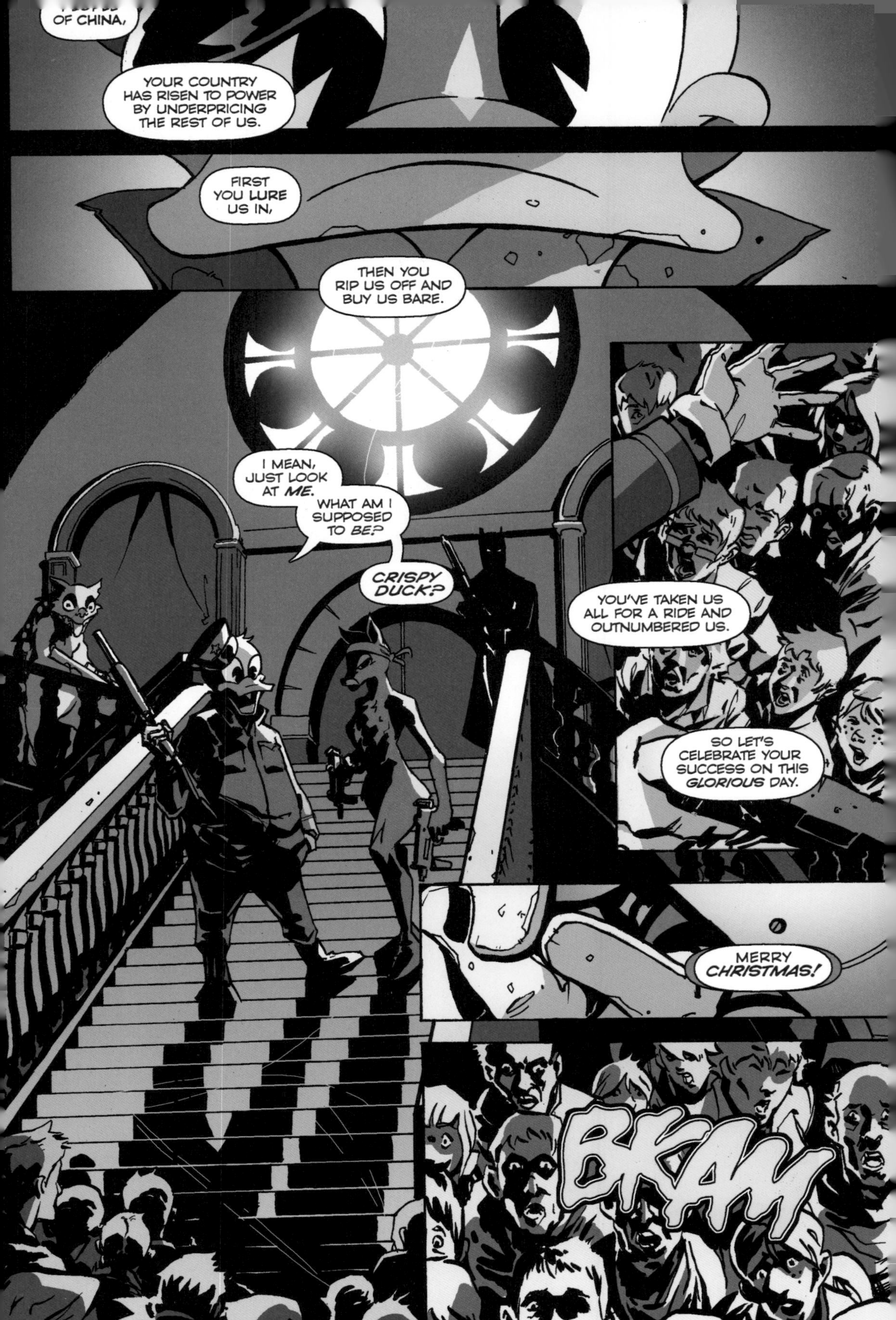
OF CHINA,
YOUR COUNTRY HAS RISEN TO POWER BY UNDERPRICING THE REST OF US.
FIRST YOU LURE US IN,
THEN YOU RIP US OFF AND BUY US BARE.
I MEAN, JUST LOOK AT *ME*.
WHAT AM I SUPPOSED TO *BE*?
CRISPY DUCK?
YOU'VE TAKEN US ALL FOR A RIDE AND OUTNUMBERED US.
SO LET'S CELEBRATE YOUR SUCCESS ON THIS *GLORIOUS* DAY.
MERRY *CHRISTMAS!*
BKAM

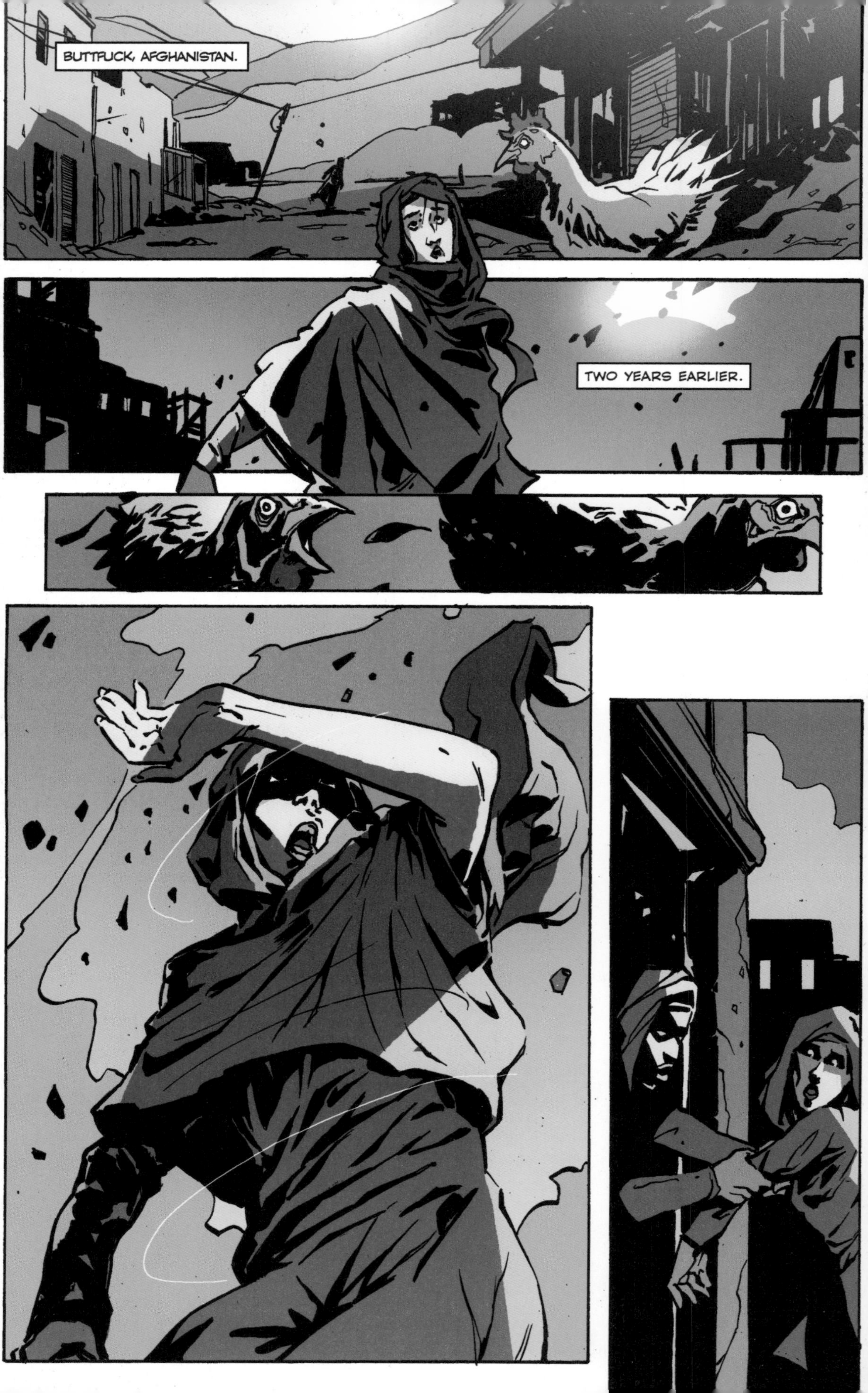
BUTTFUCK, AFGHANISTAN.
TWO YEARS EARLIER.

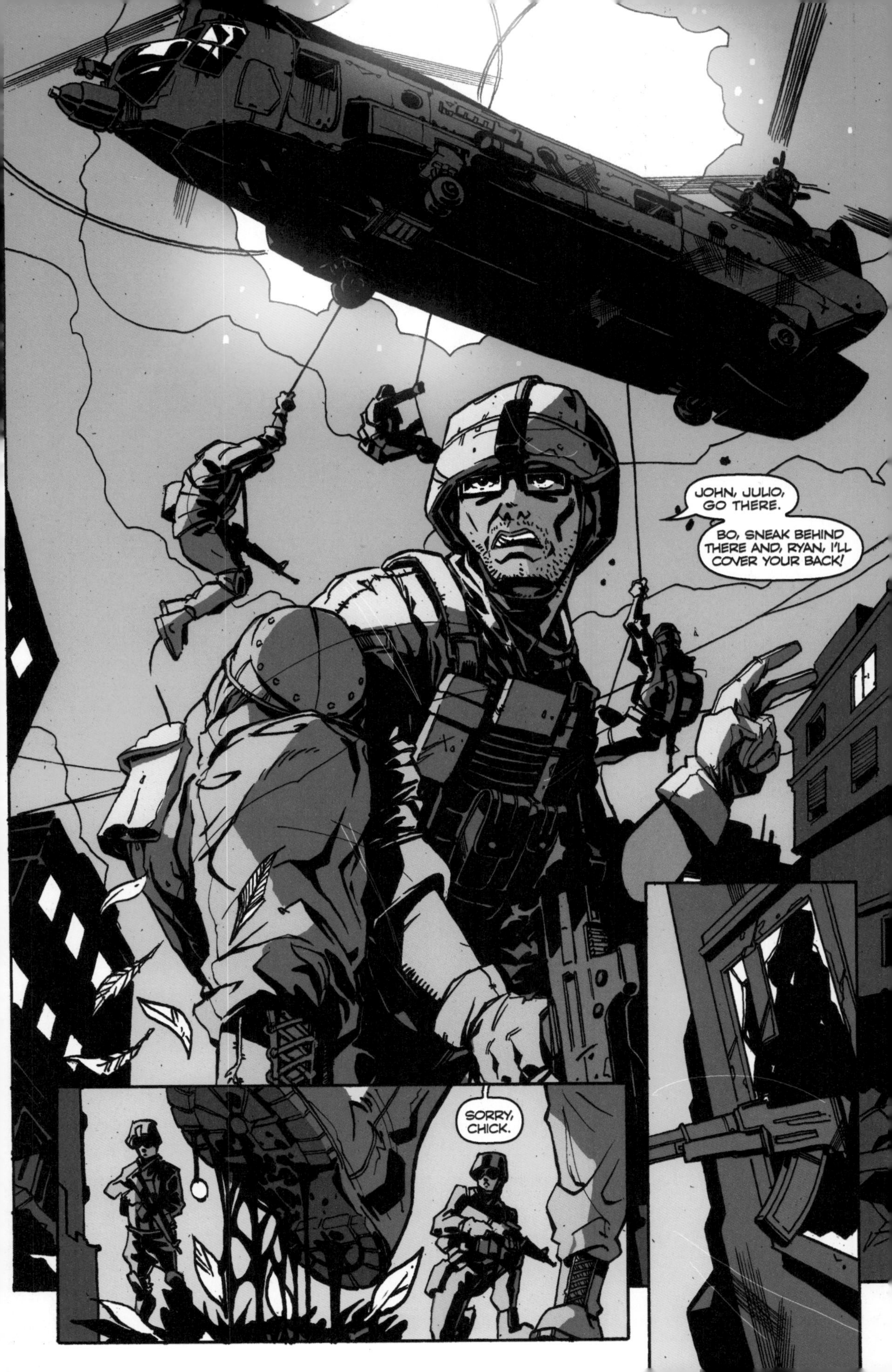
JOHN, JULIO, GO THERE.
BO, SNEAK BEHIND THERE AND, RYAN, I'LL COVER YOUR BACK!
SORRY, CHICK.

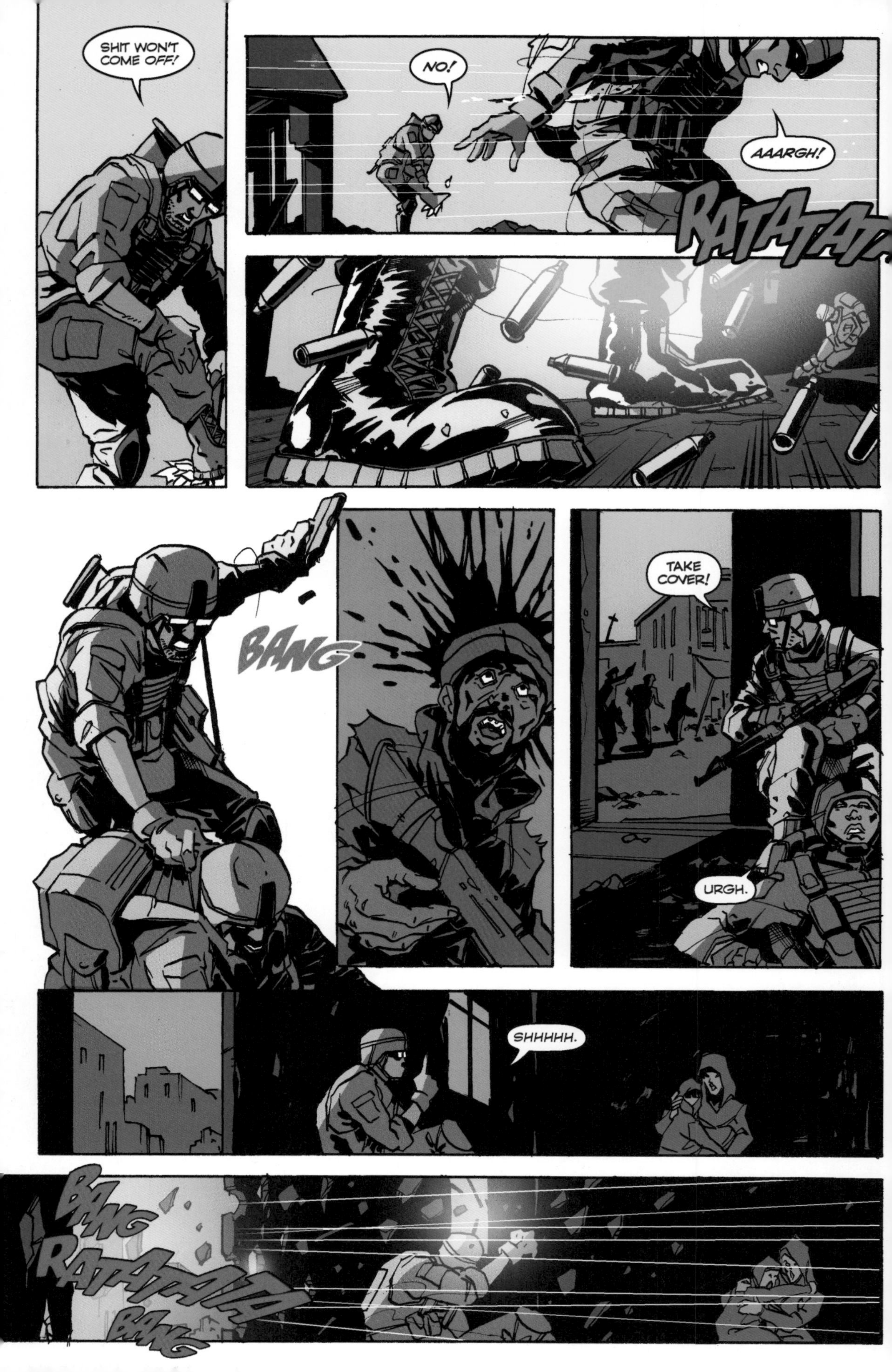
SHIT WON'T COME OFF!
NO!
AAARGH!
RATATATA
BANG
TAKE COVER!
URGH.
SHHHHH.
BANG
RATATATATA
BANG

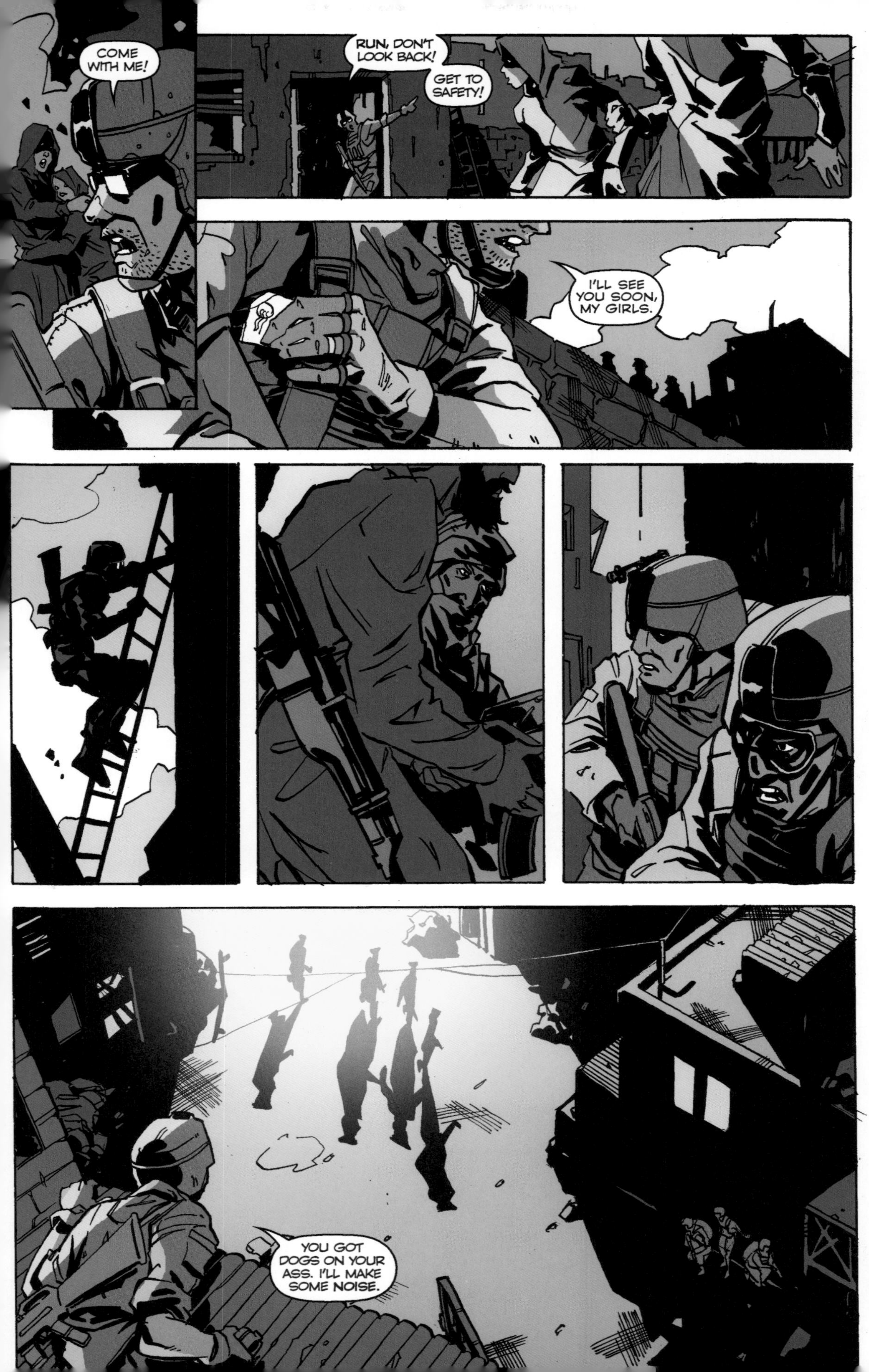
COME WITH ME!
RUN, DON'T LOOK BACK!
GET TO SAFETY!
I'LL SEE YOU SOON, MY GIRLS.
YOU GOT DOGS ON YOUR ASS. I'LL MAKE SOME NOISE.

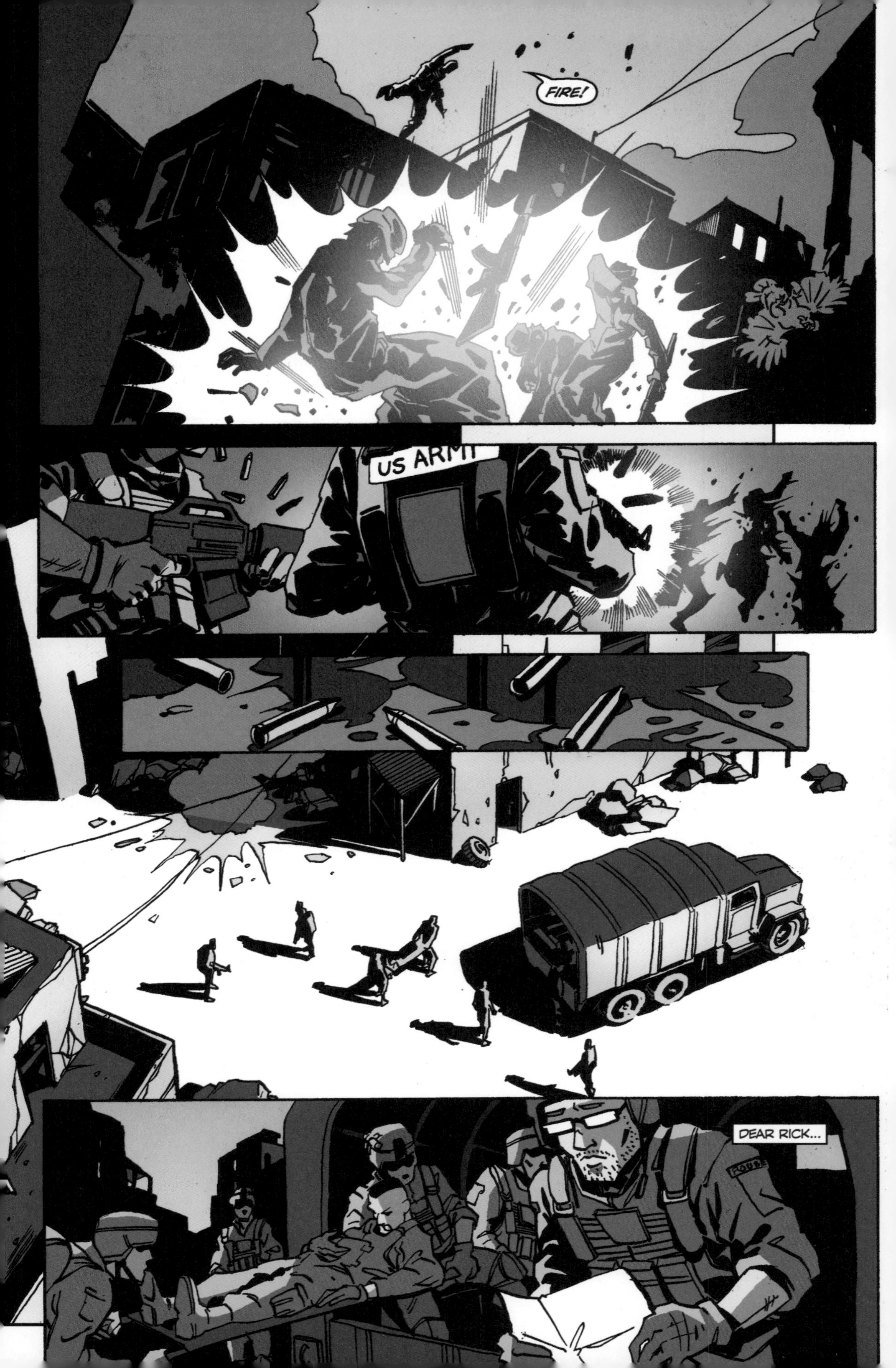
FIRE!
US ARMY
DEAR RICK...

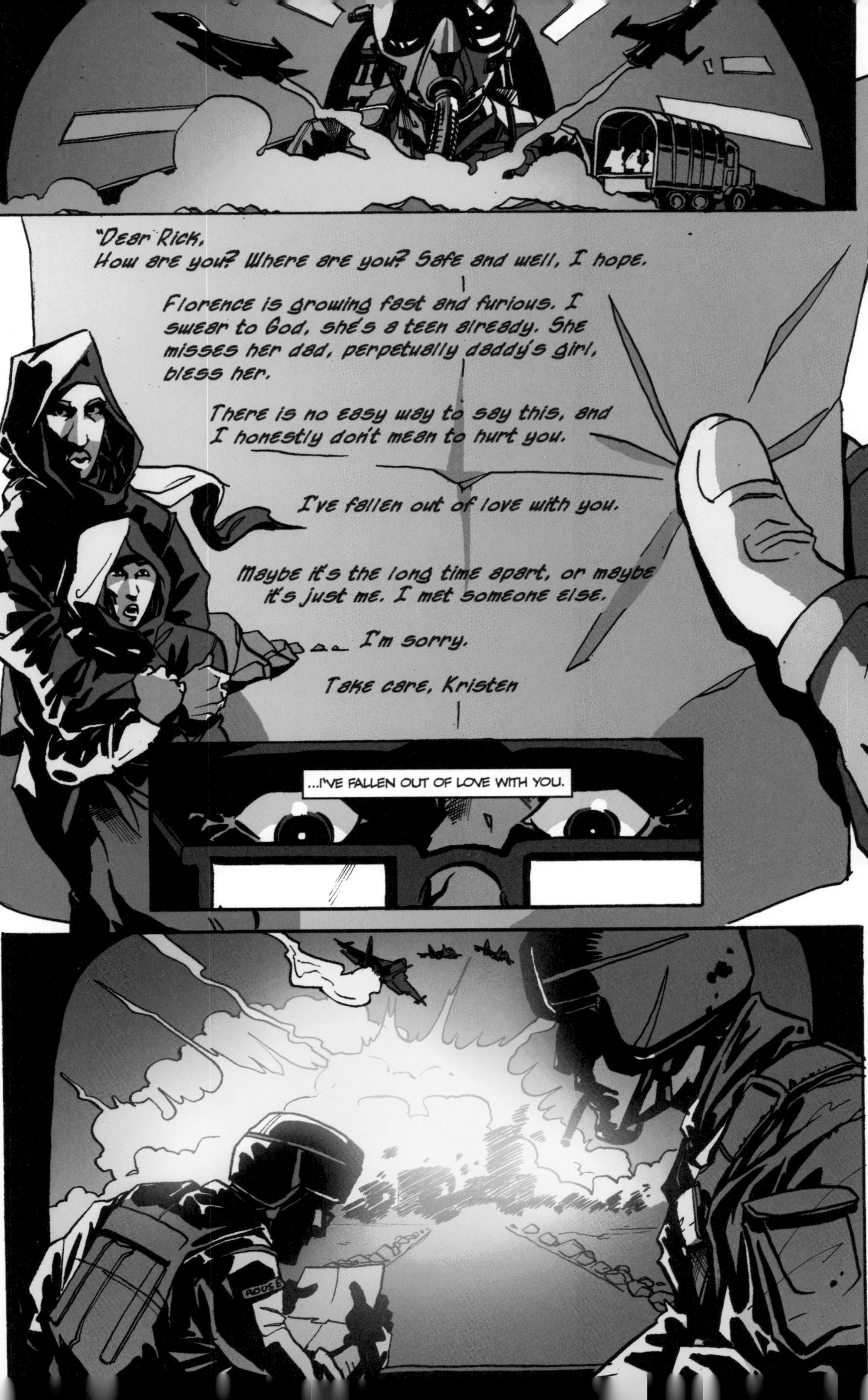
"Dear Rick,
How are you? Where are you? Safe and well, I hope.
Florence is growing fast and furious. I swear to God, she's a teen already. She misses her dad, perpetually daddy's girl, bless her.
There is no easy way to say this, and I honestly don't mean to hurt you.
I've fallen out of love with you.
Maybe it's the long time apart, or maybe it's just me. I met someone else.
... I'm sorry.
Take care, Kristen
...I'VE FALLEN OUT OF LOVE WITH YOU.

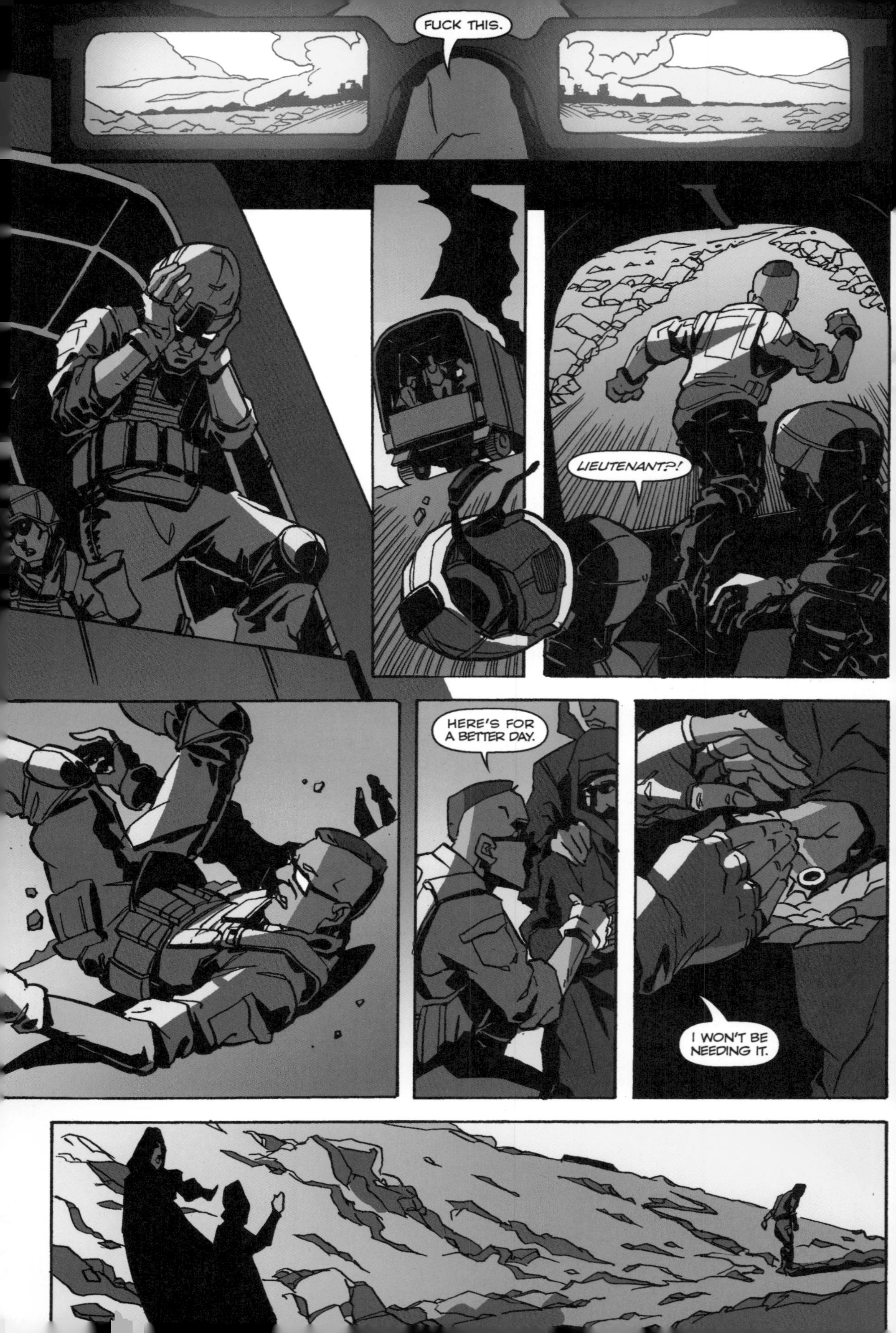
FUCK THIS.
LIEUTENANT?!
HERE'S FOR A BETTER DAY.
I WON'T BE NEEDING IT.

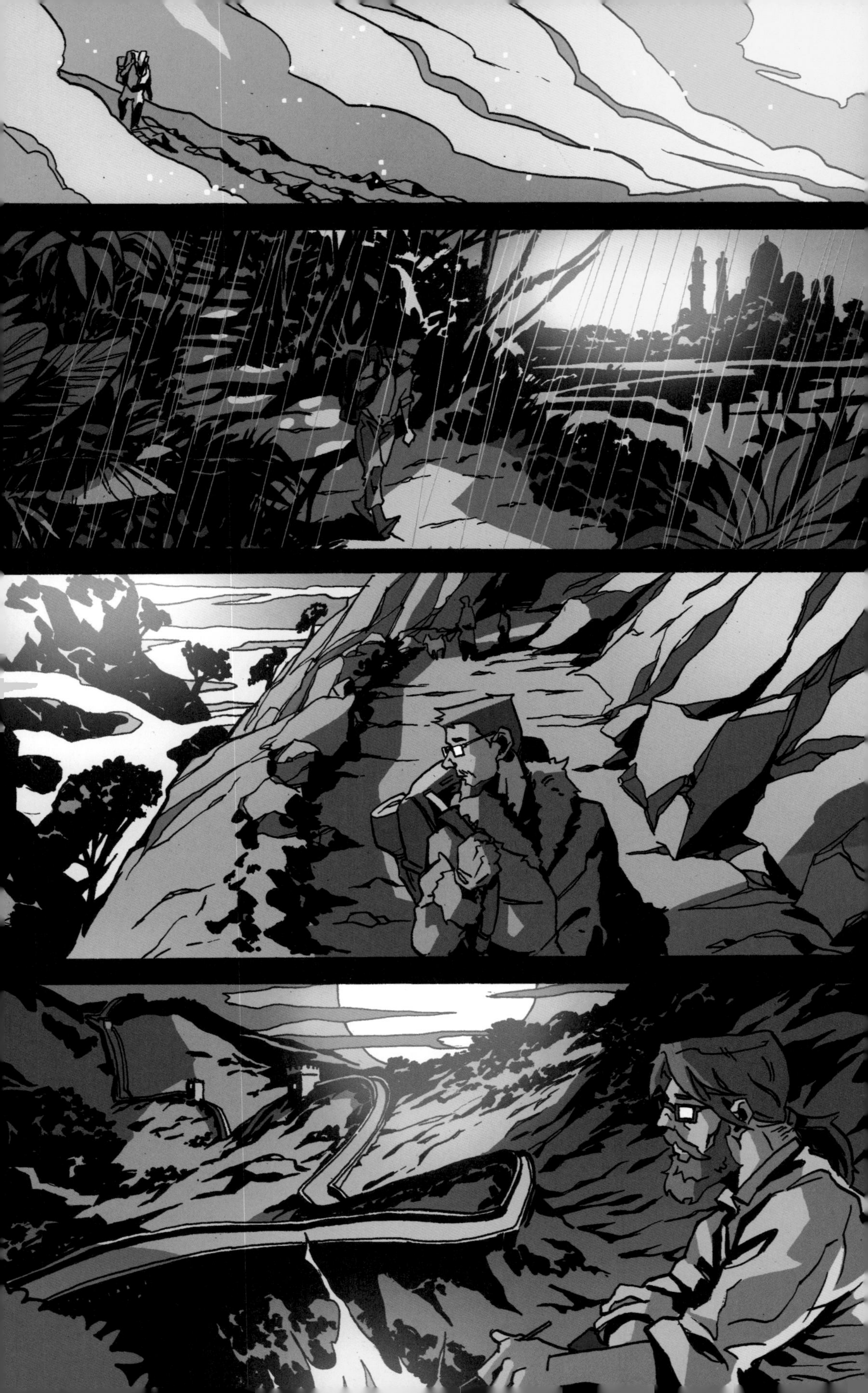

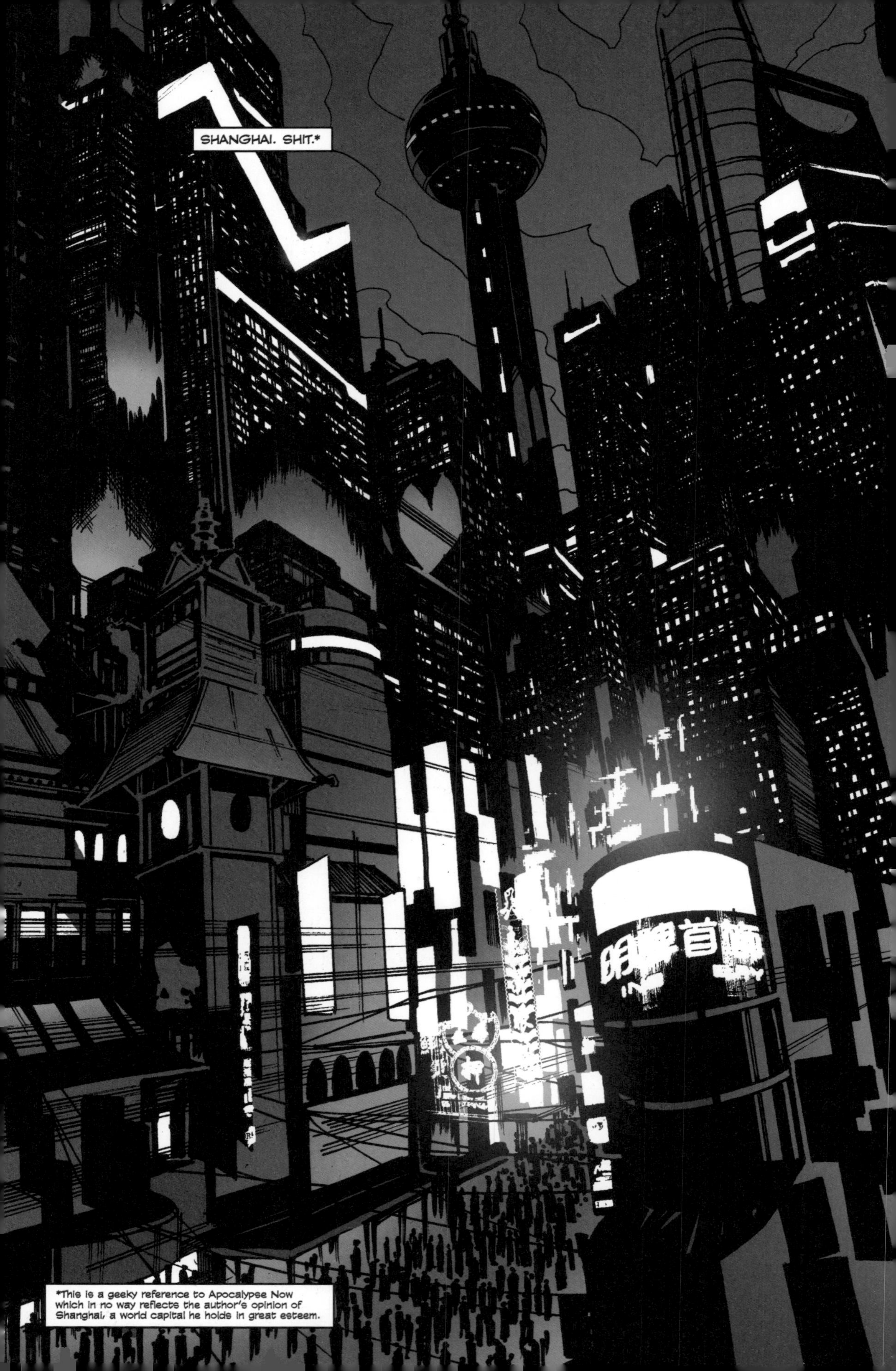
SHANGHAI. SHIT.*
*This is a geeky reference to Apocalypse Now which in no way reflects the author's opinion of Shanghai, a world capital he holds in great esteem.

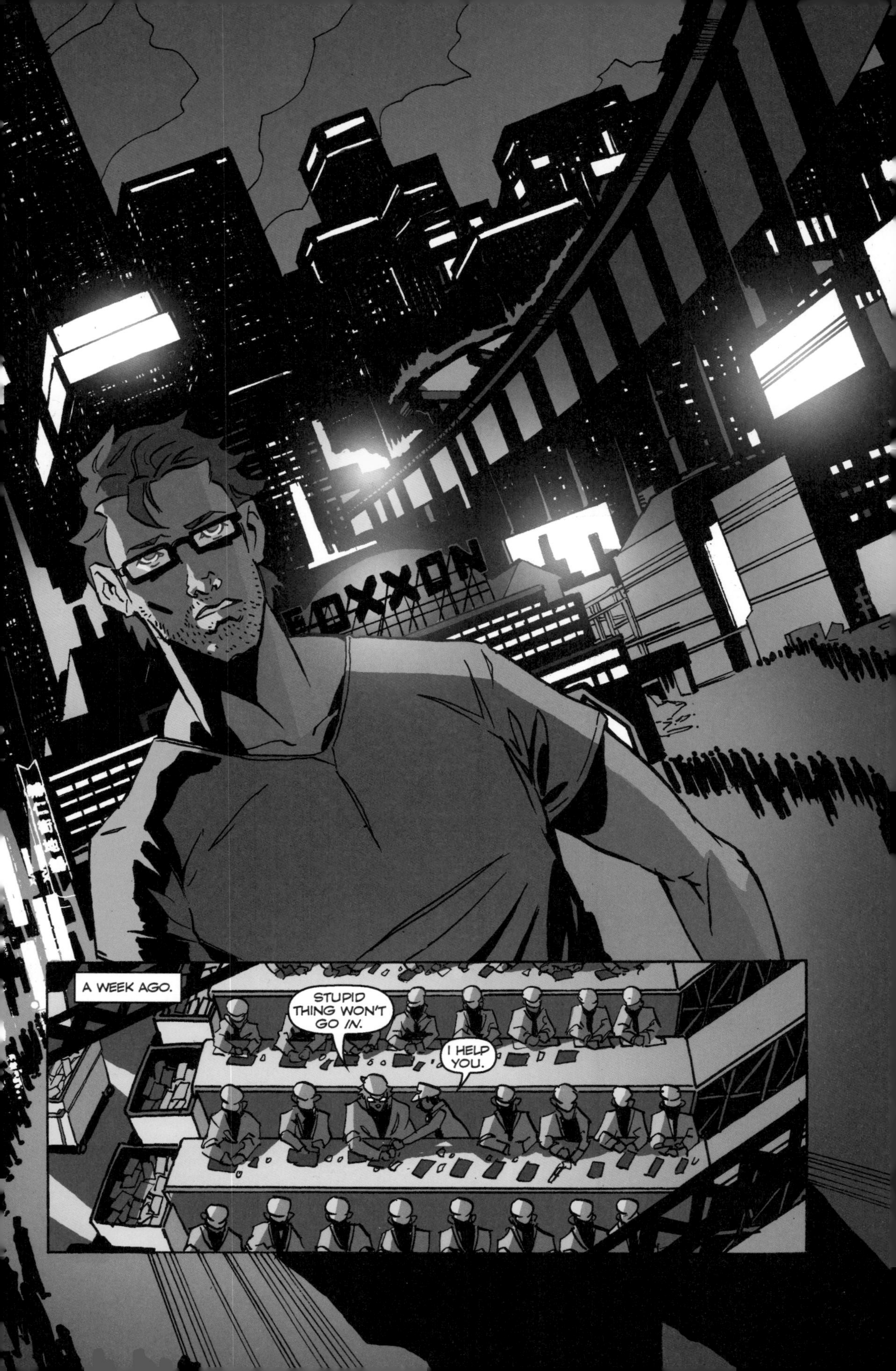

ROXXON
A WEEK AGO.
STUPID THING WON'T GO IN.
I HELP YOU.

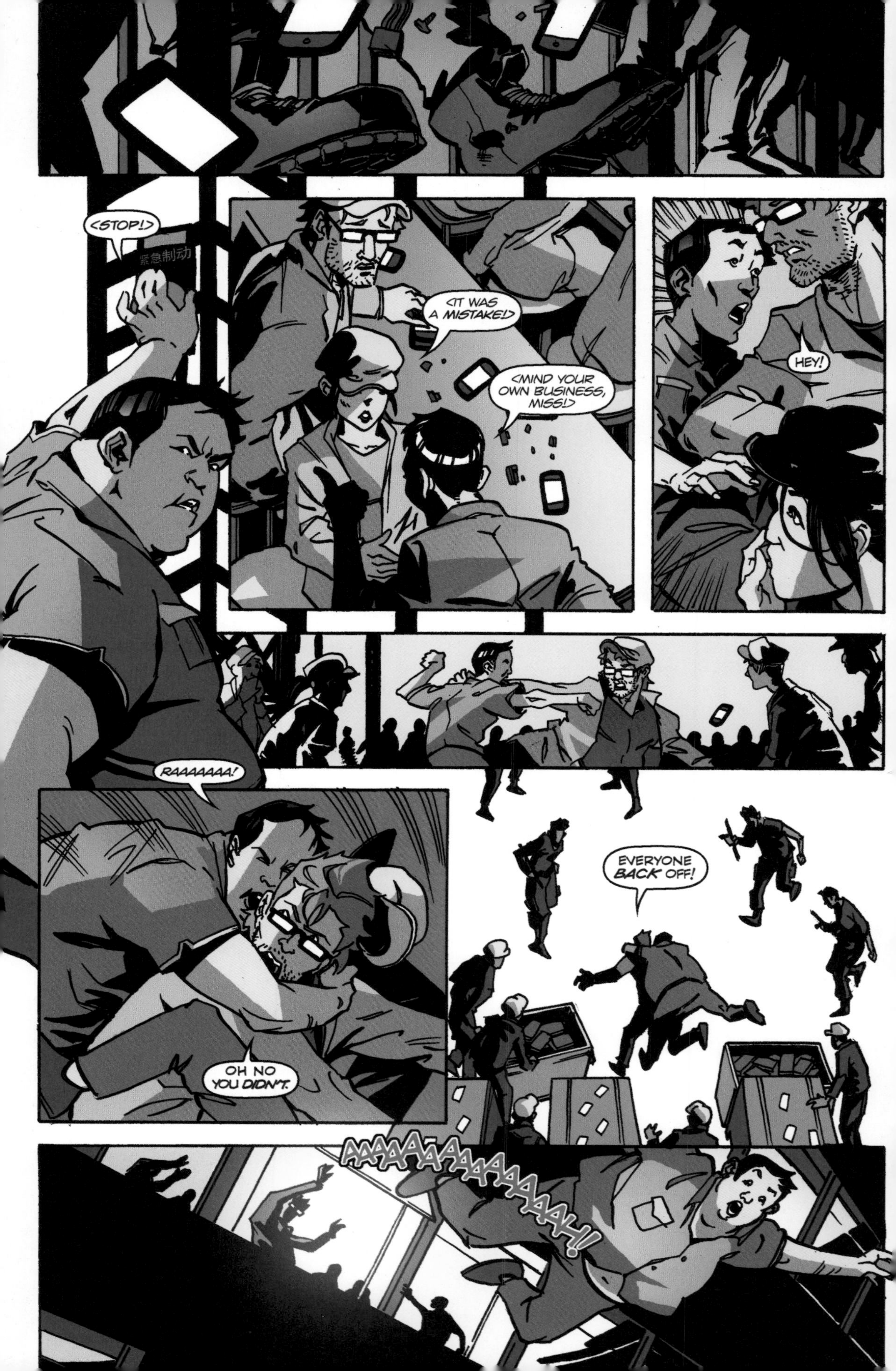
<STOP!>
紧急制动
<IT WAS A MISTAKE!>
<MIND YOUR OWN BUSINESS, MISS!>
HEY!
RAAAAAAA!
OH NO YOU DIDN'T.
EVERYONE BACK OFF!
AAAAAAAAAAAAAAAAAH!!

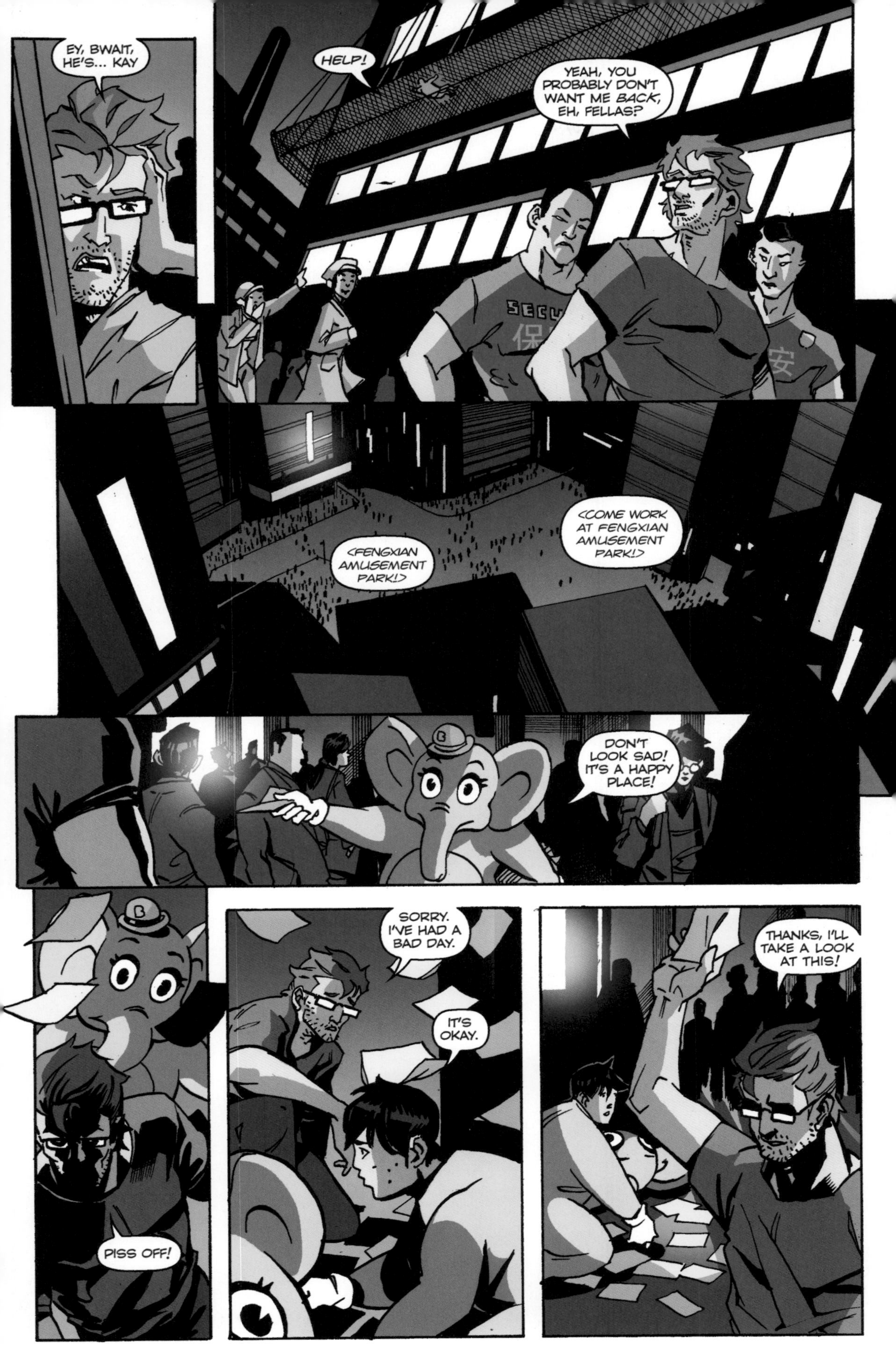
EY, BWAIT, HE'S... KAY
HELP!
YEAH, YOU PROBABLY DON'T WANT ME *BACK*, EH, FELLAS?
SECU
保
安
<FENGXIAN AMUSEMENT PARK!>
<COME WORK AT FENGXIAN AMUSEMENT PARK!>
DON'T LOOK SAD! IT'S A HAPPY PLACE!
PISS OFF!
SORRY. I'VE HAD A BAD DAY.
IT'S OKAY.
THANKS, I'LL TAKE A LOOK AT THIS!

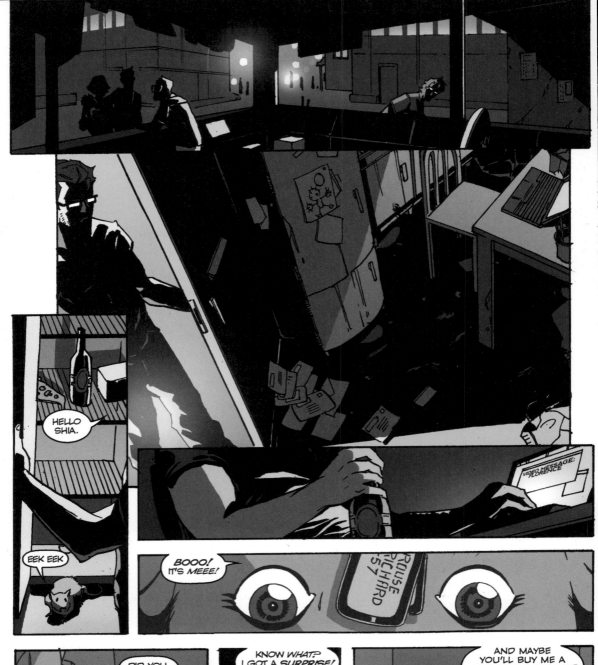

HELLO SHIA.

EEK EEK

VIDEO MESSAGE: FLORENCE

BOOO! IT'S MEEE!

DID YOU SEE THAT? I HOPE YOU SAW THAT.

KNOW WHAT? I GOT A SURPRISE! BUT YEAH,

FIRST I WANNA SAY I'M PROUD OF YOU. YOU'LL BE A GREAT FACTORY MANAGER.

AND MAYBE YOU'LL BUY ME A MOTORCYCLE ONE DAY? JUST A LITTLE ONE.

OKAY, OR A SCOOTER IF IT'S TOO MUCH.

WHO ARE YOU TALKING TO, DARLING? DON'T PUT THE LAPTOP ON THE FLOOR!

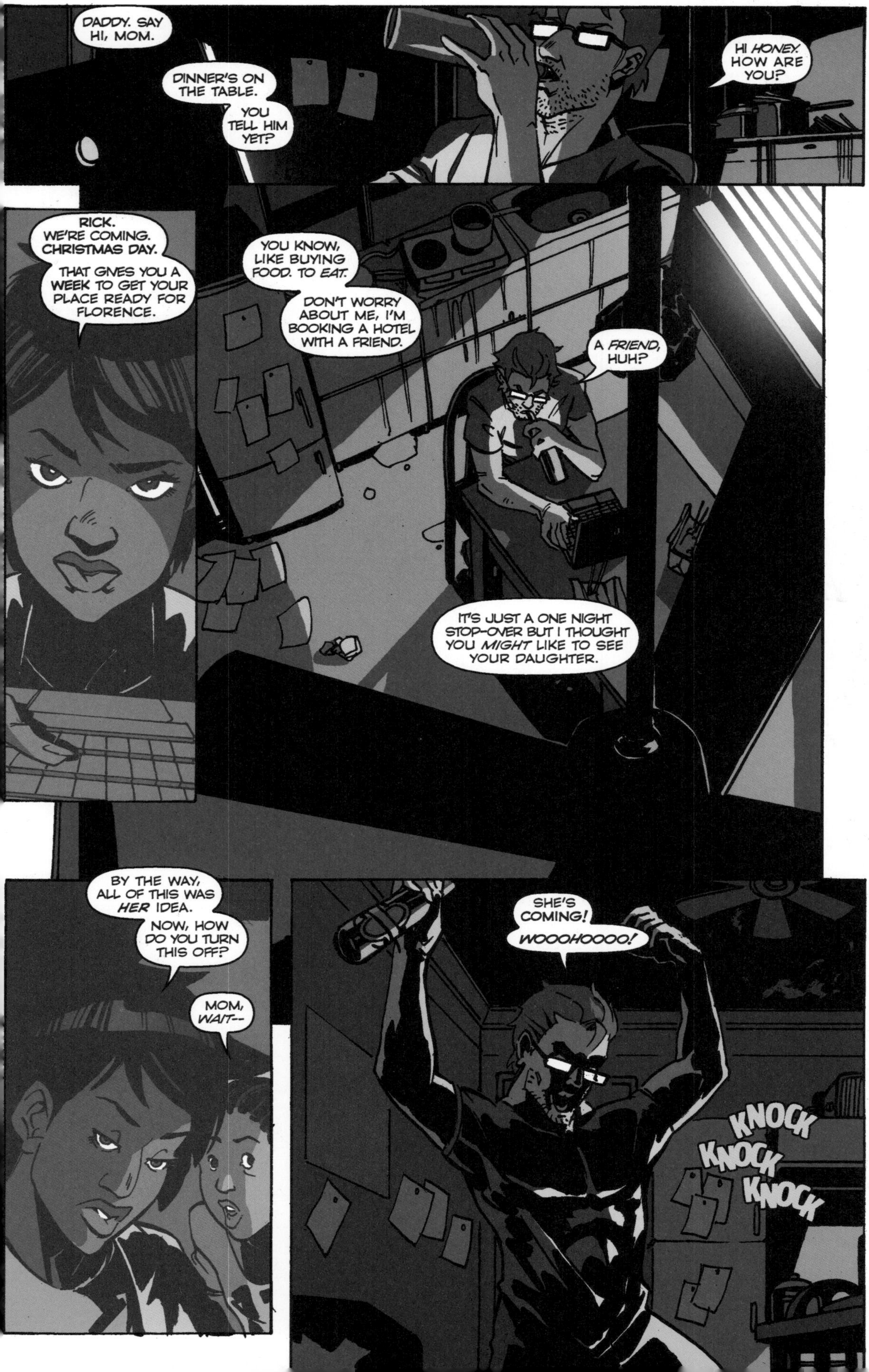
DADDY. SAY HI, MOM.
DINNER'S ON THE TABLE.
YOU TELL HIM YET?
HI HONEY. HOW ARE YOU?
RICK. WE'RE COMING. CHRISTMAS DAY.
THAT GIVES YOU A WEEK TO GET YOUR PLACE READY FOR FLORENCE.
YOU KNOW, LIKE BUYING FOOD. TO EAT.
DON'T WORRY ABOUT ME, I'M BOOKING A HOTEL WITH A FRIEND.
A FRIEND, HUH?
IT'S JUST A ONE NIGHT STOP-OVER BUT I THOUGHT YOU MIGHT LIKE TO SEE YOUR DAUGHTER.
BY THE WAY, ALL OF THIS WAS HER IDEA.
NOW, HOW DO YOU TURN THIS OFF?
MOM, WAIT--
SHE'S COMING!
WOOOHOOOO!
KNOCK
KNOCK
KNOCK

WHO'S THERE?

HELLO RICK--

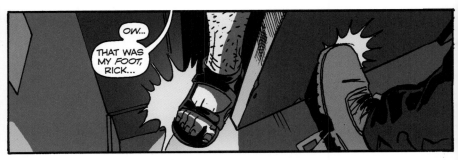

OW... THAT WAS MY *FOOT*, RICK...

MR. YU! HOW NICE TO SEE YOU!

LISTEN, TODAY IS YOUR LAST DAY. YOU GO OUT.

LISTEN, I--

NO MORE *EXCUSES*. PLEASE.

I WILL PAY YOU *TWO* MONTHS IN ADVANCE. SOON AS I HAVE IT.

I HAVE NEW TENANTS. THEY'RE MOVING IN TOMORROW.

I UNDERSTAND YOU'RE ANGRY, BUT YOU DON'T HAVE TO *BLUFF*.

I DON'T BLUFF. THIS IS THEM. YOU MOVE OUT *NOW*, OKAY?

I'M SORRY.

SURE YOU ARE. YOUR FOOT?

IT'S OKAY.

REMOVE IT.

BANG

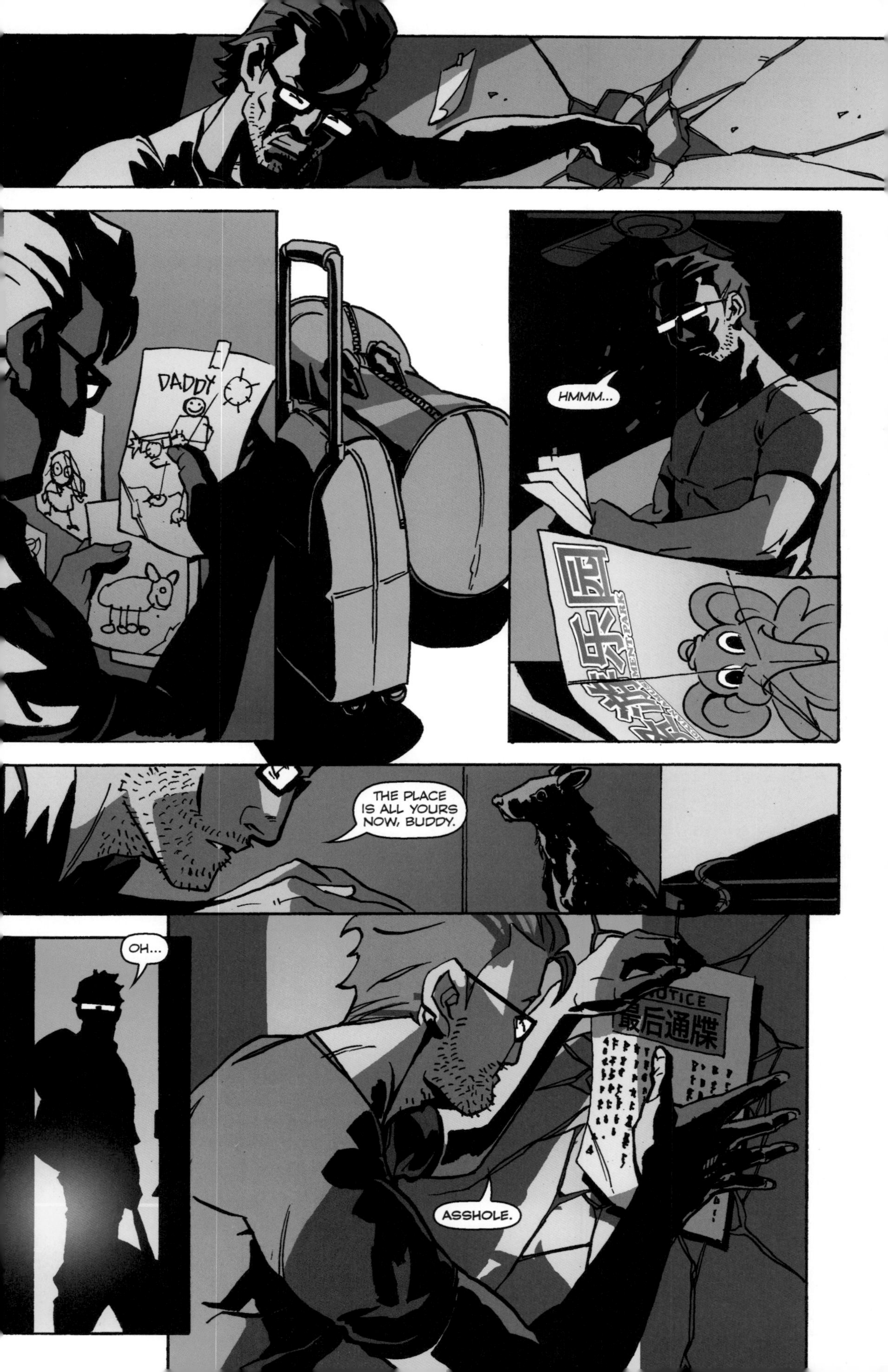
DADDY
HMMM...
THE PLACE IS ALL YOURS NOW, BUDDY.
OH...
最后通牒
ASSHOLE.

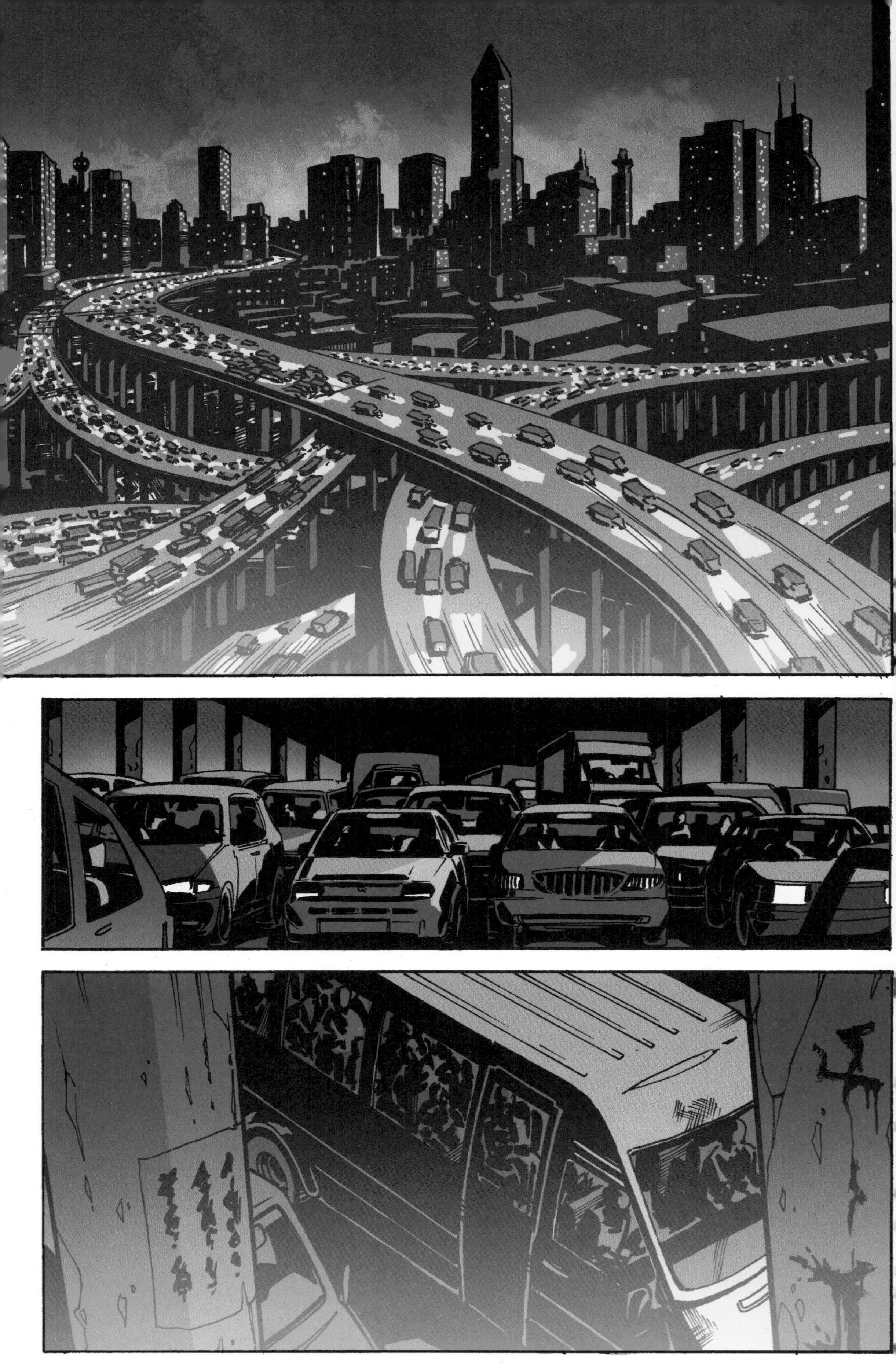

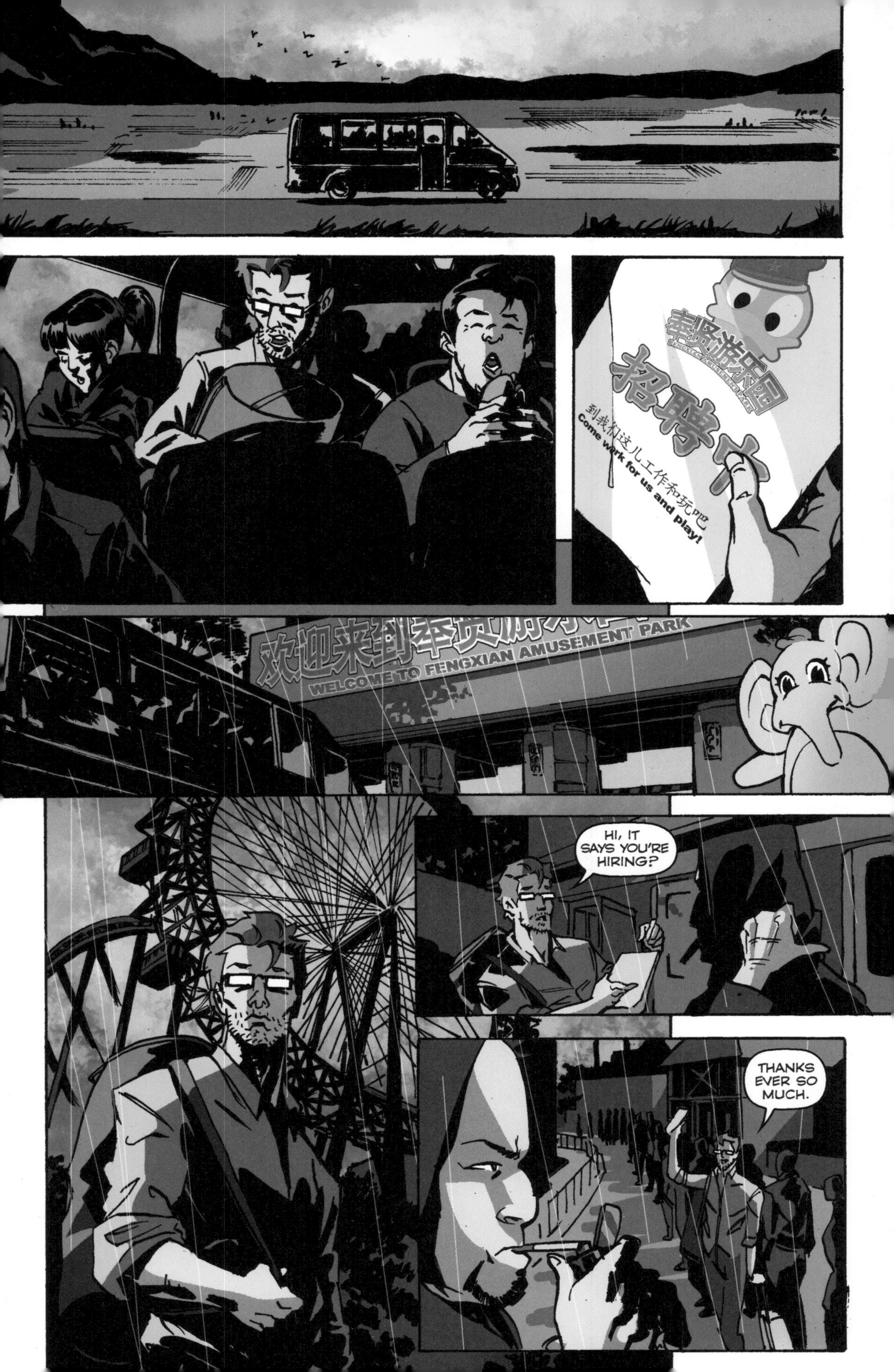
奉贤游乐园
FENGXIAN AMUSEMENT PARK
招聘中
到我们这儿工作和玩吧
Come work for us and play!
欢迎来到奉贤游乐园
FENGXIAN AMUSEMENT PARK
WELCOME TO FENGXIAN AMUSEMENT PARK
HI, IT SAYS YOU'RE HIRING?
THANKS EVER SO MUCH.

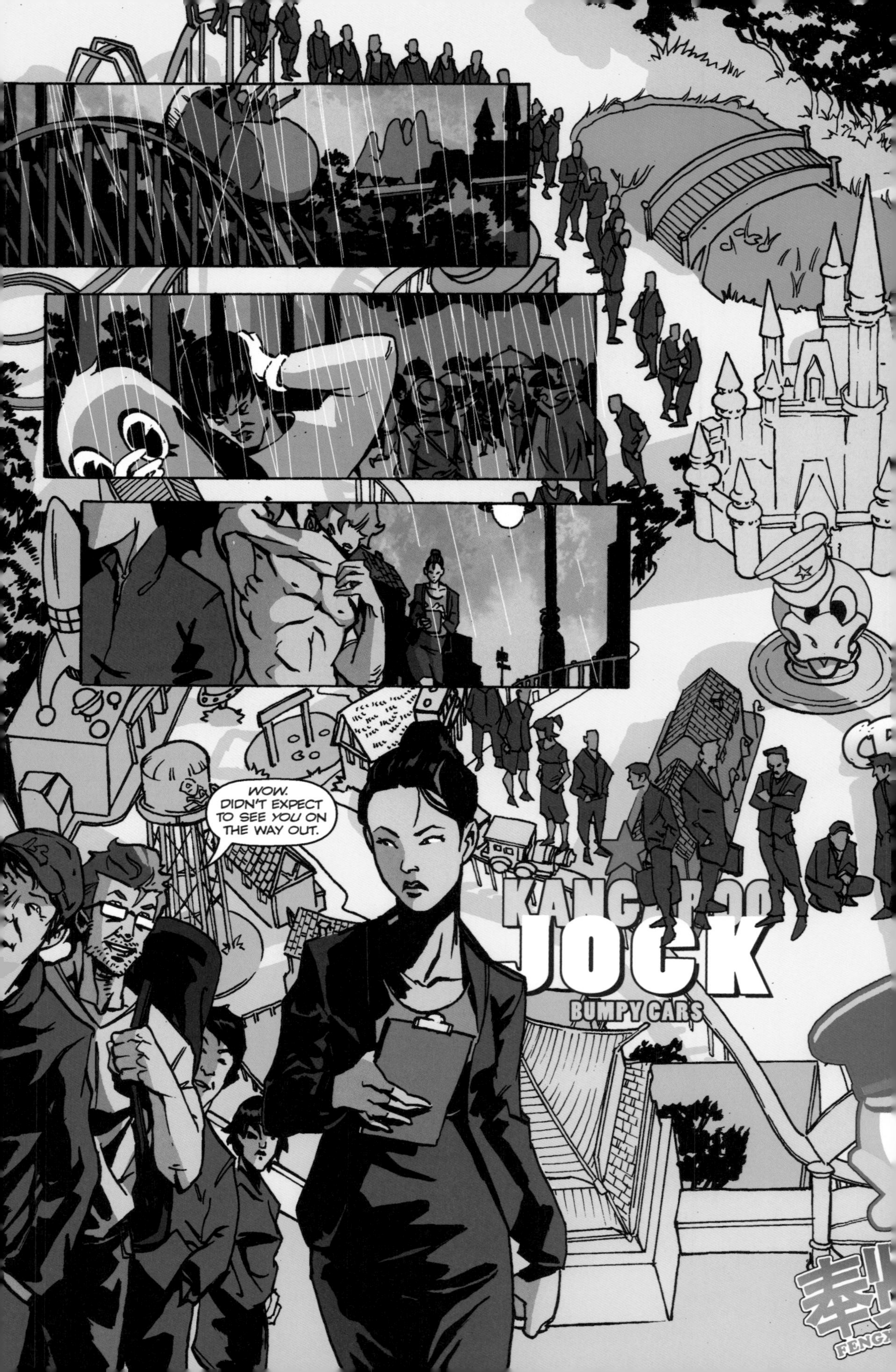
WOW. DIDN'T EXPECT TO SEE YOU ON THE WAY OUT.
JOCK
BUMPY CARS

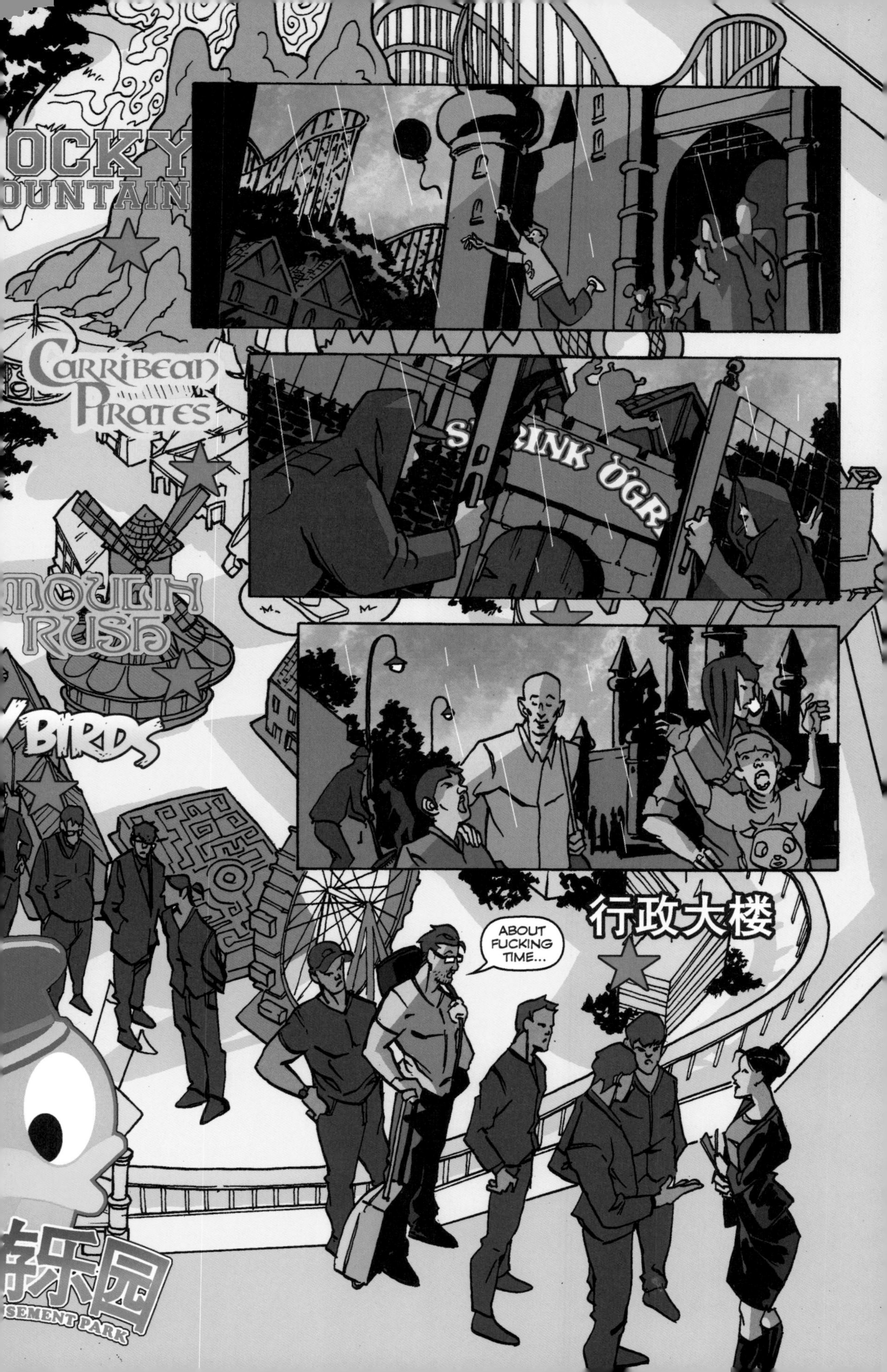
Carribean Pirates
MOULIN RUSH
行政大楼
ABOUT FUCKING TIME...

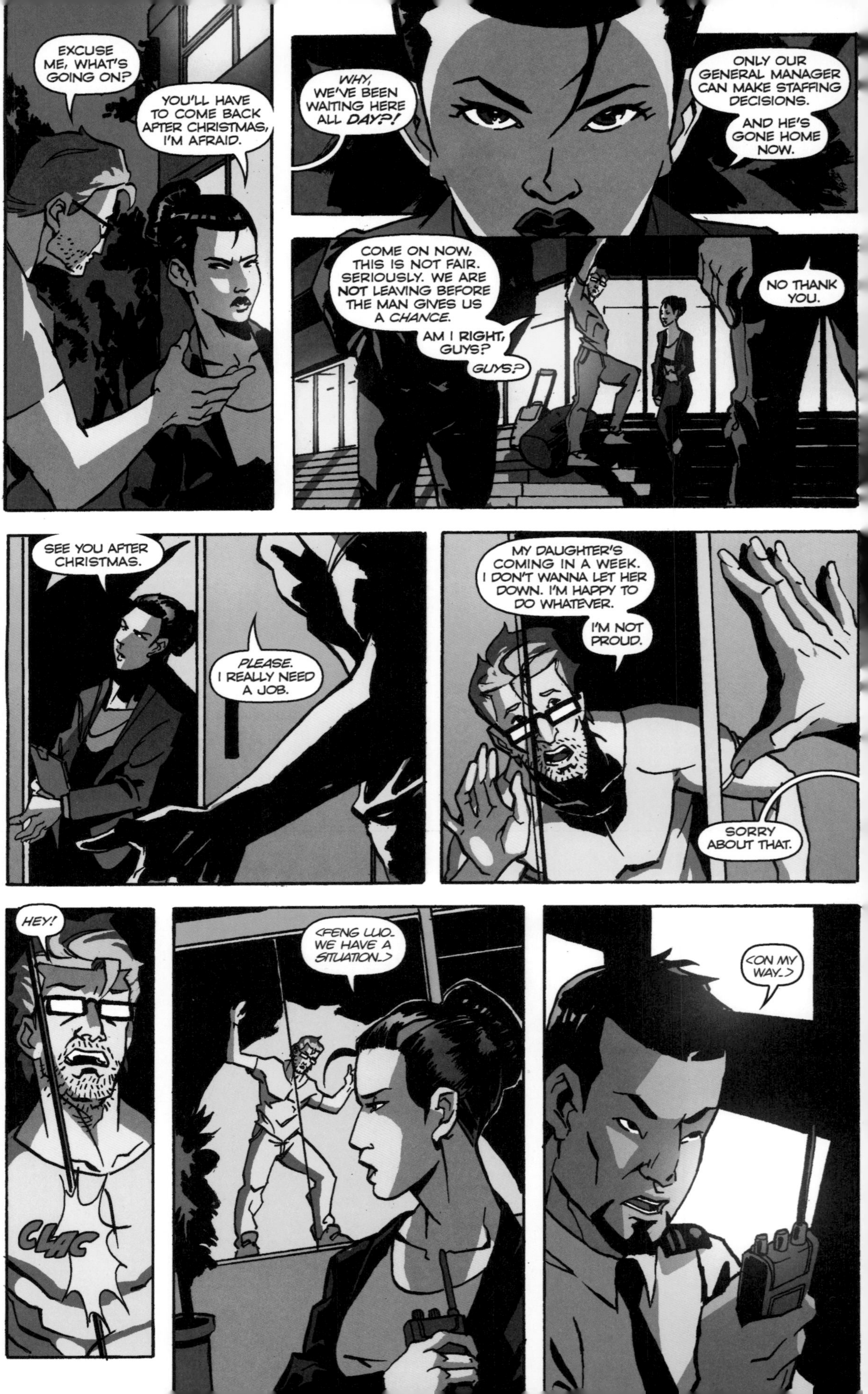
EXCUSE ME, WHAT'S GOING ON?
YOU'LL HAVE TO COME BACK AFTER CHRISTMAS, I'M AFRAID.
WHY, WE'VE BEEN WAITING HERE ALL DAY?!
ONLY OUR GENERAL MANAGER CAN MAKE STAFFING DECISIONS.
AND HE'S GONE HOME NOW.
COME ON NOW, THIS IS NOT FAIR. SERIOUSLY. WE ARE NOT LEAVING BEFORE THE MAN GIVES US A CHANCE.
AM I RIGHT, GUYS?
GUYS?
NO THANK YOU.
SEE YOU AFTER CHRISTMAS.
PLEASE. I REALLY NEED A JOB.
MY DAUGHTER'S COMING IN A WEEK. I DON'T WANNA LET HER DOWN. I'M HAPPY TO DO WHATEVER.
I'M NOT PROUD.
SORRY ABOUT THAT.
HEY!
CLAC
<FENG LUO. WE HAVE A SITUATION.>
<ON MY WAY.>

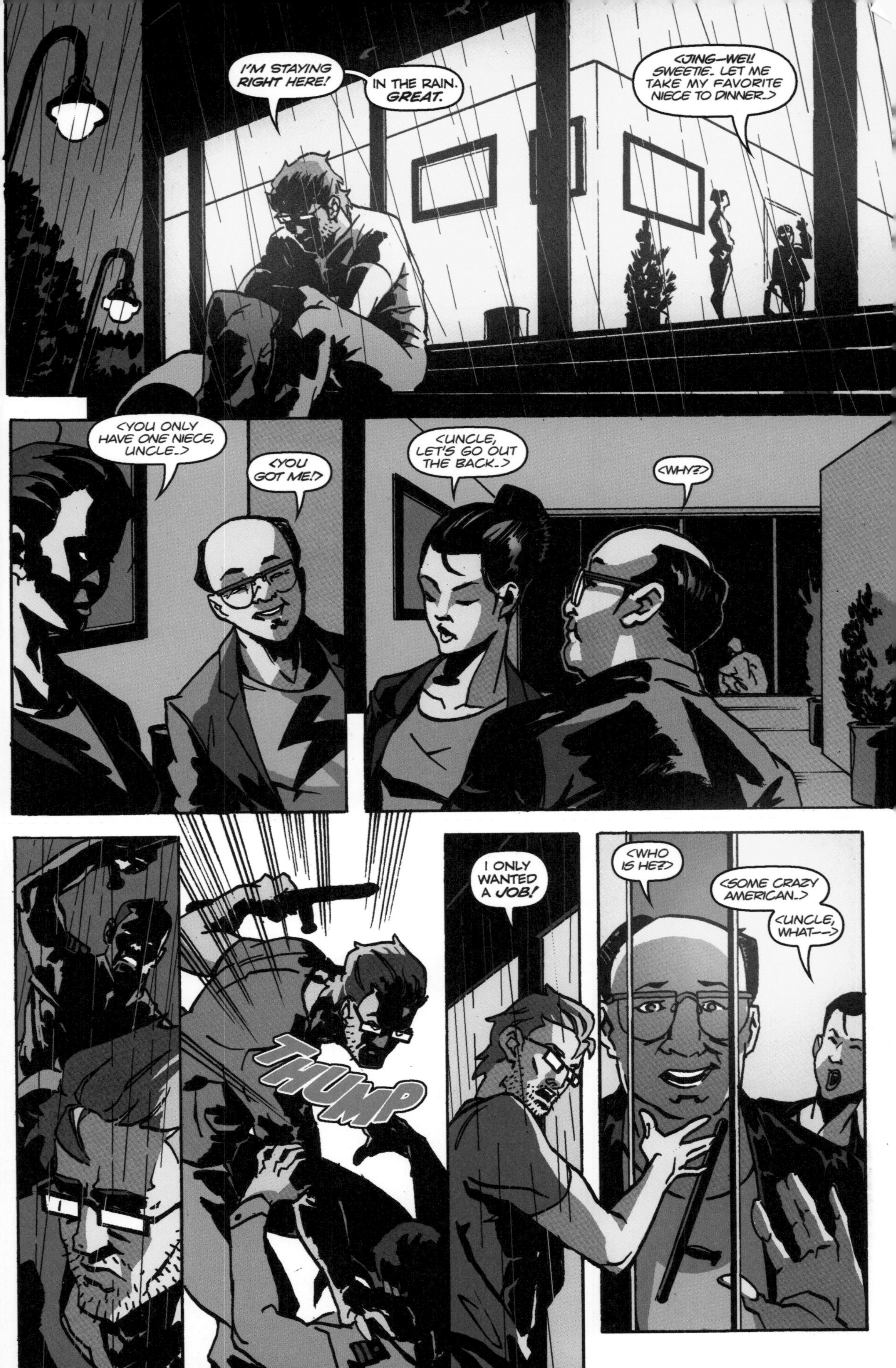
I'M STAYING RIGHT HERE!
IN THE RAIN. GREAT.
<JING-WEI! SWEETIE. LET ME TAKE MY FAVORITE NIECE TO DINNER.>
<YOU ONLY HAVE ONE NIECE, UNCLE.>
<YOU GOT ME!>
<UNCLE, LET'S GO OUT THE BACK.>
<WHY?>
THUMP
I ONLY WANTED A JOB!
<WHO IS HE?>
<SOME CRAZY AMERICAN.>
<UNCLE, WHAT-->

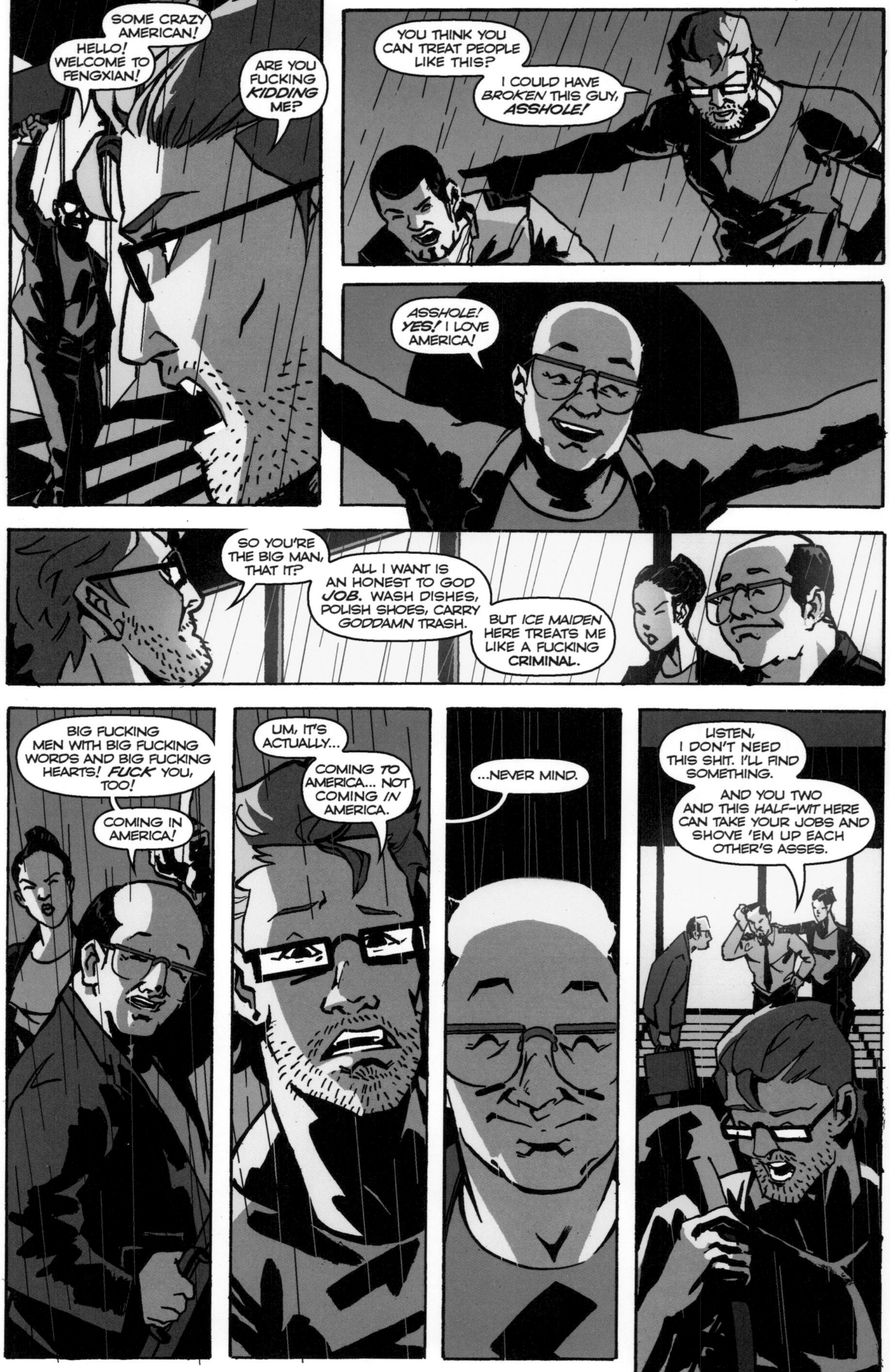
SOME CRAZY AMERICAN!
HELLO! WELCOME TO FENGXIAN!
ARE YOU FUCKING KIDDING ME?
YOU THINK YOU CAN TREAT PEOPLE LIKE THIS?
I COULD HAVE BROKEN THIS GUY, ASSHOLE!
ASSHOLE! YES! I LOVE AMERICA!
SO YOU'RE THE BIG MAN, THAT IT?
ALL I WANT IS AN HONEST TO GOD JOB. WASH DISHES, POLISH SHOES, CARRY GODDAMN TRASH.
BUT ICE MAIDEN HERE TREATS ME LIKE A FUCKING CRIMINAL.
BIG FUCKING MEN WITH BIG FUCKING WORDS AND BIG FUCKING HEARTS! FUCK YOU, TOO!
COMING IN AMERICA!
UM, IT'S ACTUALLY...
COMING TO AMERICA... NOT COMING IN AMERICA.
...NEVER MIND.
LISTEN, I DON'T NEED THIS SHIT. I'LL FIND SOMETHING.
AND YOU TWO AND THIS HALF-WIT HERE CAN TAKE YOUR JOBS AND SHOVE 'EM UP EACH OTHER'S ASSES.

YOU NEED A JOB? I THINK WE NEED BETTER SECURITY.

WHAT'S YOUR NAME, MY FRIEND?

RICK.

RICK...?

RICHARD ROUSE.

RICKY... ROUSE. PERFECT.

I MAY HAVE A JOB FOR YOU.

UNCLE, I DON'T THINK—

OOOMPH!

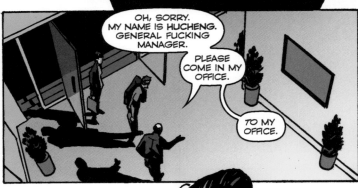

OH, SORRY. MY NAME IS HUCHENG. GENERAL FUCKING MANAGER.

PLEASE COME IN MY OFFICE.

TO MY OFFICE.

THANK YOU, JING-WEI, NOW PLEASE SAVE MR. ROUSE'S THINGS FROM THE RAIN.

I WON'T BE LONG.

I APOLOGIZE FOR JING-WEI. SHE IS ONLY PROTECTING HER UNCLE.

GOOD TO HAVE A GUARDIAN ANGEL.

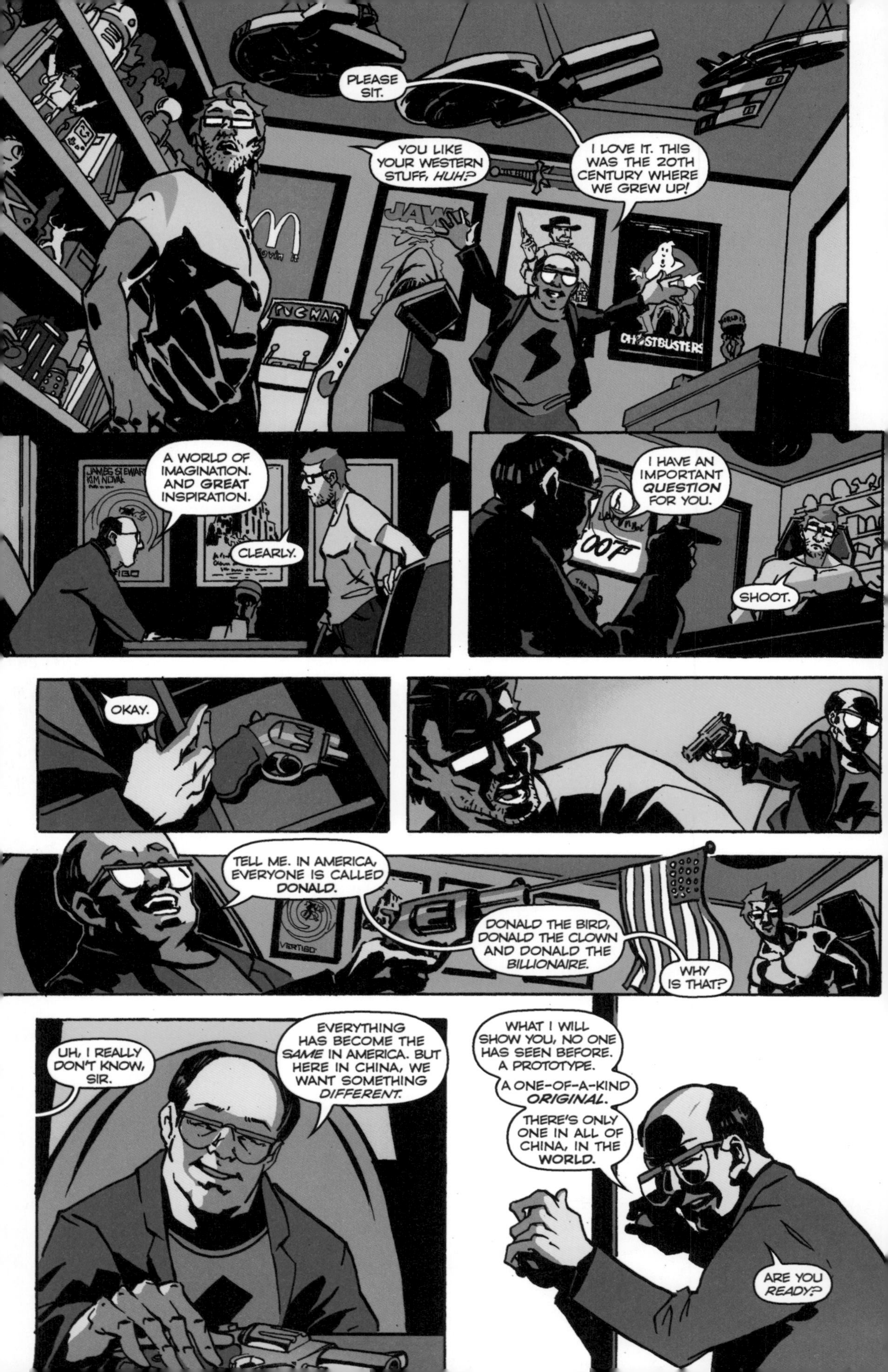
PLEASE SIT.
YOU LIKE YOUR WESTERN STUFF, *HUH?*
I LOVE IT. THIS WAS THE 20TH CENTURY WHERE WE GREW UP!
JAWS
PACMAN
GHOSTBUSTERS
A WORLD OF IMAGINATION. AND GREAT INSPIRATION.
CLEARLY.
I HAVE AN IMPORTANT *QUESTION* FOR YOU.
007
SHOOT.
OKAY.
TELL ME. IN AMERICA, EVERYONE IS CALLED DONALD.
DONALD THE BIRD, DONALD THE CLOWN AND DONALD THE *BILLIONAIRE.*
WHY IS THAT?
VERTIGO
UH, I REALLY DON'T KNOW, SIR.
EVERYTHING HAS BECOME THE *SAME* IN AMERICA. BUT HERE IN CHINA, WE WANT SOMETHING *DIFFERENT.*
WHAT I WILL SHOW YOU, NO ONE HAS SEEN BEFORE. A PROTOTYPE.
A ONE-OF-A-KIND ***ORIGINAL.***
THERE'S ONLY ONE IN ALL OF CHINA, IN THE WORLD.
ARE YOU *READY?*

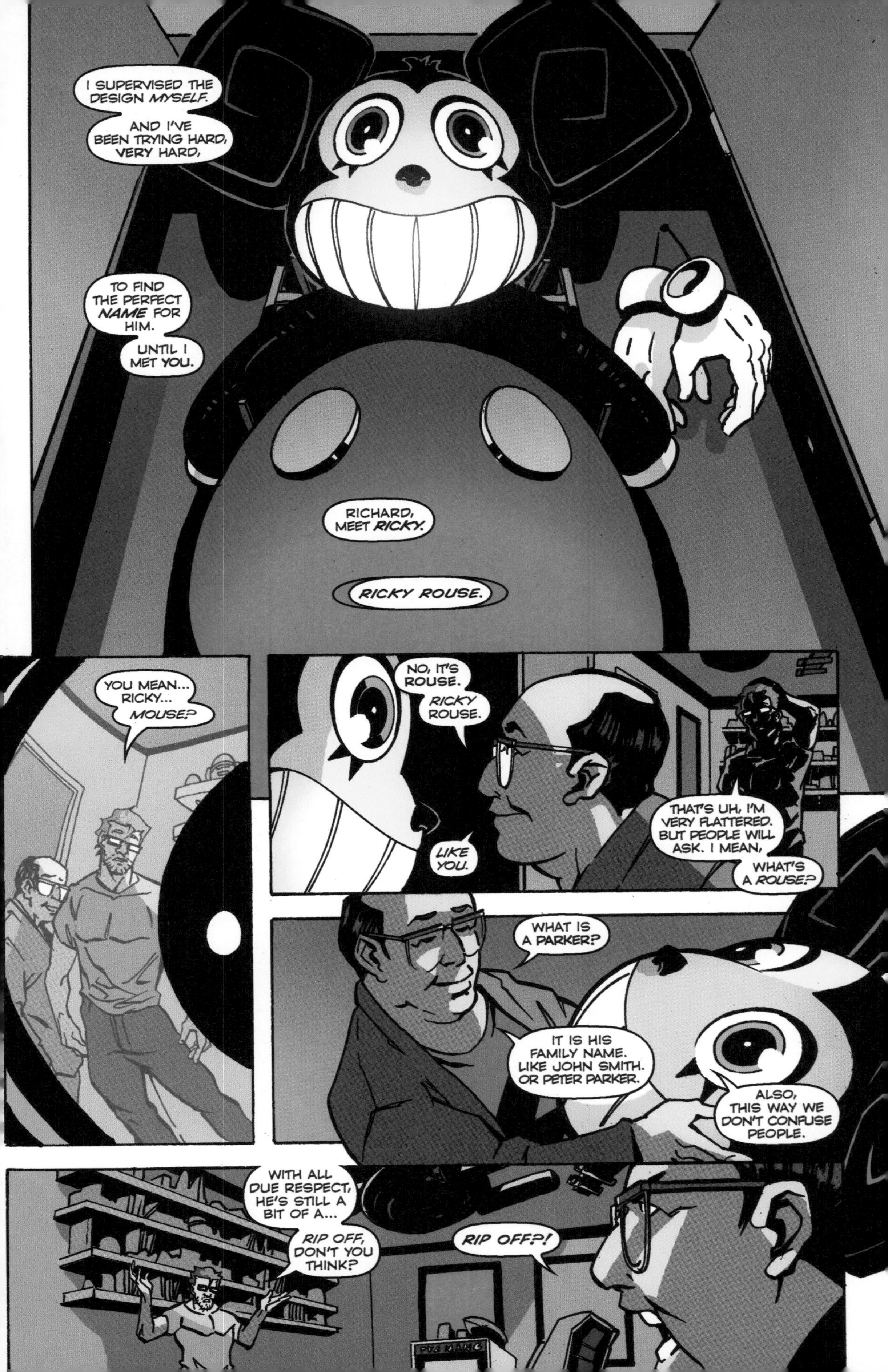
I SUPERVISED THE DESIGN MYSELF.
AND I'VE BEEN TRYING HARD, VERY HARD,
TO FIND THE PERFECT NAME FOR HIM.
UNTIL I MET YOU.
RICHARD, MEET RICKY.
RICKY ROUSE.
YOU MEAN... RICKY... MOUSE?
NO, IT'S ROUSE. RICKY ROUSE.
LIKE YOU.
THAT'S UH, I'M VERY FLATTERED. BUT PEOPLE WILL ASK. I MEAN,
WHAT'S A ROUSE?
WHAT IS A PARKER?
IT IS HIS FAMILY NAME. LIKE JOHN SMITH. OR PETER PARKER.
ALSO, THIS WAY WE DON'T CONFUSE PEOPLE.
WITH ALL DUE RESPECT, HE'S STILL A BIT OF A...
RIP OFF, DON'T YOU THINK?
RIP OFF?!

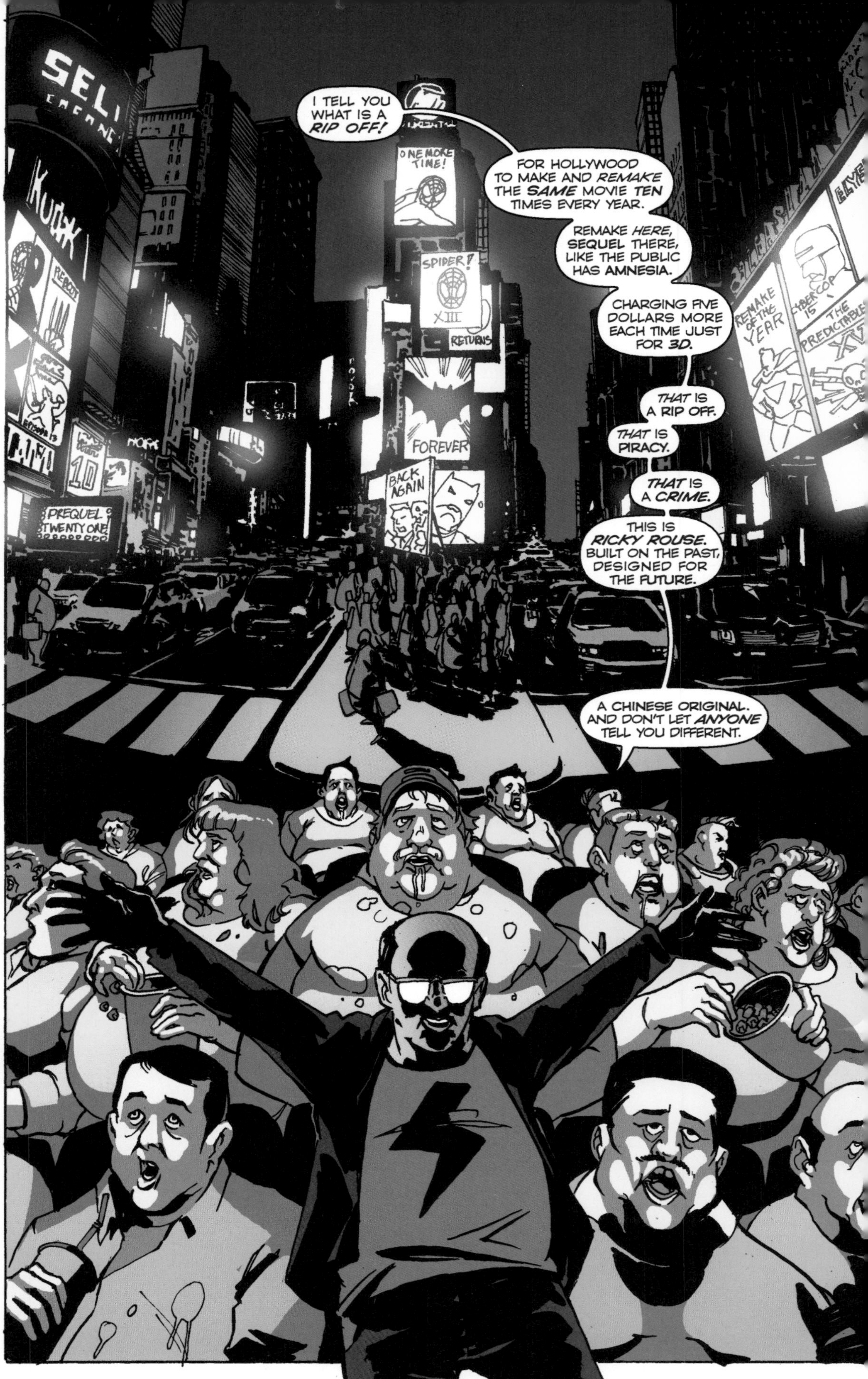
I TELL YOU WHAT IS A RIP OFF!
FOR HOLLYWOOD TO MAKE AND REMAKE THE SAME MOVIE TEN TIMES EVERY YEAR.
REMAKE HERE, SEQUEL THERE, LIKE THE PUBLIC HAS AMNESIA.
CHARGING FIVE DOLLARS MORE EACH TIME JUST FOR 3D.
THAT IS A RIP OFF.
THAT IS PIRACY.
THAT IS A CRIME.
THIS IS RICKY ROUSE. BUILT ON THE PAST, DESIGNED FOR THE FUTURE.
A CHINESE ORIGINAL. AND DON'T LET ANYONE TELL YOU DIFFERENT.
ONE MORE TIME!
SPIDER! XIII
RETURNS
FOREVER
BACK AGAIN
PREQUEL TWENTY ONE
REBOOT
REMAKE OF THE YEAR
CYBER COP 15
THE PREDICTABLE XV
10

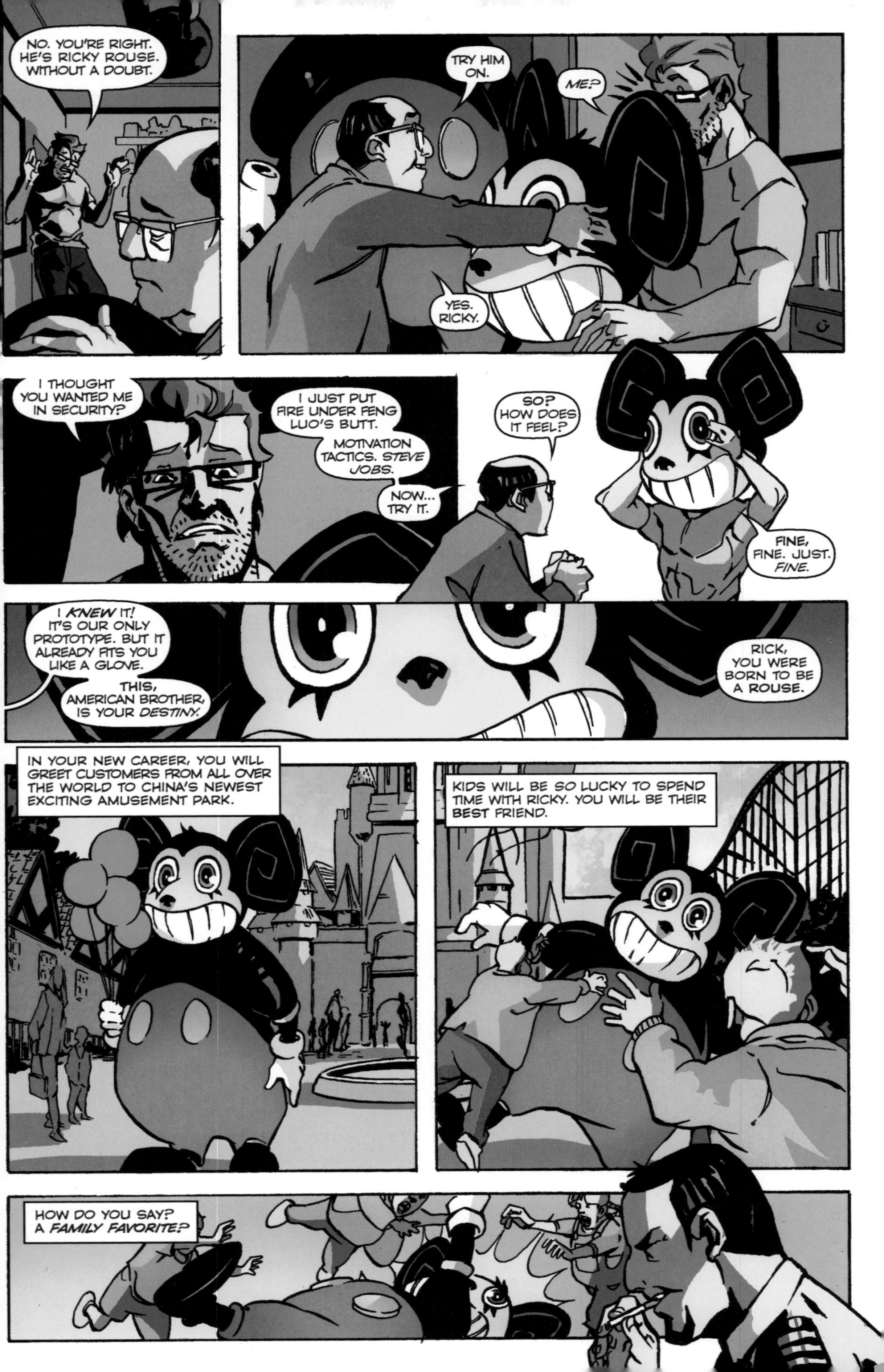

NO. YOU'RE RIGHT. HE'S RICKY ROUSE. WITHOUT A DOUBT.
TRY HIM ON.
ME?
YES. RICKY.
I THOUGHT YOU WANTED ME IN SECURITY?
I JUST PUT FIRE UNDER FENG LUO'S BUTT.
MOTIVATION TACTICS. *STEVE JOBS*.
NOW... TRY IT.
SO? HOW DOES IT FEEL?
FINE, FINE. JUST. *FINE*.
I ***KNEW*** IT! IT'S OUR ONLY PROTOTYPE. BUT IT ALREADY FITS YOU LIKE A GLOVE.
THIS, AMERICAN BROTHER, IS YOUR *DESTINY*.
RICK, YOU WERE BORN TO BE A ROUSE.
IN YOUR NEW CAREER, YOU WILL GREET CUSTOMERS FROM ALL OVER THE WORLD TO CHINA'S NEWEST EXCITING AMUSEMENT PARK.
KIDS WILL BE SO LUCKY TO SPEND TIME WITH RICKY. YOU WILL BE THEIR **BEST** FRIEND.
HOW DO YOU SAY? A *FAMILY FAVORITE*?

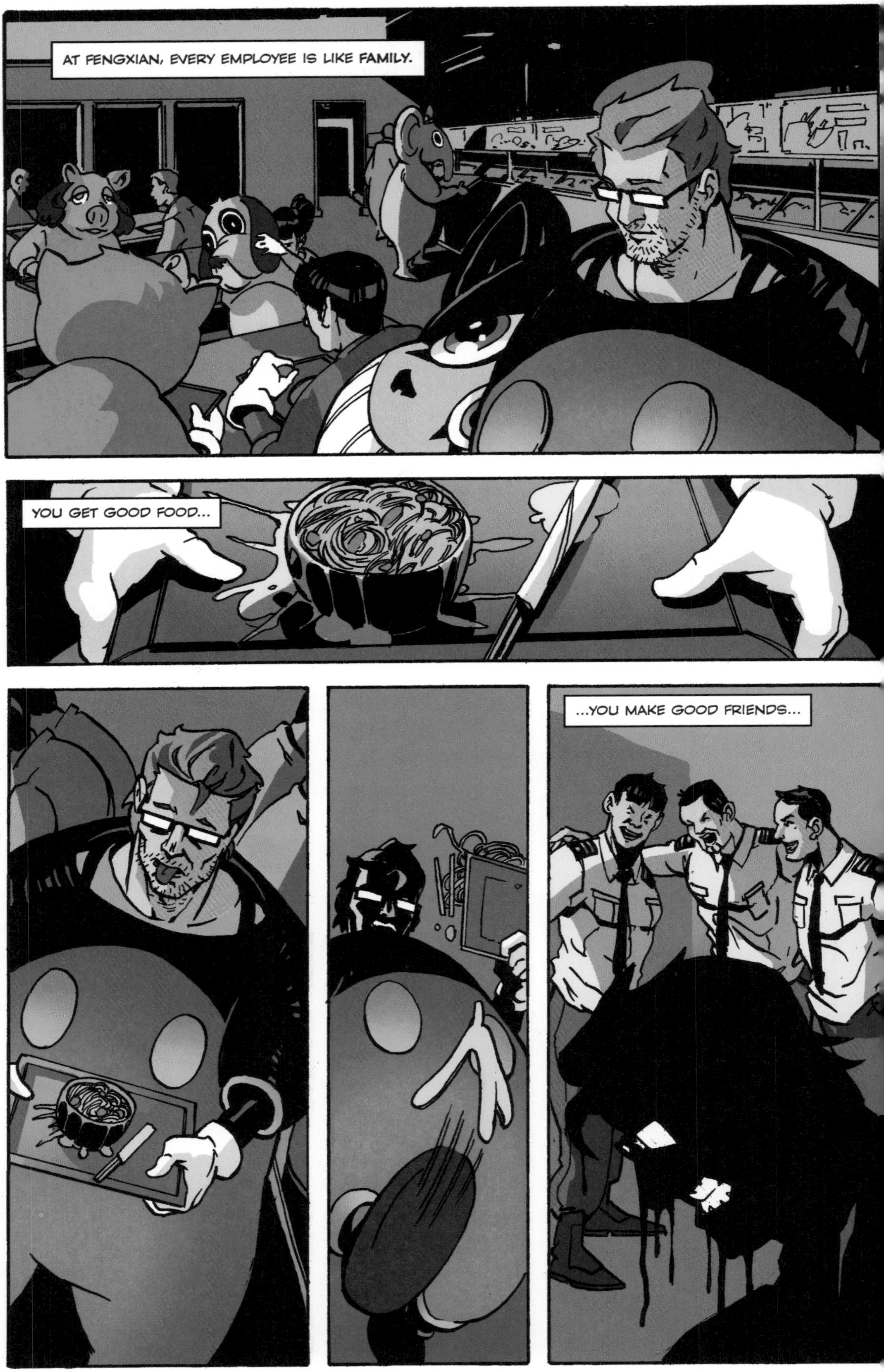
AT FENGXIAN, EVERY EMPLOYEE IS LIKE FAMILY.
YOU GET GOOD FOOD...
...YOU MAKE GOOD FRIENDS...

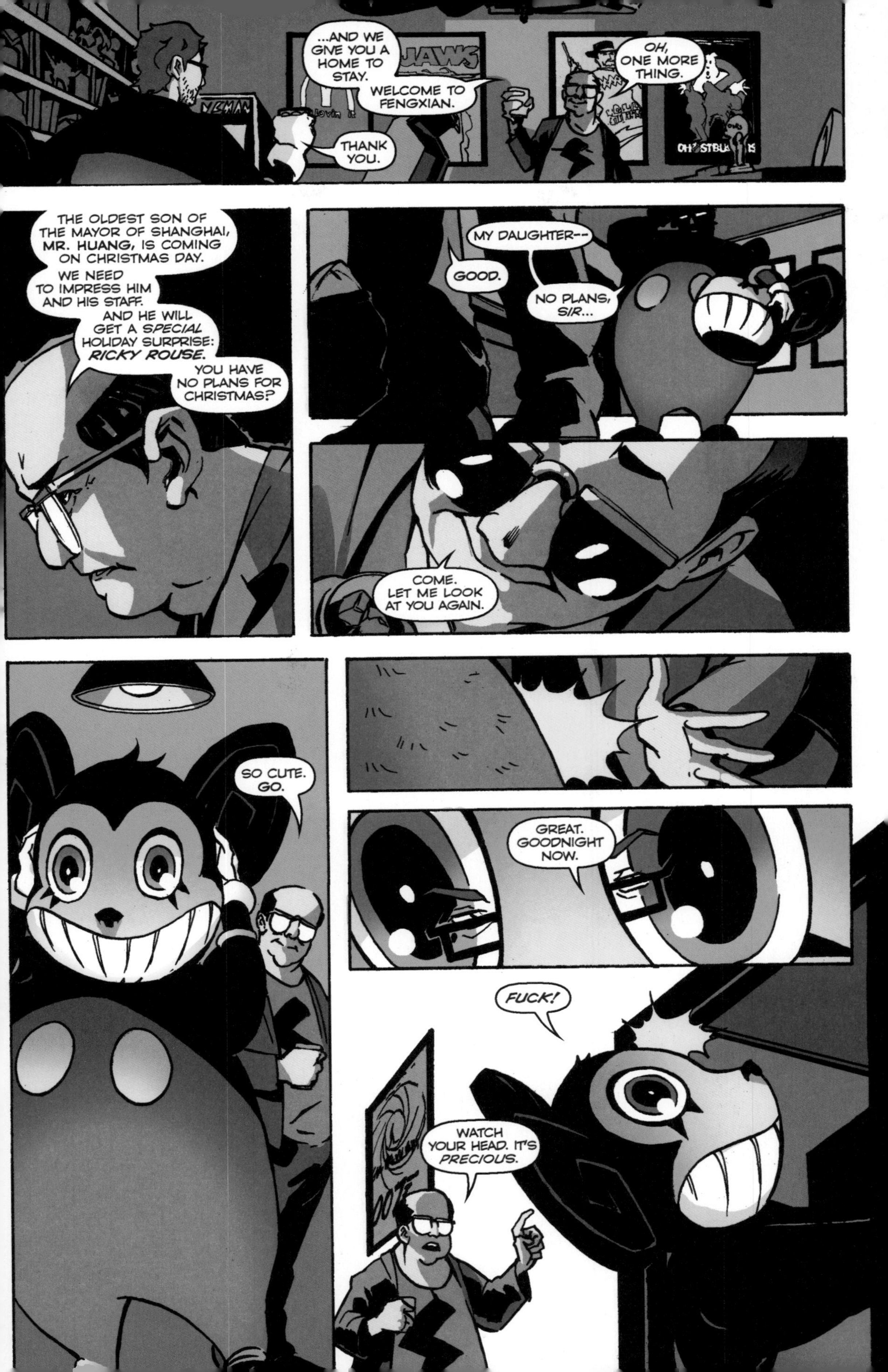
...AND WE GIVE YOU A HOME TO STAY.
WELCOME TO FENGXIAN.
THANK YOU.
OH, ONE MORE THING.
JAWS
GHOSTBUSTERS
THE OLDEST SON OF THE MAYOR OF SHANGHAI, MR. HUANG, IS COMING ON CHRISTMAS DAY.
WE NEED TO IMPRESS HIM AND HIS STAFF.
AND HE WILL GET A SPECIAL HOLIDAY SURPRISE: RICKY ROUSE.
YOU HAVE NO PLANS FOR CHRISTMAS?
NO PLANS, SIR...
MY DAUGHTER--
GOOD.
COME. LET ME LOOK AT YOU AGAIN.
SO CUTE. GO.
GREAT. GOODNIGHT NOW.
FUCK!
WATCH YOUR HEAD. IT'S PRECIOUS.

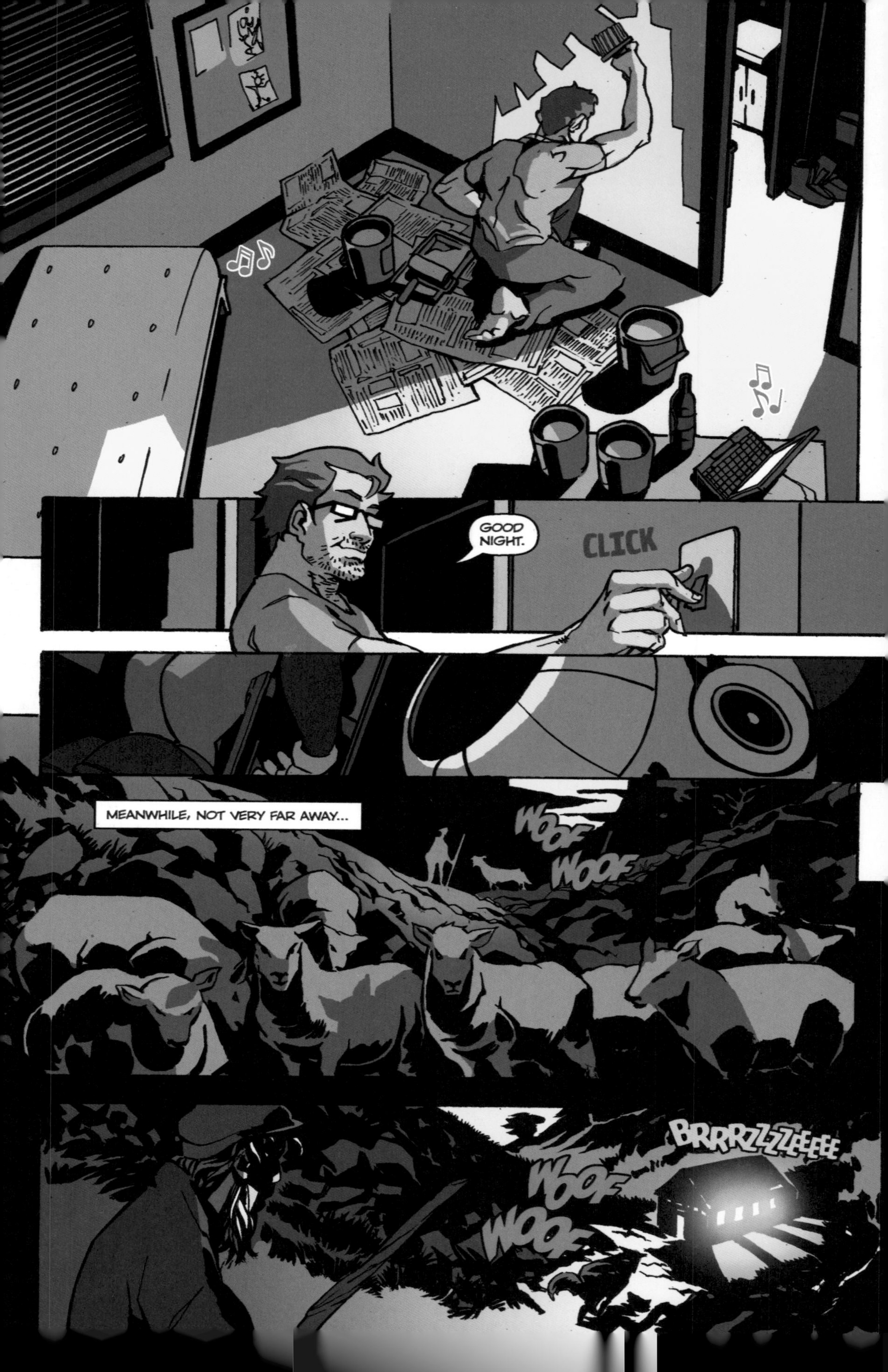
GOOD NIGHT.
CLICK
MEANWHILE, NOT VERY FAR AWAY...
WOOF
WOOF
BRRRZZZZZEEEEE
WOOF
WOOF

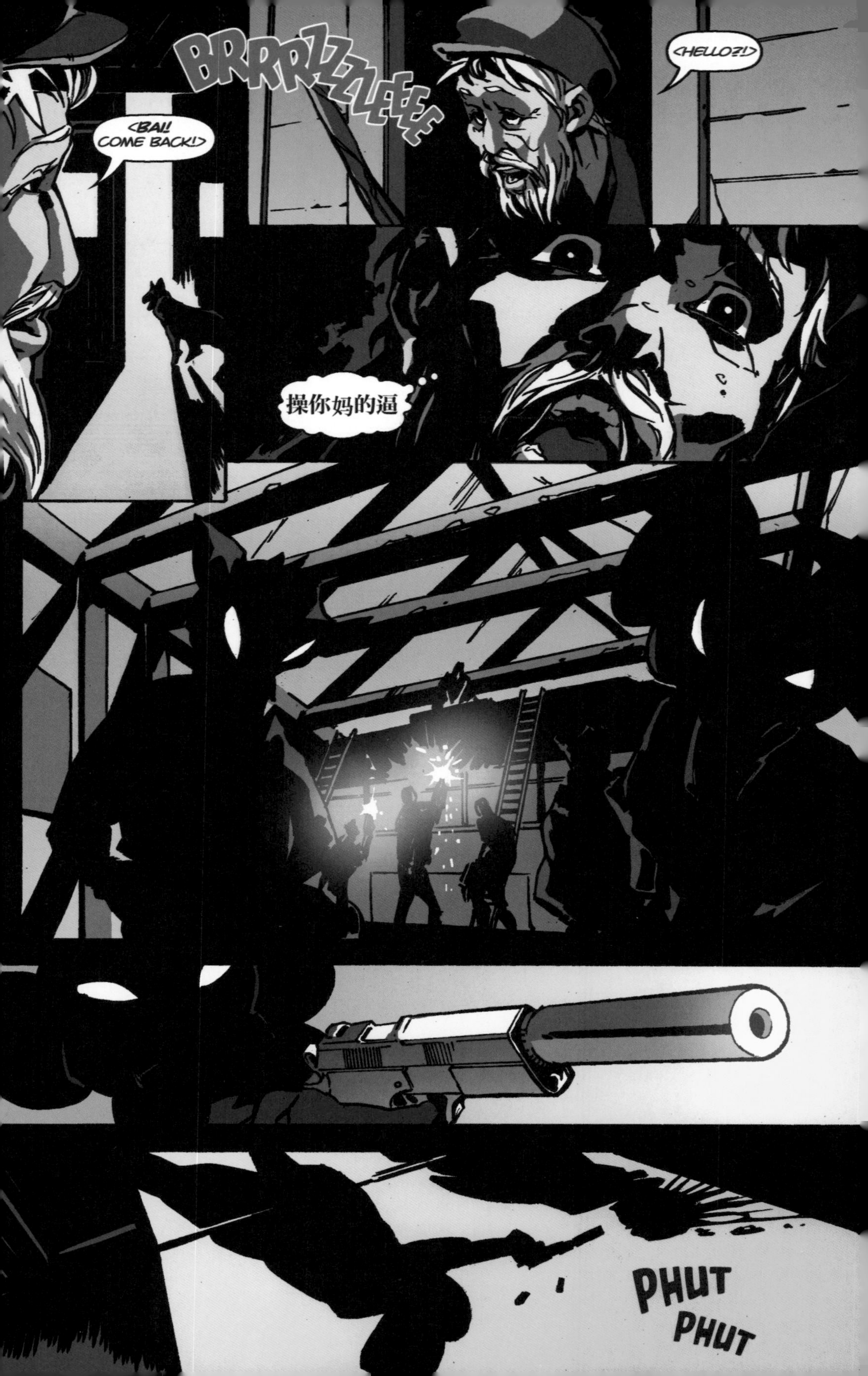
BRRRRZZZLEEEE
<HELLO?!>
<BAI! COME BACK!>
操你妈的逼
PHUT
PHUT

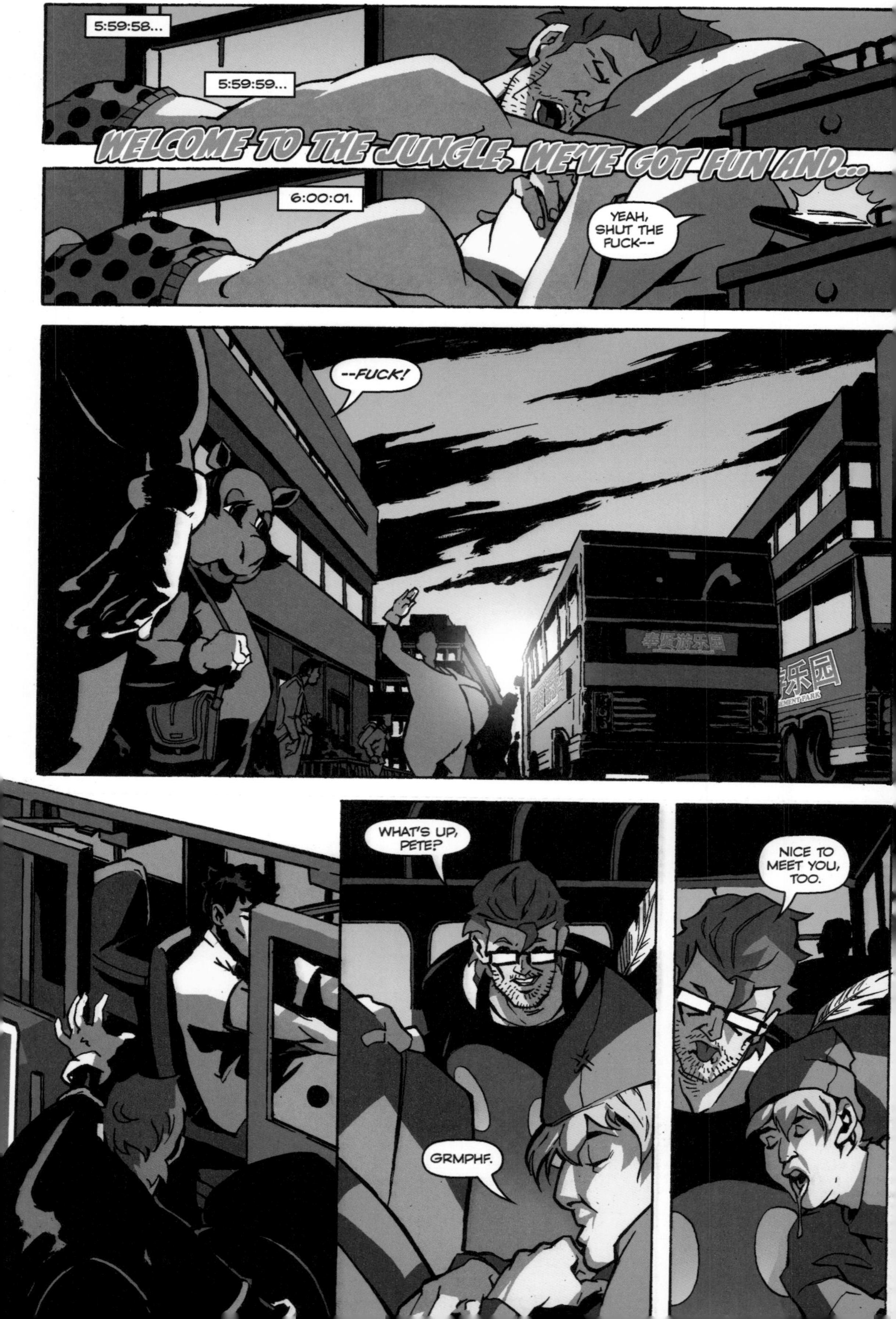
5:59:58...
5:59:59...
WELCOME TO THE JUNGLE, WE'VE GOT FUN AND...
6:00:01.
YEAH, SHUT THE FUCK--
--FUCK!
奉贤游乐园
WHAT'S UP, PETE?
GRMPHF.
NICE TO MEET YOU, TOO.

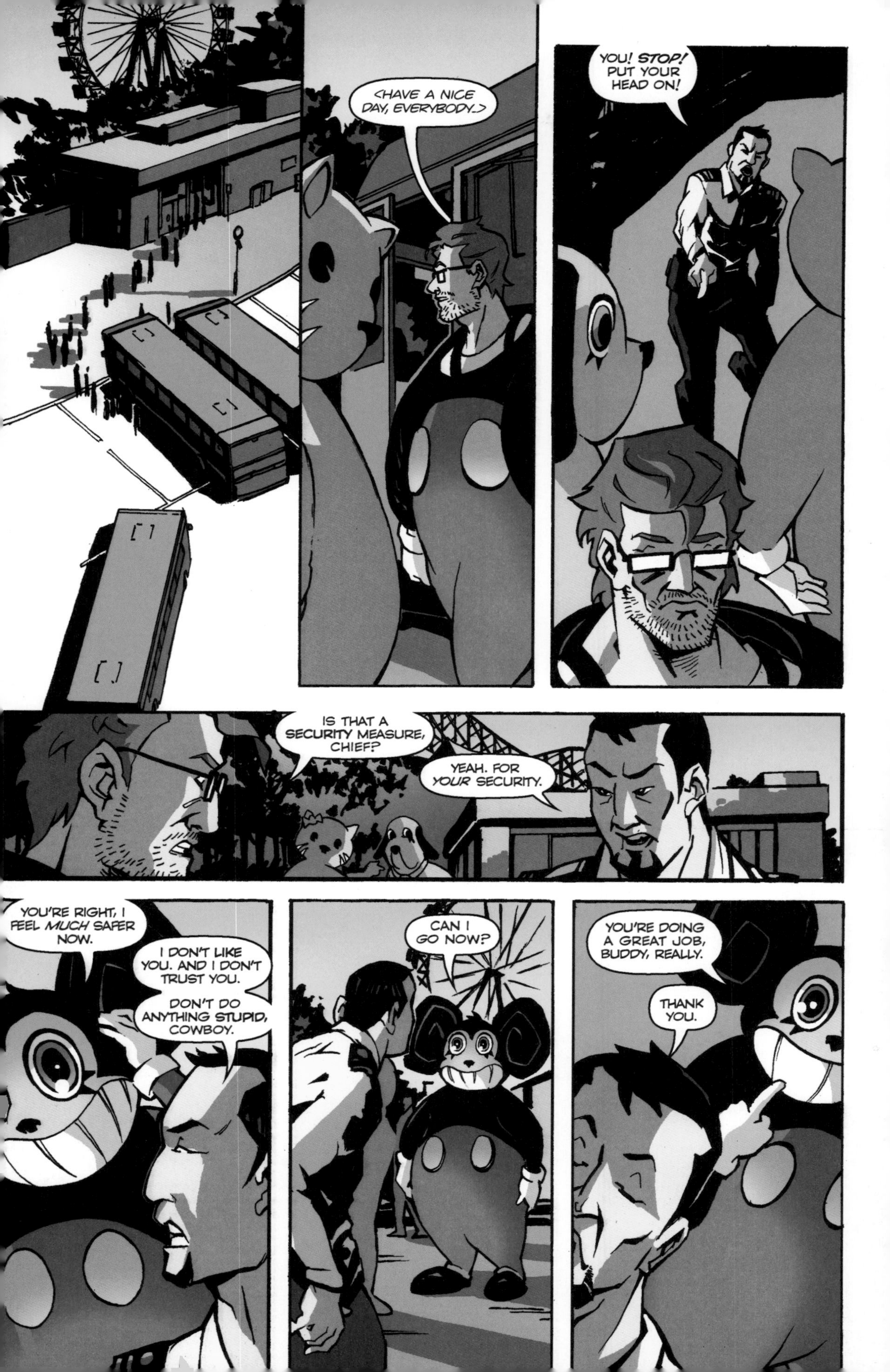
<HAVE A NICE DAY, EVERYBODY.>
YOU! *STOP!* PUT YOUR HEAD ON!
IS THAT A SECURITY MEASURE, CHIEF?
YEAH. FOR *YOUR* SECURITY.
YOU'RE RIGHT, I FEEL *MUCH* SAFER NOW.
I DON'T LIKE YOU. AND I DON'T TRUST YOU.
DON'T DO ANYTHING STUPID, COWBOY.
CAN I GO NOW?
YOU'RE DOING A GREAT JOB, BUDDY, REALLY.
THANK YOU.

THE HAMSTER HAS FLEAS, GRANDMA.

THAT'S NICE, DEAR.

SKRITCH SKRITCH

FUCKING PLASTIC JUNKSUIT--

HANG ON A SECOND...

RUSTLE RUSTLE

闲人免进
NO ENTRY

HEY, KID!

CLICK CLICK CLICK CLICK

HEY YOU!

YOU WEREN'T SUPPOSED TO BE THERE.

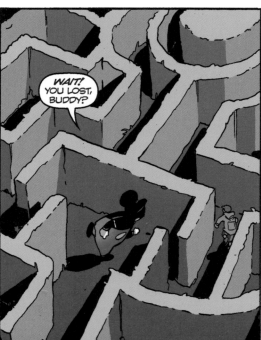

WAIT! YOU LOST, BUDDY?

WHERE ARE YOUR FOLKS?

HEY!

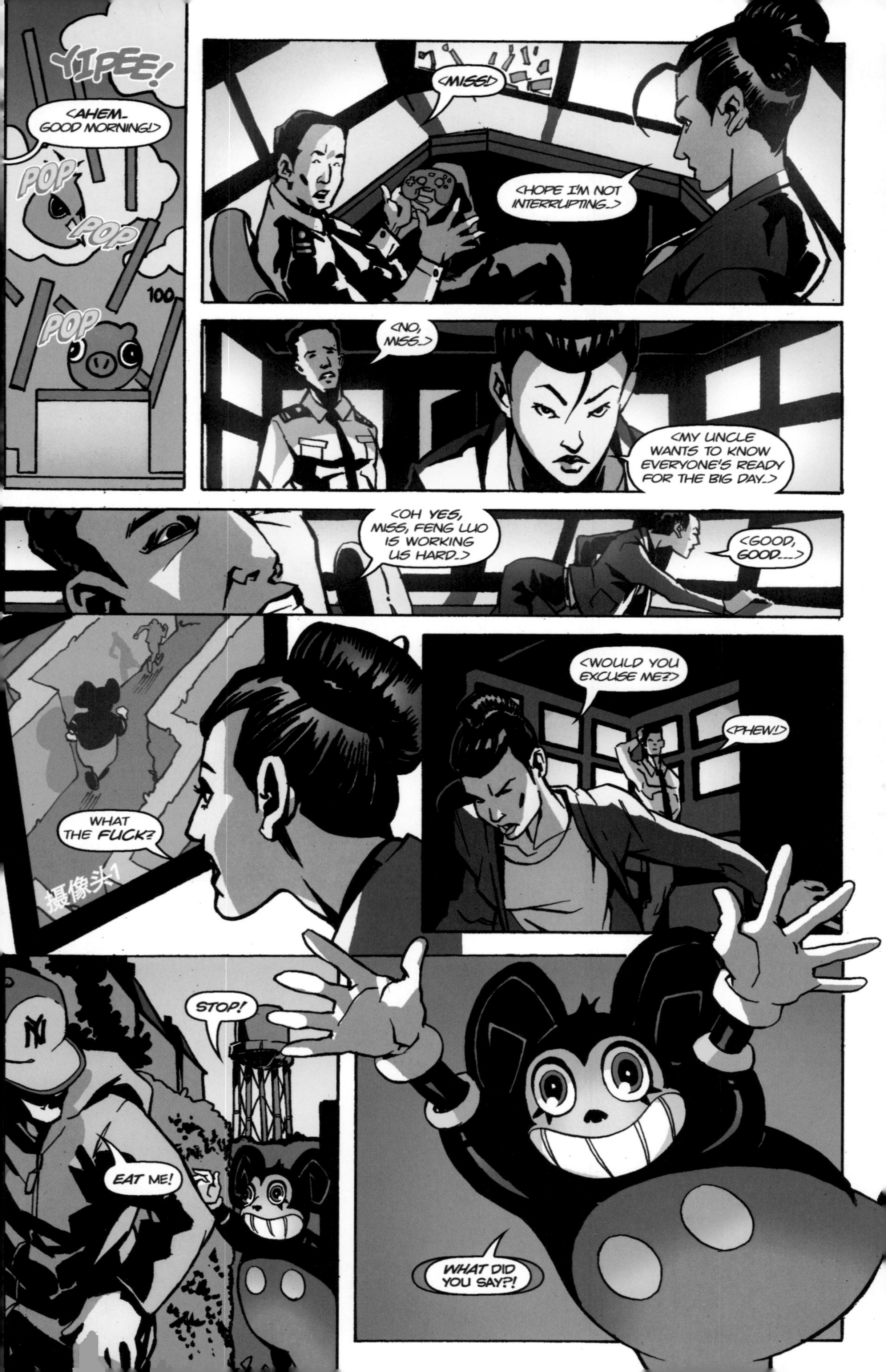
YIPEE!
<AHEM. GOOD MORNING!>
POP
POP
100
POP
<MISS!>
<HOPE I'M NOT INTERRUPTING.>
<NO, MISS.>
<MY UNCLE WANTS TO KNOW EVERYONE'S READY FOR THE BIG DAY.>
<OH YES, MISS, FENG LUO IS WORKING US HARD.>
<GOOD, GOOD...>
<WOULD YOU EXCUSE ME?>
<PHEW!>
WHAT THE FUCK?
摄像头1
STOP!
EAT ME!
WHAT DID YOU SAY?!

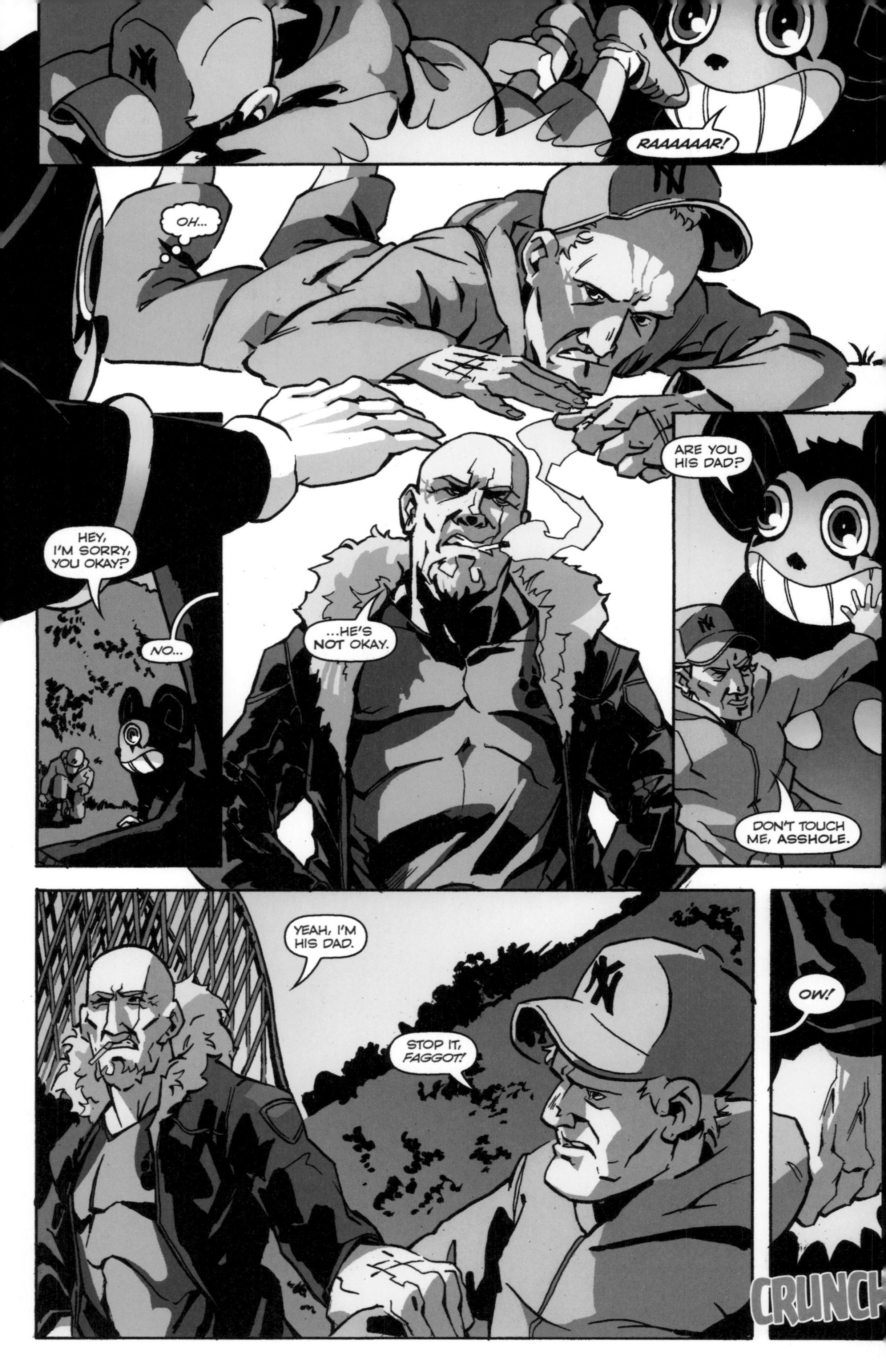
RAAAAAAR!
OH...
HEY, I'M SORRY, YOU OKAY?
NO...
...HE'S NOT OKAY.
ARE YOU HIS DAD?
DON'T TOUCH ME, ASSHOLE.
YEAH, I'M HIS DAD.
STOP IT, FAGGOT!
OW!
CRUNCH

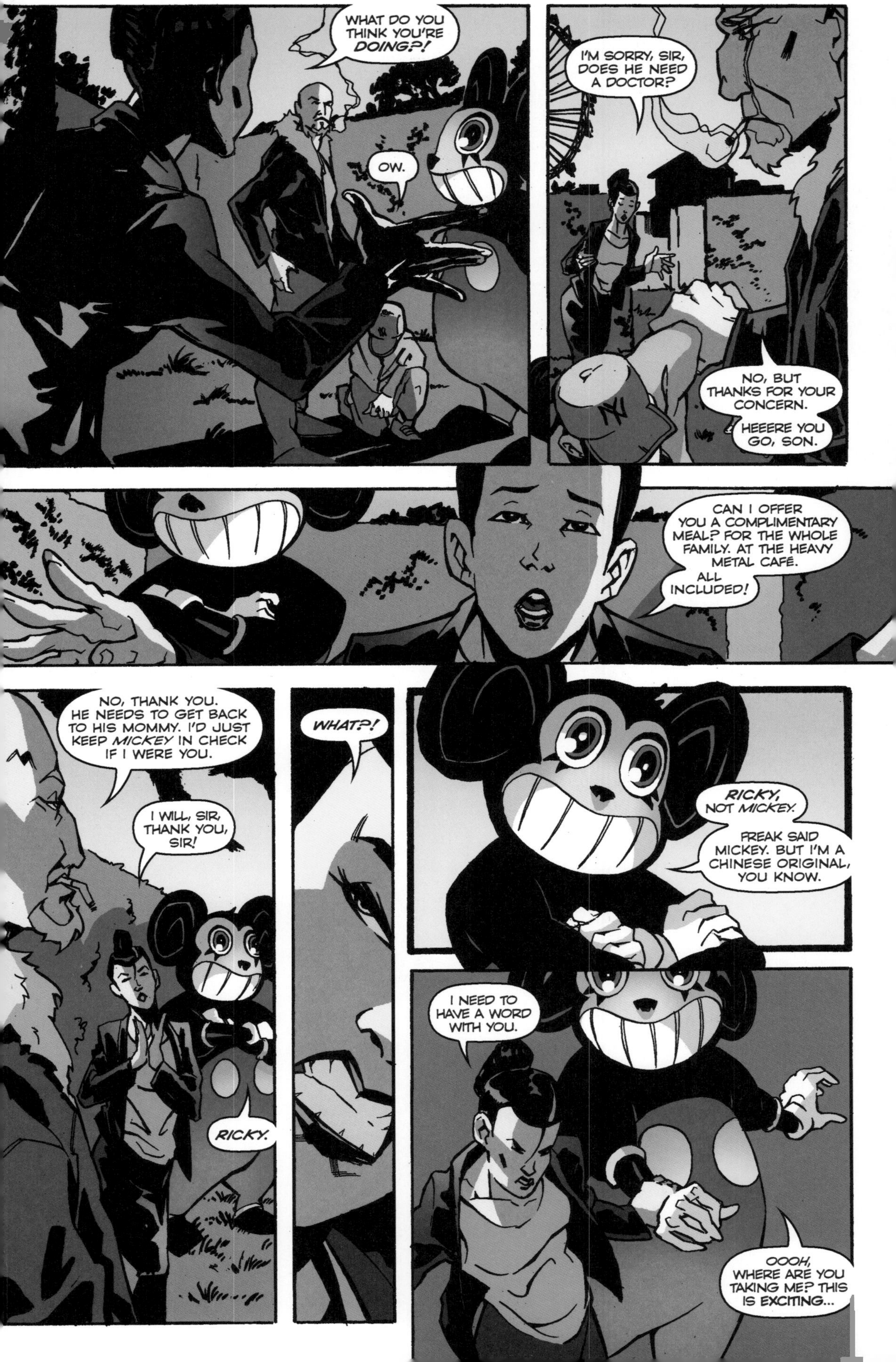
WHAT DO YOU THINK YOU'RE *DOING?!*
OW.
I'M SORRY, SIR, DOES HE NEED A DOCTOR?
NO, BUT THANKS FOR YOUR CONCERN.
HEEERE YOU GO, SON.
CAN I OFFER YOU A COMPLIMENTARY MEAL? FOR THE WHOLE FAMILY. AT THE HEAVY METAL CAFÉ.
ALL INCLUDED!
NO, THANK YOU. HE NEEDS TO GET BACK TO HIS MOMMY. I'D JUST KEEP *MICKEY* IN CHECK IF I WERE YOU.
I WILL, SIR, THANK YOU, SIR!
RICKY.
WHAT?!
RICKY, NOT *MICKEY.*
FREAK SAID MICKEY. BUT I'M A CHINESE ORIGINAL, YOU KNOW.
I NEED TO HAVE A WORD WITH YOU.
OOOH, WHERE ARE YOU TAKING ME? THIS IS EXCITING...

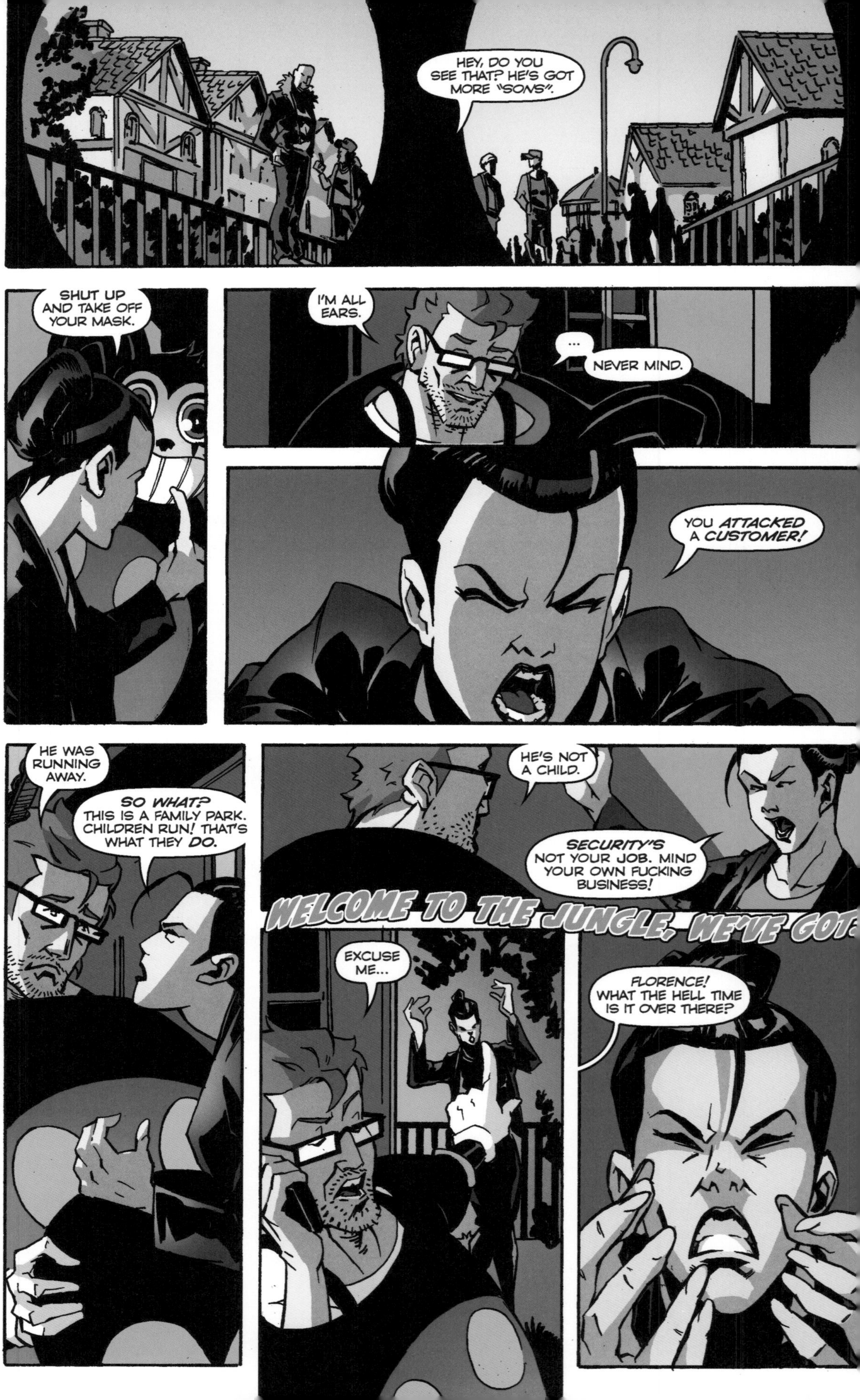
HEY, DO YOU SEE THAT? HE'S GOT MORE "SONS".
SHUT UP AND TAKE OFF YOUR MASK.
I'M ALL EARS.
...
NEVER MIND.
YOU ATTACKED A CUSTOMER!
HE WAS RUNNING AWAY.
SO WHAT? THIS IS A FAMILY PARK. CHILDREN RUN! THAT'S WHAT THEY DO.
HE'S NOT A CHILD.
SECURITY'S NOT YOUR JOB. MIND YOUR OWN FUCKING BUSINESS!
WELCOME TO THE JUNGLE, WE'VE GOT
EXCUSE ME...
FLORENCE! WHAT THE HELL TIME IS IT OVER THERE?

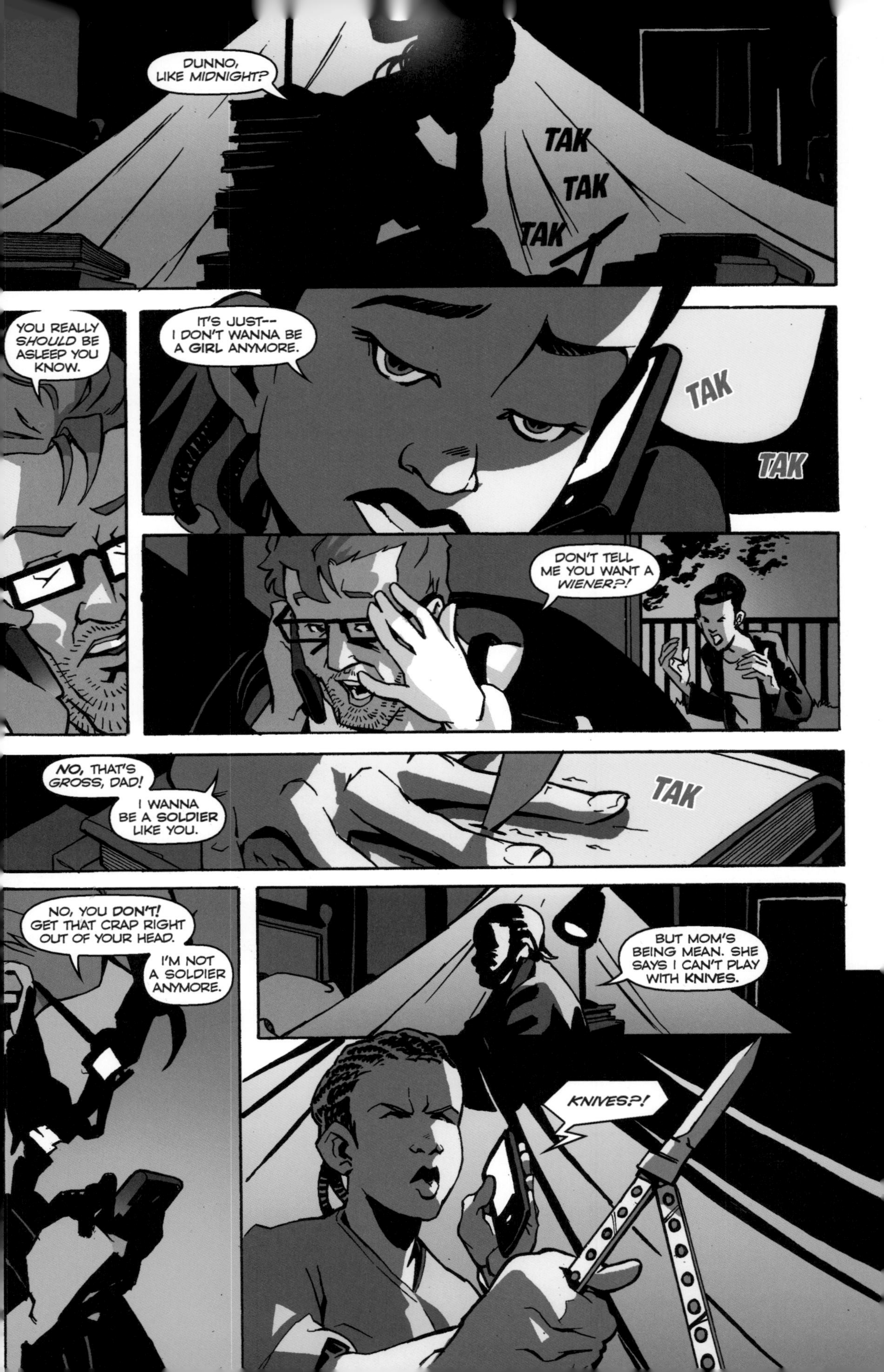
DUNNO, LIKE MIDNIGHT?
TAK
TAK
TAK
YOU REALLY SHOULD BE ASLEEP YOU KNOW.
IT'S JUST-- I DON'T WANNA BE A GIRL ANYMORE.
TAK
TAK
DON'T TELL ME YOU WANT A WIENER?!
NO, THAT'S GROSS, DAD!
I WANNA BE A SOLDIER LIKE YOU.
TAK
NO, YOU DON'T! GET THAT CRAP RIGHT OUT OF YOUR HEAD.
I'M NOT A SOLDIER ANYMORE.
BUT MOM'S BEING MEAN. SHE SAYS I CAN'T PLAY WITH KNIVES.
KNIVES?!

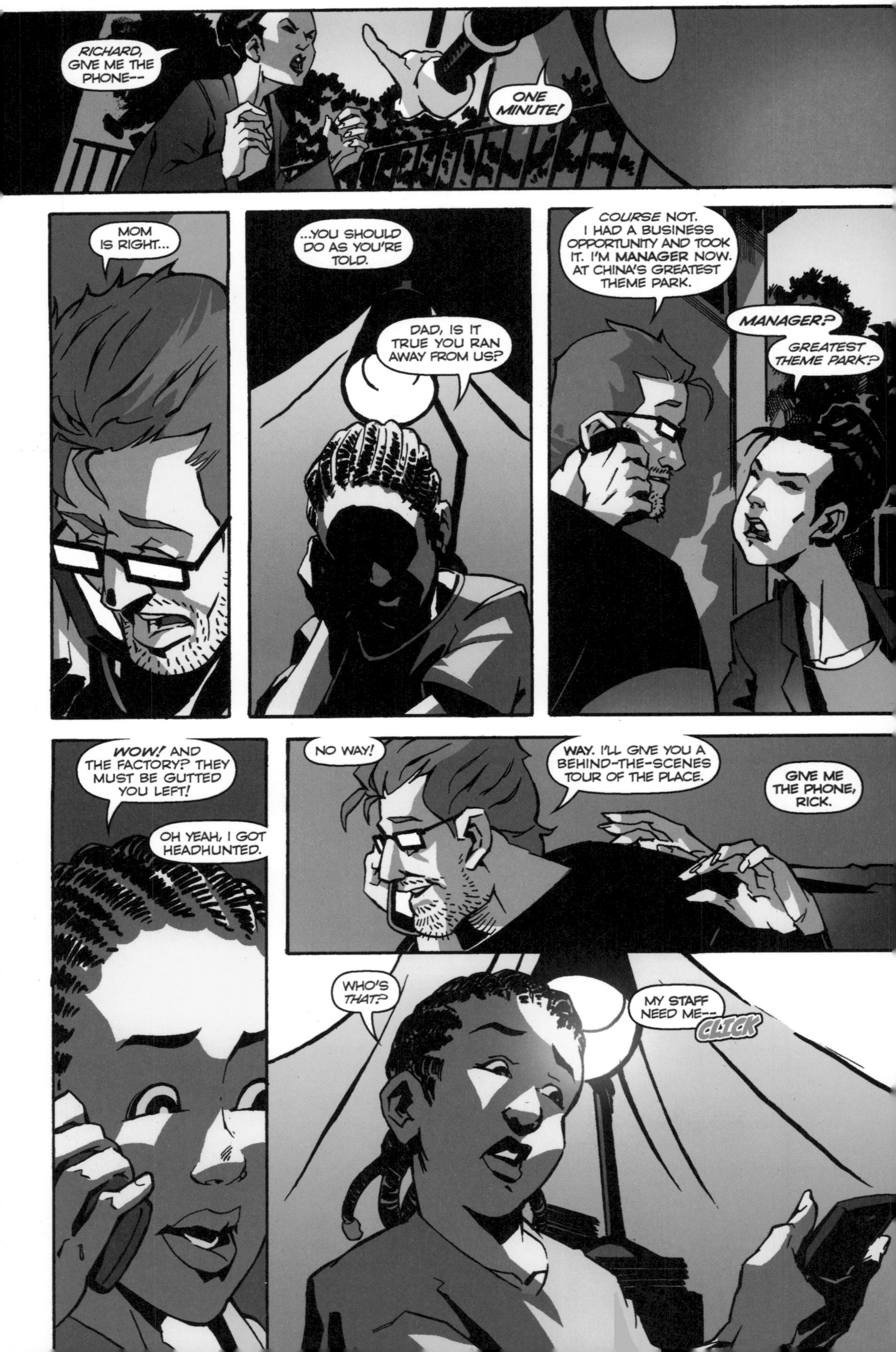
RICHARD, GIVE ME THE PHONE--
ONE MINUTE!
MOM IS RIGHT...
...YOU SHOULD DO AS YOU'RE TOLD.
DAD, IS IT TRUE YOU RAN AWAY FROM US?
COURSE NOT. I HAD A BUSINESS OPPORTUNITY AND TOOK IT. I'M MANAGER NOW. AT CHINA'S GREATEST THEME PARK.
MANAGER? GREATEST THEME PARK?
WOW! AND THE FACTORY? THEY MUST BE GUTTED YOU LEFT!
OH YEAH, I GOT HEADHUNTED.
NO WAY!
WAY. I'LL GIVE YOU A BEHIND-THE-SCENES TOUR OF THE PLACE.
GIVE ME THE PHONE, RICK.
WHO'S THAT?
MY STAFF NEED ME--
CLICK

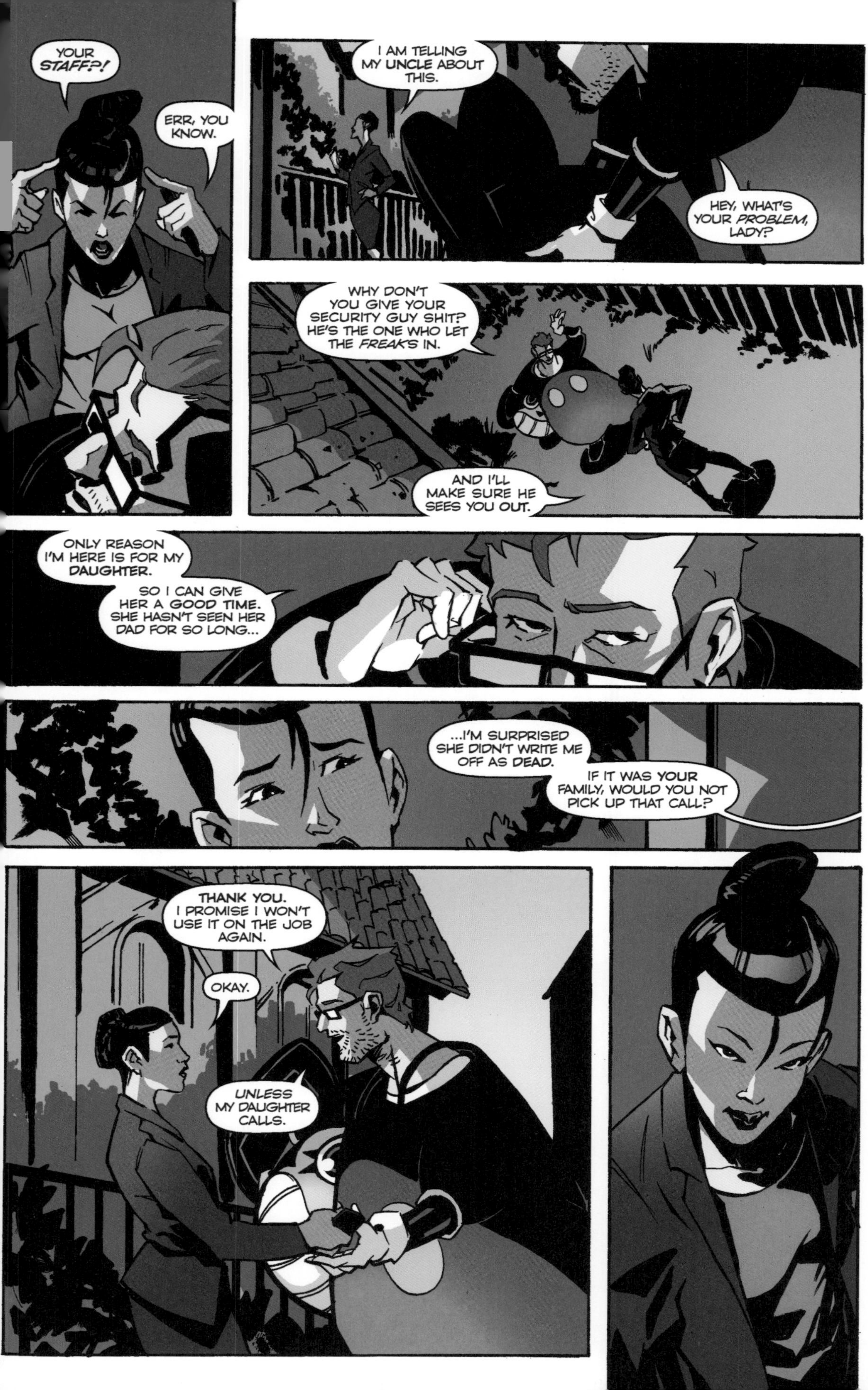
YOUR STAFF?!
ERR, YOU KNOW.
I AM TELLING MY UNCLE ABOUT THIS.
HEY, WHAT'S YOUR PROBLEM, LADY?
WHY DON'T YOU GIVE YOUR SECURITY GUY SHIT? HE'S THE ONE WHO LET THE FREAKS IN.
AND I'LL MAKE SURE HE SEES YOU OUT.
ONLY REASON I'M HERE IS FOR MY DAUGHTER.
SO I CAN GIVE HER A GOOD TIME. SHE HASN'T SEEN HER DAD FOR SO LONG...
...I'M SURPRISED SHE DIDN'T WRITE ME OFF AS DEAD.
IF IT WAS YOUR FAMILY, WOULD YOU NOT PICK UP THAT CALL?
THANK YOU. I PROMISE I WON'T USE IT ON THE JOB AGAIN.
OKAY.
UNLESS MY DAUGHTER CALLS.

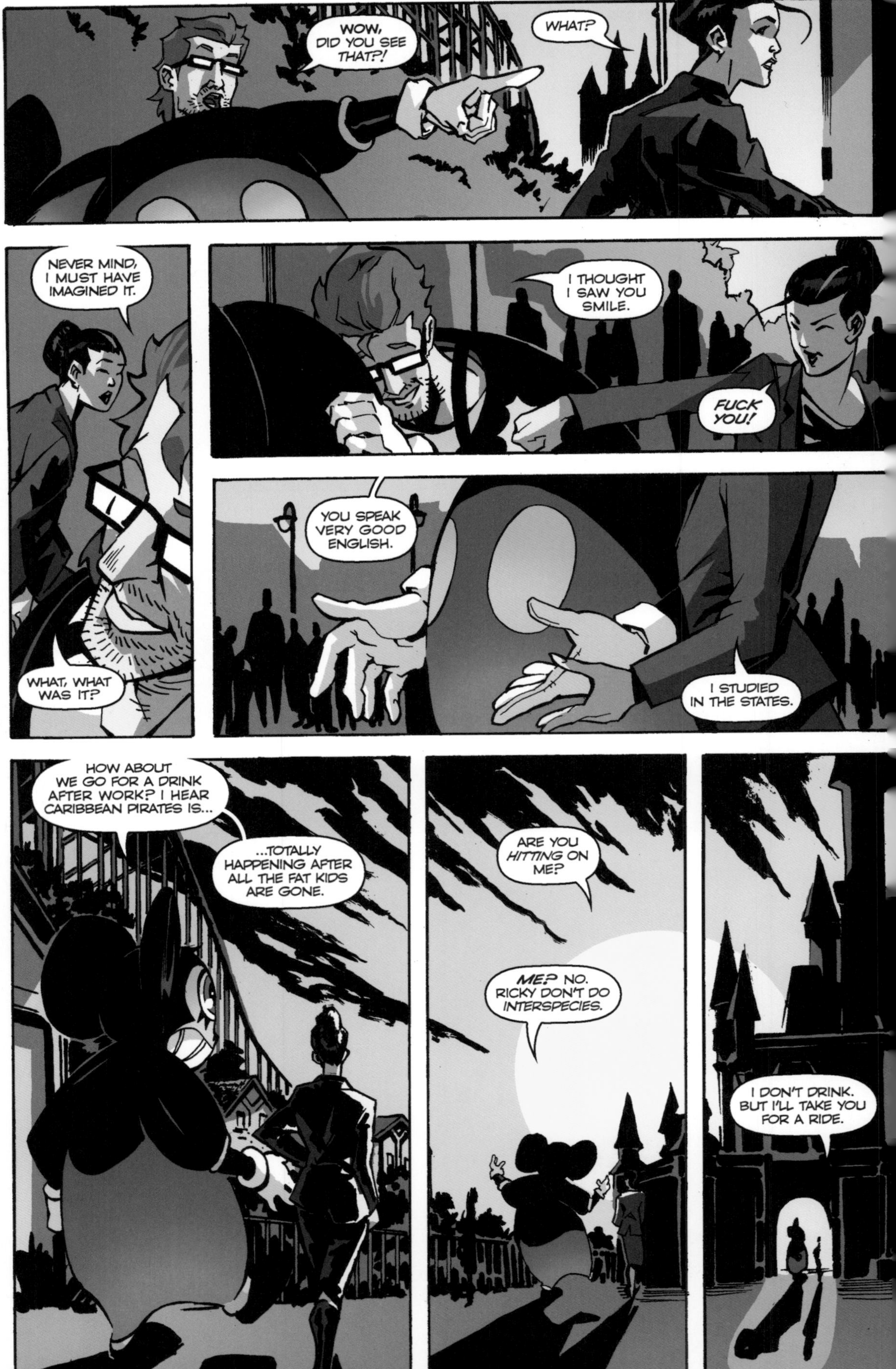
WOW, DID YOU SEE THAT?!
WHAT?
NEVER MIND, I MUST HAVE IMAGINED IT.
WHAT, WHAT WAS IT?
I THOUGHT I SAW YOU SMILE.
FUCK YOU!
YOU SPEAK VERY GOOD ENGLISH.
I STUDIED IN THE STATES.
HOW ABOUT WE GO FOR A DRINK AFTER WORK? I HEAR CARIBBEAN PIRATES IS...
...TOTALLY HAPPENING AFTER ALL THE FAT KIDS ARE GONE.
ARE YOU HITTING ON ME?
ME? NO. RICKY DON'T DO INTERSPECIES.
I DON'T DRINK. BUT I'LL TAKE YOU FOR A RIDE.

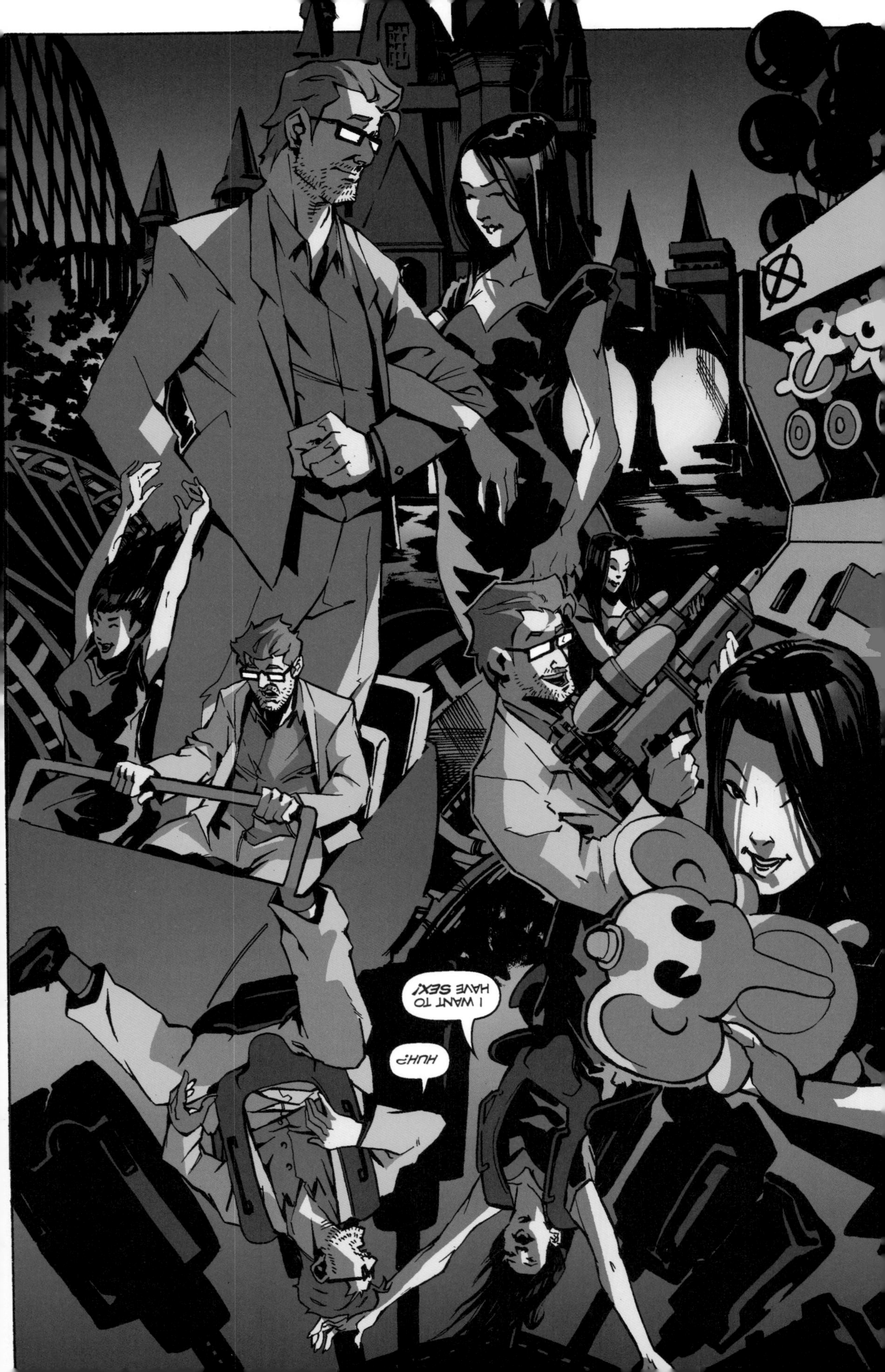
I WANT TO
HAVE SEX!
HUH?

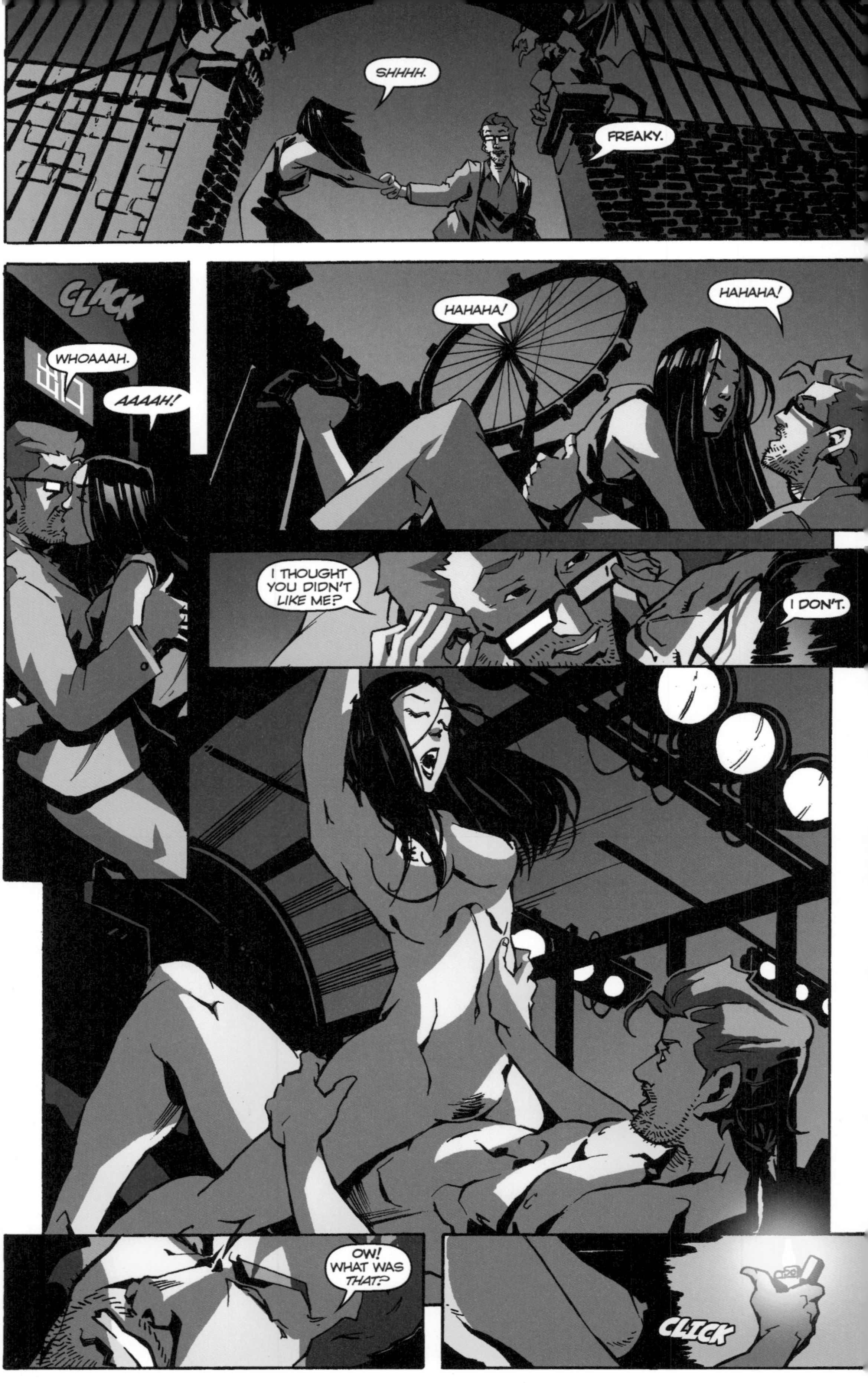
SHHHH.
FREAKY.
CLACK
WHOAAAH.
AAAAH!
HAHAHA!
HAHAHA!
I THOUGHT YOU DIDN'T LIKE ME?
I DON'T.
OW! WHAT WAS *THAT?*
CLICK

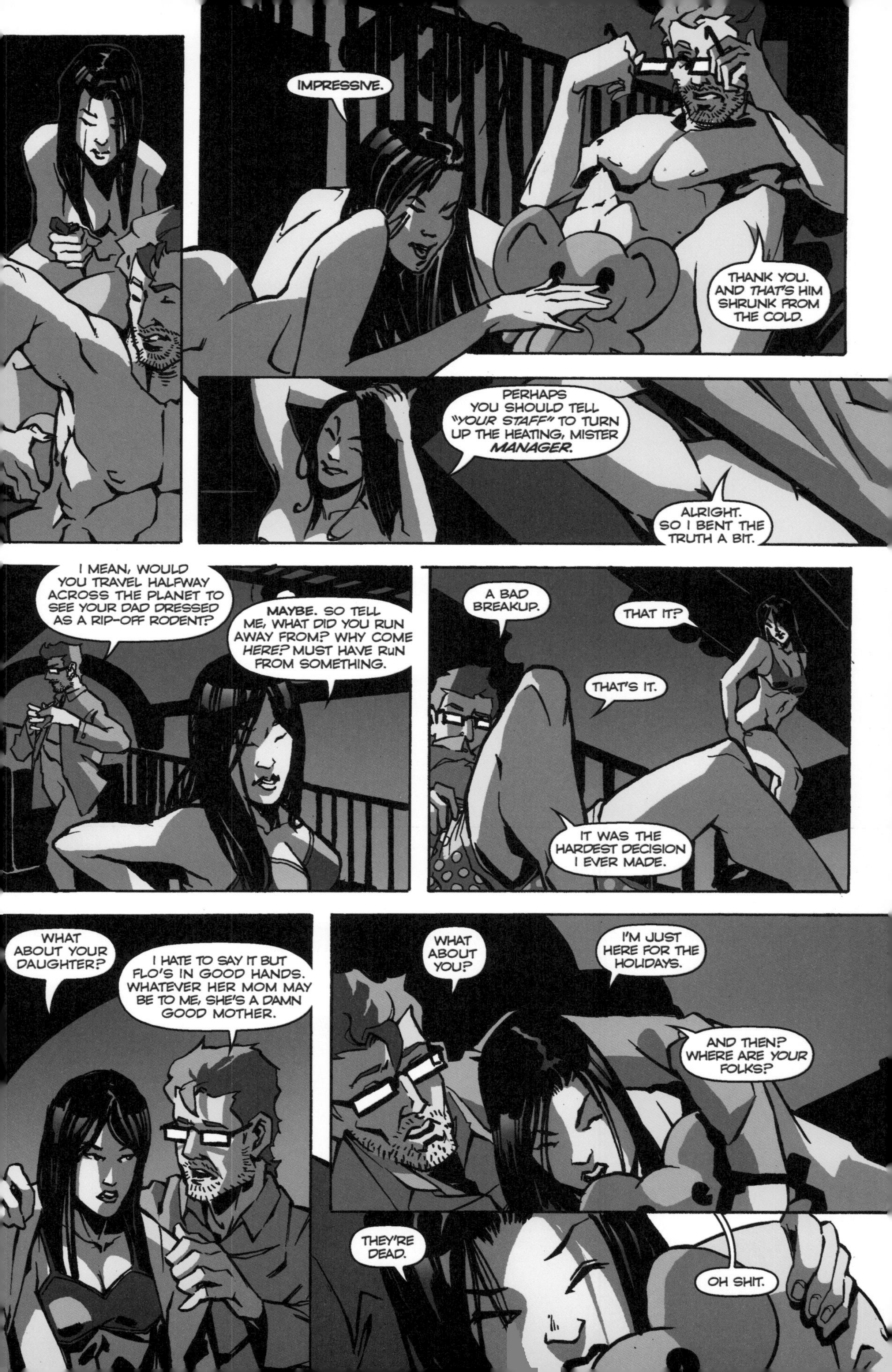

IMPRESSIVE.
THANK YOU. AND THAT'S HIM SHRUNK FROM THE COLD.
PERHAPS YOU SHOULD TELL "YOUR STAFF" TO TURN UP THE HEATING, MISTER MANAGER.
ALRIGHT. SO I BENT THE TRUTH A BIT.
I MEAN, WOULD YOU TRAVEL HALFWAY ACROSS THE PLANET TO SEE YOUR DAD DRESSED AS A RIP-OFF RODENT?
MAYBE. SO TELL ME, WHAT DID YOU RUN AWAY FROM? WHY COME HERE? MUST HAVE RUN FROM SOMETHING.
A BAD BREAKUP.
THAT IT?
THAT'S IT.
IT WAS THE HARDEST DECISION I EVER MADE.
WHAT ABOUT YOUR DAUGHTER?
I HATE TO SAY IT BUT FLO'S IN GOOD HANDS. WHATEVER HER MOM MAY BE TO ME, SHE'S A DAMN GOOD MOTHER.
WHAT ABOUT YOU?
I'M JUST HERE FOR THE HOLIDAYS.
AND THEN? WHERE ARE YOUR FOLKS?
THEY'RE DEAD.
OH SHIT.

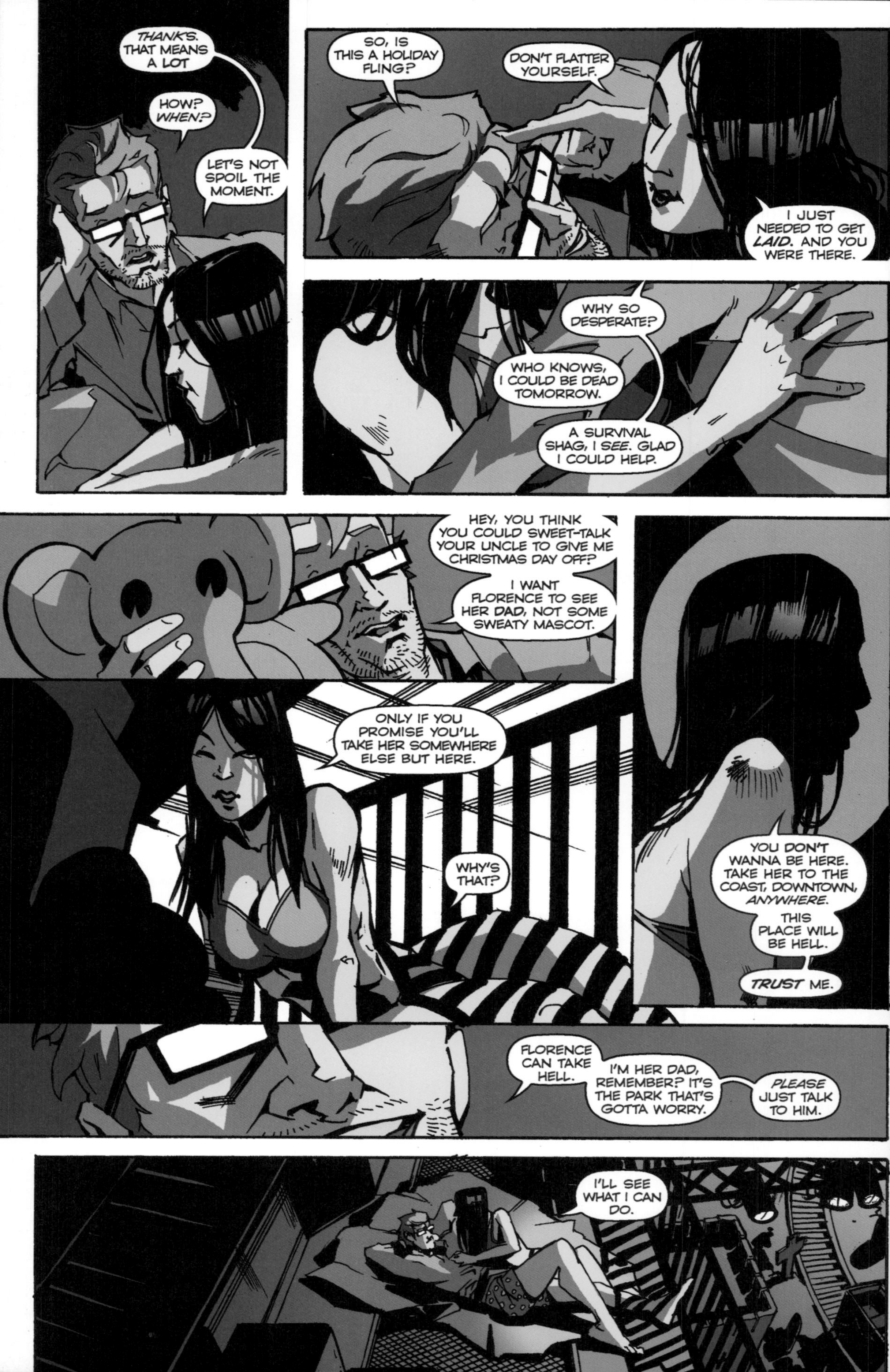
THANKS. THAT MEANS A LOT
HOW? WHEN?
LET'S NOT SPOIL THE MOMENT.
SO, IS THIS A HOLIDAY FLING?
DON'T FLATTER YOURSELF.
I JUST NEEDED TO GET LAID. AND YOU WERE THERE.
WHY SO DESPERATE?
WHO KNOWS, I COULD BE DEAD TOMORROW.
A SURVIVAL SHAG, I SEE. GLAD I COULD HELP.
HEY, YOU THINK YOU COULD SWEET-TALK YOUR UNCLE TO GIVE ME CHRISTMAS DAY OFF?
I WANT FLORENCE TO SEE HER DAD, NOT SOME SWEATY MASCOT.
ONLY IF YOU PROMISE YOU'LL TAKE HER SOMEWHERE ELSE BUT HERE.
WHY'S THAT?
YOU DON'T WANNA BE HERE. TAKE HER TO THE COAST, DOWNTOWN, ANYWHERE.
THIS PLACE WILL BE HELL.
TRUST ME.
FLORENCE CAN TAKE HELL.
I'M HER DAD, REMEMBER? IT'S THE PARK THAT'S GOTTA WORRY.
PLEASE JUST TALK TO HIM.
I'LL SEE WHAT I CAN DO.

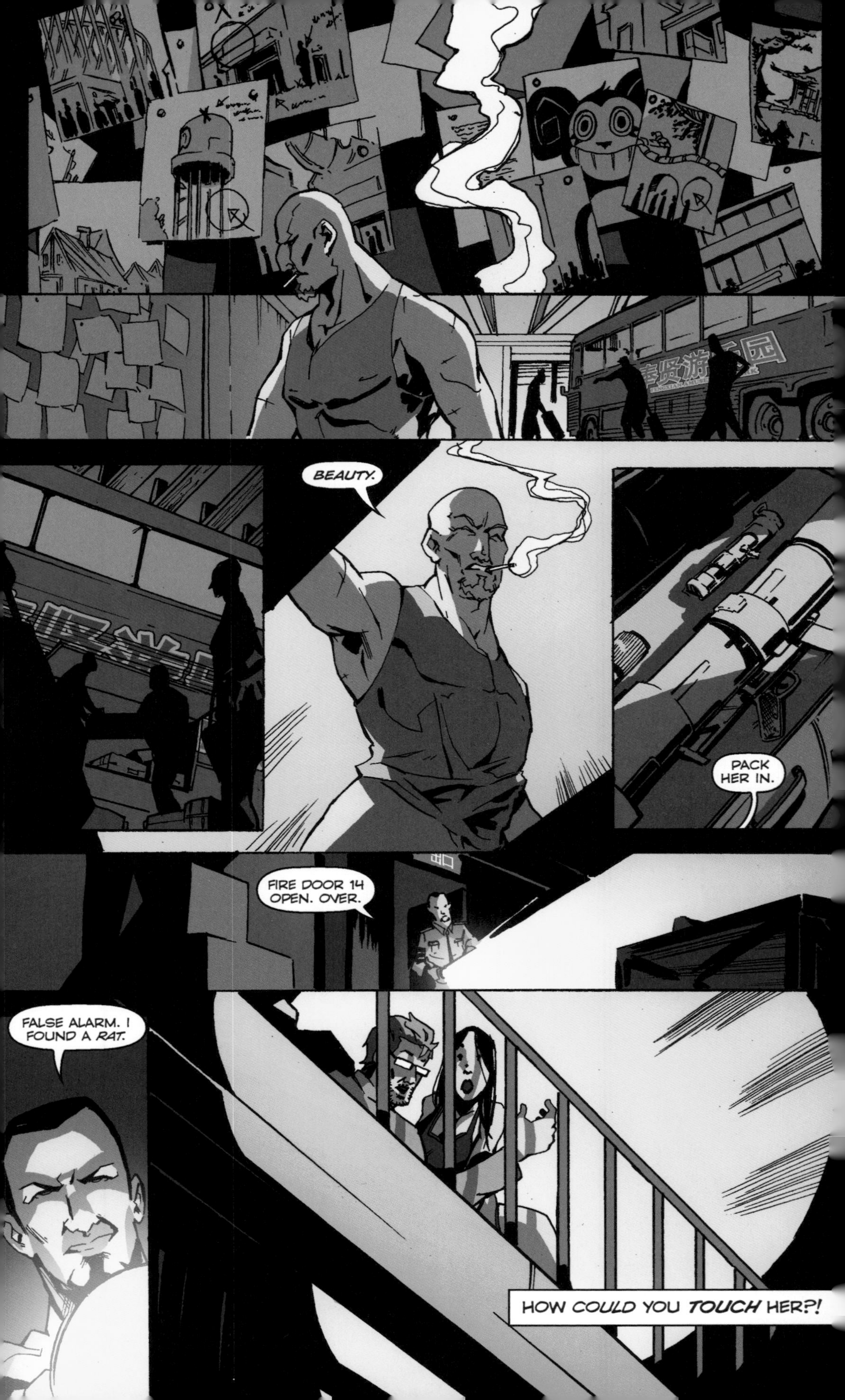

BEAUTY.
PACK HER IN.
FIRE DOOR 14 OPEN. OVER.
FALSE ALARM. I FOUND A RAT.
HOW COULD YOU TOUCH HER?!

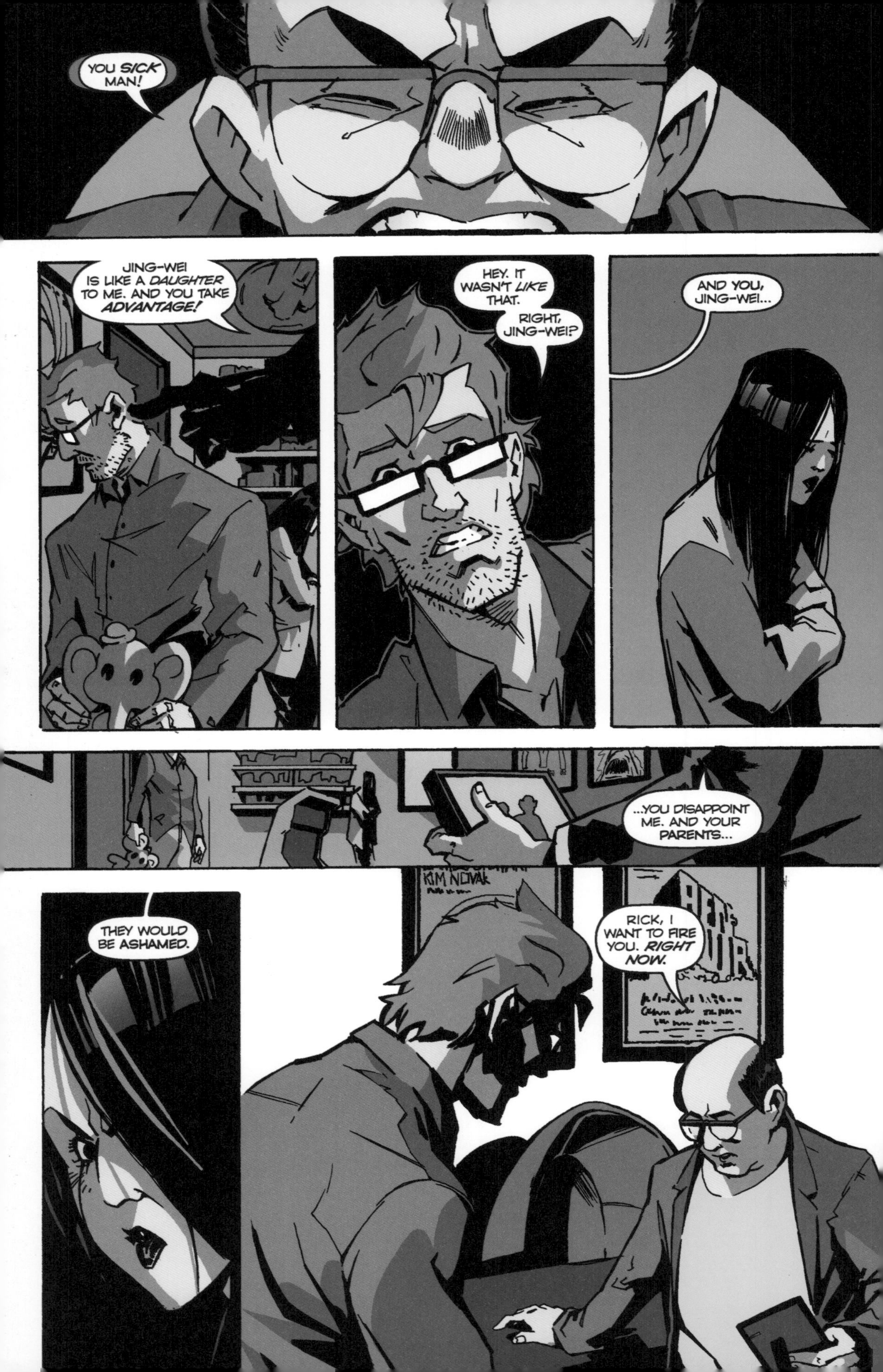
YOU SICK MAN!
JING-WEI IS LIKE A DAUGHTER TO ME. AND YOU TAKE ADVANTAGE!
HEY. IT WASN'T LIKE THAT.
RIGHT, JING-WEI?
AND YOU, JING-WEI...
...YOU DISAPPOINT ME. AND YOUR PARENTS...
THEY WOULD BE ASHAMED.
KIM NOVAK
RICK, I WANT TO FIRE YOU. RIGHT NOW.

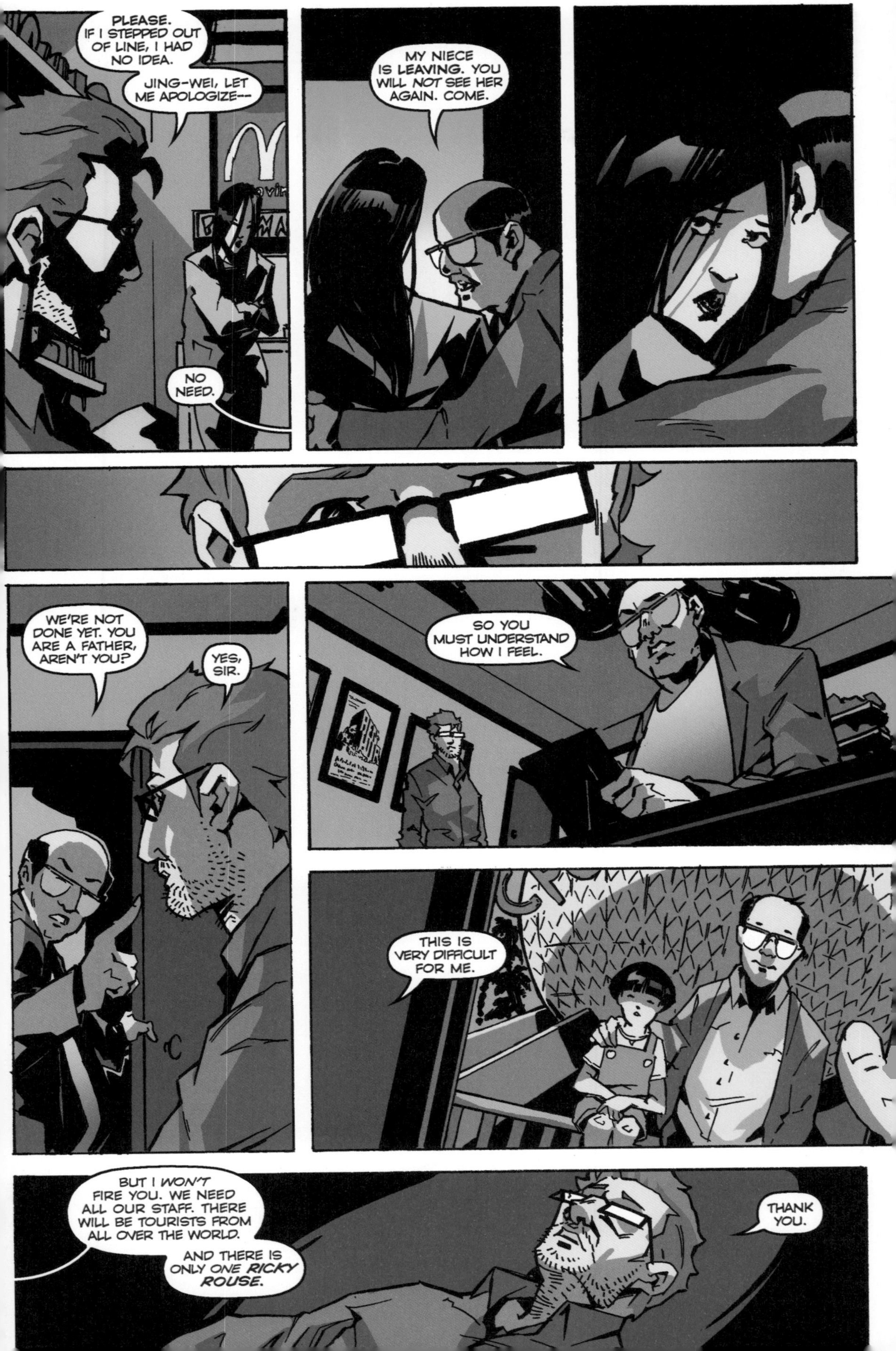
PLEASE. IF I STEPPED OUT OF LINE, I HAD NO IDEA.
JING-WEI, LET ME APOLOGIZE--
NO NEED.
MY NIECE IS LEAVING. YOU WILL *NOT* SEE HER AGAIN. COME.
WE'RE NOT DONE YET. YOU ARE A FATHER, AREN'T YOU?
YES, SIR.
SO YOU MUST UNDERSTAND HOW I FEEL.
THIS IS VERY DIFFICULT FOR ME.
BUT I *WON'T* FIRE YOU. WE NEED ALL OUR STAFF. THERE WILL BE TOURISTS FROM ALL OVER THE WORLD.
AND THERE IS ONLY *ONE RICKY ROUSE*.
THANK YOU.

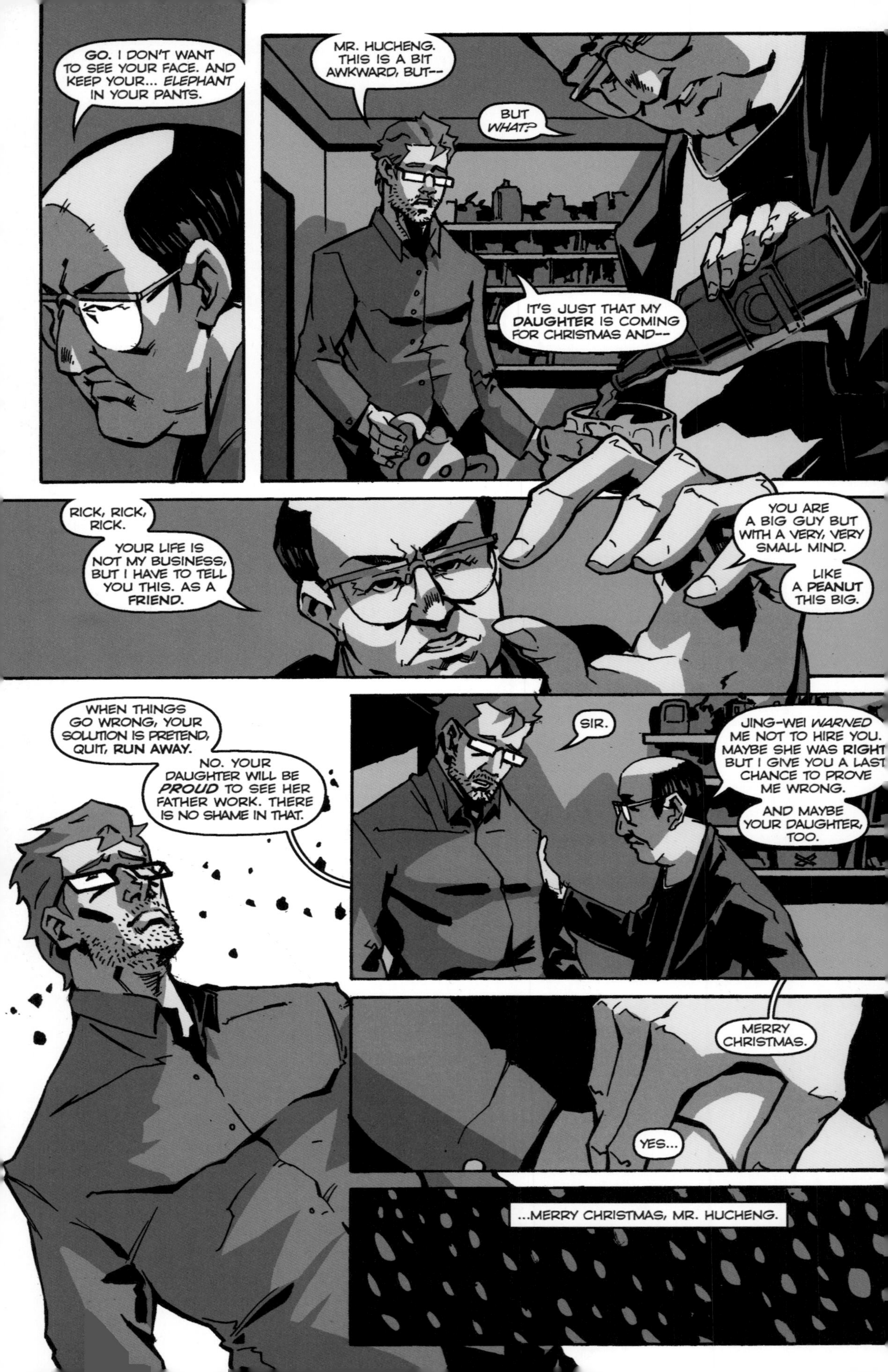
GO. I DON'T WANT TO SEE YOUR FACE. AND KEEP YOUR... ELEPHANT IN YOUR PANTS.
MR. HUCHENG. THIS IS A BIT AWKWARD, BUT--
BUT WHAT?
IT'S JUST THAT MY DAUGHTER IS COMING FOR CHRISTMAS AND--
RICK, RICK, RICK.
YOUR LIFE IS NOT MY BUSINESS, BUT I HAVE TO TELL YOU THIS. AS A FRIEND.
YOU ARE A BIG GUY BUT WITH A VERY, VERY SMALL MIND.
LIKE A PEANUT THIS BIG.
WHEN THINGS GO WRONG, YOUR SOLUTION IS PRETEND, QUIT, RUN AWAY.
NO. YOUR DAUGHTER WILL BE PROUD TO SEE HER FATHER WORK. THERE IS NO SHAME IN THAT.
SIR.
JING-WEI WARNED ME NOT TO HIRE YOU. MAYBE SHE WAS RIGHT BUT I GIVE YOU A LAST CHANCE TO PROVE ME WRONG.
AND MAYBE YOUR DAUGHTER, TOO.
MERRY CHRISTMAS.
YES...
...MERRY CHRISTMAS, MR. HUCHENG.

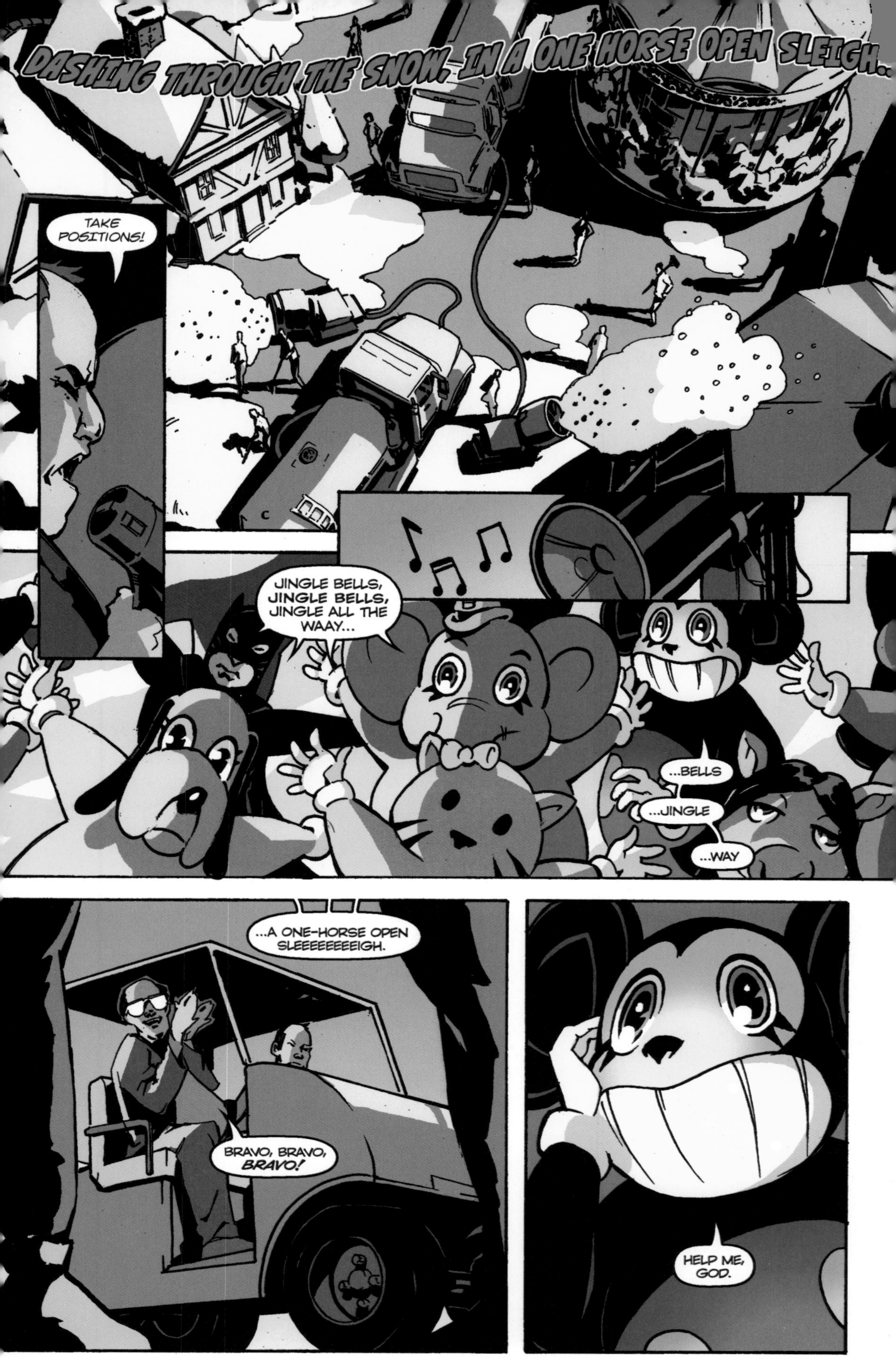

DASHING THROUGH THE SNOW, IN A ONE HORSE OPEN SLEIGH..
TAKE POSITIONS!
JINGLE BELLS, JINGLE BELLS, JINGLE ALL THE WAAY...
...BELLS
...JINGLE
...WAY
...A ONE-HORSE OPEN SLEEEEEEEEEIGH.
BRAVO, BRAVO, *BRAVO!*
HELP ME, GOD.

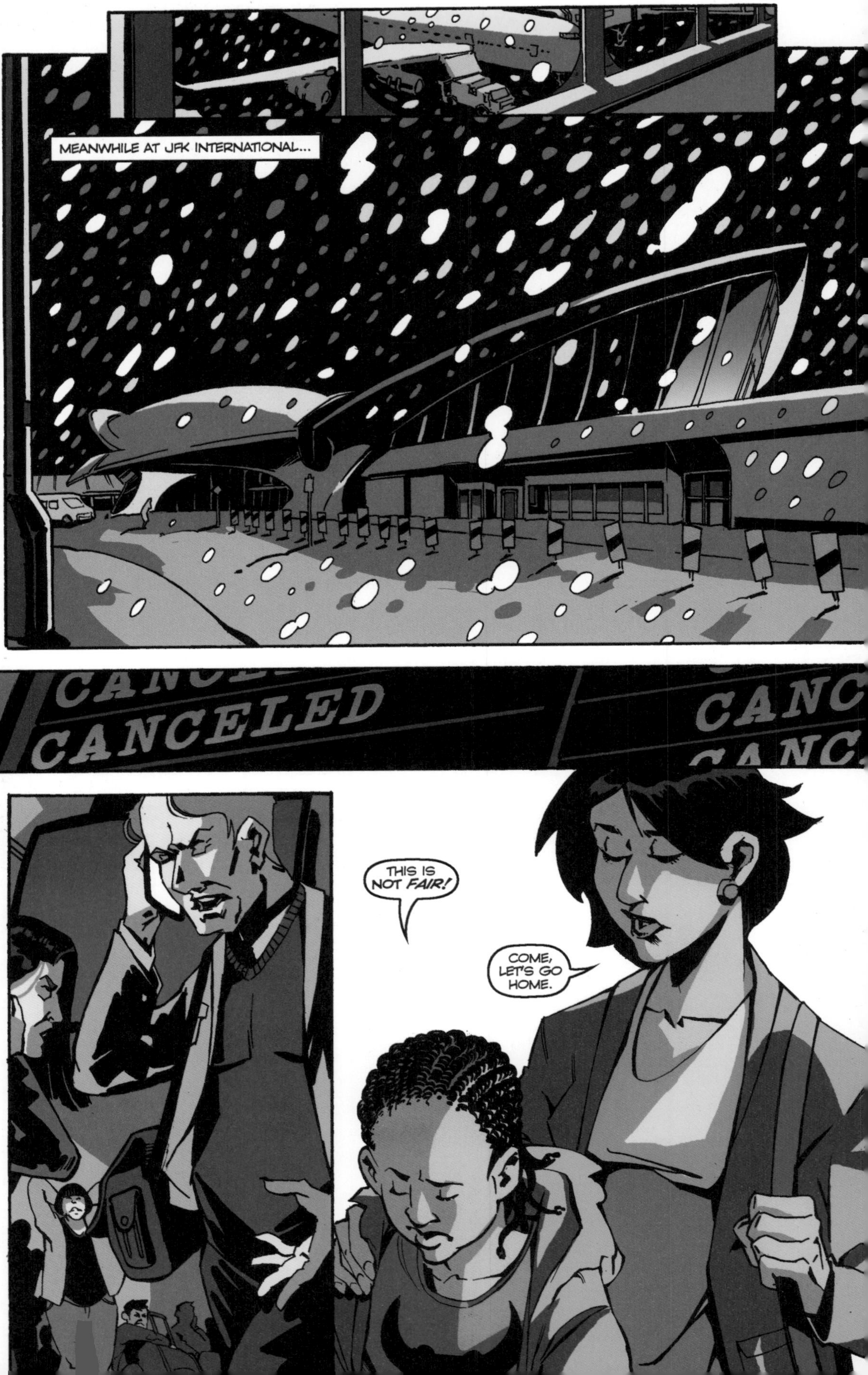
MEANWHILE AT JFK INTERNATIONAL...
CANCELED
CANCELED
THIS IS NOT FAIR!
COME, LET'S GO HOME.

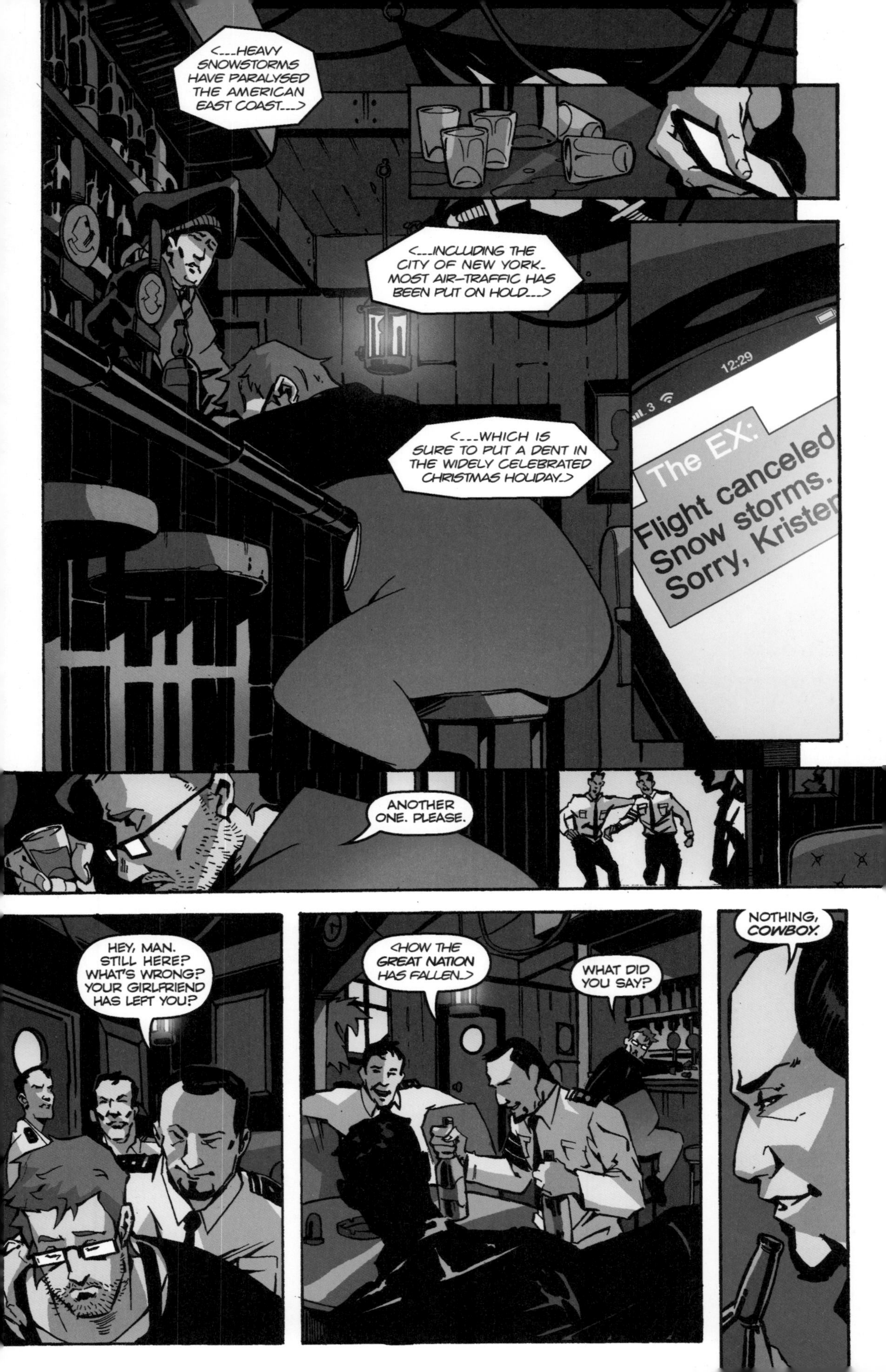
<...HEAVY SNOWSTORMS HAVE PARALYSED THE AMERICAN EAST COAST...>
<...INCLUDING THE CITY OF NEW YORK. MOST AIR-TRAFFIC HAS BEEN PUT ON HOLD...>
12:29
The EX:
Flight canceled
Snow storms.
Sorry, Kriste
<...WHICH IS SURE TO PUT A DENT IN THE WIDELY CELEBRATED CHRISTMAS HOLIDAY.>
ANOTHER ONE. PLEASE.
HEY, MAN. STILL HERE? WHAT'S WRONG? YOUR GIRLFRIEND HAS LEFT YOU?
<HOW THE GREAT NATION HAS FALLEN.>
WHAT DID YOU SAY?
NOTHING, *COWBOY.*

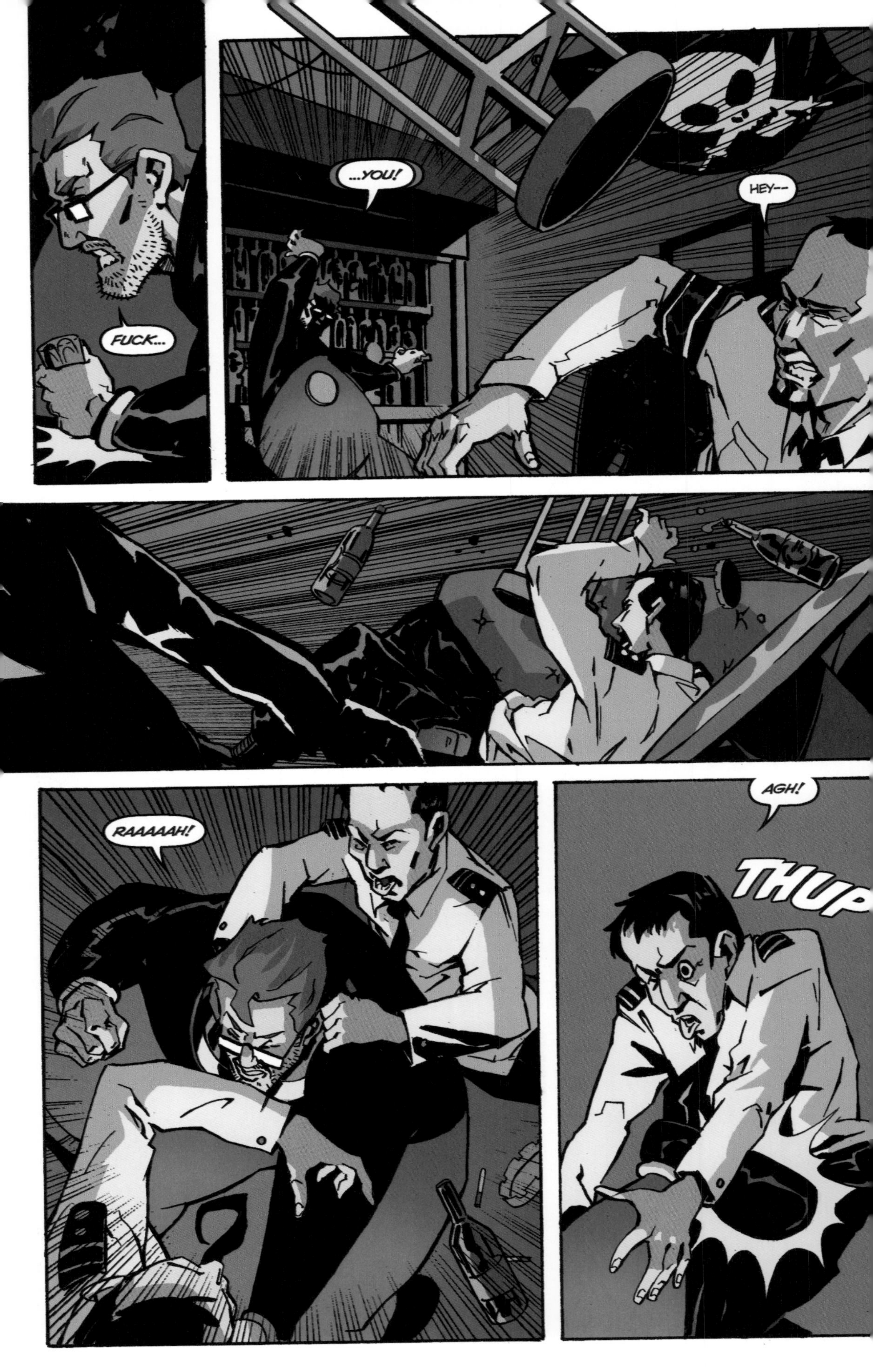
FUCK...
...YOU!
HEY--
RAAAAAH!
AGH!
THUP

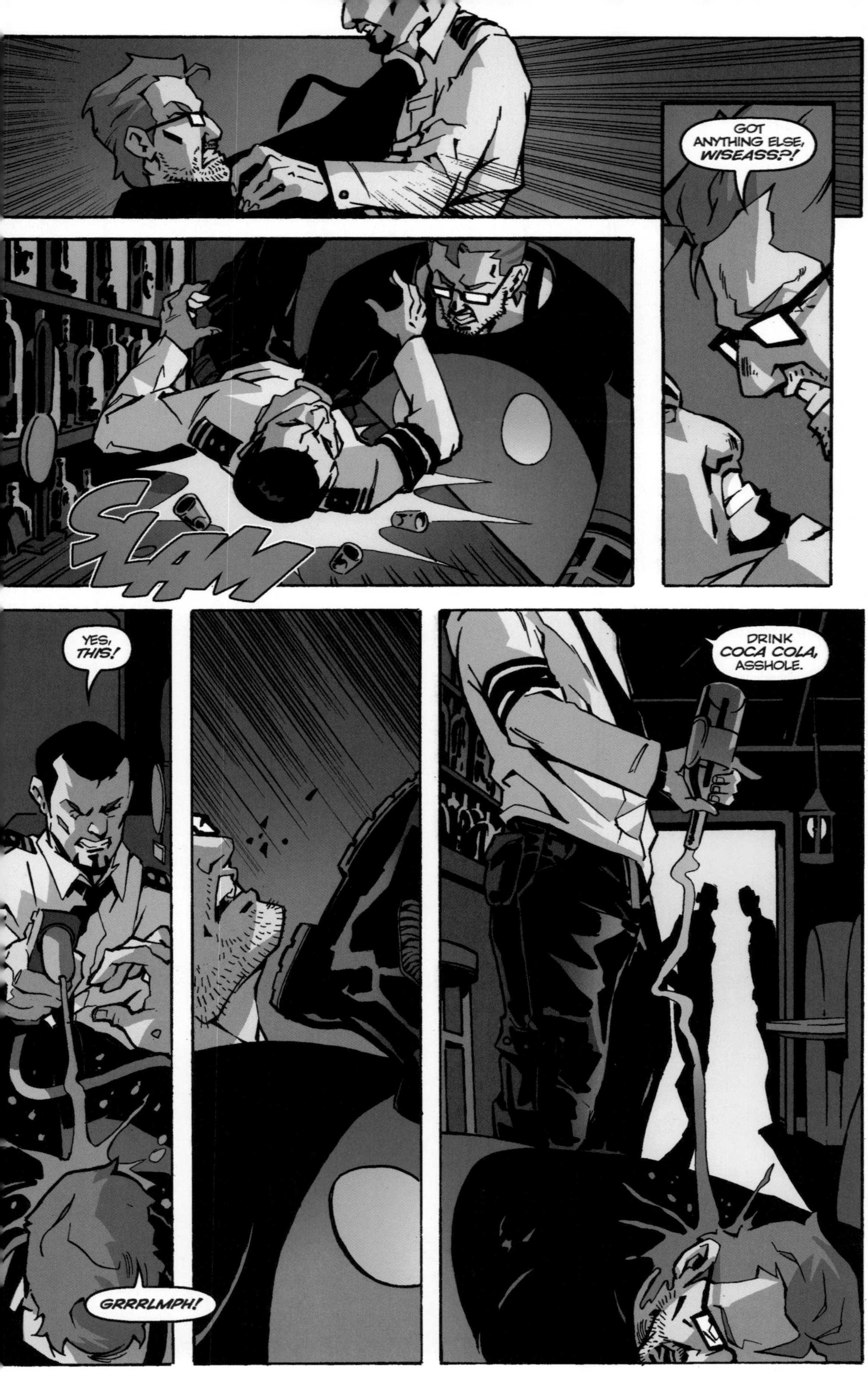
GOT ANYTHING ELSE, WISEASS?!
SLAM
YES, THIS!
GRRRLMPH!
DRINK COCA COLA, ASSHOLE.

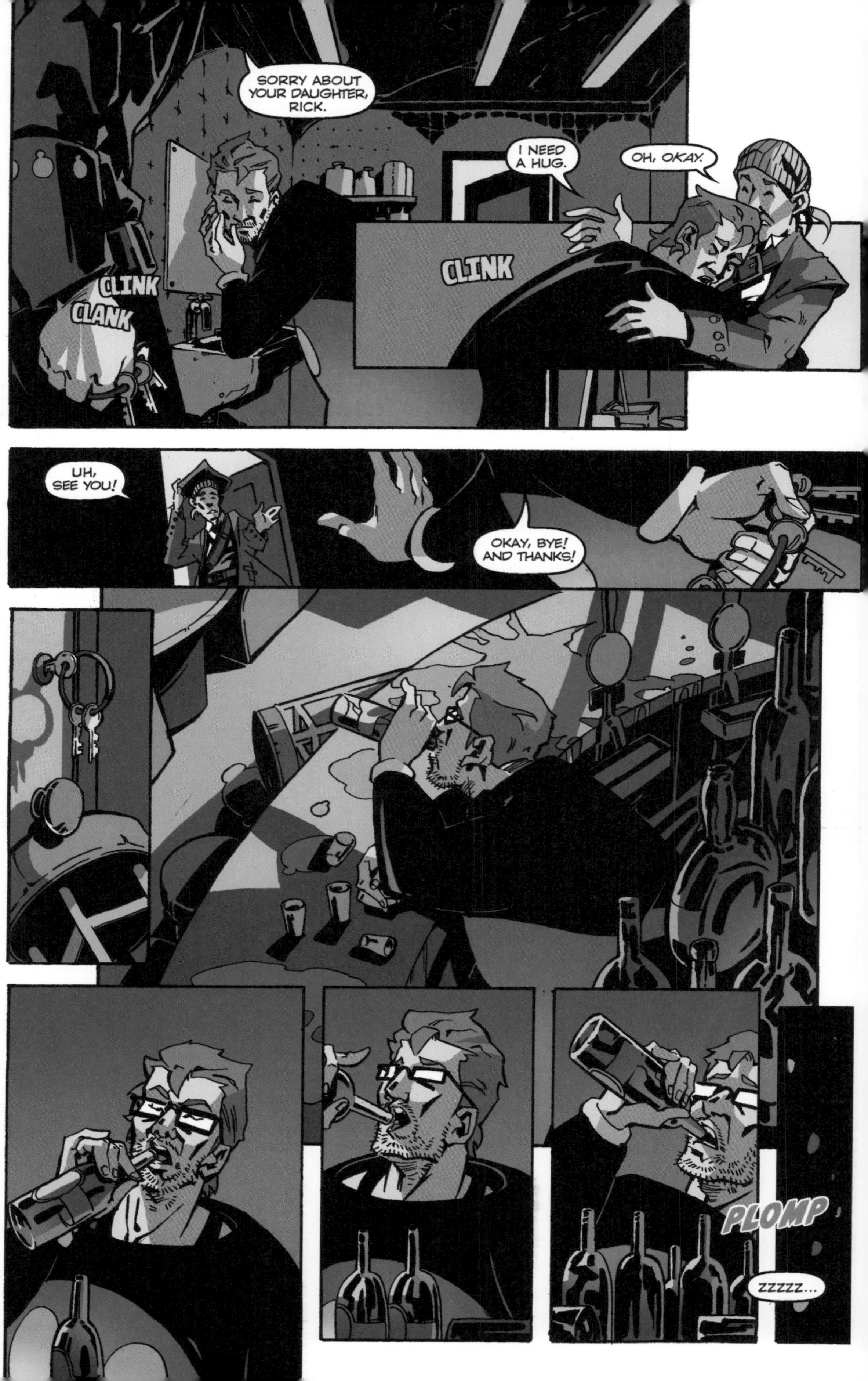
SORRY ABOUT YOUR DAUGHTER, RICK.
CLINK
CLANK
I NEED A HUG.
OH, OKAY.
CLINK
UH, SEE YOU!
OKAY, BYE! AND THANKS!
PLOMP
ZZZZZ...

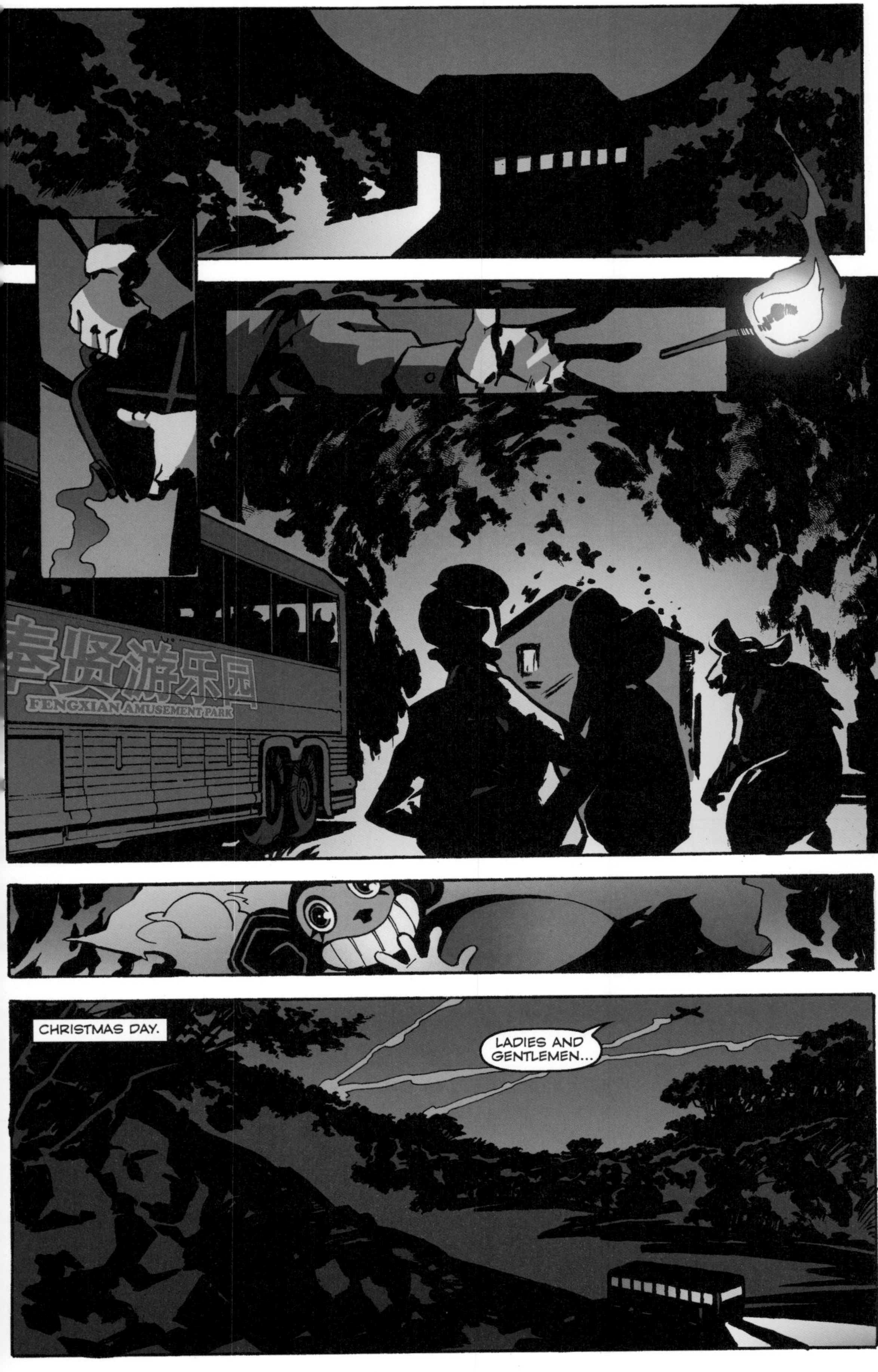
奉贤游乐园
FENGXIAN AMUSEMENT PARK
CHRISTMAS DAY.
LADIES AND GENTLEMEN...

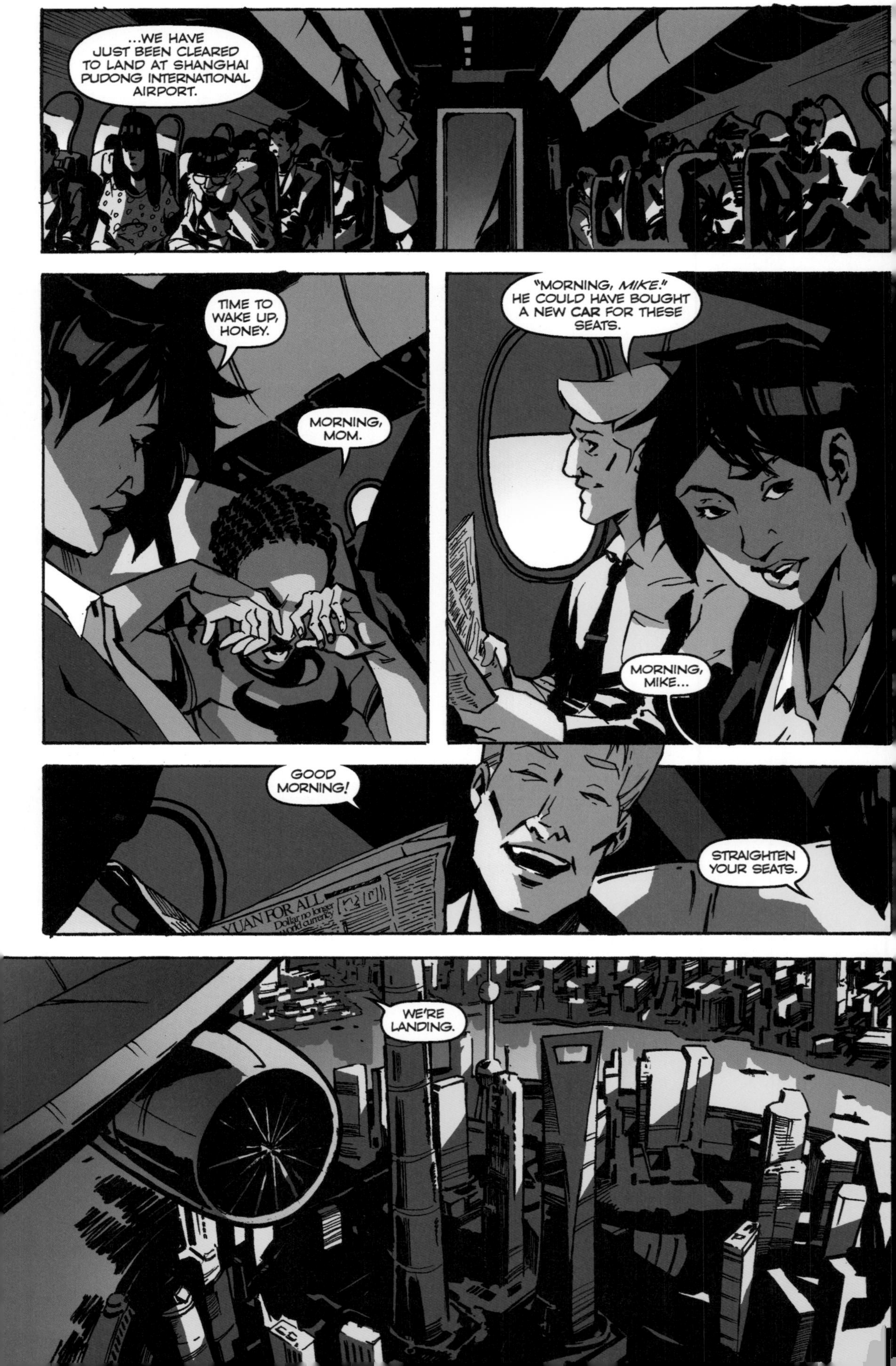
...WE HAVE JUST BEEN CLEARED TO LAND AT SHANGHAI PUDONG INTERNATIONAL AIRPORT.
TIME TO WAKE UP, HONEY.
MORNING, MOM.
"MORNING, MIKE." HE COULD HAVE BOUGHT A NEW CAR FOR THESE SEATS.
MORNING, MIKE...
GOOD MORNING!
YUAN FOR ALL
Dollar no longer world currency
STRAIGHTEN YOUR SEATS.
WE'RE LANDING.

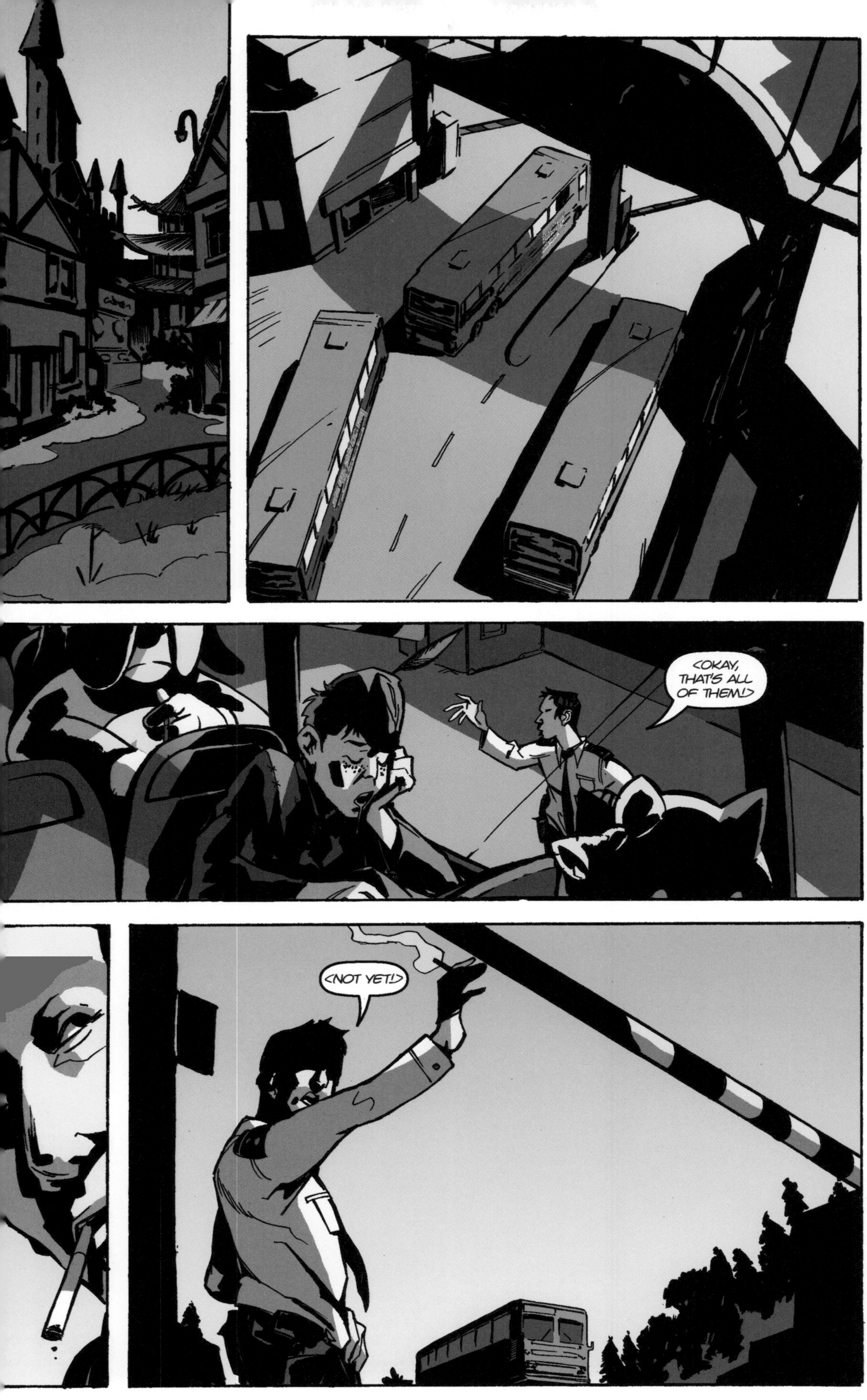
<OKAY, THAT'S ALL OF THEM!>
<NOT YET!>

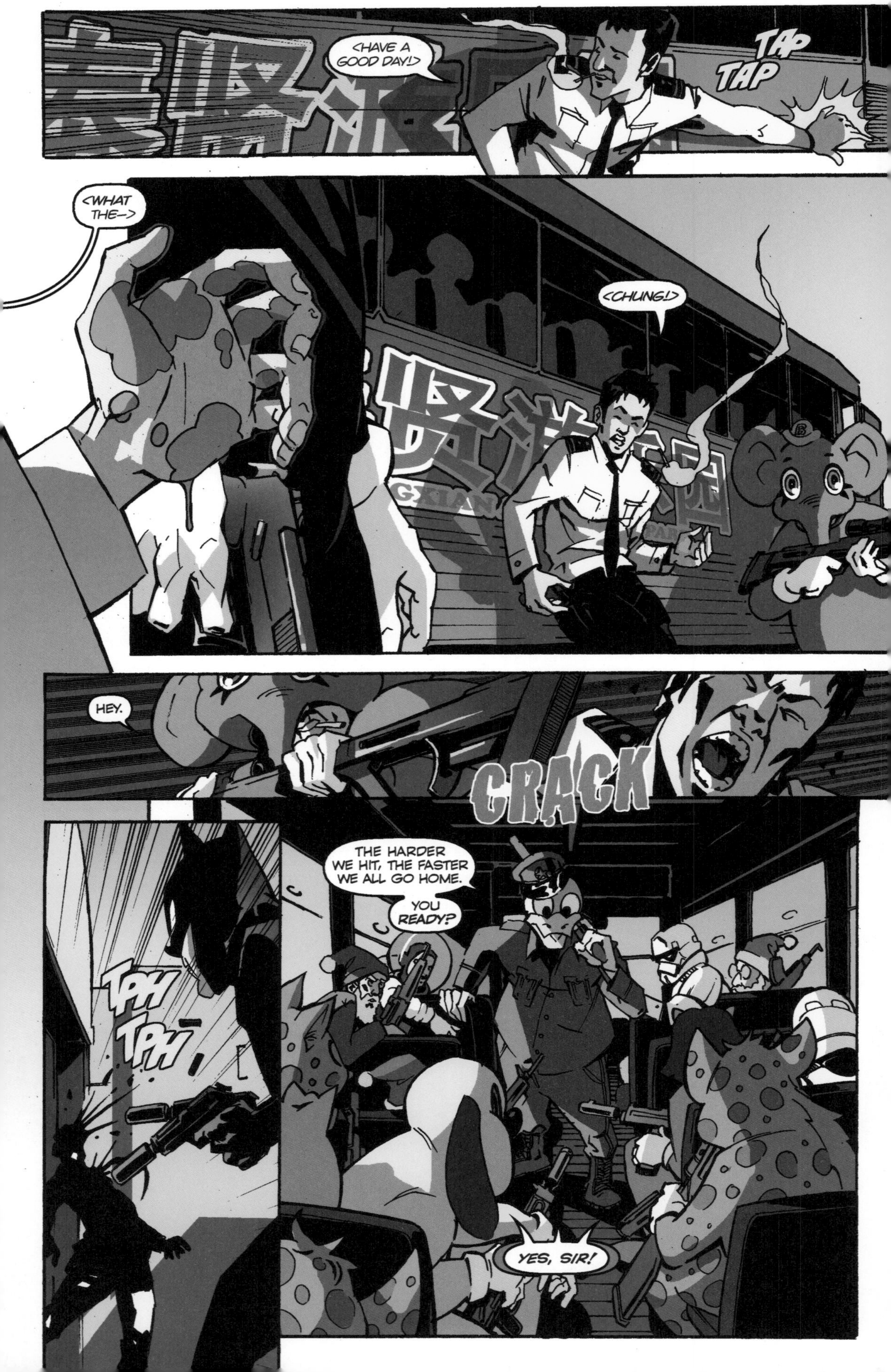

<HAVE A GOOD DAY!>
TAP TAP
<WHAT THE-->
<CHUNG!>
HEY.
CRACK
THE HARDER WE HIT, THE FASTER WE ALL GO HOME.
YOU READY?
TPH TPH
YES, SIR!

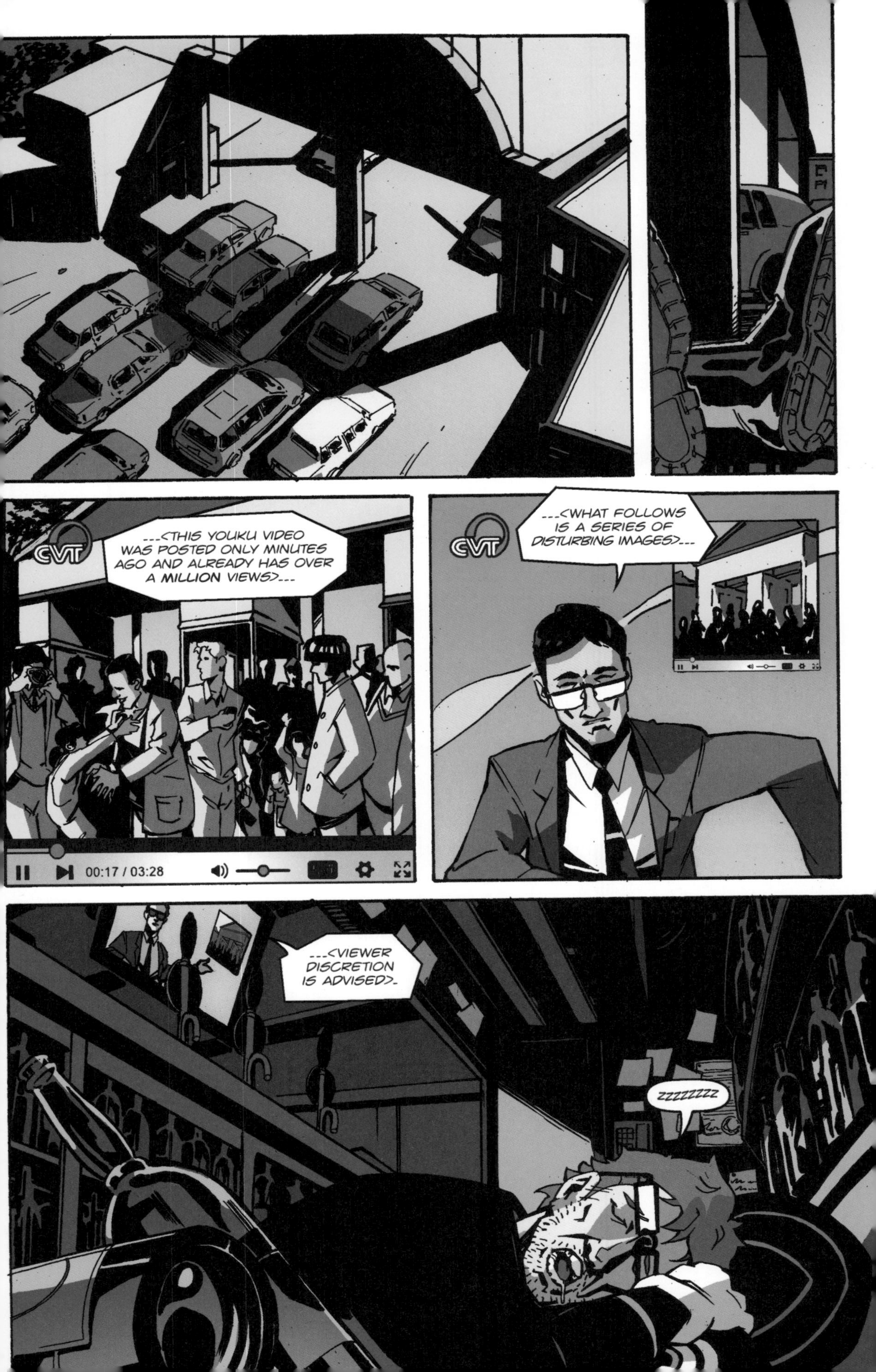
CVT
...<THIS YOUKU VIDEO WAS POSTED ONLY MINUTES AGO AND ALREADY HAS OVER A MILLION VIEWS>...
00:17 / 03:28
CVT
...<WHAT FOLLOWS IS A SERIES OF DISTURBING IMAGES>...
...<VIEWER DISCRETION IS ADVISED>.
ZZZZZZZZ

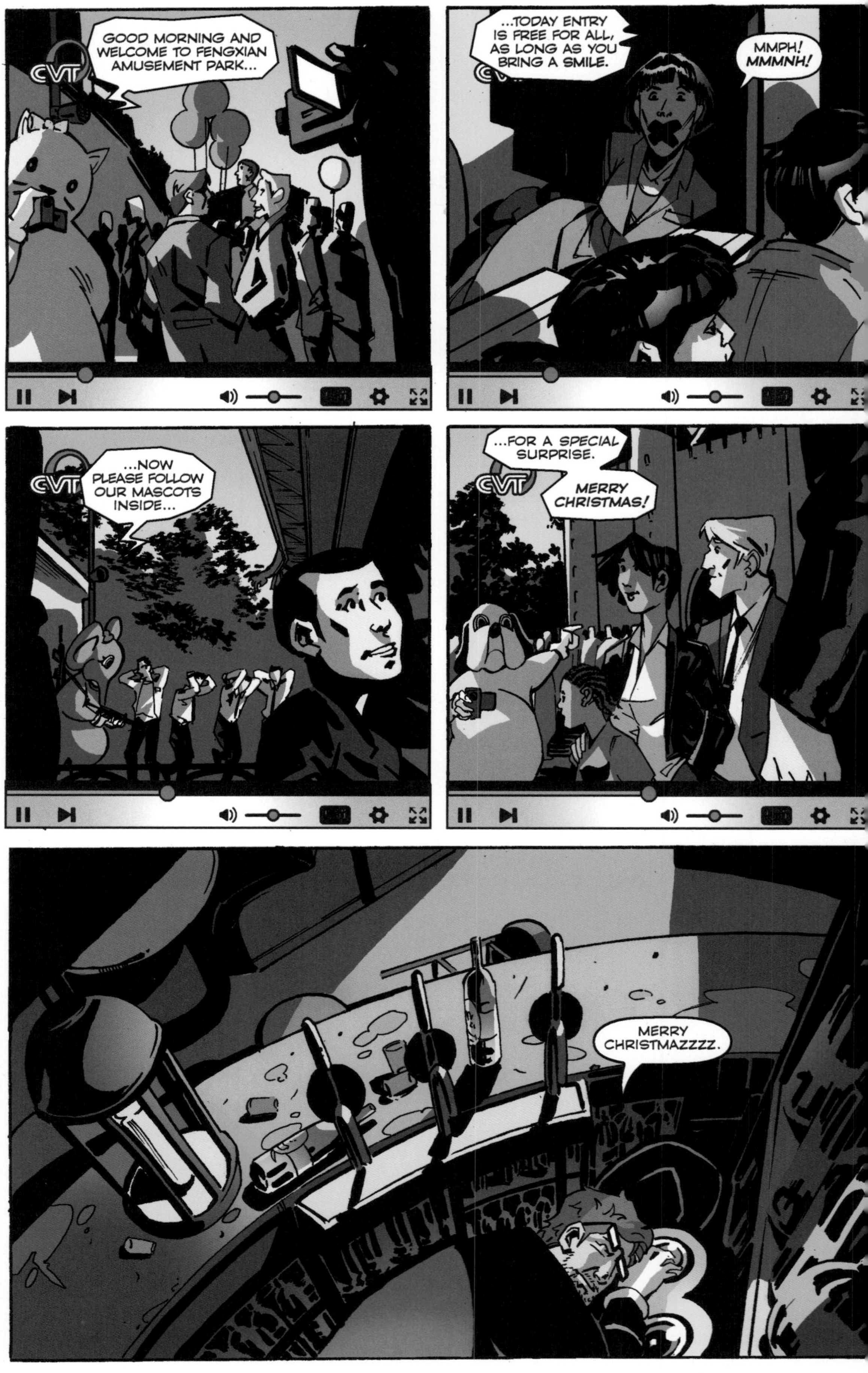
GOOD MORNING AND WELCOME TO FENGXIAN AMUSEMENT PARK...
...TODAY ENTRY IS FREE FOR ALL, AS LONG AS YOU BRING A SMILE.
MMPH! MMMNH!
...NOW PLEASE FOLLOW OUR MASCOTS INSIDE...
...FOR A SPECIAL SURPRISE.
MERRY CHRISTMAS!
MERRY CHRISTMAZZZZ.

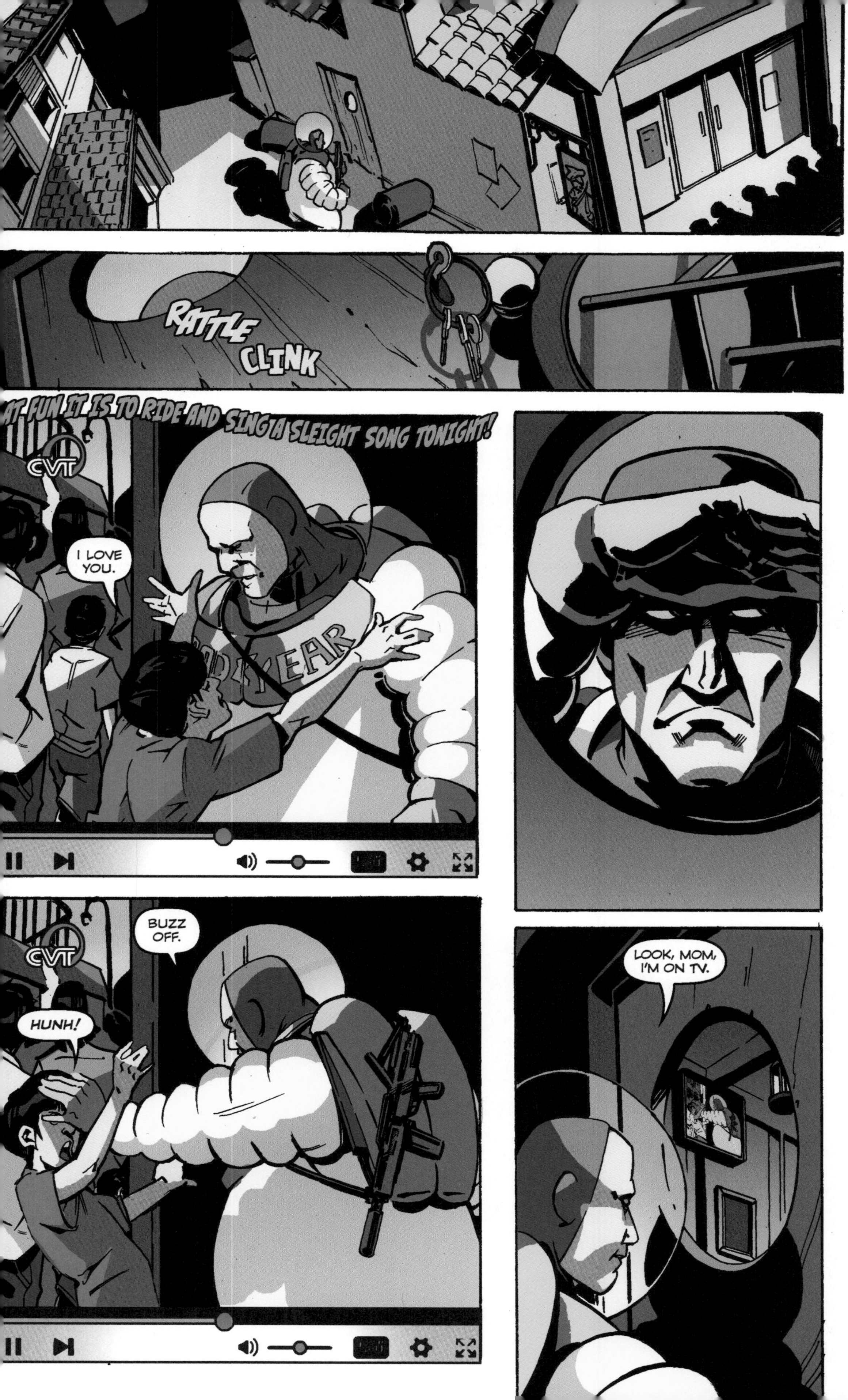
RATTLE
CLINK
AT FUN IT IS TO RIDE AND SING A SLEIGHT SONG TONIGHT!
CVT
I LOVE YOU.
CVT
BUZZ OFF.
HUNH!
LOOK, MOM, I'M ON TV.

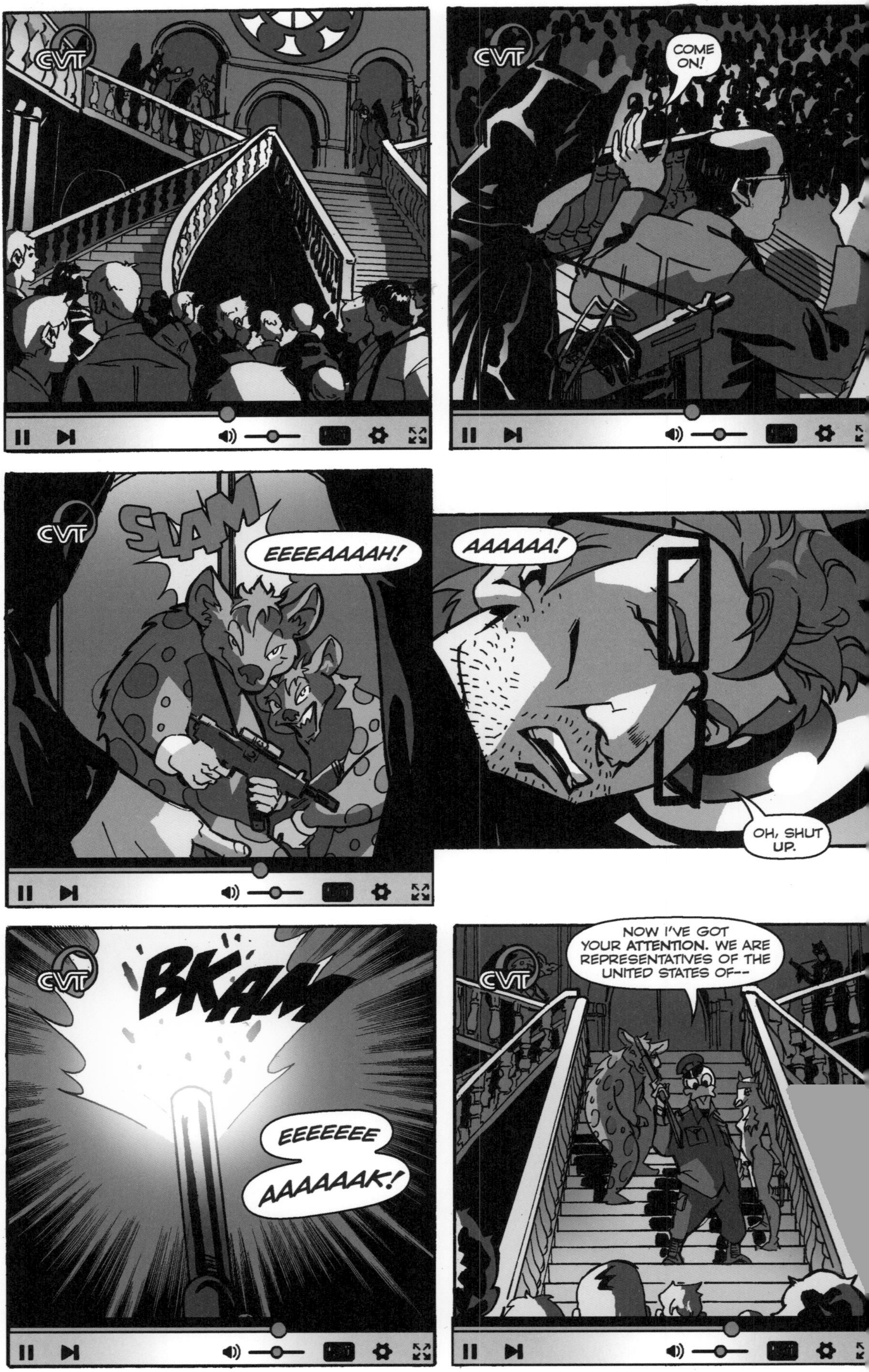
CVT
COME ON!
SLAM
EEEEAAAAH!
AAAAAA!
OH, SHUT UP.
BKAM
EEEEEEE AAAAAAK!
NOW I'VE GOT YOUR ATTENTION. WE ARE REPRESENTATIVES OF THE UNITED STATES OF--

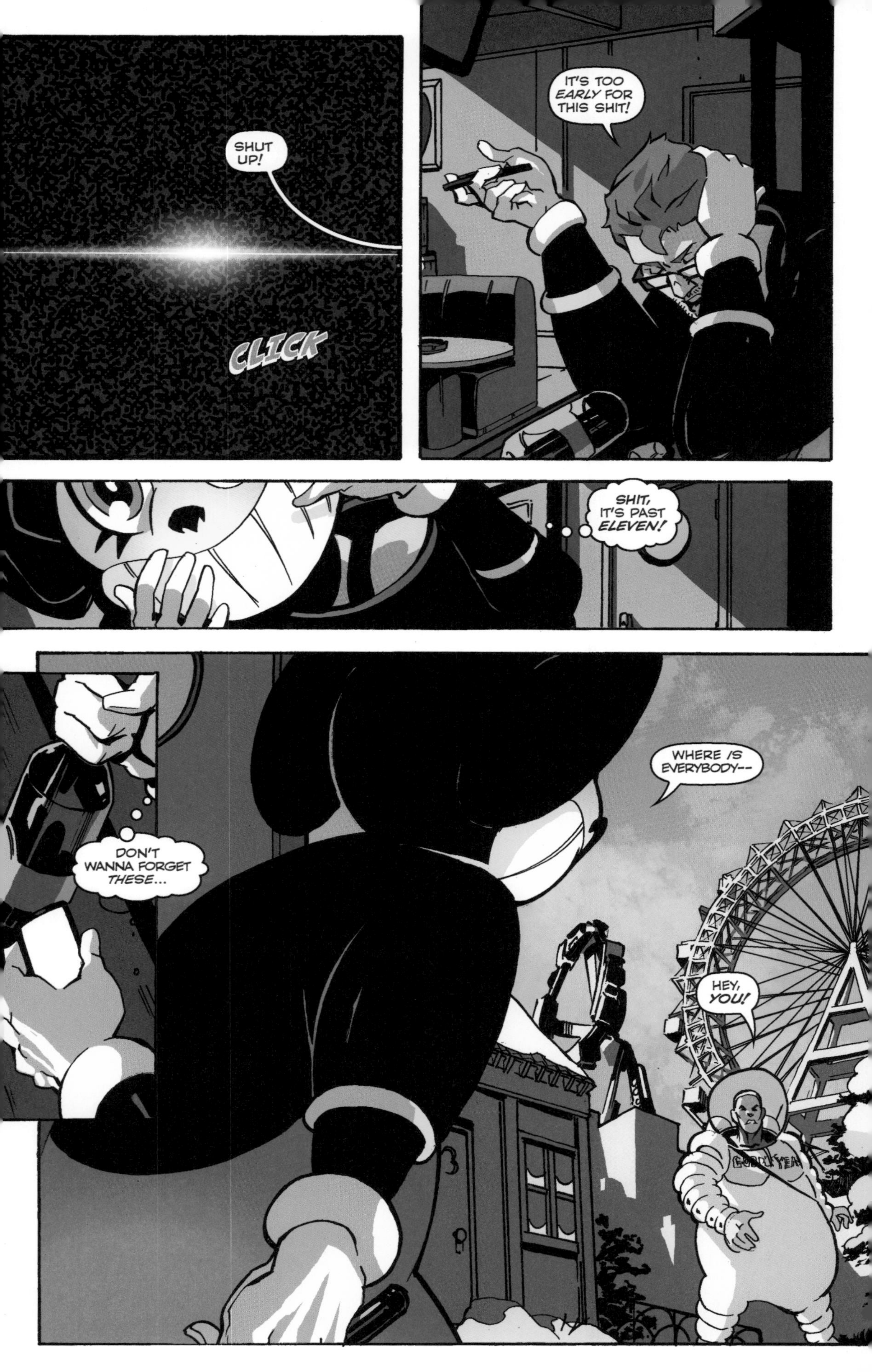
SHUT UP!
CLICK
IT'S TOO EARLY FOR THIS SHIT!
SHIT, IT'S PAST ELEVEN!
DON'T WANNA FORGET THESE...
WHERE IS EVERYBODY--
HEY, YOU!

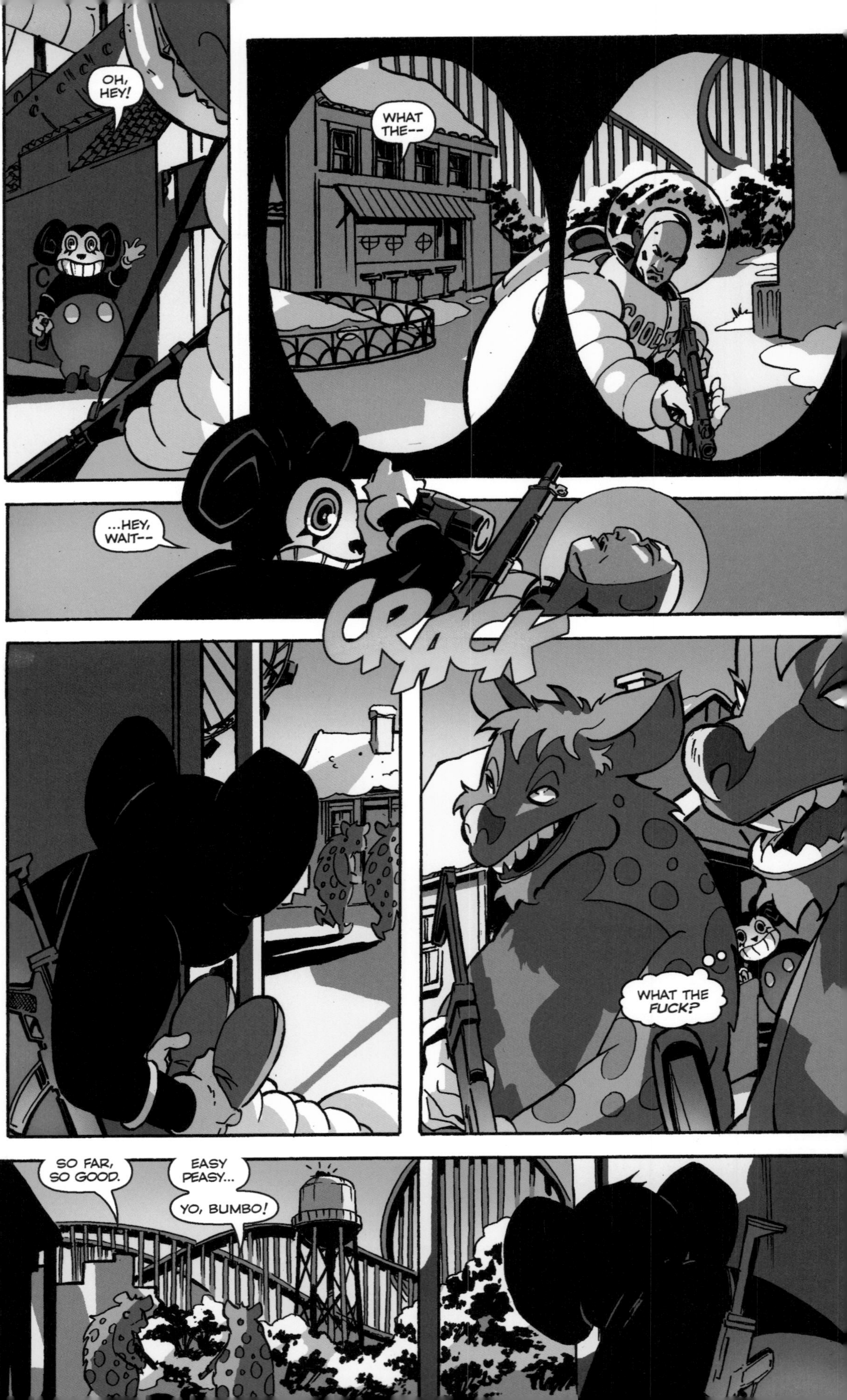
OH, HEY!
WHAT THE--
...HEY, WAIT--
CRACK
WHAT THE FUCK?
SO FAR, SO GOOD.
EASY PEASY...
YO, BUMBO!

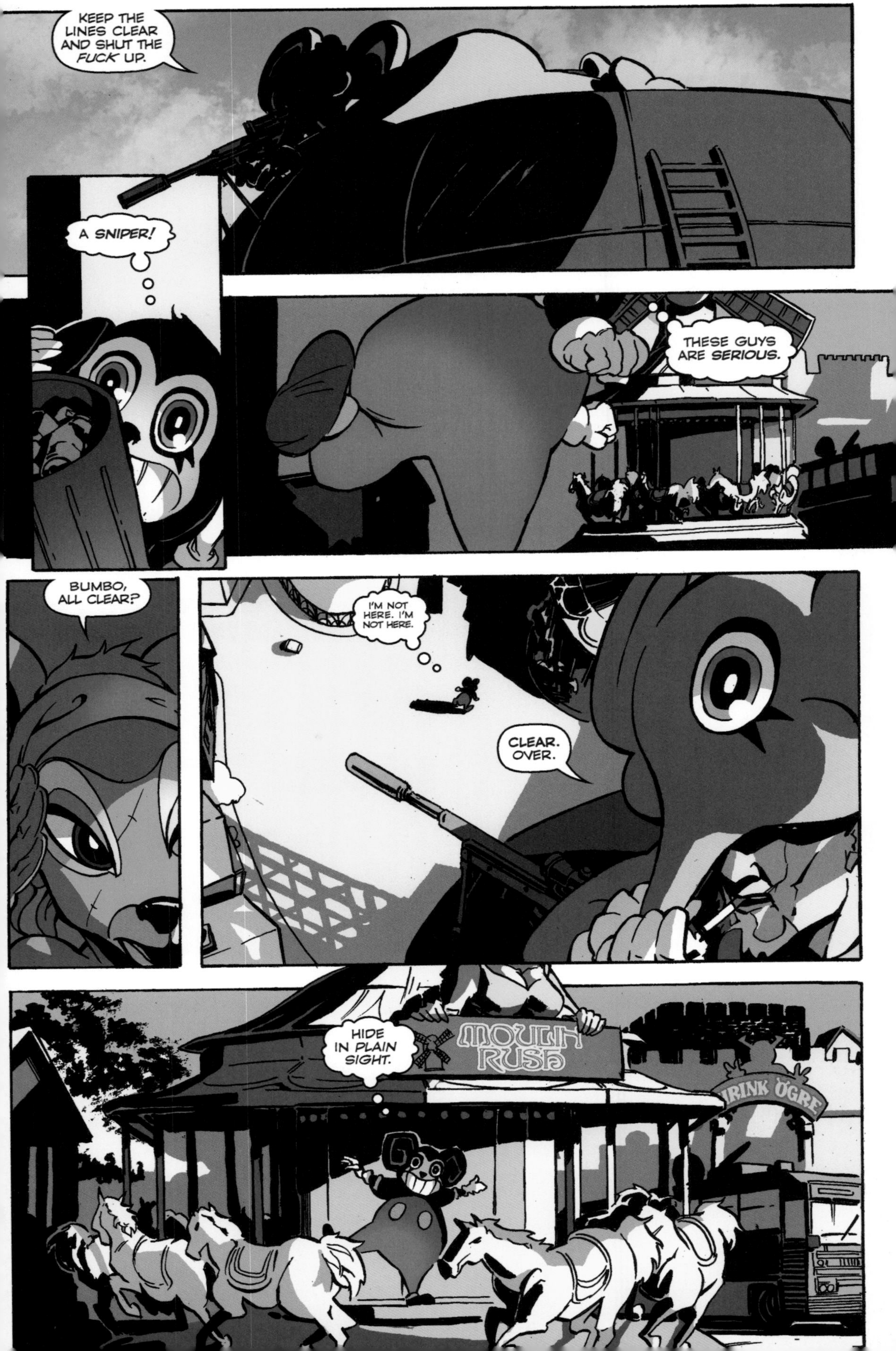
KEEP THE LINES CLEAR AND SHUT THE FUCK UP.
A SNIPER!
THESE GUYS ARE SERIOUS.
BUMBO, ALL CLEAR?
I'M NOT HERE. I'M NOT HERE.
CLEAR. OVER.
HIDE IN PLAIN SIGHT.
MOUTH RUSH
DRINK OGRE

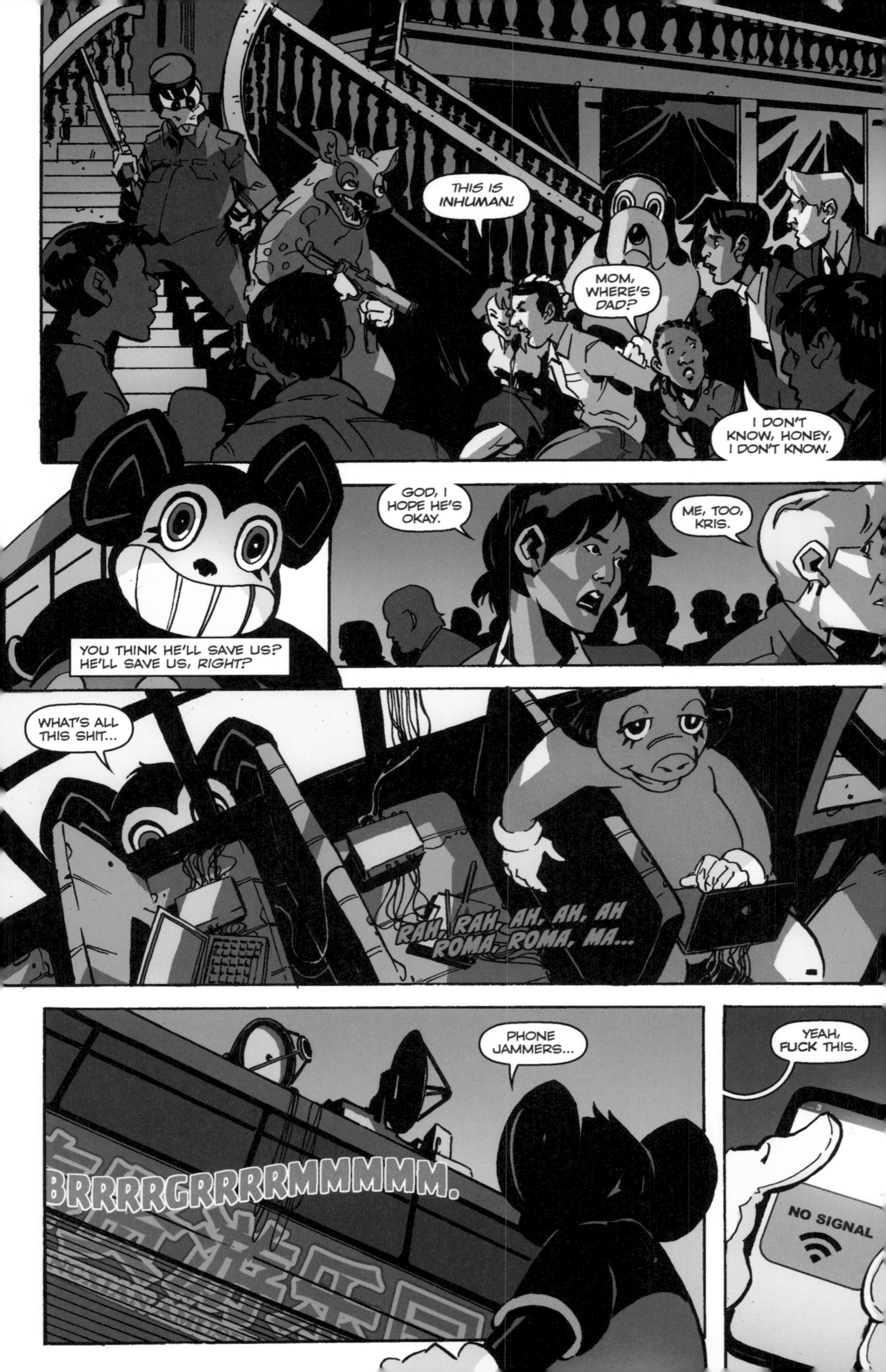
THIS IS INHUMAN!
MOM, WHERE'S DAD?
I DON'T KNOW, HONEY, I DON'T KNOW.
YOU THINK HE'LL SAVE US? HE'LL SAVE US, RIGHT?
GOD, I HOPE HE'S OKAY.
ME, TOO, KRIS.
WHAT'S ALL THIS SHIT...
RAH, RAH, AH, AH, AH ROMA, ROMA, MA...
PHONE JAMMERS...
BRRRRGRRRRRMMMMMM.
YEAH, FUCK THIS.
NO SIGNAL

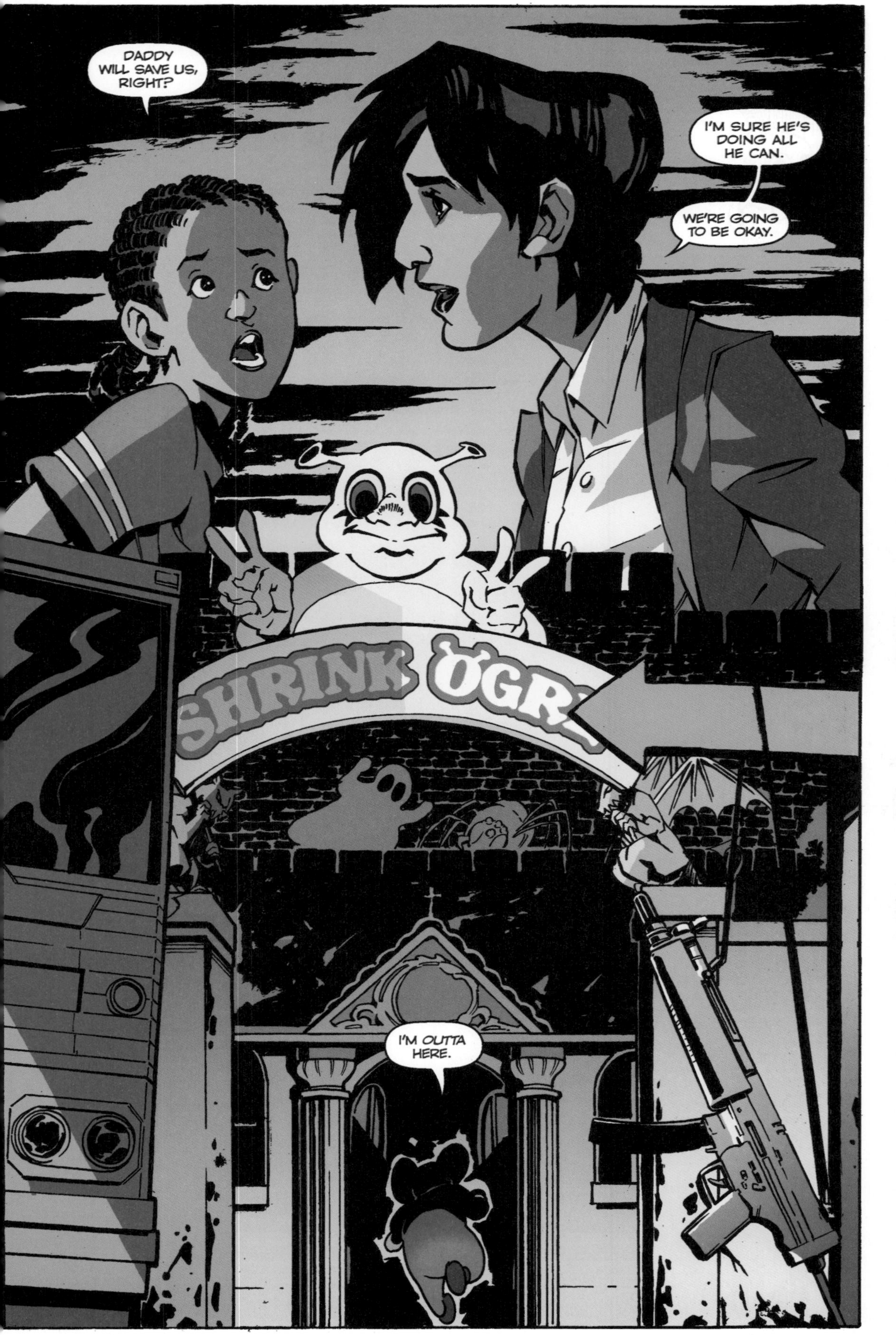
DADDY WILL SAVE US, RIGHT?
I'M SURE HE'S DOING ALL HE CAN.
WE'RE GOING TO BE OKAY.
SHRINK OGR
I'M OUTTA HERE.

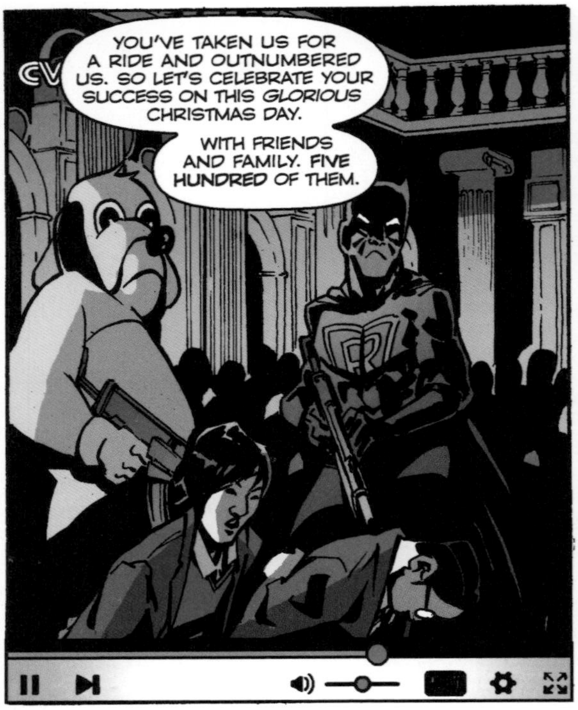
YOU'VE TAKEN US FOR A RIDE AND OUTNUMBERED US. SO LET'S CELEBRATE YOUR SUCCESS ON THIS GLORIOUS CHRISTMAS DAY.
WITH FRIENDS AND FAMILY. FIVE HUNDRED OF THEM.

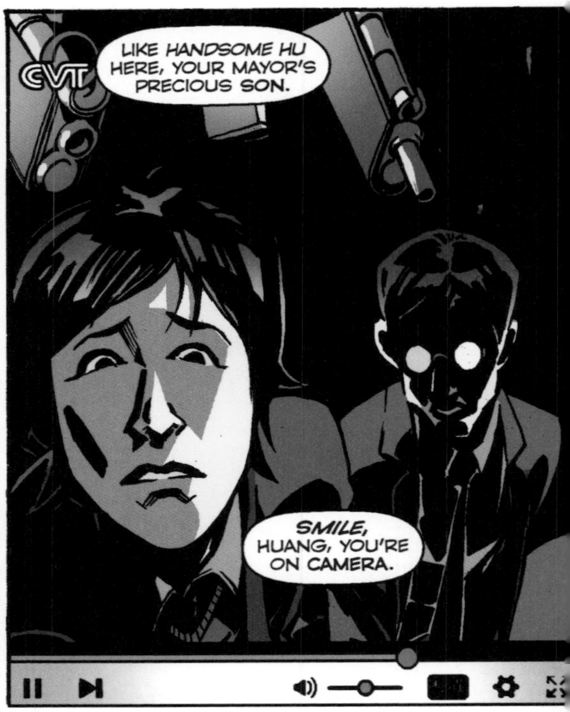
LIKE HANDSOME HU HERE, YOUR MAYOR'S PRECIOUS SON.
SMILE, HUANG, YOU'RE ON CAMERA.

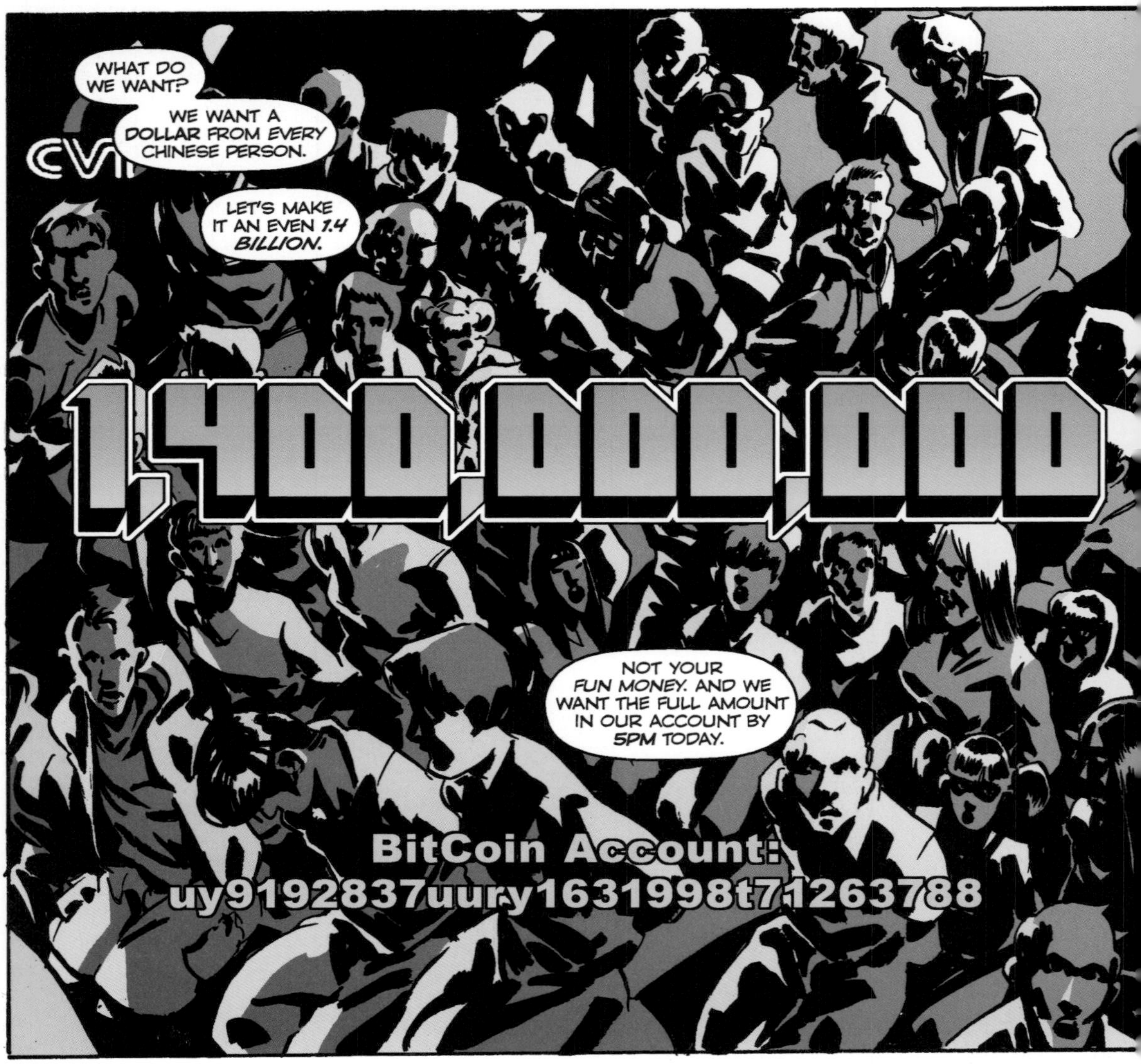
WHAT DO WE WANT?
WE WANT A DOLLAR FROM EVERY CHINESE PERSON.
LET'S MAKE IT AN EVEN 1.4 BILLION.
1,400,000,000
NOT YOUR FUN MONEY. AND WE WANT THE FULL AMOUNT IN OUR ACCOUNT BY 5PM TODAY.
BitCoin Account:
uy9192837uury1631998t71263788

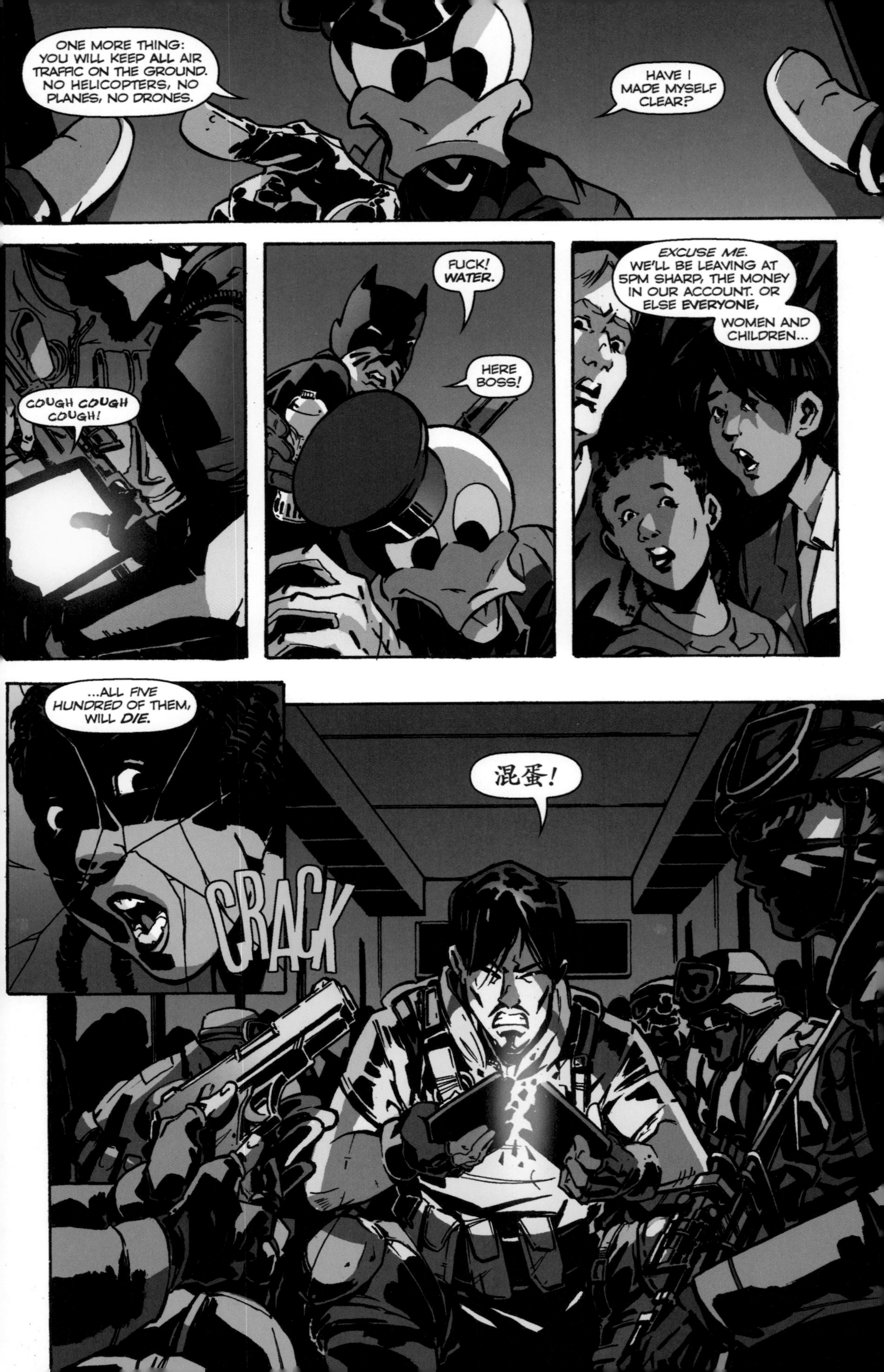
ONE MORE THING: YOU WILL KEEP ALL AIR TRAFFIC ON THE GROUND. NO HELICOPTERS, NO PLANES, NO DRONES.
HAVE I MADE MYSELF CLEAR?
COUGH COUGH COUGH!
FUCK! WATER.
HERE BOSS!
EXCUSE ME. WE'LL BE LEAVING AT 5PM SHARP, THE MONEY IN OUR ACCOUNT. OR ELSE EVERYONE,
WOMEN AND CHILDREN...
...ALL FIVE HUNDRED OF THEM, WILL DIE.
CRACK
混蛋!

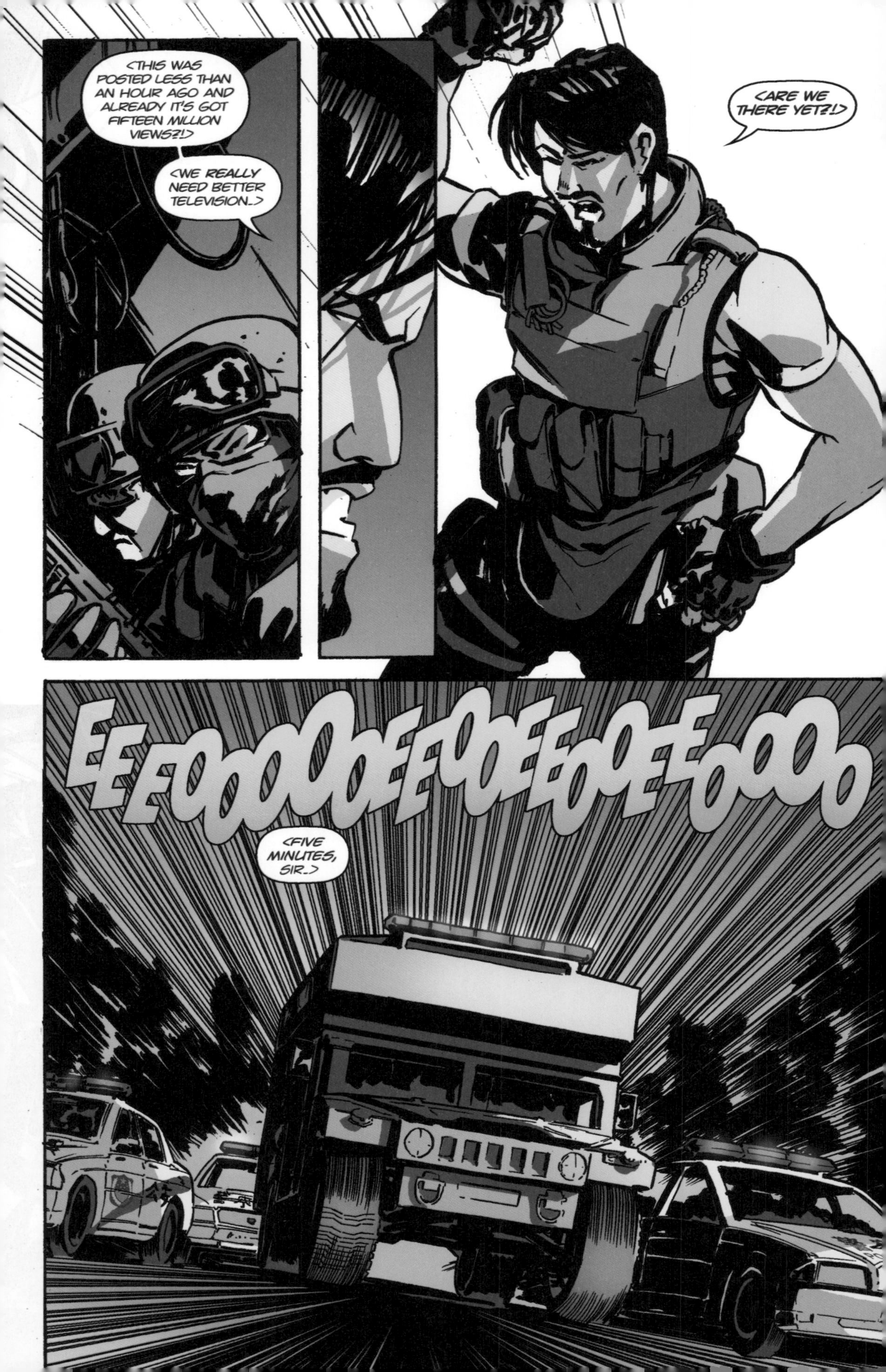
<THIS WAS POSTED LESS THAN AN HOUR AGO AND ALREADY IT'S GOT FIFTEEN MILLION VIEWS?!>
<WE REALLY NEED BETTER TELEVISION...>
<ARE WE THERE YET?!>
EEEOOOOOEEOOEEOOEEOOOO
<FIVE MINUTES, SIR...>

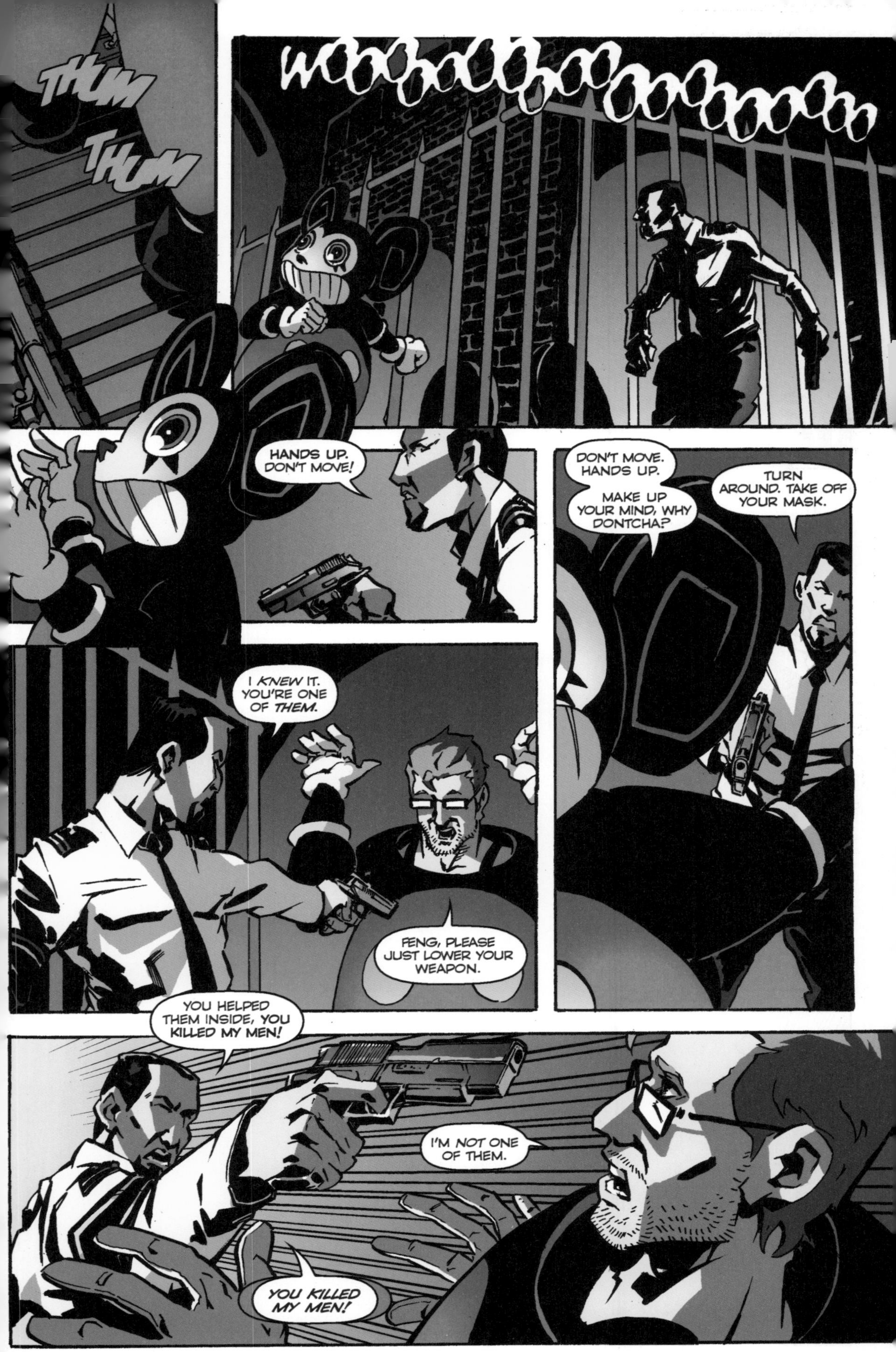
THUM
THUM
WOOOOOOOOOOOOOOOOOO
HANDS UP. DON'T MOVE!
DON'T MOVE. HANDS UP.
MAKE UP YOUR MIND, WHY DONTCHA?
TURN AROUND. TAKE OFF YOUR MASK.
I *KNEW* IT. YOU'RE ONE OF *THEM*.
FENG, PLEASE JUST LOWER YOUR WEAPON.
YOU HELPED THEM INSIDE, YOU KILLED MY MEN!
I'M *NOT* ONE OF THEM.
YOU KILLED MY MEN!

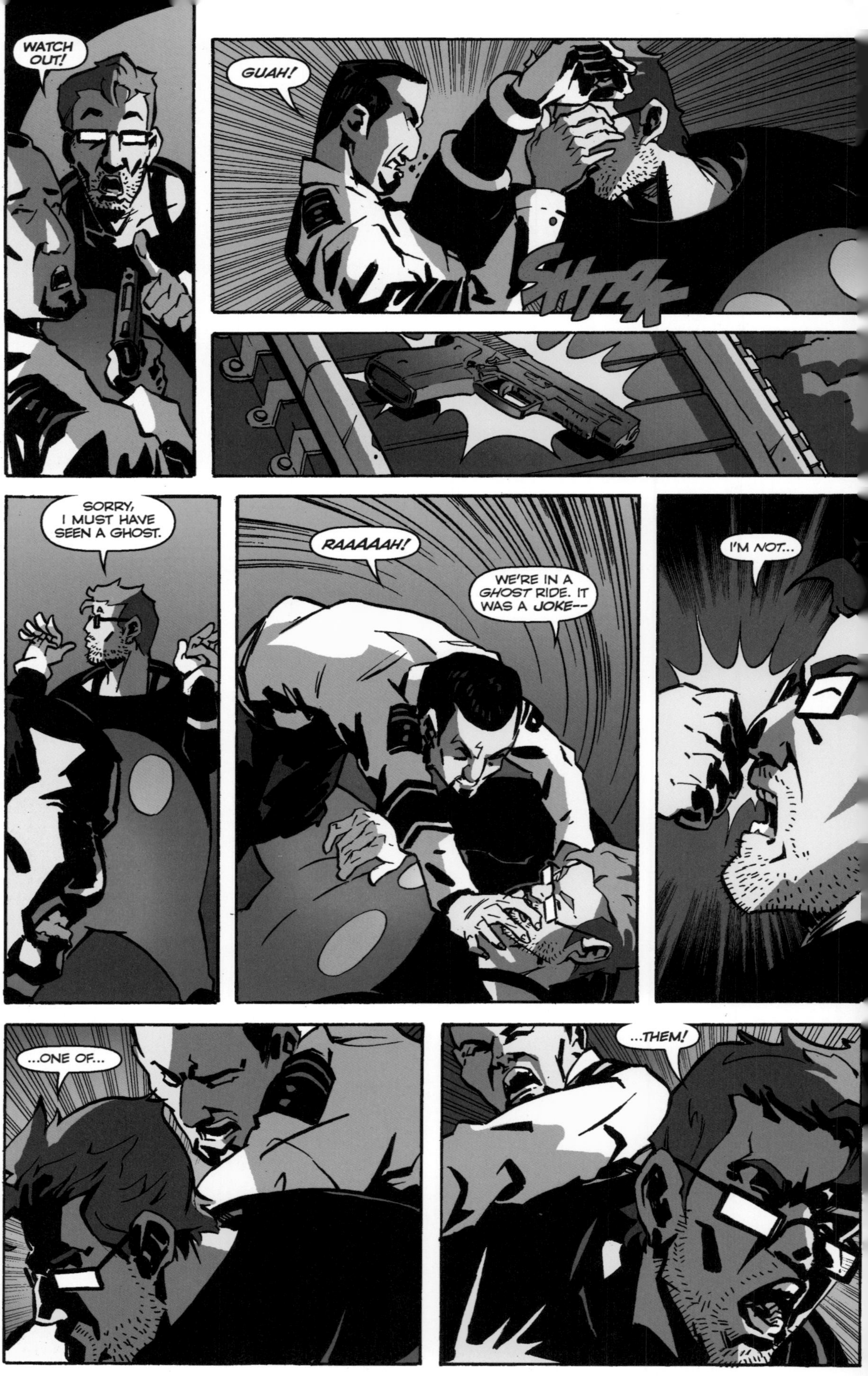
WATCH OUT!
GUAH!
SHTAK
SORRY, I MUST HAVE SEEN A GHOST.
RAAAAAH!
WE'RE IN A GHOST RIDE. IT WAS A JOKE--
I'M NOT...
...ONE OF...
...THEM!

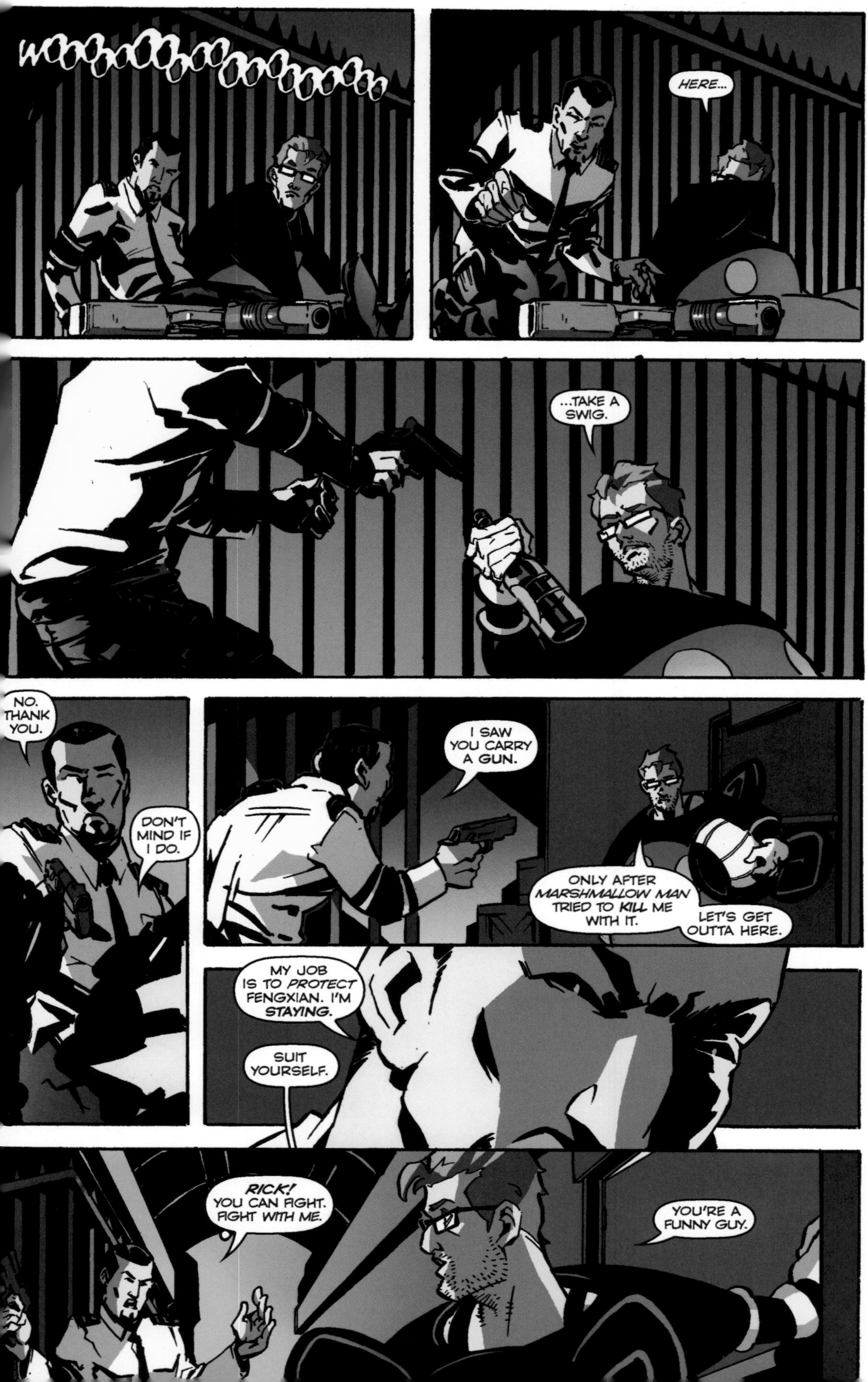
WOOOOOOOOOOOOOOOOOOOOO
HERE...
...TAKE A SWIG.
NO. THANK YOU.
DON'T MIND IF I DO.
I SAW YOU CARRY A GUN.
ONLY AFTER MARSHMALLOW MAN TRIED TO KILL ME WITH IT.
LET'S GET OUTTA HERE.
MY JOB IS TO PROTECT FENGXIAN. I'M STAYING.
SUIT YOURSELF.
RICK! YOU CAN FIGHT. FIGHT WITH ME.
YOU'RE A FUNNY GUY.

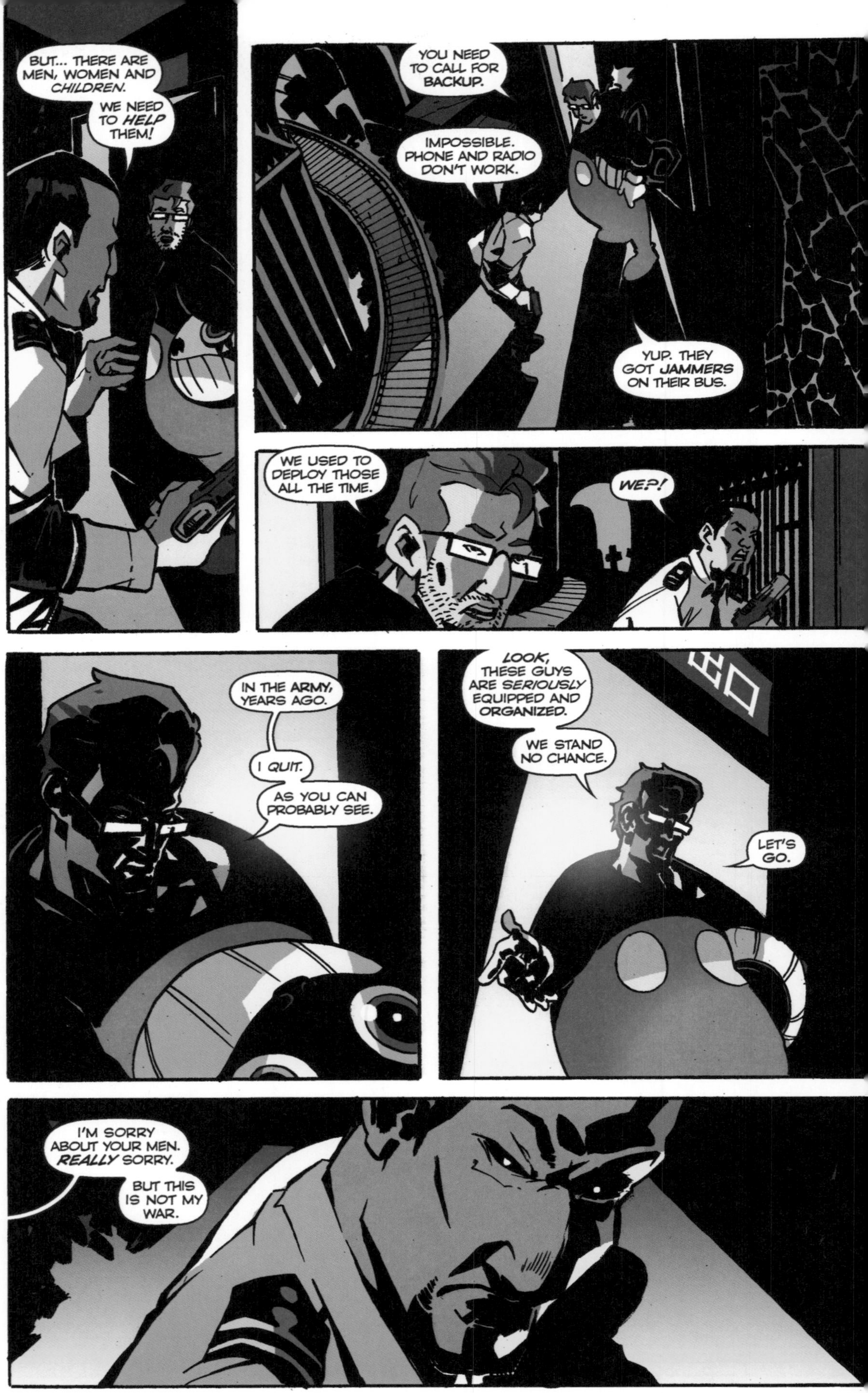

BUT... THERE ARE MEN, WOMEN AND *CHILDREN*.
WE NEED TO *HELP* THEM!
YOU NEED TO CALL FOR BACKUP.
IMPOSSIBLE. PHONE AND RADIO DON'T WORK.
YUP. THEY GOT **JAMMERS** ON THEIR BUS.
WE USED TO DEPLOY THOSE ALL THE TIME.
WE?!
IN THE **ARMY**, YEARS AGO.
I *QUIT*.
AS YOU CAN PROBABLY SEE.
LOOK, THESE GUYS ARE *SERIOUSLY* EQUIPPED AND ORGANIZED.
WE STAND NO CHANCE.
LET'S GO.
I'M SORRY ABOUT YOUR MEN. *REALLY* SORRY.
BUT THIS IS NOT MY WAR.

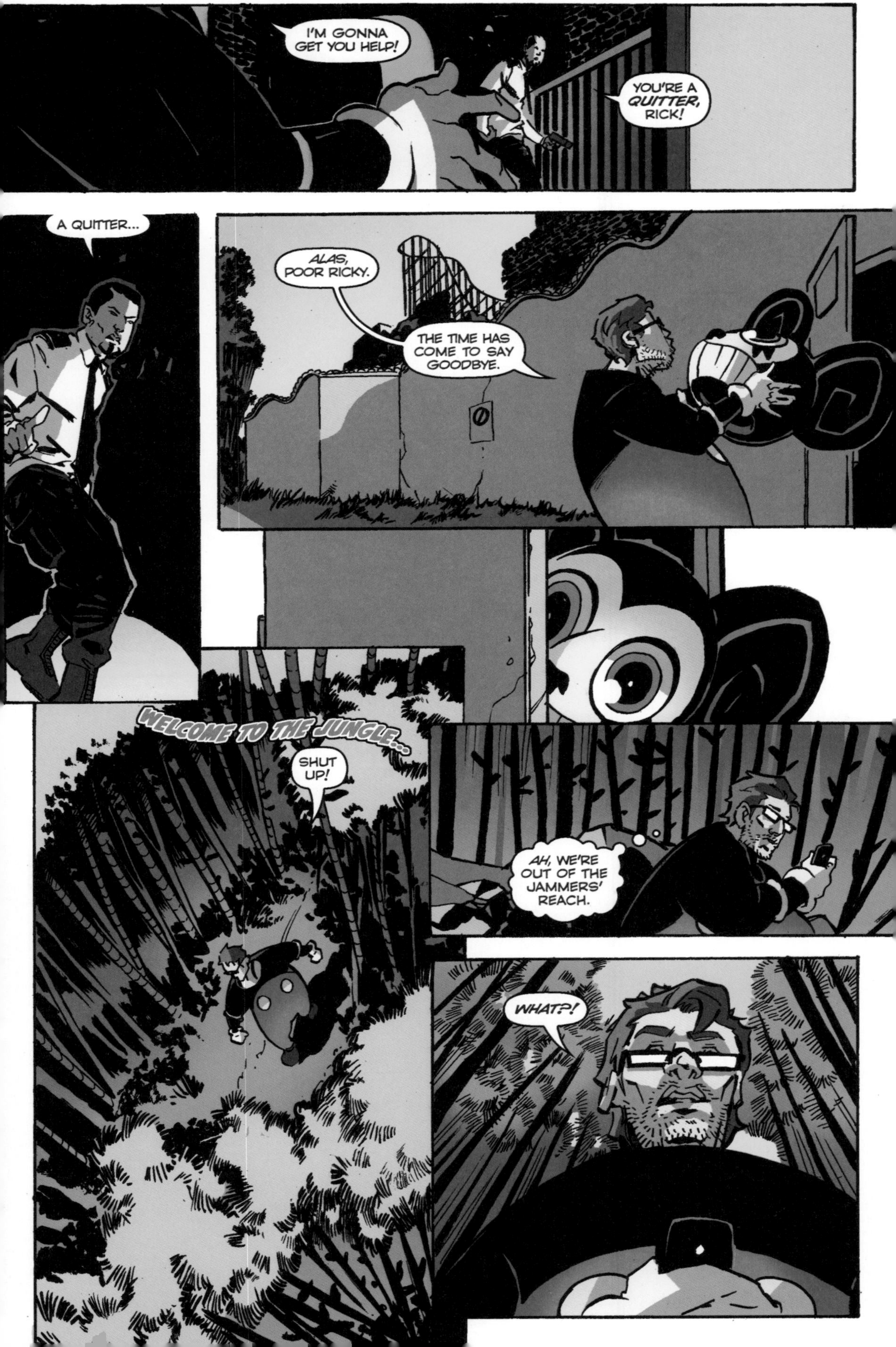
I'M GONNA GET YOU HELP!
YOU'RE A *QUITTER*, RICK!
A QUITTER...
ALAS, POOR RICKY.
THE TIME HAS COME TO SAY GOODBYE.
WELCOME TO THE JUNGLE...
SHUT UP!
AH, WE'RE OUT OF THE JAMMERS' REACH.
WHAT?!

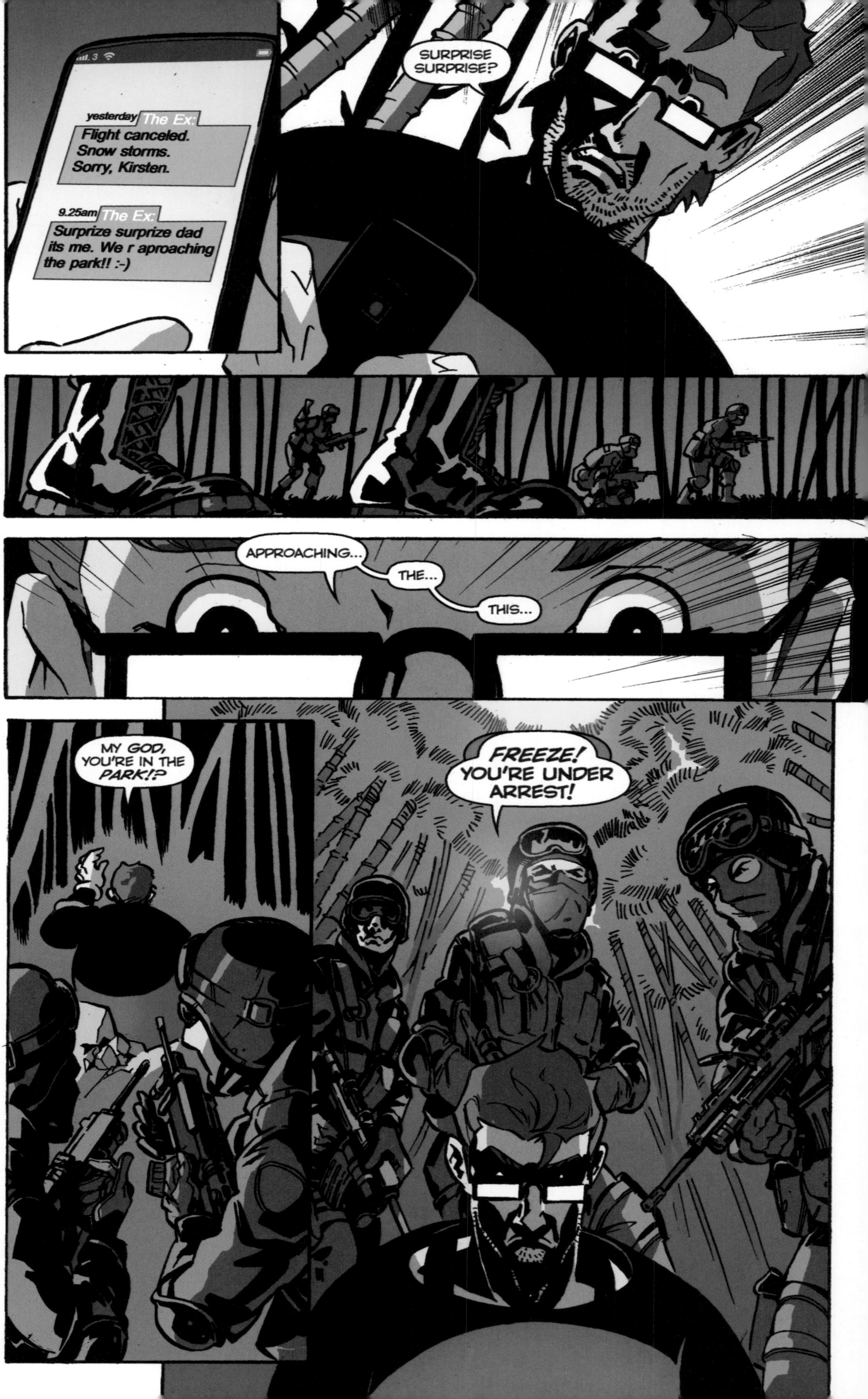
yesterday The Ex:
Flight canceled. Snow storms. Sorry, Kirsten.
9.25am The Ex:
Surprize surprize dad its me. We r aproaching the park!! :-)
SURPRISE SURPRISE?
APPROACHING...
THE...
THIS...
MY GOD, YOU'RE IN THE PARK!?
FREEZE! YOU'RE UNDER ARREST!

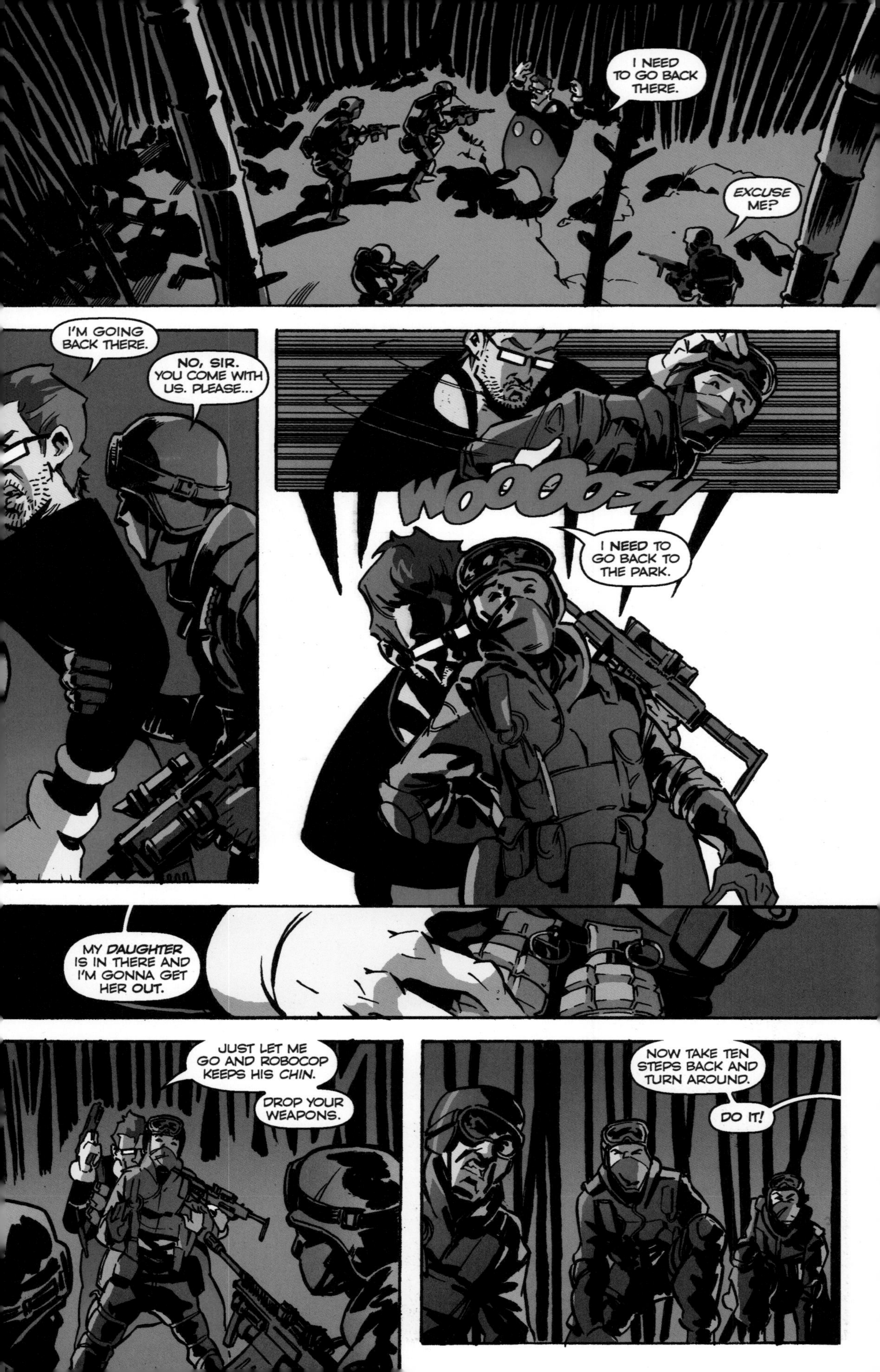
I NEED TO GO BACK THERE.
EXCUSE ME?
I'M GOING BACK THERE.
NO, SIR. YOU COME WITH US. PLEASE...
WOOOOSH
I NEED TO GO BACK TO THE PARK.
MY DAUGHTER IS IN THERE AND I'M GONNA GET HER OUT.
JUST LET ME GO AND ROBOCOP KEEPS HIS CHIN.
DROP YOUR WEAPONS.
NOW TAKE TEN STEPS BACK AND TURN AROUND.
DO IT!

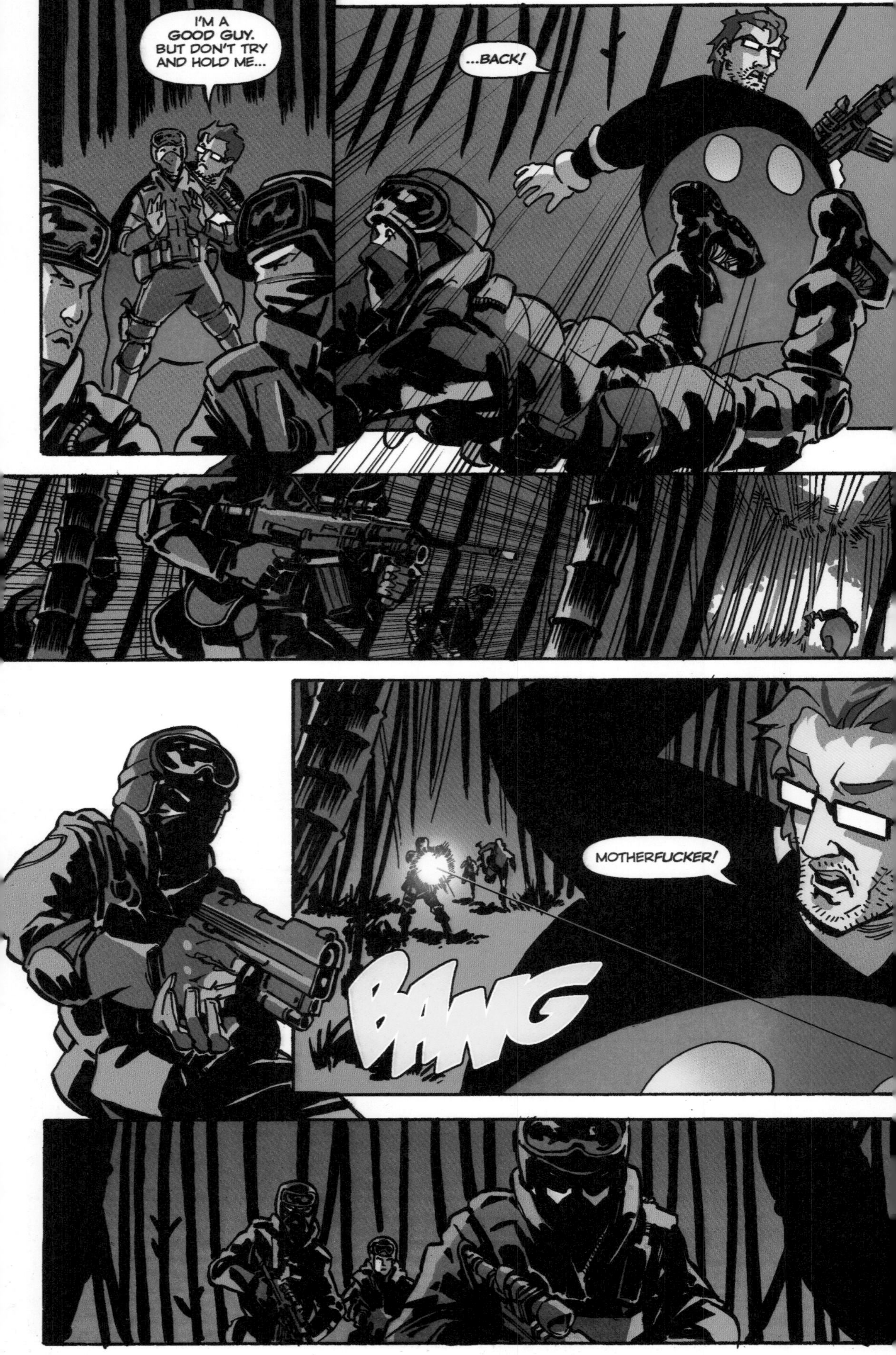
I'M A GOOD GUY. BUT DON'T TRY AND HOLD ME...
...BACK!
MOTHERFUCKER!
BANG

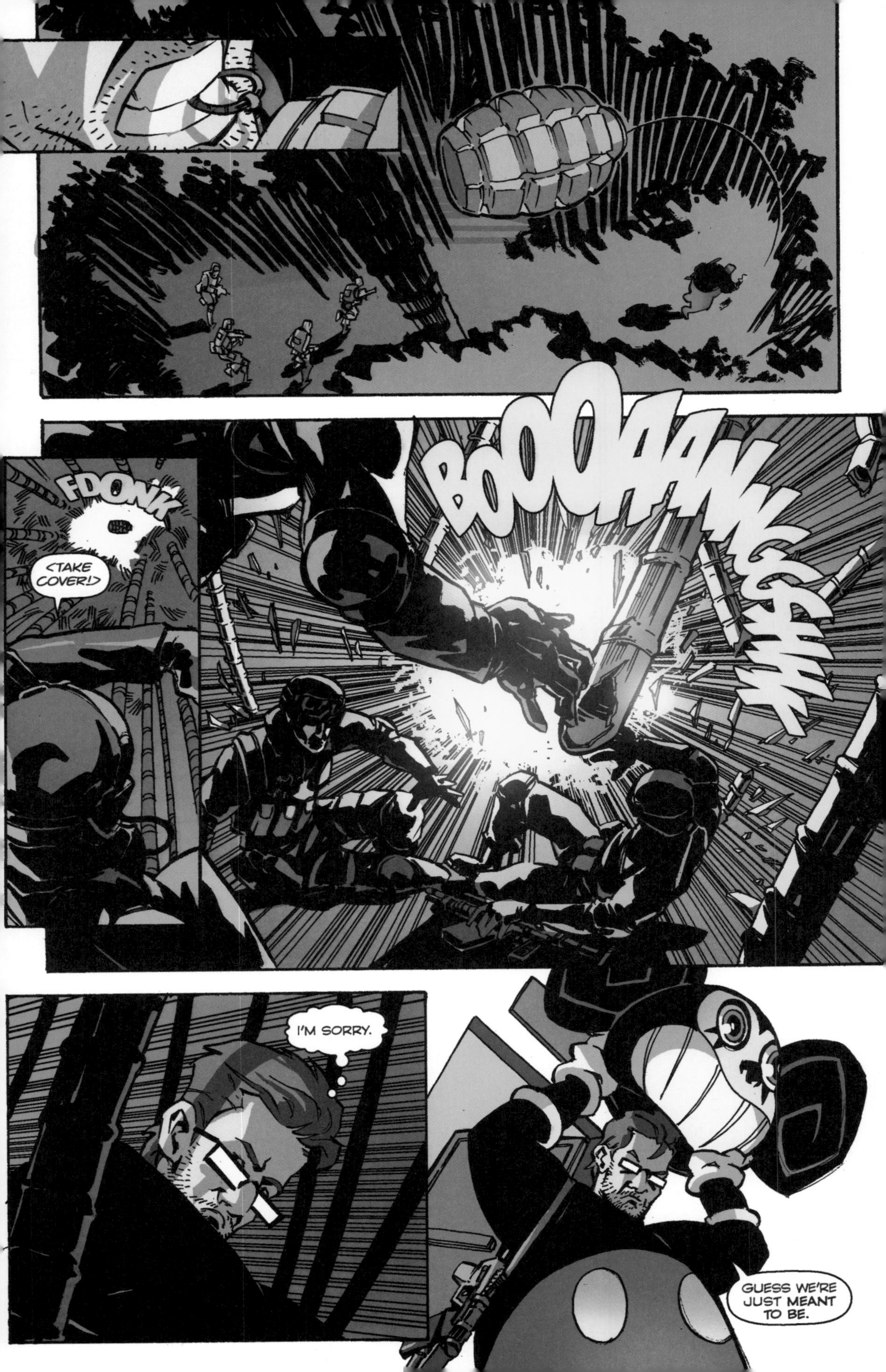
FDONK
<TAKE COVER!>
BOOOAAANGGCHHK
I'M SORRY.
GUESS WE'RE JUST MEANT TO BE.

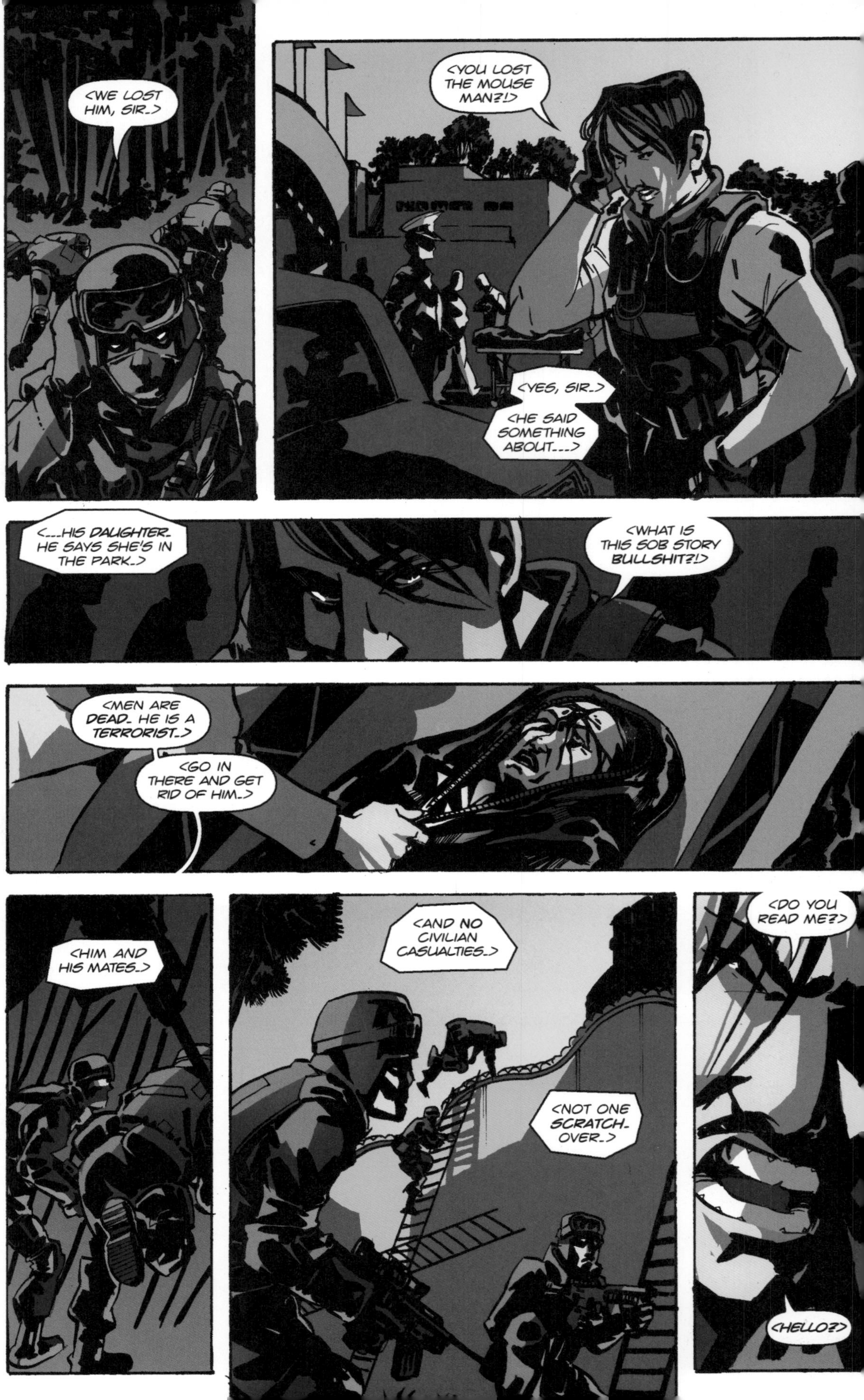
<WE LOST HIM, SIR.>
<YOU LOST THE MOUSE MAN?!>
<YES, SIR.>
<HE SAID SOMETHING ABOUT...>
<...HIS DAUGHTER. HE SAYS SHE'S IN THE PARK.>
<WHAT IS THIS SOB STORY BULLSHIT?!>
<MEN ARE DEAD. HE IS A TERRORIST.>
<GO IN THERE AND GET RID OF HIM.>
<HIM AND HIS MATES.>
<AND NO CIVILIAN CASUALTIES.>
<NOT ONE SCRATCH. OVER.>
<DO YOU READ ME?>
<HELLO?>

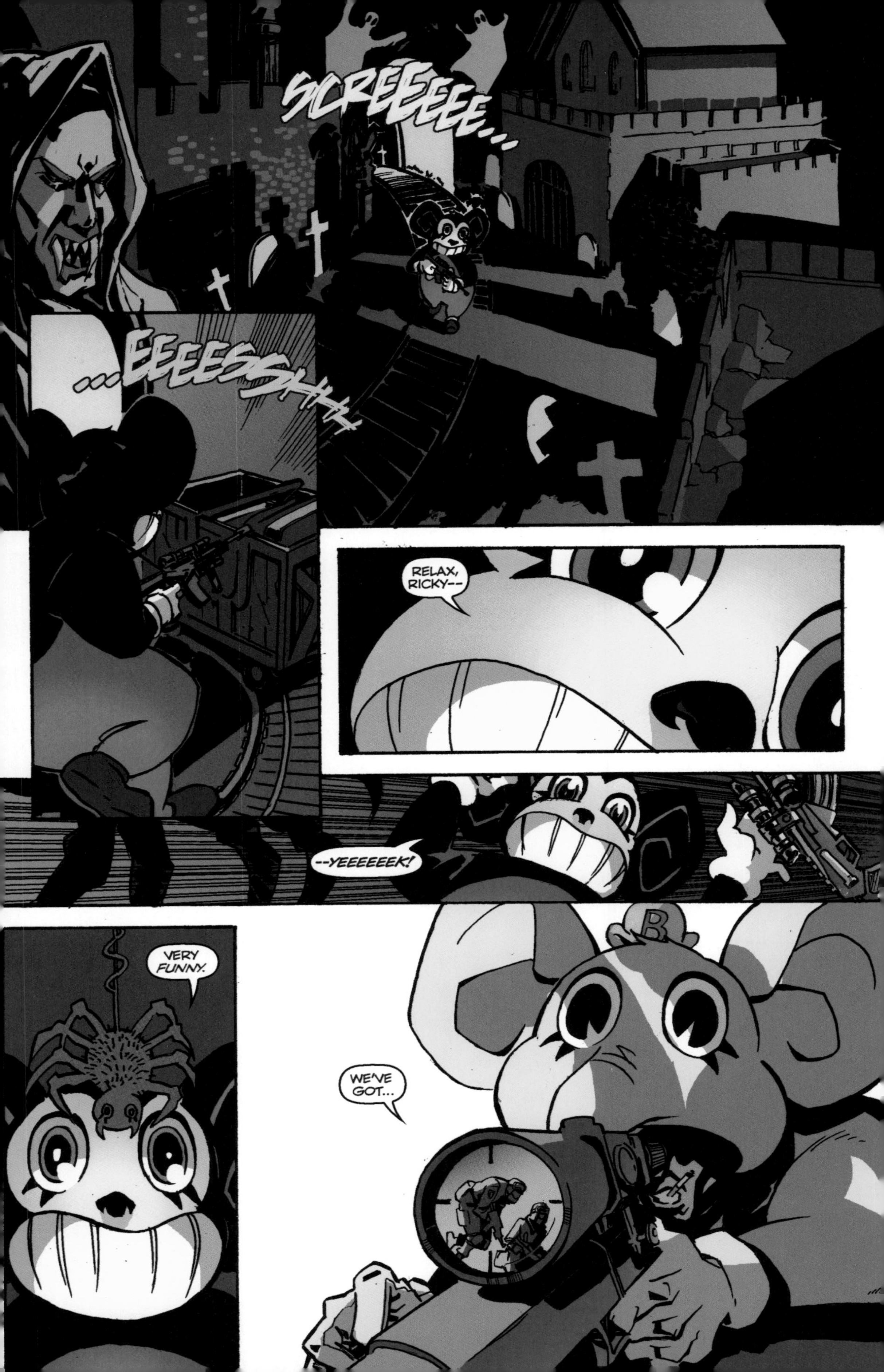
SCREEEEEE...
...EEEESSHHH
RELAX, RICKY--
--YEEEEEEK!
VERY FUNNY.
WE'VE GOT...

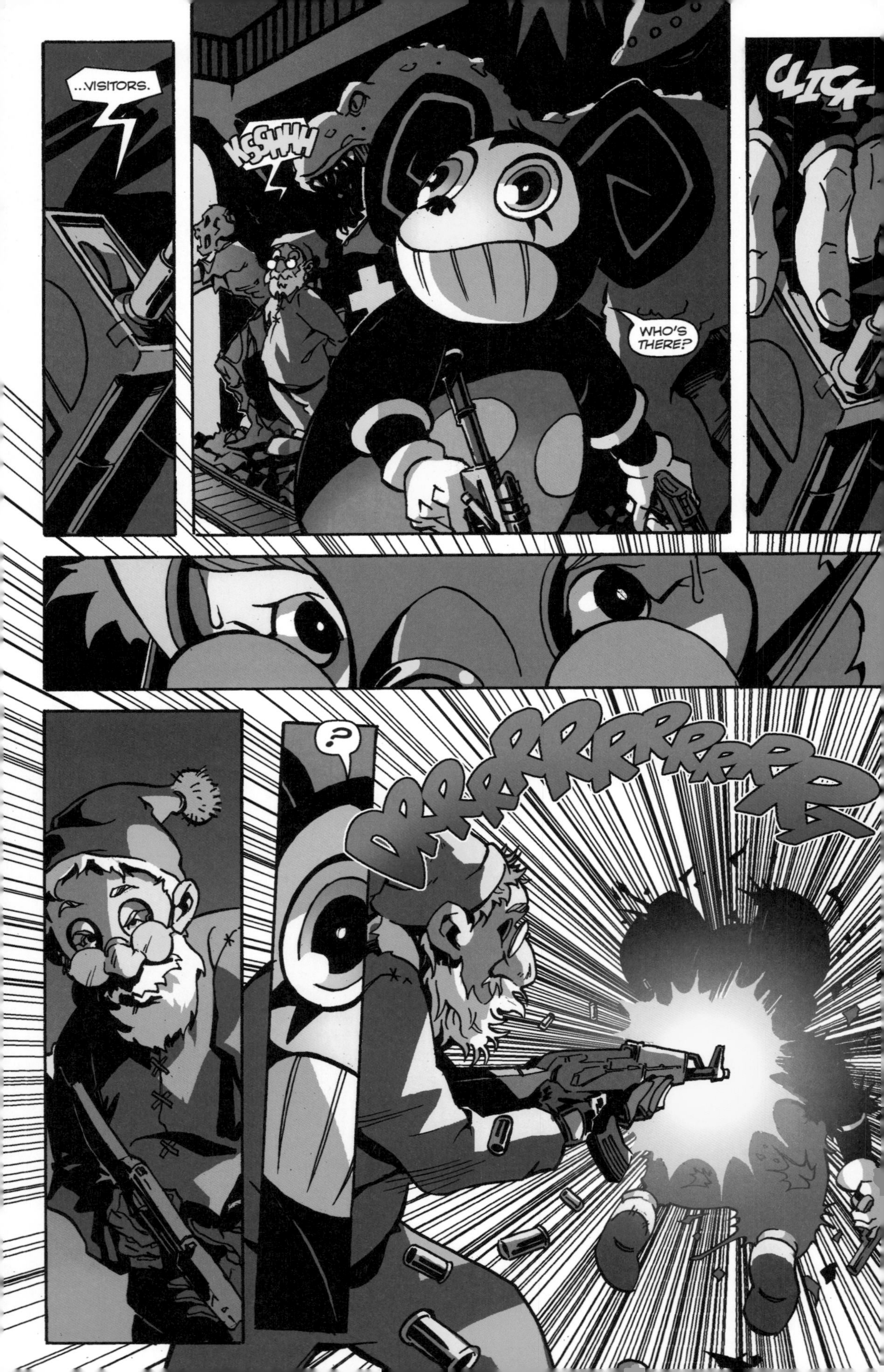
...VISITORS.
KSSHHH
WHO'S THERE?
CLICK
?
BRRRRRRRRRRRR

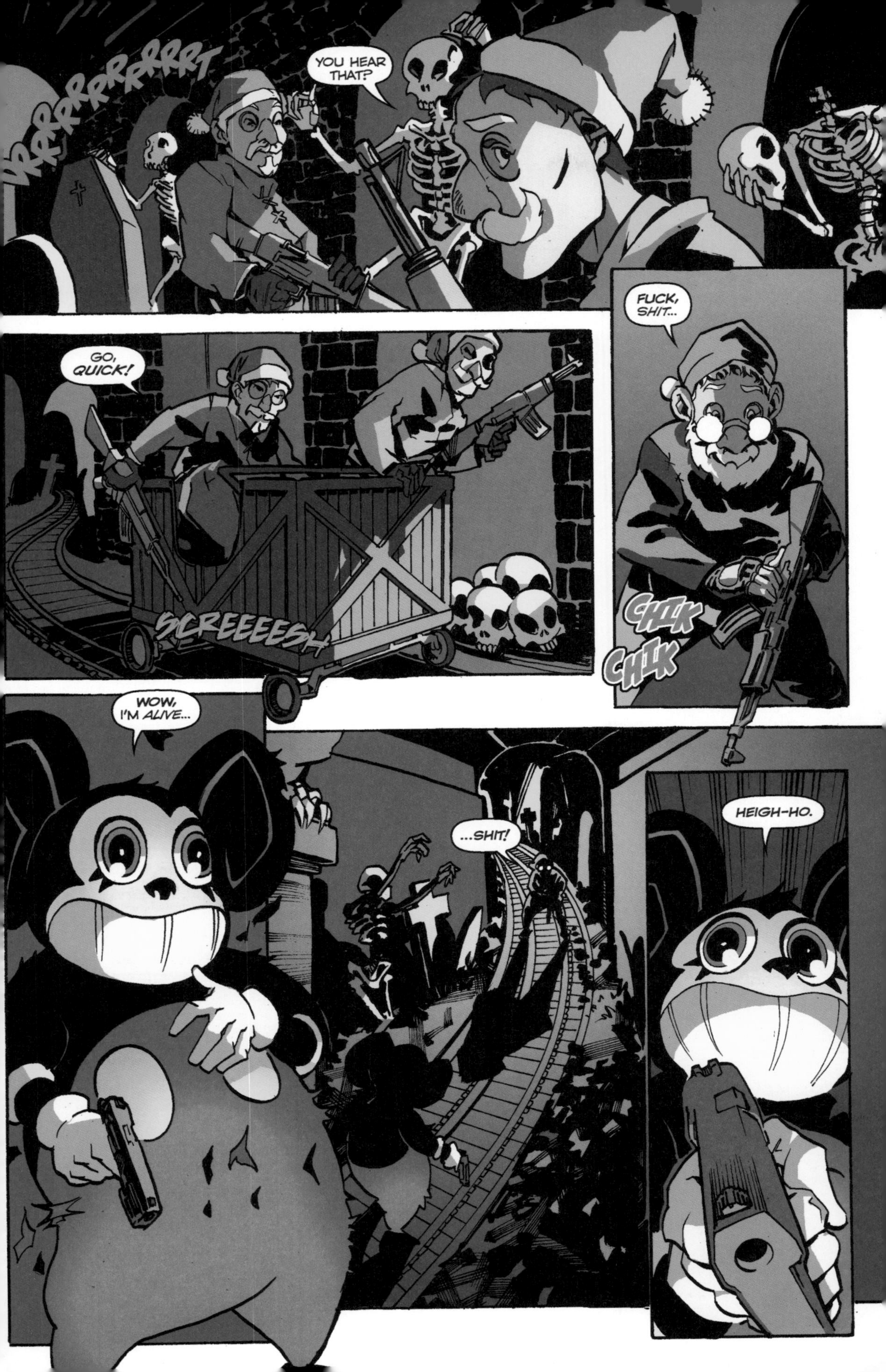
VRRRRRRRRRRRRT
YOU HEAR THAT?
GO, QUICK!
SCREEEEESH
FUCK, SHIT...
CHIK
CHIK
WOW, I'M ALIVE...
...SHIT!
HEIGH-HO.

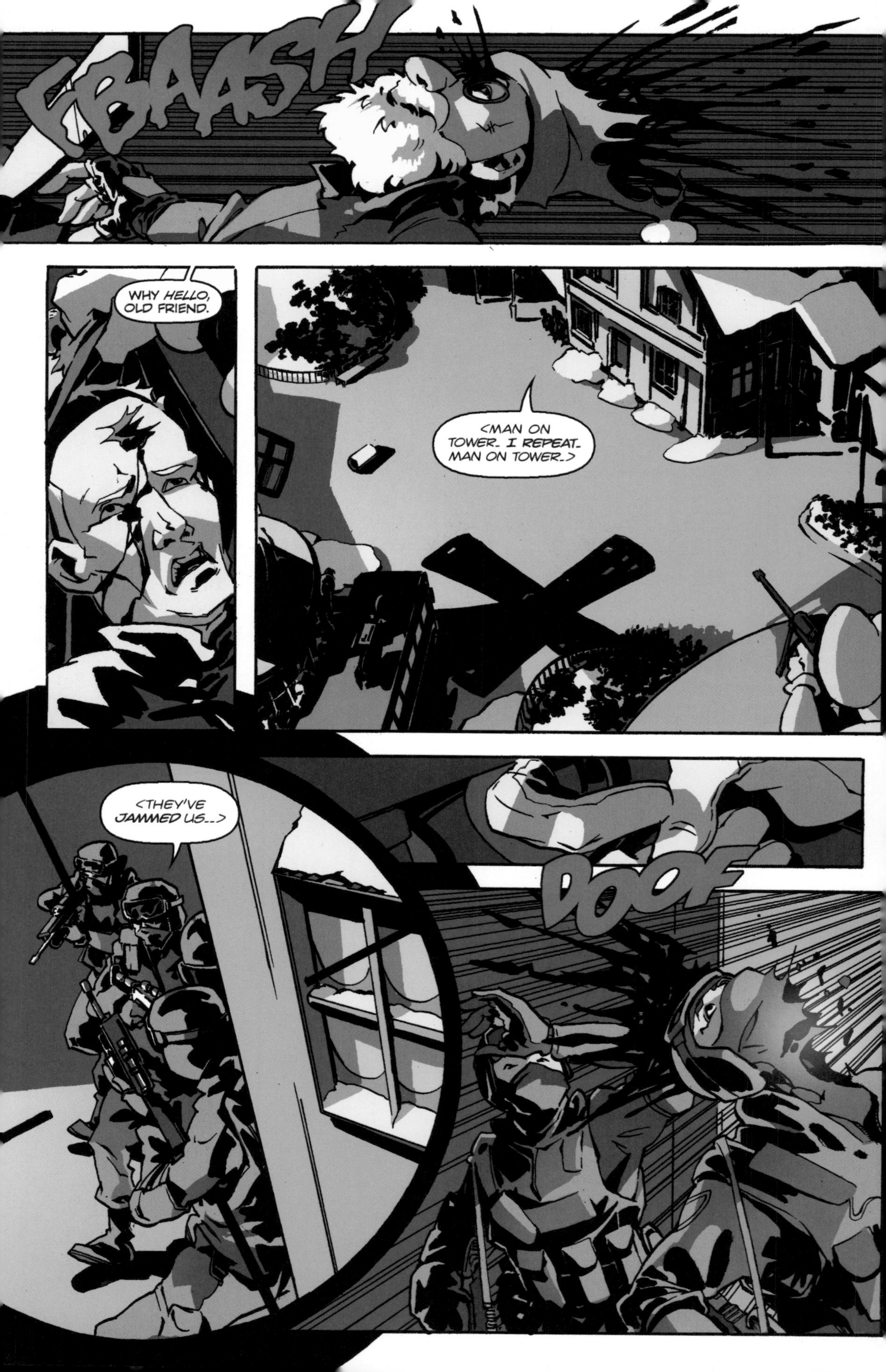
FBAASH
WHY HELLO, OLD FRIEND.
<MAN ON TOWER. I REPEAT. MAN ON TOWER.>
<THEY'VE JAMMED US...>
DOOF

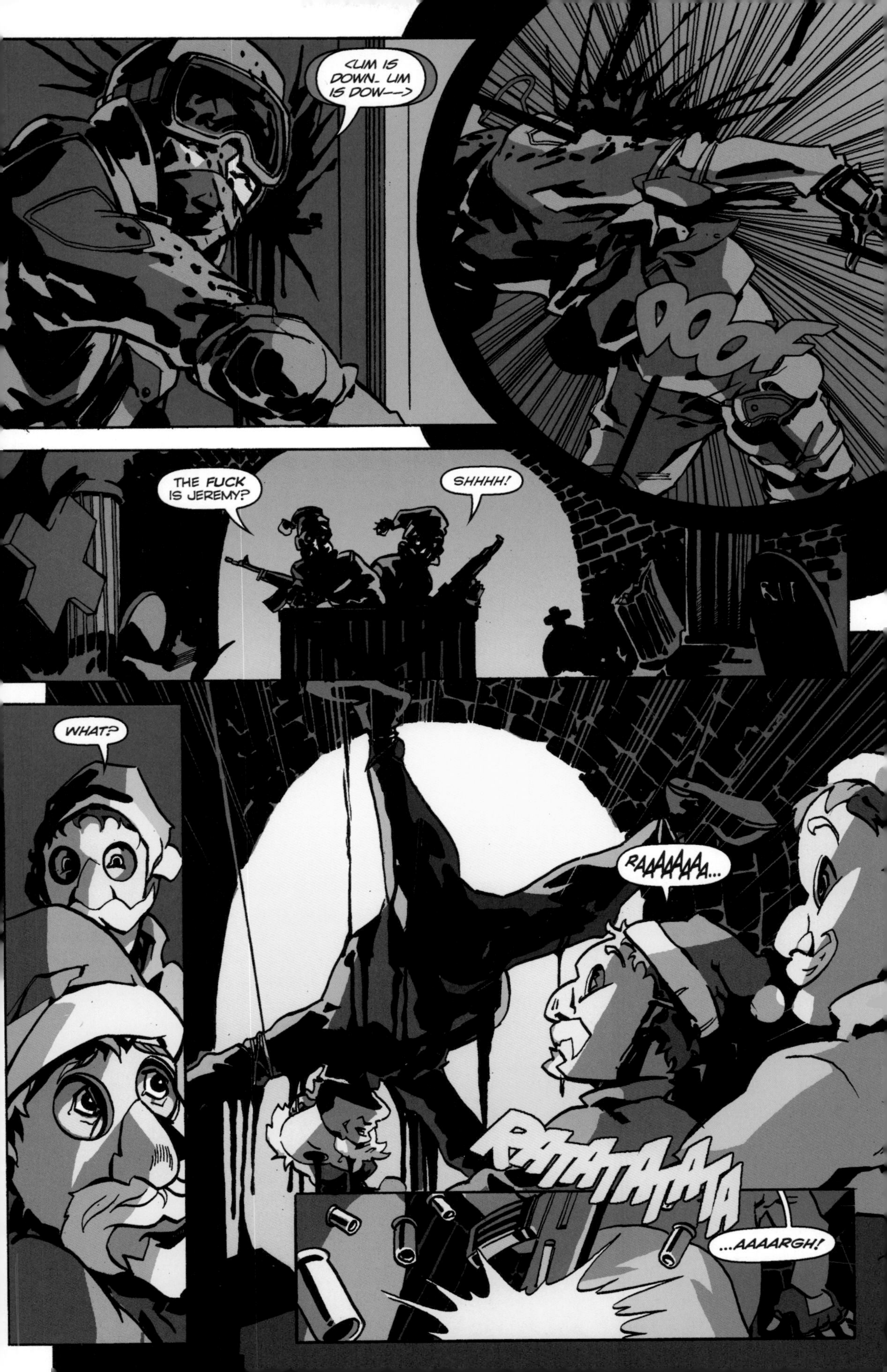
<UM IS DOWN. UM IS DOW-->
DOOF
THE FUCK IS JEREMY?
SHHHH!
WHAT?
RAAAAAAA...
RATATATATA
...AAAARGH!

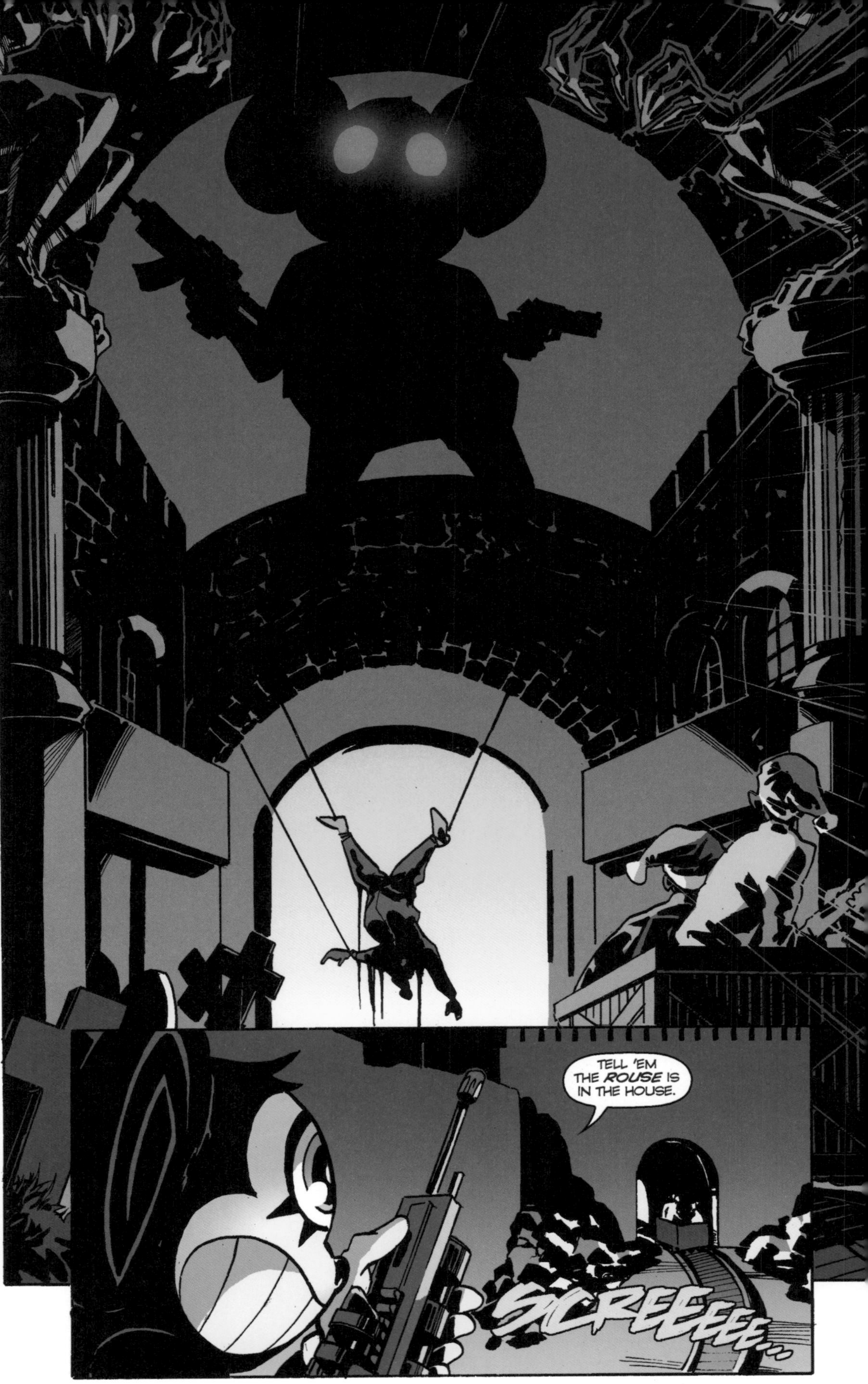

TELL 'EM THE *ROUSE* IS IN THE HOUSE.
SKREEEEEEE...

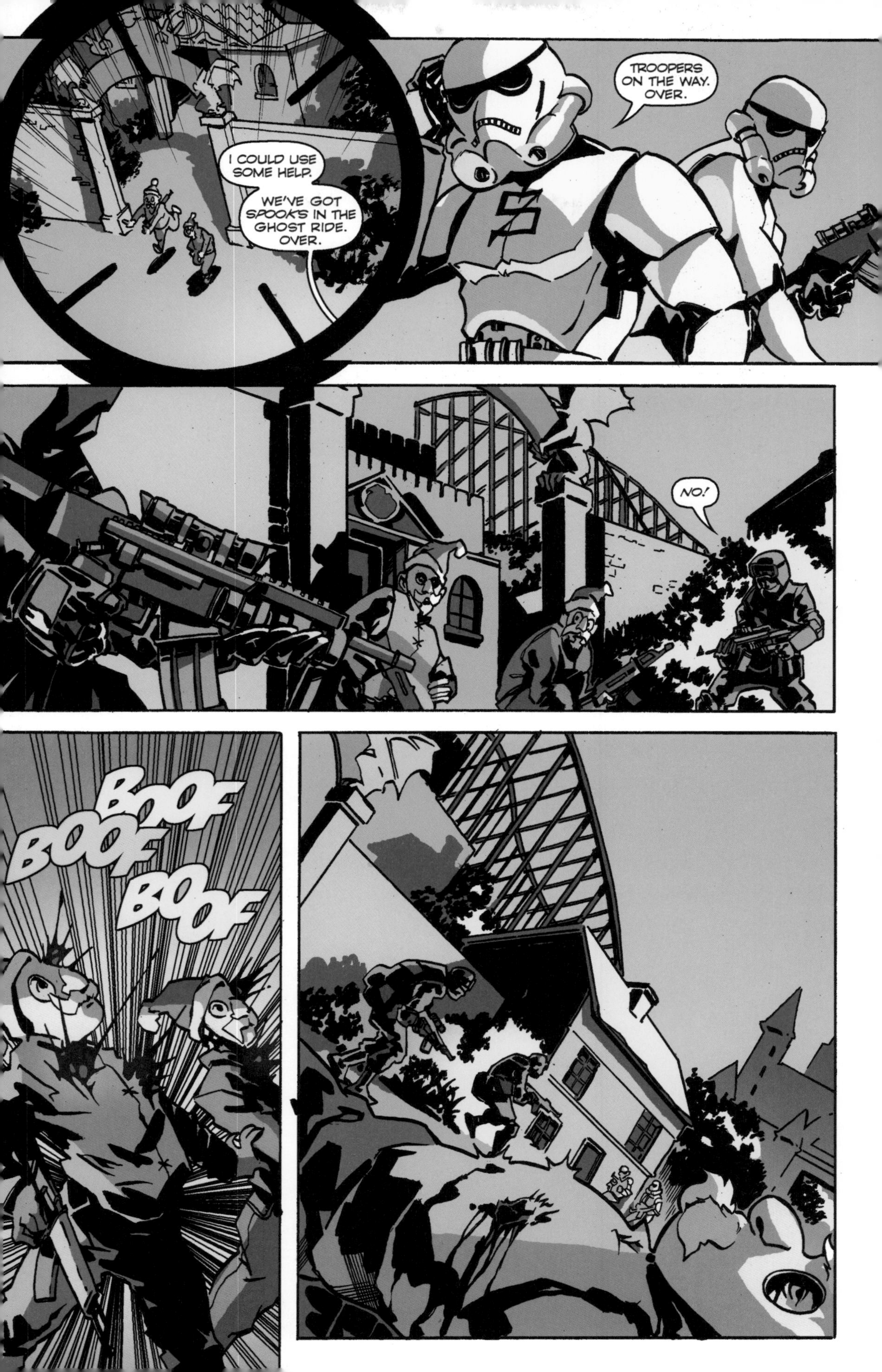

I COULD USE SOME HELP.
WE'VE GOT SPOOKS IN THE GHOST RIDE. OVER.
TROOPERS ON THE WAY. OVER.
NO!
BOOF
BOOF
BOOF

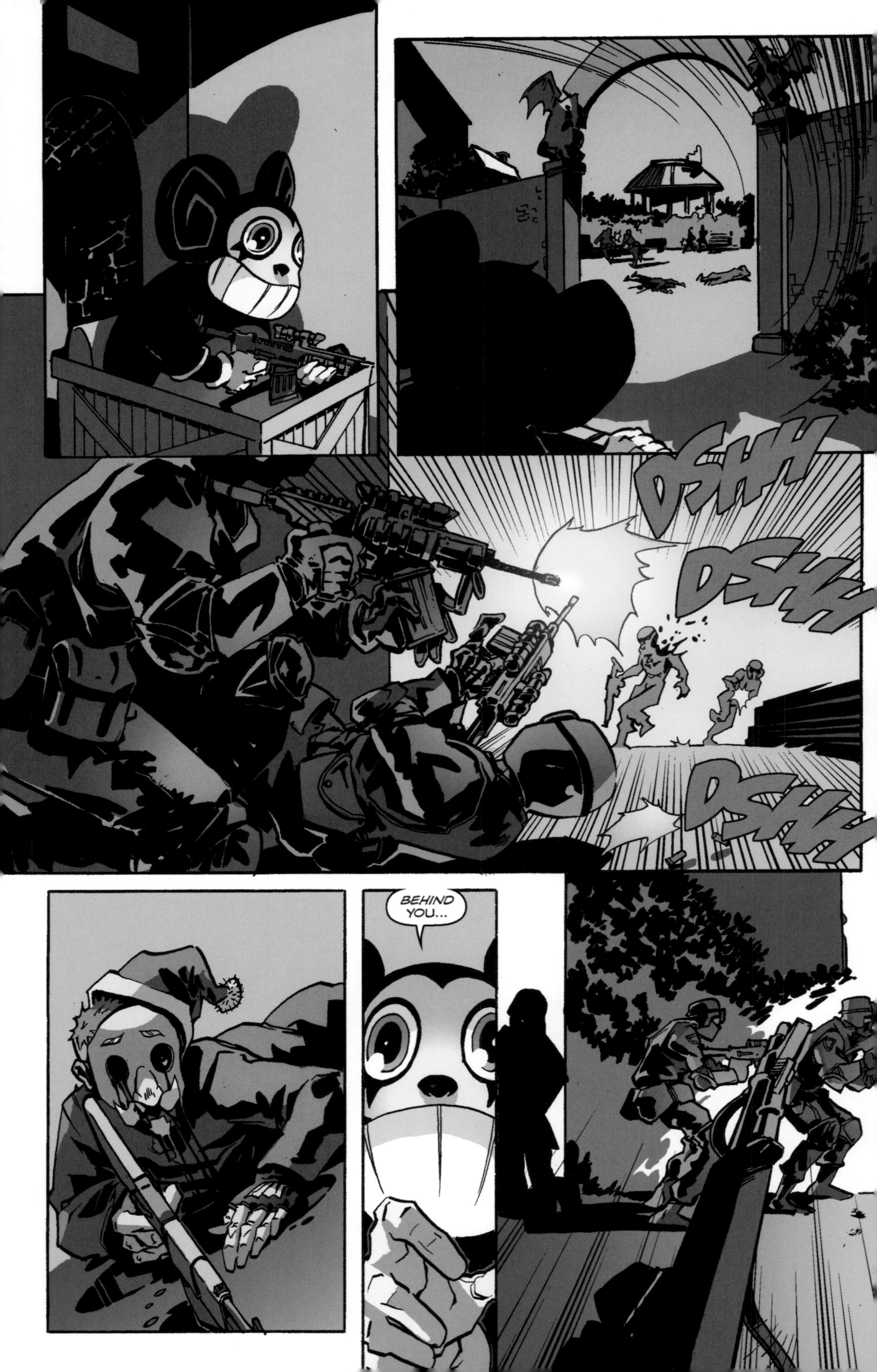
DSHH
DSHH
DSHH
BEHIND YOU...

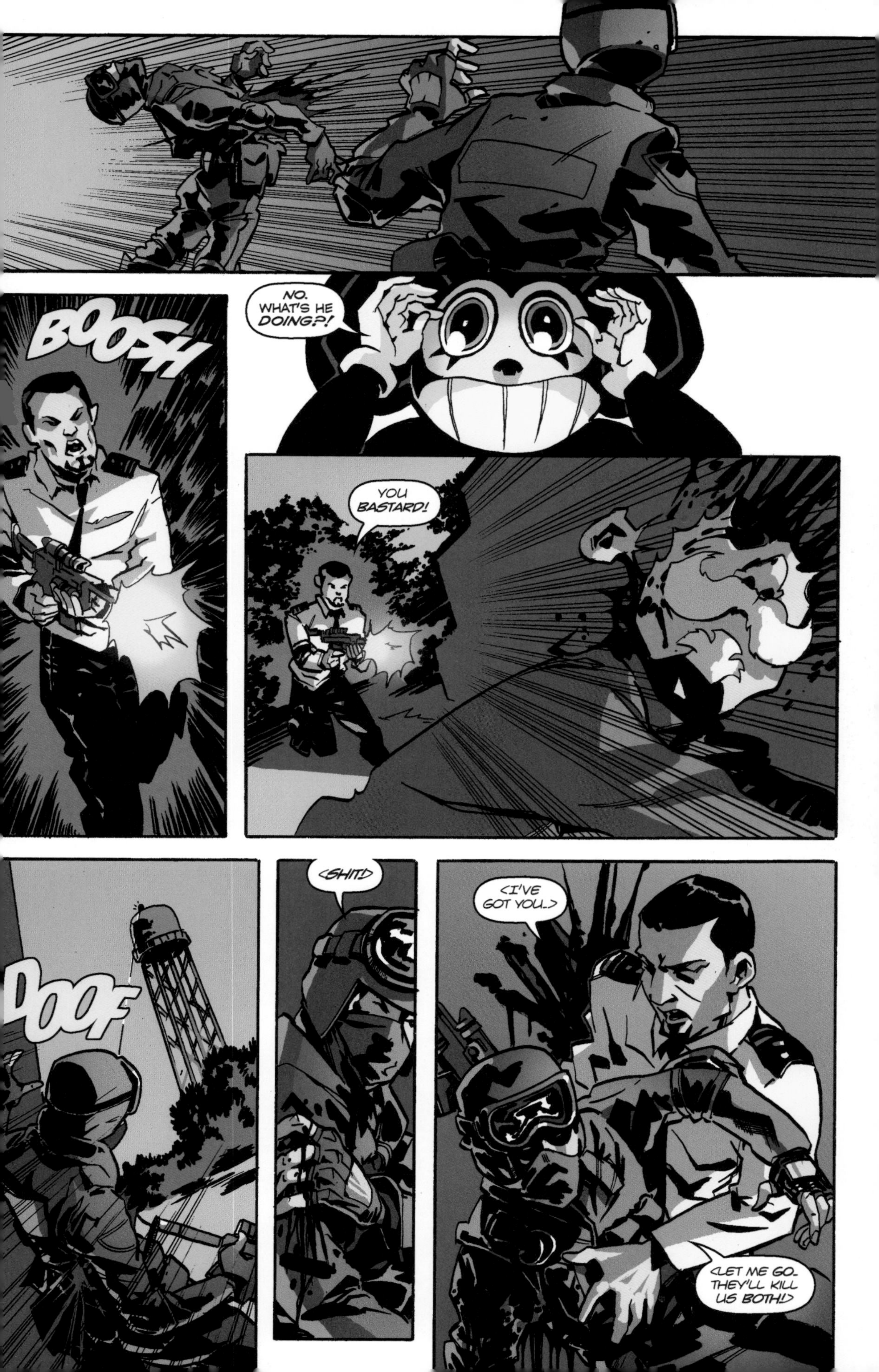
BOOSH
NO. WHAT'S HE DOING?!
YOU BASTARD!
DOOF
<SHIT!>
<I'VE GOT YOU.>
<LET ME GO. THEY'LL KILL US BOTH!>

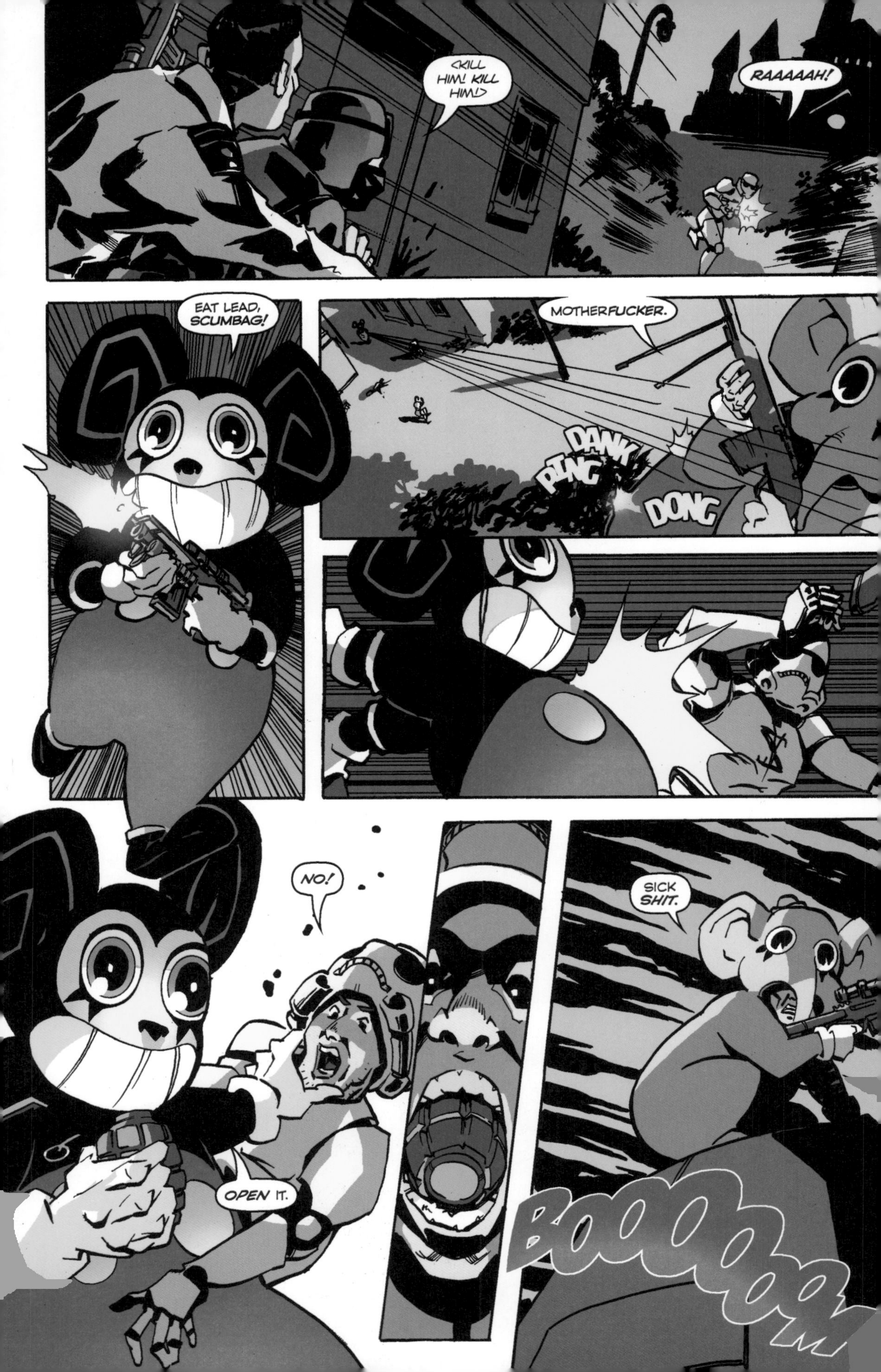

<KILL HIM! KILL HIM!>
RAAAAAH!
EAT LEAD, SCUMBAG!
MOTHERFUCKER.
DANK
PING
DONG
NO!
OPEN IT.
SICK SHIT.
BOOOOOOM

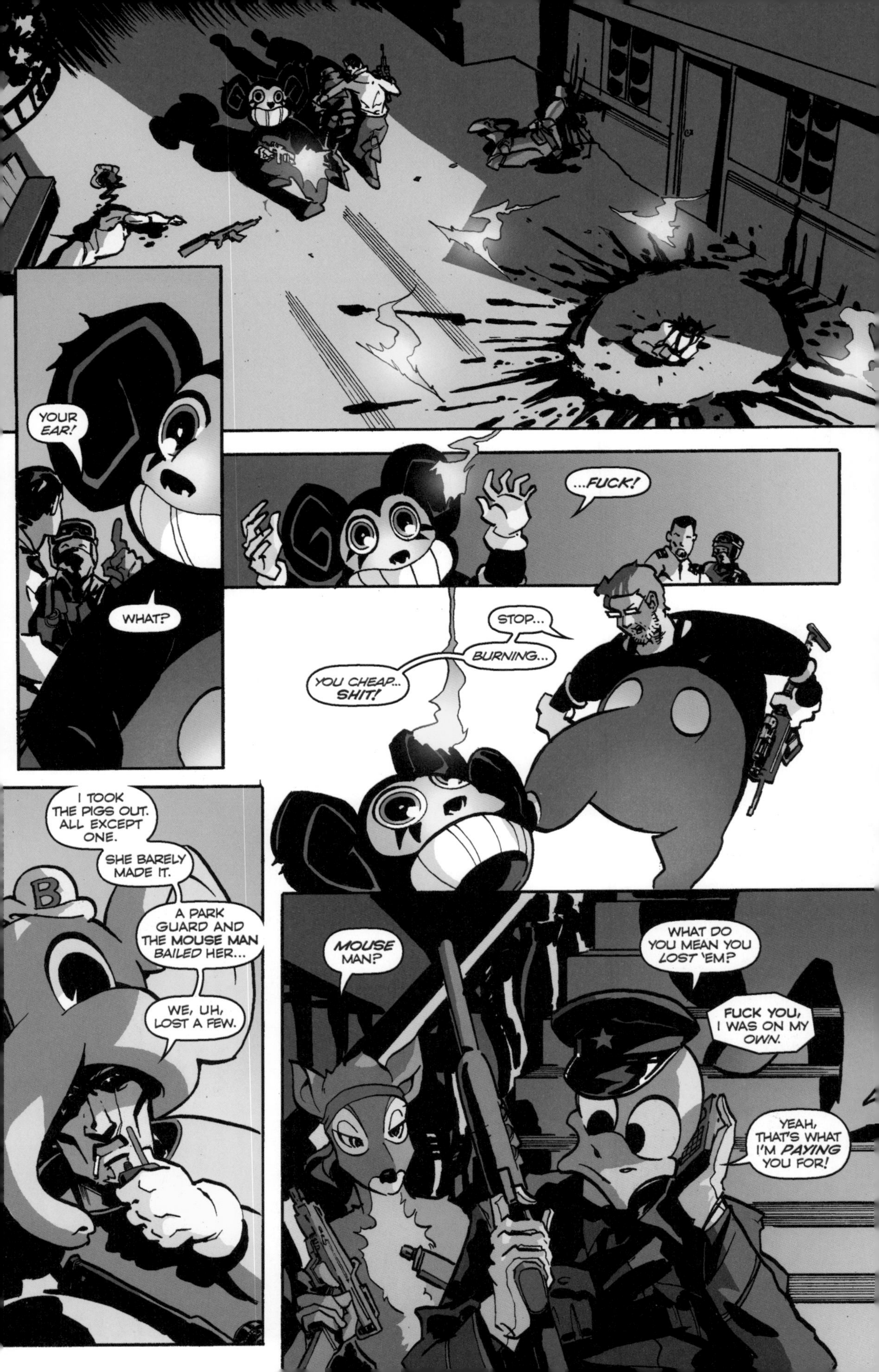

YOUR EAR!
WHAT?
...FUCK!
STOP...
BURNING...
YOU CHEAP... SHIT!
I TOOK THE PIGS OUT. ALL EXCEPT ONE.
SHE BARELY MADE IT.
A PARK GUARD AND THE MOUSE MAN BAILED HER...
WE, UH, LOST A FEW.
MOUSE MAN?
WHAT DO YOU MEAN YOU LOST 'EM?
FUCK YOU, I WAS ON MY OWN.
YEAH, THAT'S WHAT I'M PAYING YOU FOR!

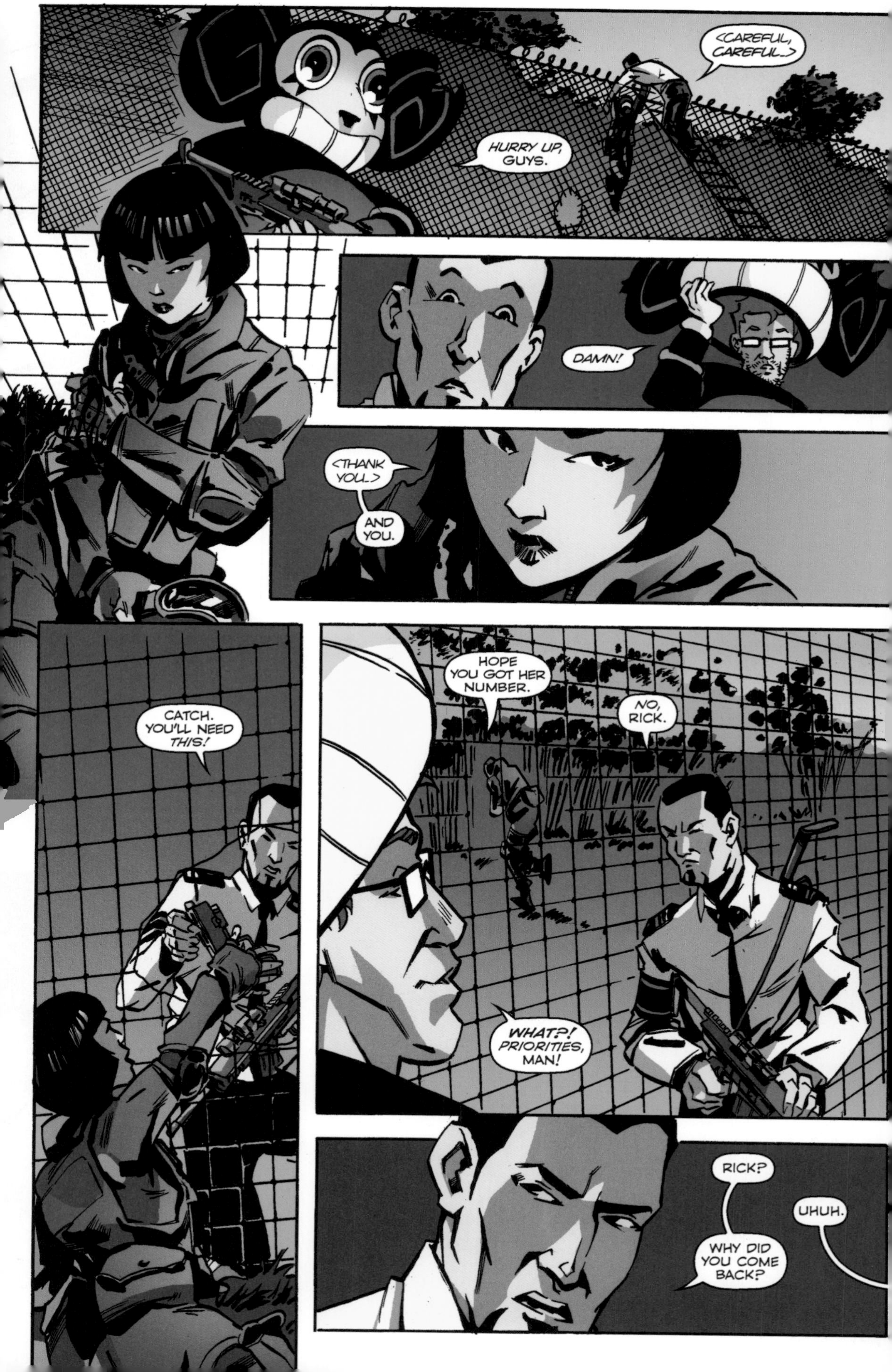
<CAREFUL, CAREFUL.>
HURRY UP, GUYS.
DAMN!
<THANK YOU.>
AND YOU.
CATCH. YOU'LL NEED THIS!
HOPE YOU GOT HER NUMBER.
NO, RICK.
WHAT?! PRIORITIES, MAN!
RICK?
WHY DID YOU COME BACK?
UHUH.

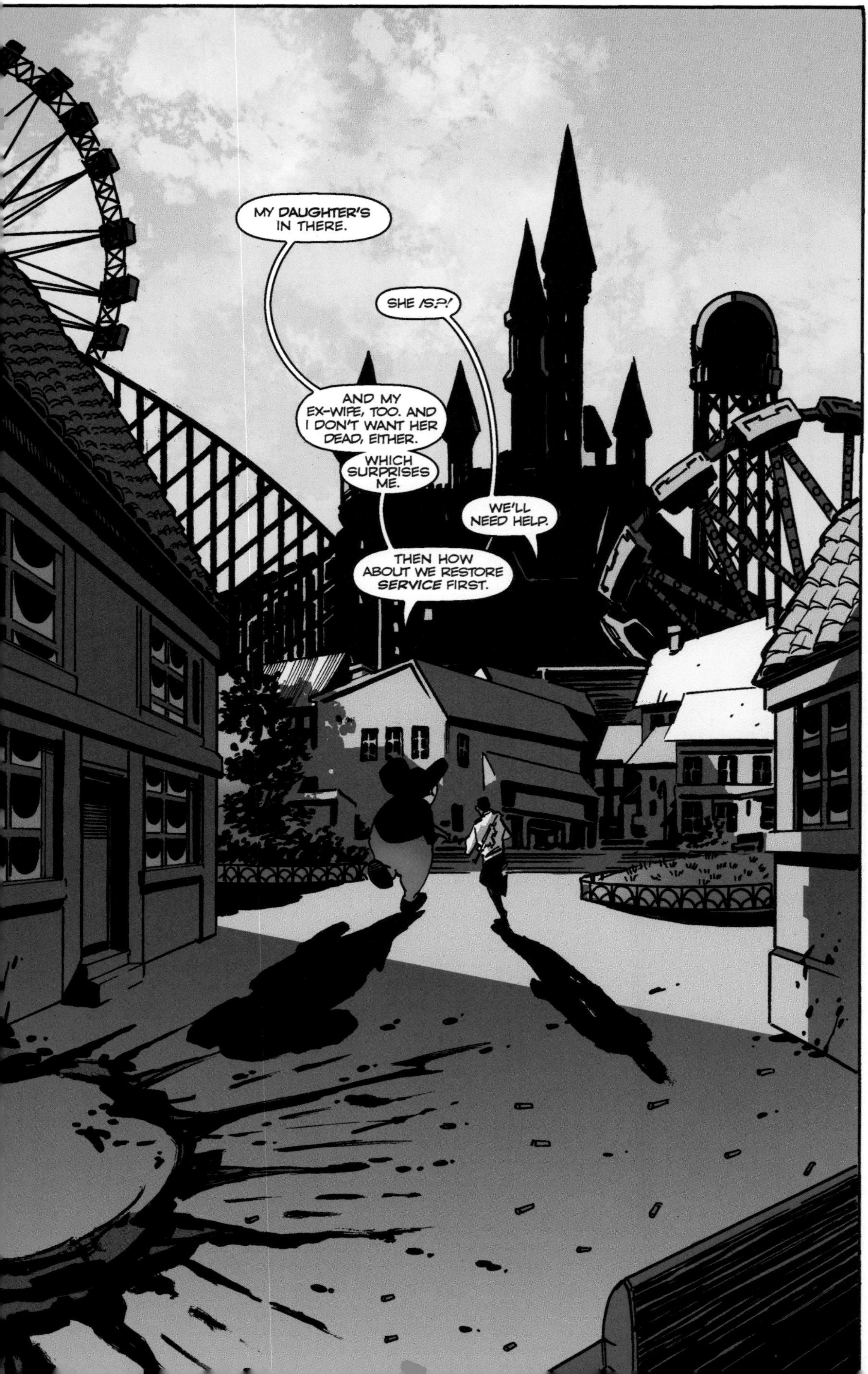
MY DAUGHTER'S IN THERE.
SHE IS?!
AND MY EX-WIFE, TOO. AND I DON'T WANT HER DEAD, EITHER.
WHICH SURPRISES ME.
WE'LL NEED HELP.
THEN HOW ABOUT WE RESTORE SERVICE FIRST.

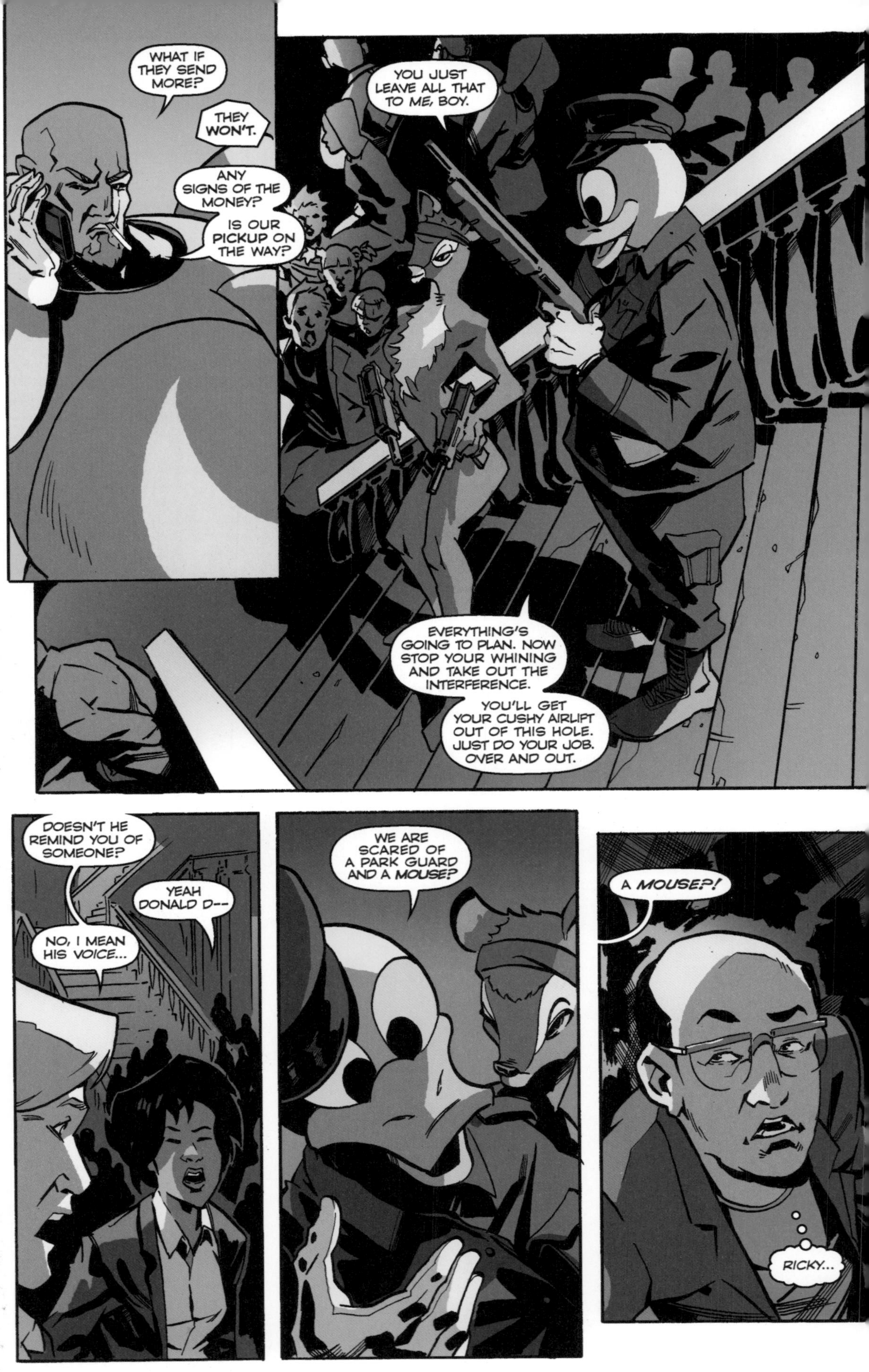
WHAT IF THEY SEND MORE?
THEY WON'T.
ANY SIGNS OF THE MONEY?
IS OUR PICKUP ON THE WAY?
YOU JUST LEAVE ALL THAT TO ME, BOY.
EVERYTHING'S GOING TO PLAN. NOW STOP YOUR WHINING AND TAKE OUT THE INTERFERENCE.
YOU'LL GET YOUR CUSHY AIRLIFT OUT OF THIS HOLE. JUST DO YOUR JOB. OVER AND OUT.
DOESN'T HE REMIND YOU OF SOMEONE?
YEAH DONALD D--
NO, I MEAN HIS VOICE...
WE ARE SCARED OF A PARK GUARD AND A MOUSE?
A MOUSE?!
RICKY...

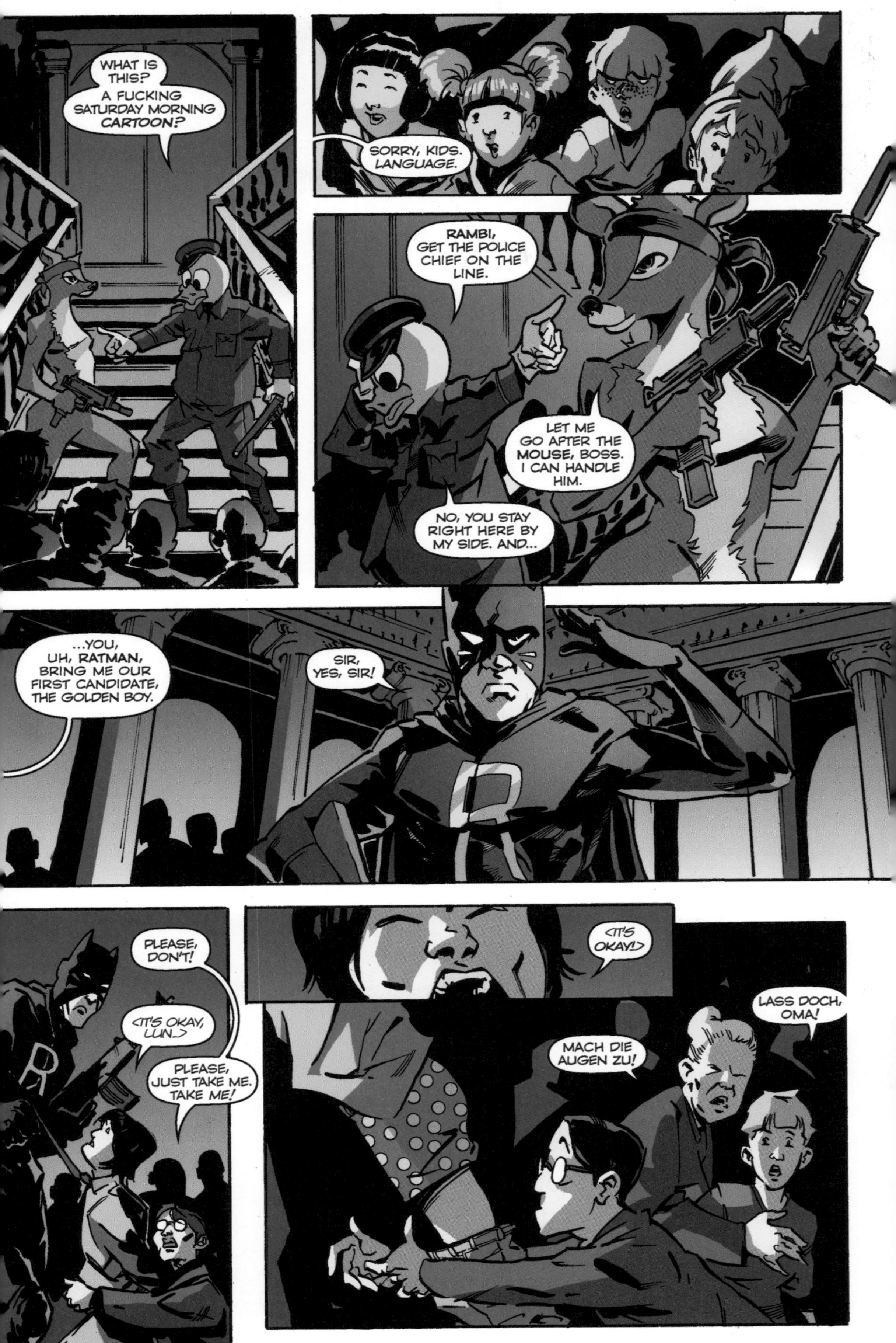

WHAT IS THIS? A FUCKING SATURDAY MORNING CARTOON?
SORRY, KIDS. LANGUAGE.
RAMBI, GET THE POLICE CHIEF ON THE LINE.
LET ME GO AFTER THE MOUSE, BOSS. I CAN HANDLE HIM.
NO, YOU STAY RIGHT HERE BY MY SIDE. AND...
...YOU, UH, RATMAN, BRING ME OUR FIRST CANDIDATE, THE GOLDEN BOY.
SIR, YES, SIR!
PLEASE, DON'T!
<IT'S OKAY, LUN.>
PLEASE, JUST TAKE ME. TAKE ME!
<IT'S OKAY!>
LASS DOCH, OMA!
MACH DIE AUGEN ZU!

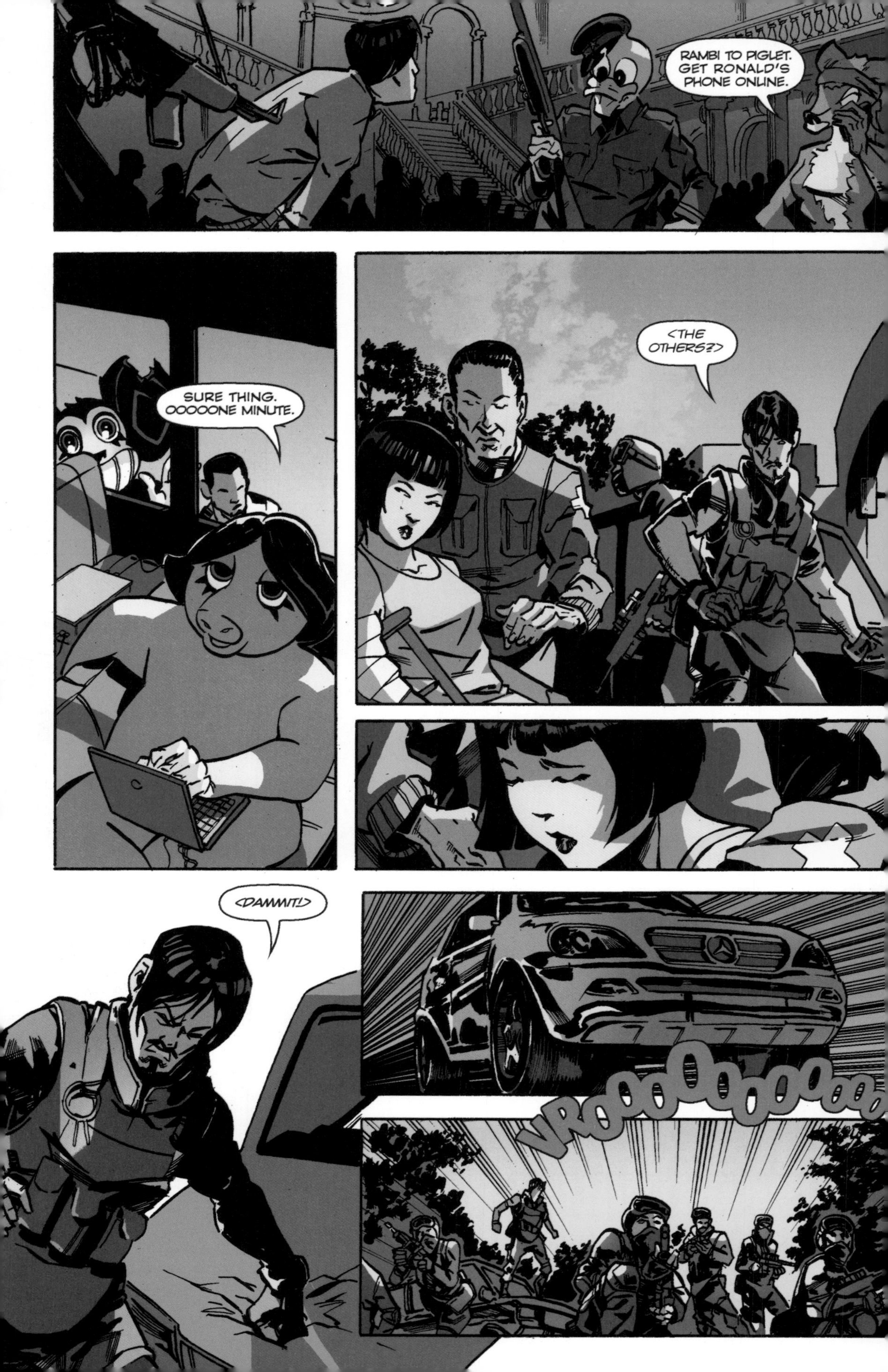

RAMBI TO PIGLET. GET RONALD'S PHONE ONLINE.
SURE THING. OOOOONE MINUTE.
<THE OTHERS?>
<DAMMIT!>
VROOOOOOOOOO

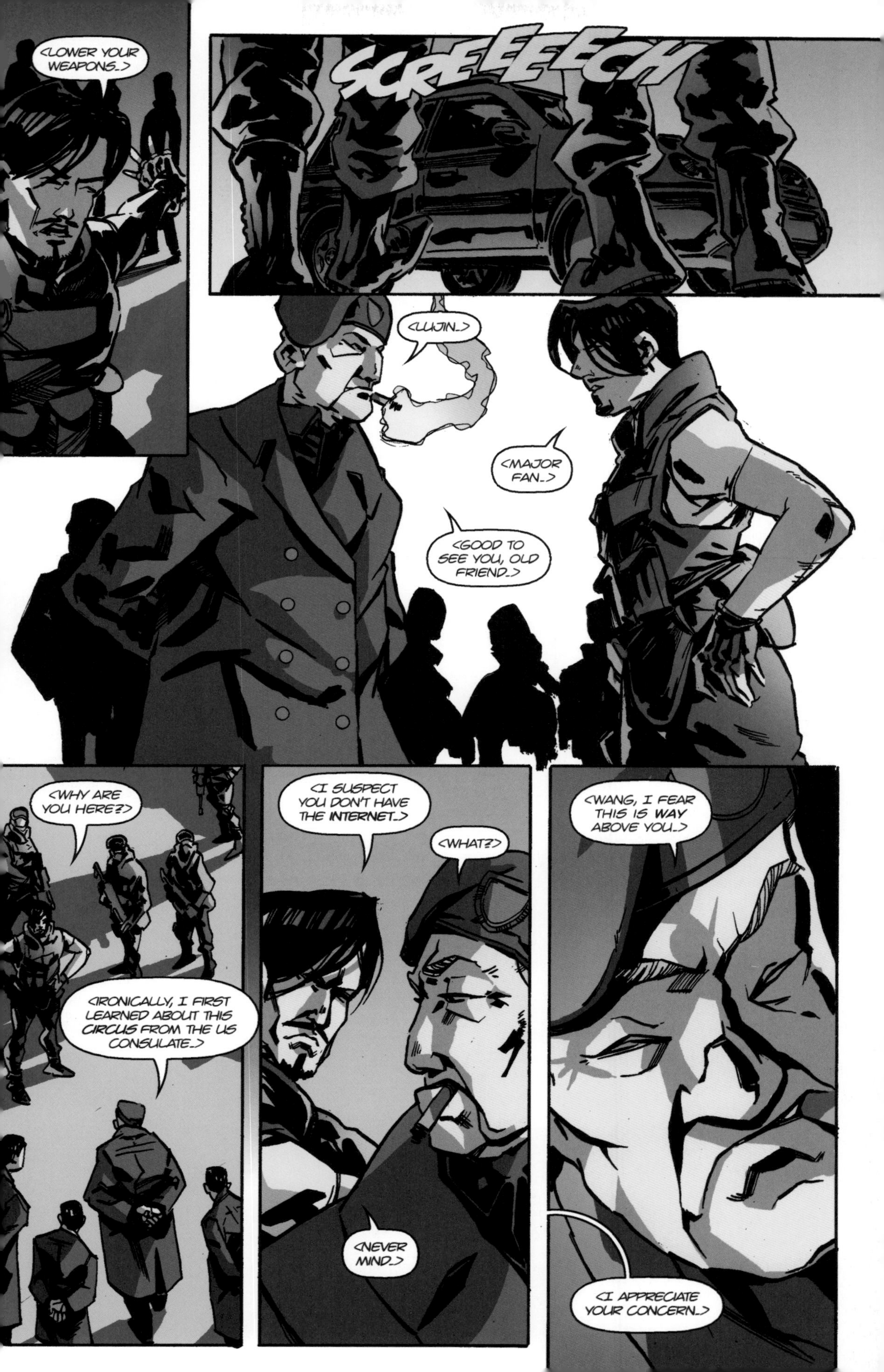
<LOWER YOUR WEAPONS.>
SCREEEECH
<LUJIN.>
<MAJOR FAN.>
<GOOD TO SEE YOU, OLD FRIEND.>
<WHY ARE YOU HERE?>
<IRONICALLY, I FIRST LEARNED ABOUT THIS CIRCUS FROM THE US CONSULATE.>
<I SUSPECT YOU DON'T HAVE THE INTERNET.>
<WHAT?>
<NEVER MIND.>
<WANG, I FEAR THIS IS WAY ABOVE YOU.>
<I APPRECIATE YOUR CONCERN.>

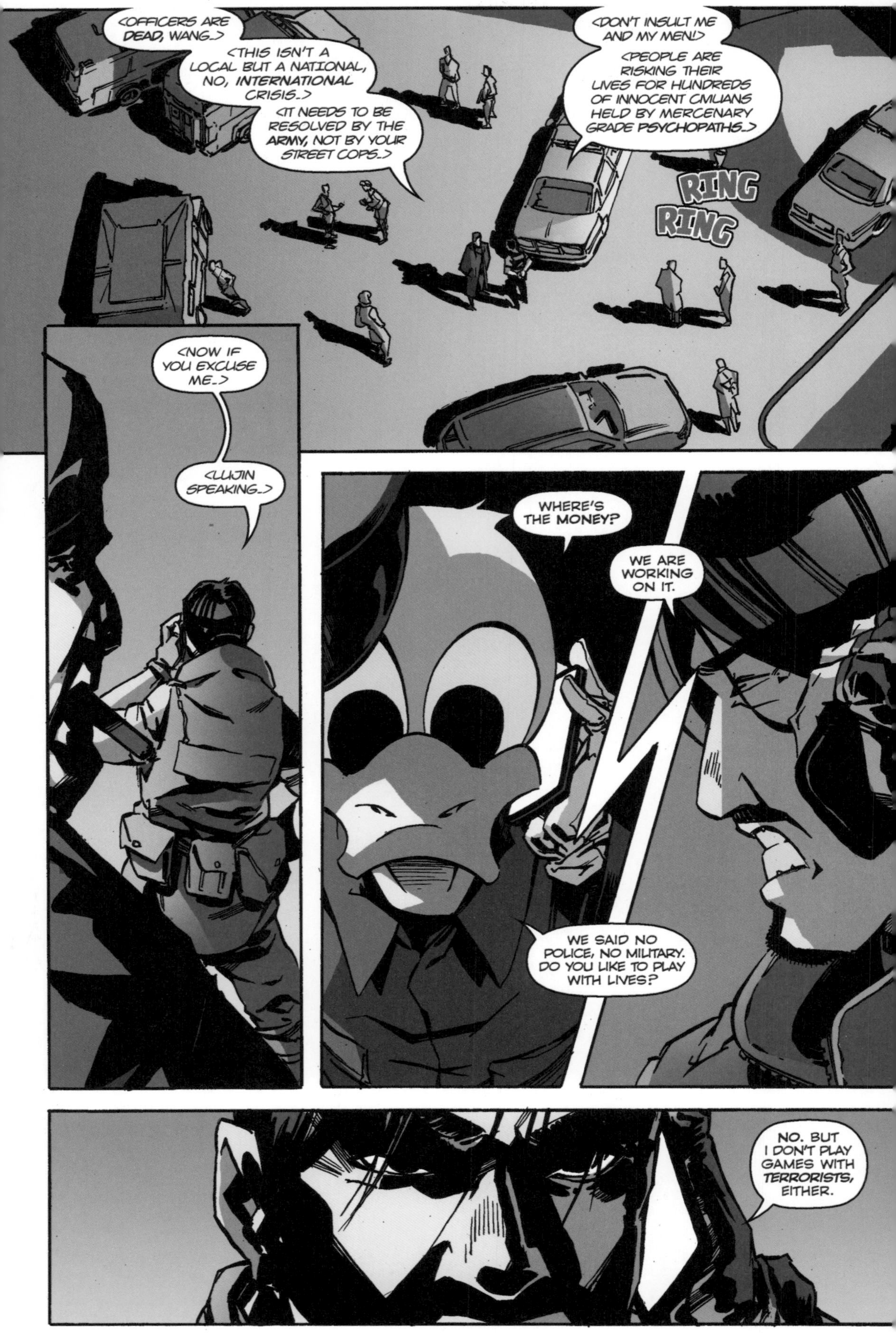

<OFFICERS ARE DEAD, WANG.>
<THIS ISN'T A LOCAL BUT A NATIONAL, NO, INTERNATIONAL CRISIS.>
<IT NEEDS TO BE RESOLVED BY THE ARMY, NOT BY YOUR STREET COPS.>
<DON'T INSULT ME AND MY MEN!>
<PEOPLE ARE RISKING THEIR LIVES FOR HUNDREDS OF INNOCENT CIVILIANS HELD BY MERCENARY GRADE PSYCHOPATHS.>
RING
RING
<NOW IF YOU EXCUSE ME.>
<LIUJIN SPEAKING.>
WHERE'S THE MONEY?
WE ARE WORKING ON IT.
WE SAID NO POLICE, NO MILITARY. DO YOU LIKE TO PLAY WITH LIVES?
NO. BUT I DON'T PLAY GAMES WITH TERRORISTS, EITHER.

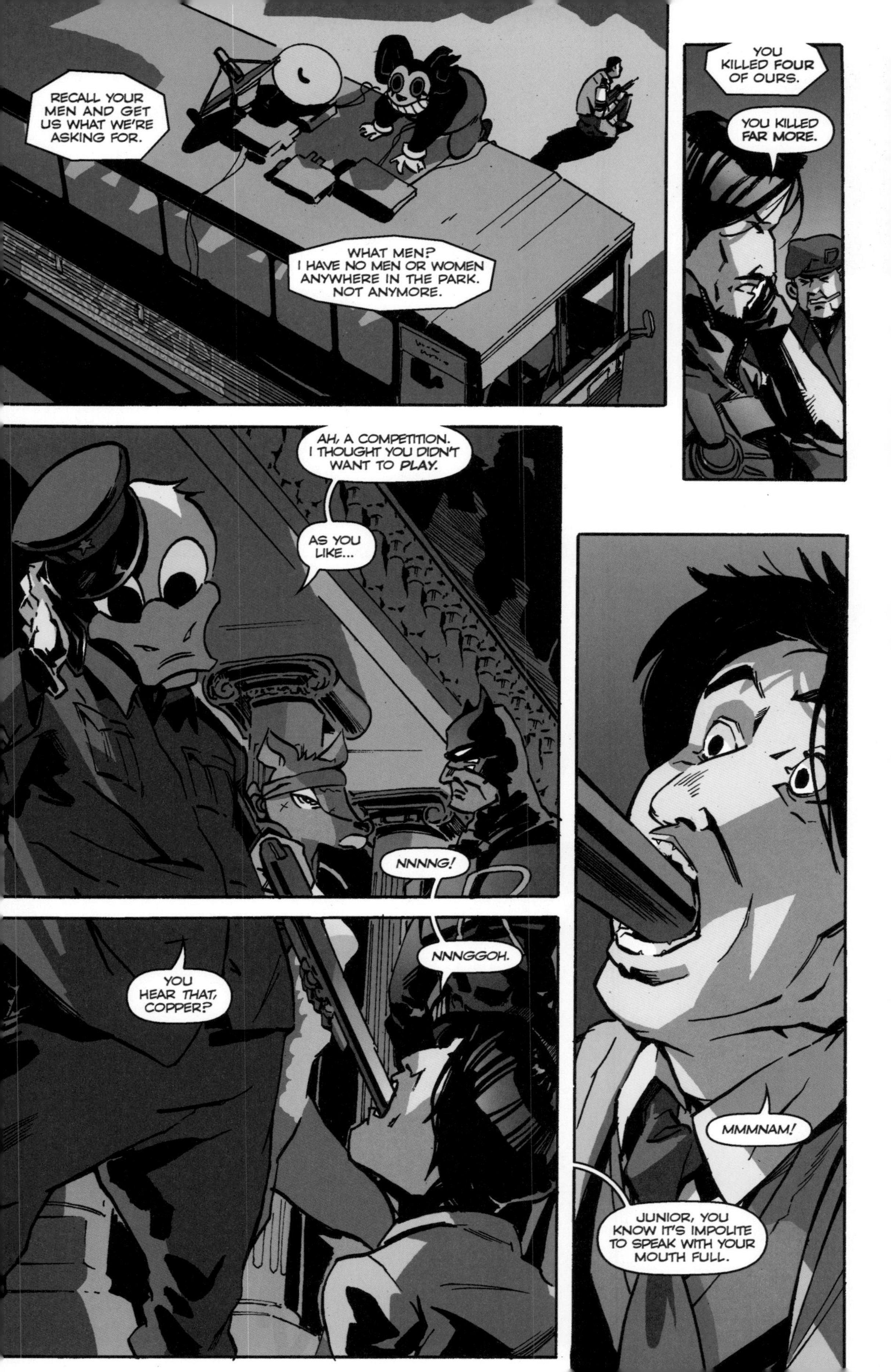
RECALL YOUR MEN AND GET US WHAT WE'RE ASKING FOR.
WHAT MEN? I HAVE NO MEN OR WOMEN ANYWHERE IN THE PARK. NOT ANYMORE.
YOU KILLED FOUR OF OURS.
YOU KILLED FAR MORE.
AH, A COMPETITION. I THOUGHT YOU DIDN'T WANT TO PLAY.
AS YOU LIKE...
NNNNG!
NNNGGOH.
YOU HEAR THAT, COPPER?
MMMNAM!
JUNIOR, YOU KNOW IT'S IMPOLITE TO SPEAK WITH YOUR MOUTH FULL.

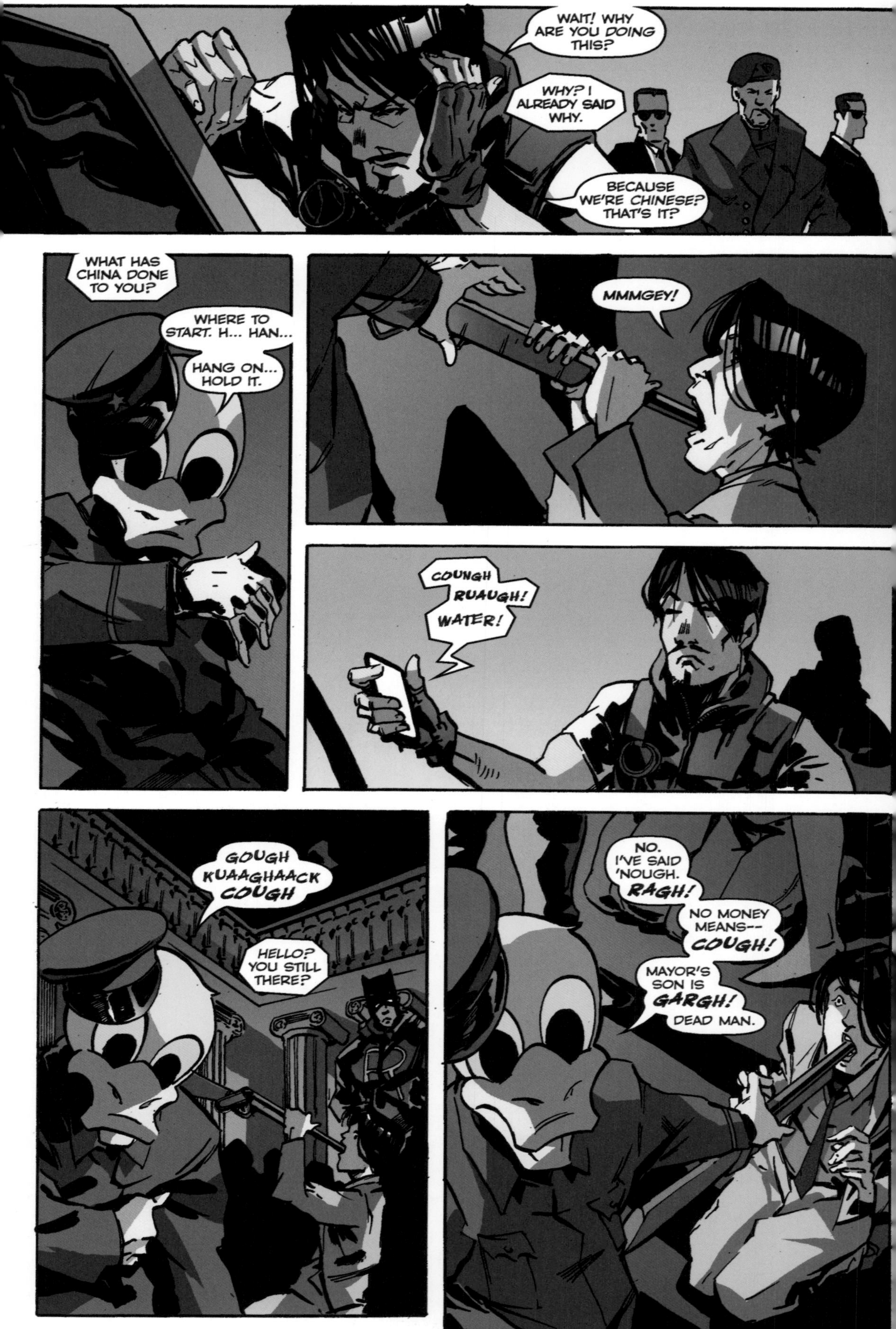
WAIT! WHY ARE YOU DOING THIS?
WHY? I ALREADY SAID WHY.
BECAUSE WE'RE CHINESE? THAT'S IT?
WHAT HAS CHINA DONE TO YOU?
WHERE TO START. H... HAN...
HANG ON... HOLD IT.
MMMGEY!
COUGH RUAUGH! WATER!
GOUGH KUAAGHAACK COUGH
HELLO? YOU STILL THERE?
NO. I'VE SAID 'NOUGH. RAGH!
NO MONEY MEANS-- COUGH!
MAYOR'S SON IS GARGH! DEAD MAN.

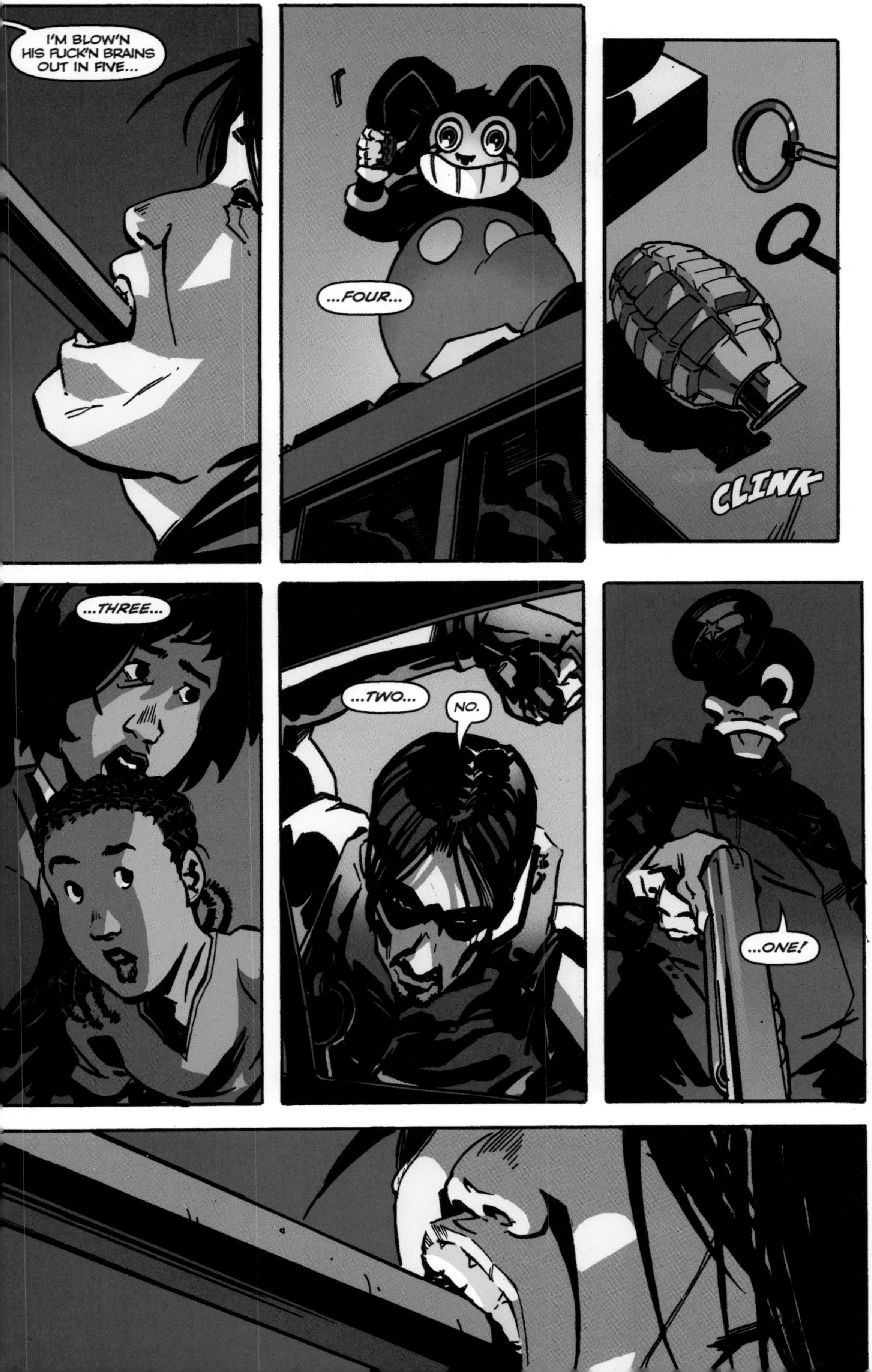
I'M BLOW'N HIS FUCK'N BRAINS OUT IN FIVE...
...FOUR...
CLINK
...THREE...
...TWO...
NO.
...ONE!

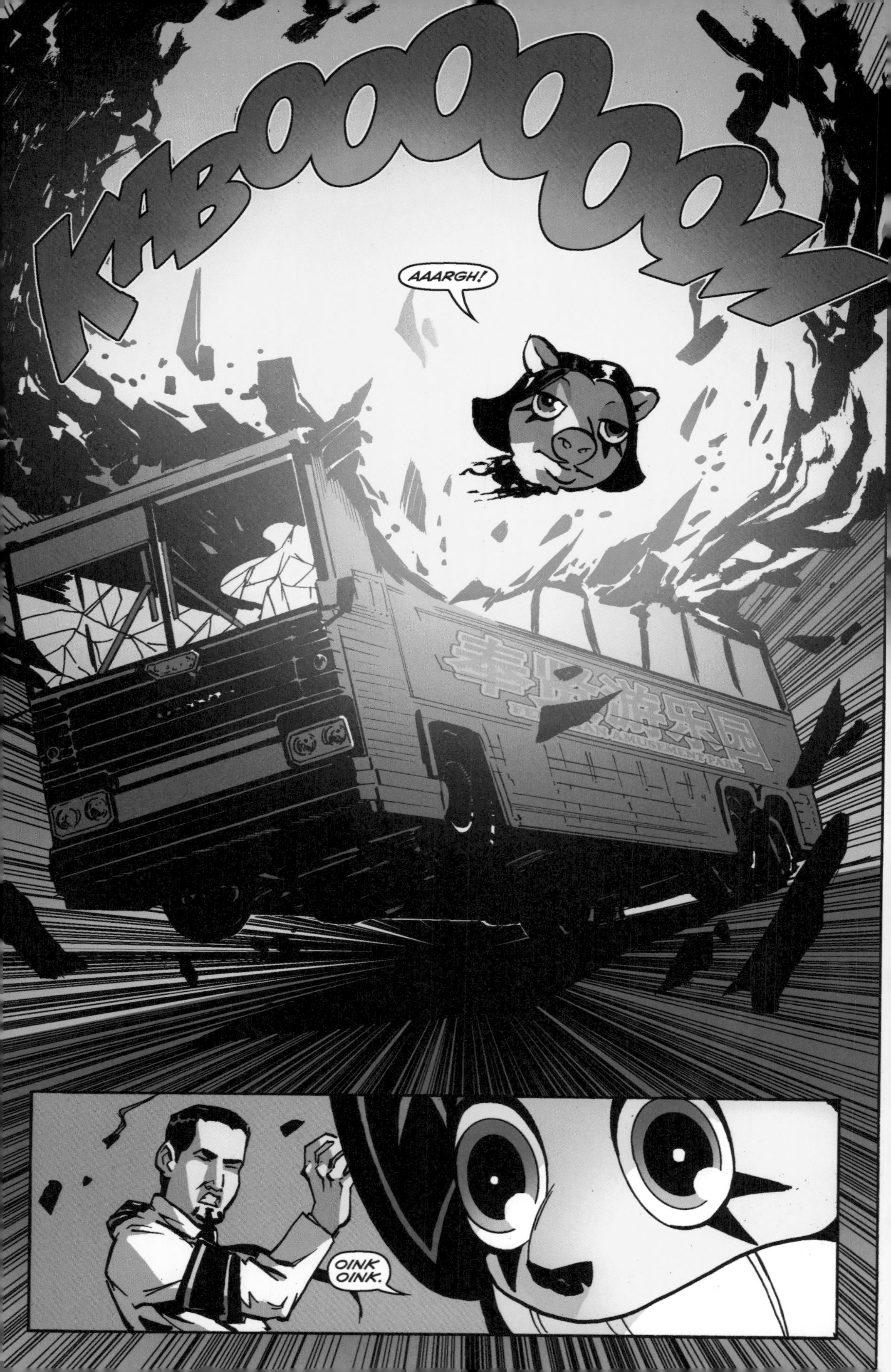
KABOOOOOOM
AAARGH!
AMUSEMENT PARK
OINK OINK.

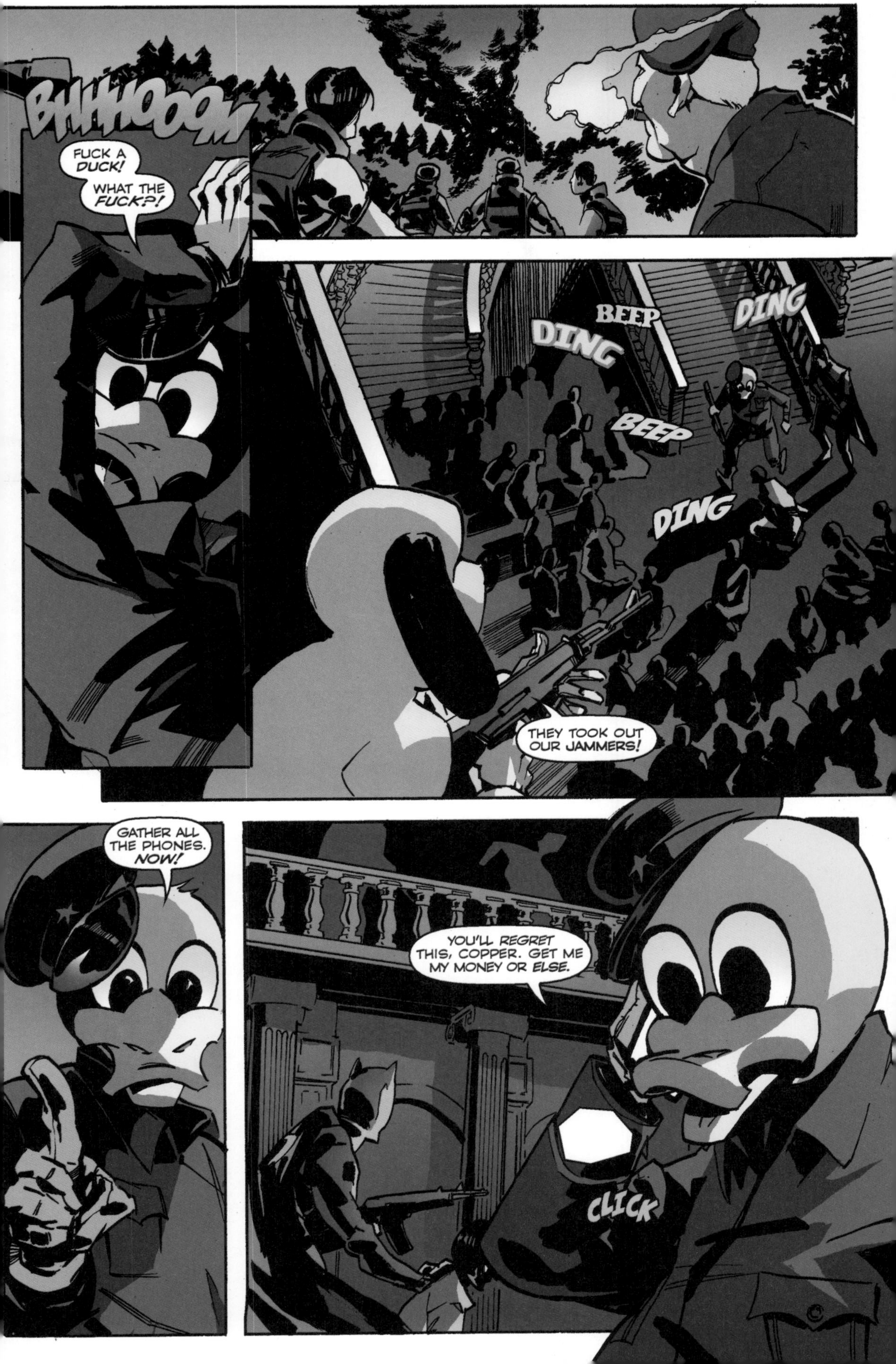
BHHOOOM
FUCK A DUCK!
WHAT THE FUCK?!
BEEP
DING
DING
BEEP
DING
THEY TOOK OUT OUR JAMMERS!
GATHER ALL THE PHONES. NOW!
YOU'LL REGRET THIS, COPPER. GET ME MY MONEY OR ELSE.
CLICK

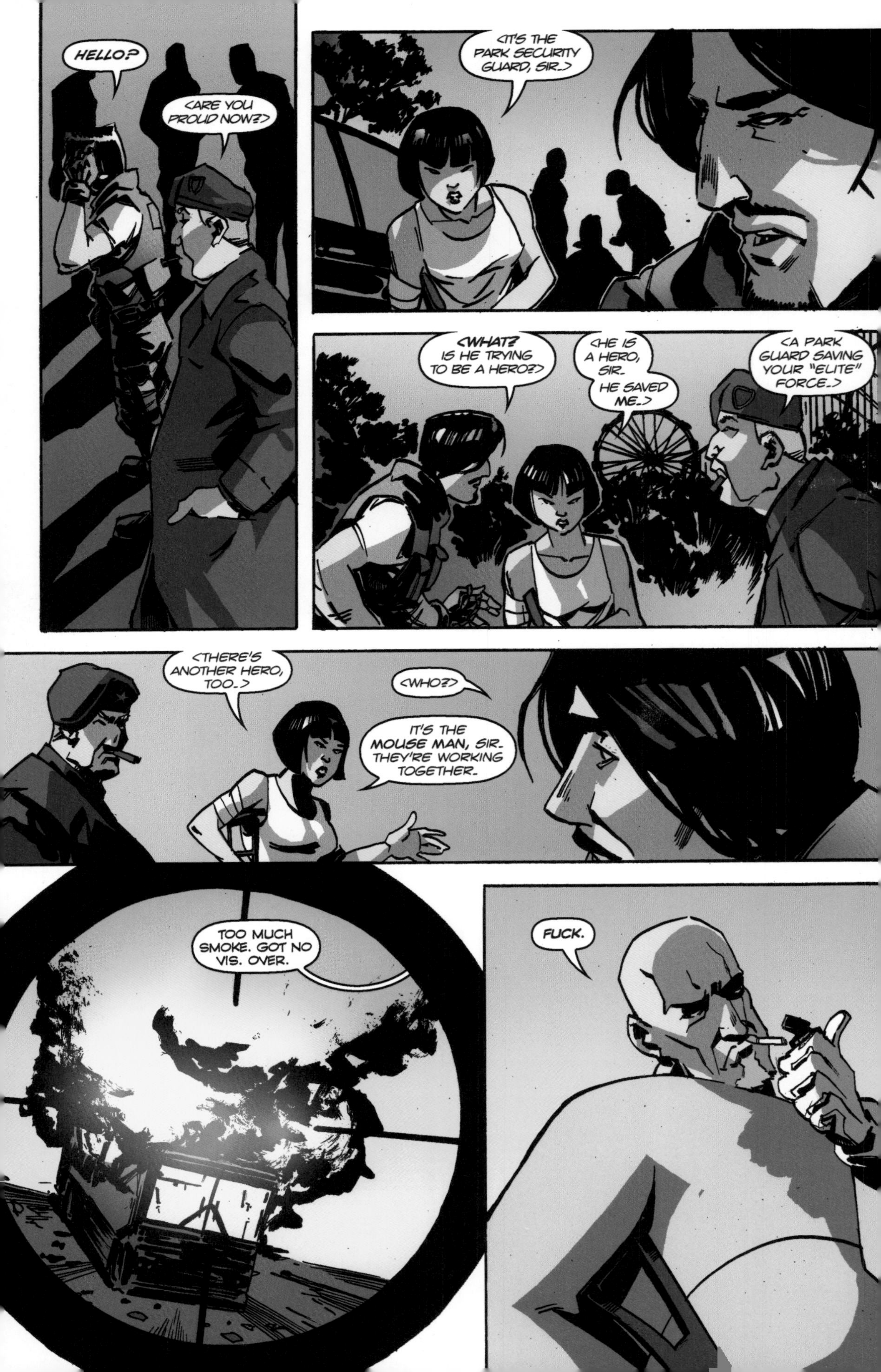
HELLO?
<ARE YOU PROUD NOW?>
<IT'S THE PARK SECURITY GUARD, SIR.>
<WHAT? IS HE TRYING TO BE A HERO?>
<HE IS A HERO, SIR.
HE SAVED ME.>
<A PARK GUARD SAVING YOUR "ELITE" FORCE.>
<THERE'S ANOTHER HERO, TOO.>
<WHO?>
IT'S THE MOUSE MAN, SIR. THEY'RE WORKING TOGETHER.
TOO MUCH SMOKE. GOT NO VIS. OVER.
FUCK.

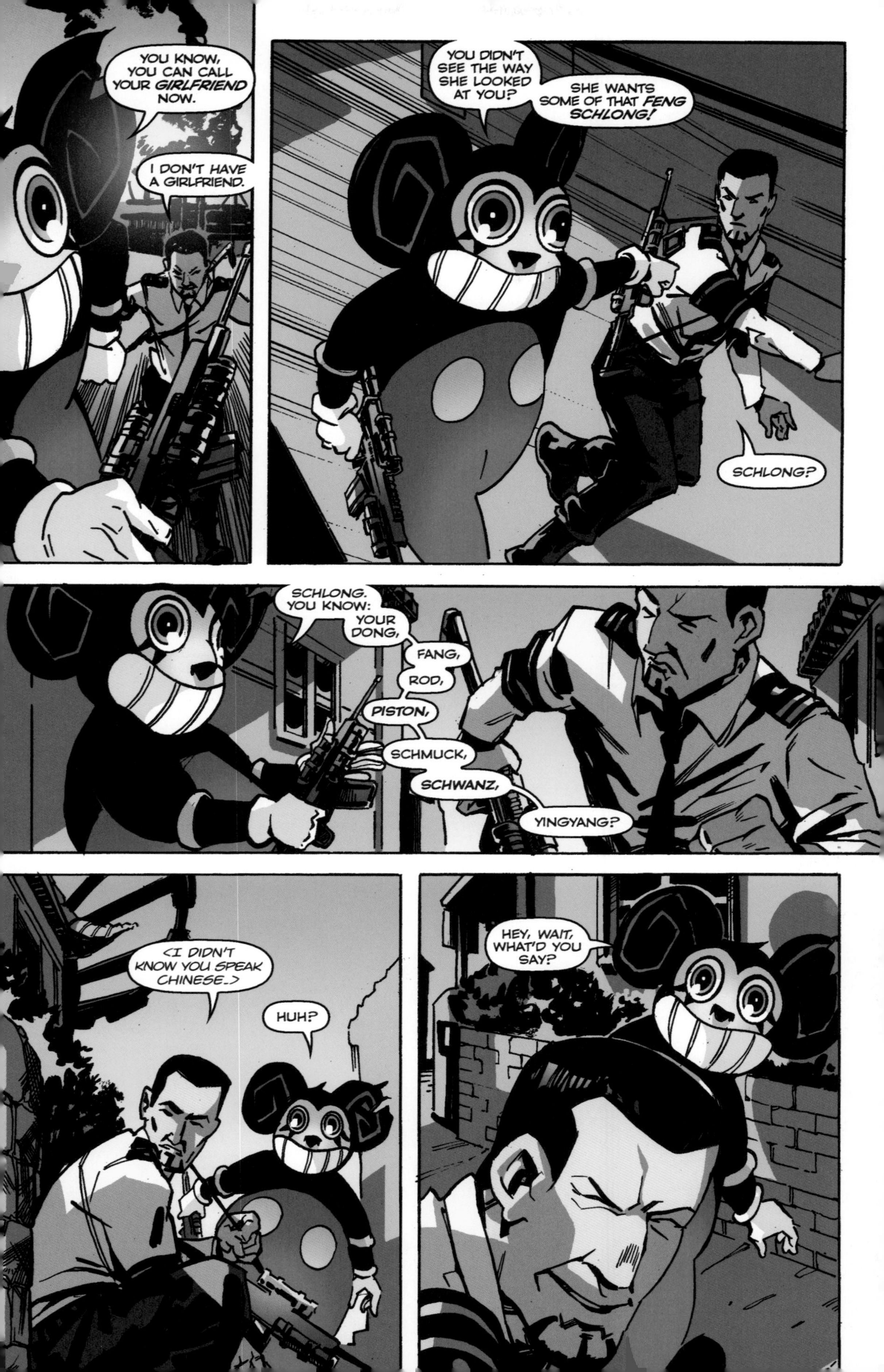
YOU KNOW, YOU CAN CALL YOUR GIRLFRIEND NOW.
I DON'T HAVE A GIRLFRIEND.
YOU DIDN'T SEE THE WAY SHE LOOKED AT YOU?
SHE WANTS SOME OF THAT FENG SCHLONG!
SCHLONG?
SCHLONG. YOU KNOW:
YOUR DONG,
FANG,
ROD,
PISTON,
SCHMUCK,
SCHWANZ,
YINGYANG?
<I DIDN'T KNOW YOU SPEAK CHINESE.>
HUH?
HEY, WAIT, WHAT'D YOU SAY?

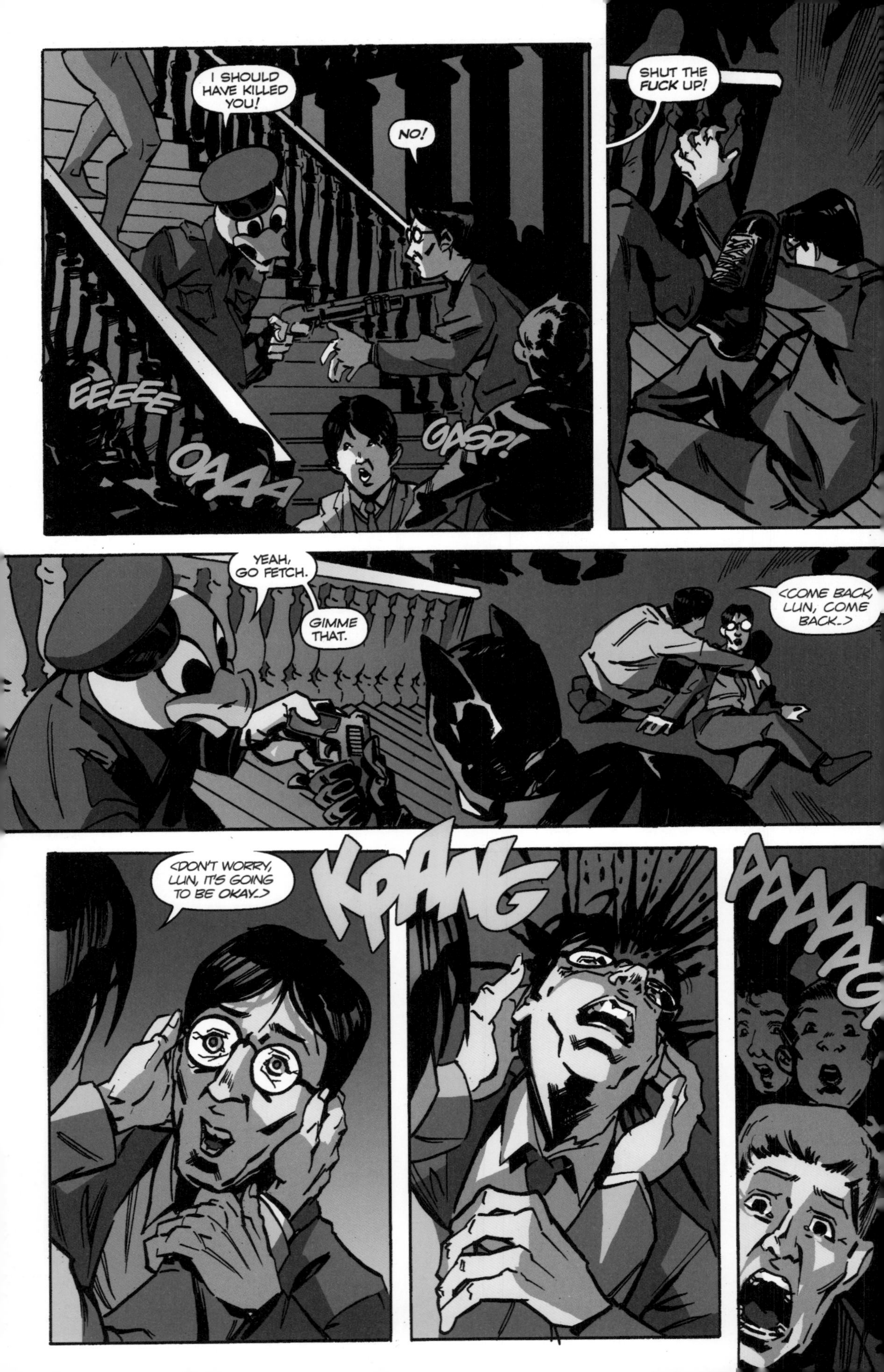
I SHOULD HAVE KILLED YOU!
NO!
EEEEEE
OAAAA
GASP!
SHUT THE FUCK UP!
YEAH, GO FETCH.
GIMME THAT.
<COME BACK, LUN, COME BACK.>
<DON'T WORRY, LUN, IT'S GOING TO BE OKAY.>
KPANG
AAAAAGH

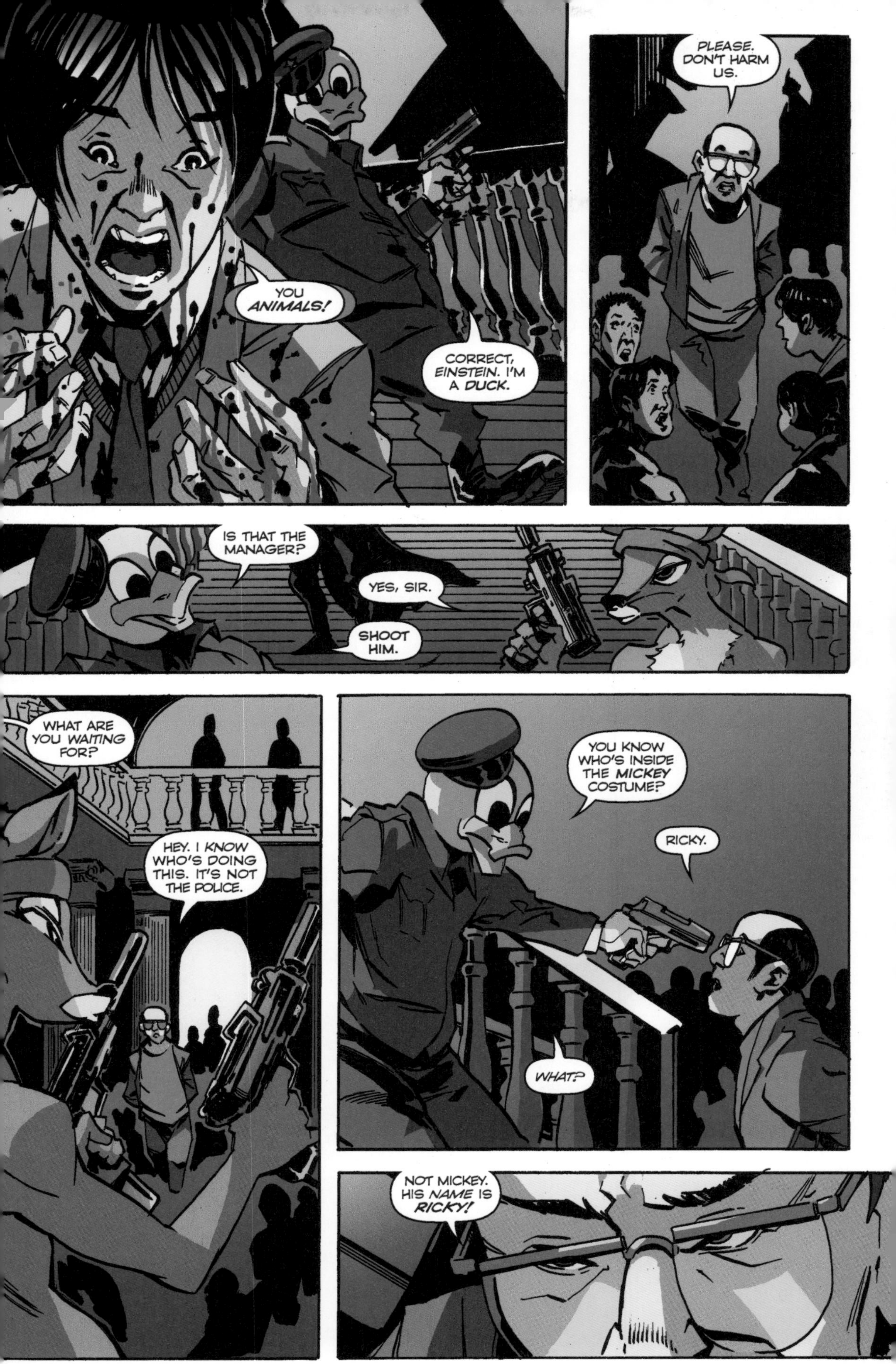
YOU ANIMALS!
CORRECT, EINSTEIN. I'M A DUCK.
PLEASE. DON'T HARM US.
IS THAT THE MANAGER?
YES, SIR.
SHOOT HIM.
WHAT ARE YOU WAITING FOR?
HEY. I KNOW WHO'S DOING THIS. IT'S NOT THE POLICE.
YOU KNOW WHO'S INSIDE THE MICKEY COSTUME?
RICKY.
WHAT?
NOT MICKEY. HIS NAME IS RICKY!

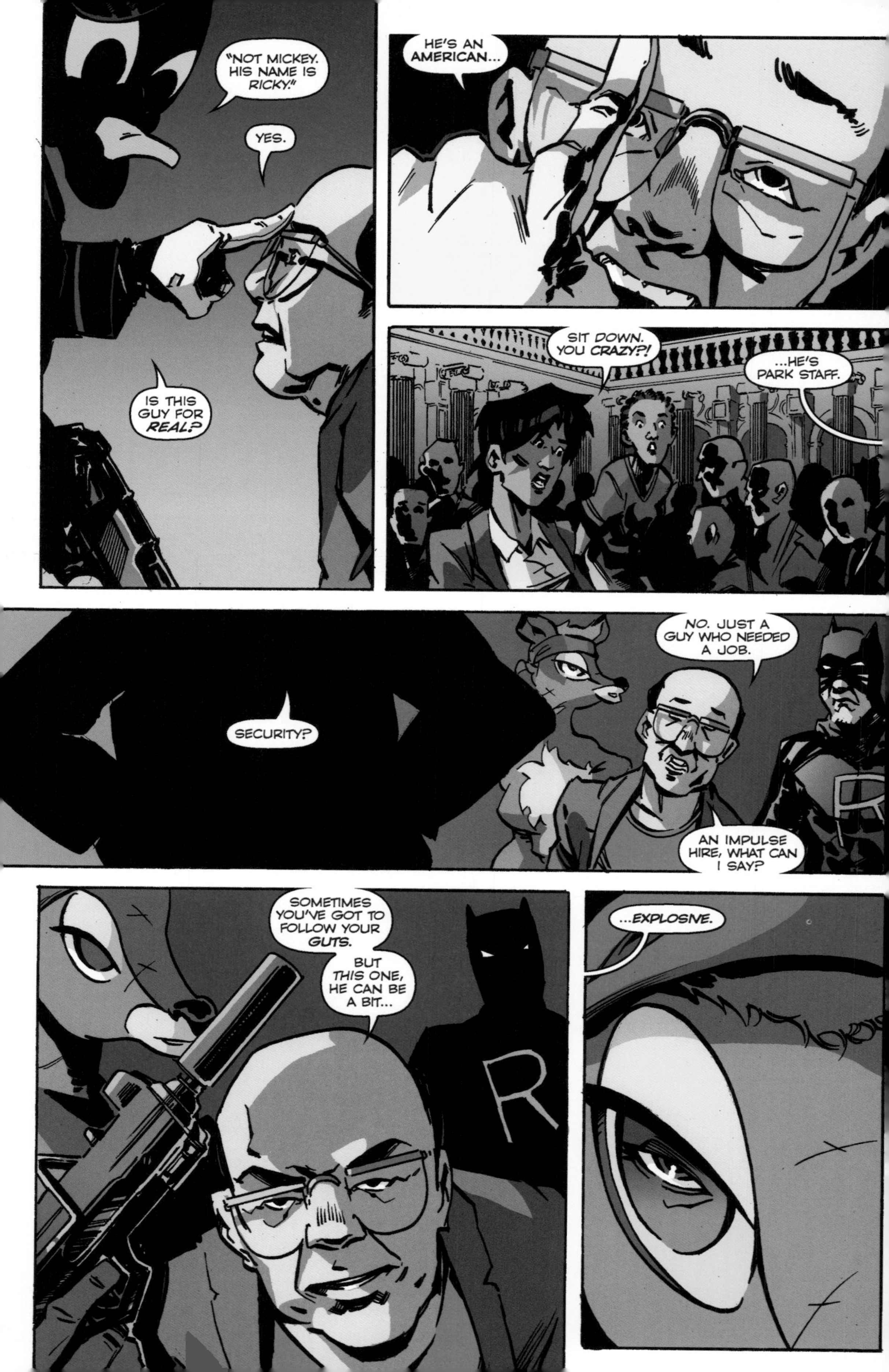
"NOT MICKEY. HIS NAME IS *RICKY.*"
YES.
IS THIS GUY FOR *REAL?*
HE'S AN AMERICAN...
SIT *DOWN.* YOU *CRAZY?!*
...HE'S PARK STAFF.
SECURITY?
NO. JUST A GUY WHO NEEDED A JOB.
AN IMPULSE HIRE, WHAT CAN I SAY?
SOMETIMES YOU'VE GOT TO FOLLOW YOUR *GUTS.*
BUT *THIS ONE,* HE CAN BE A BIT...
...*EXPLOSIVE.*

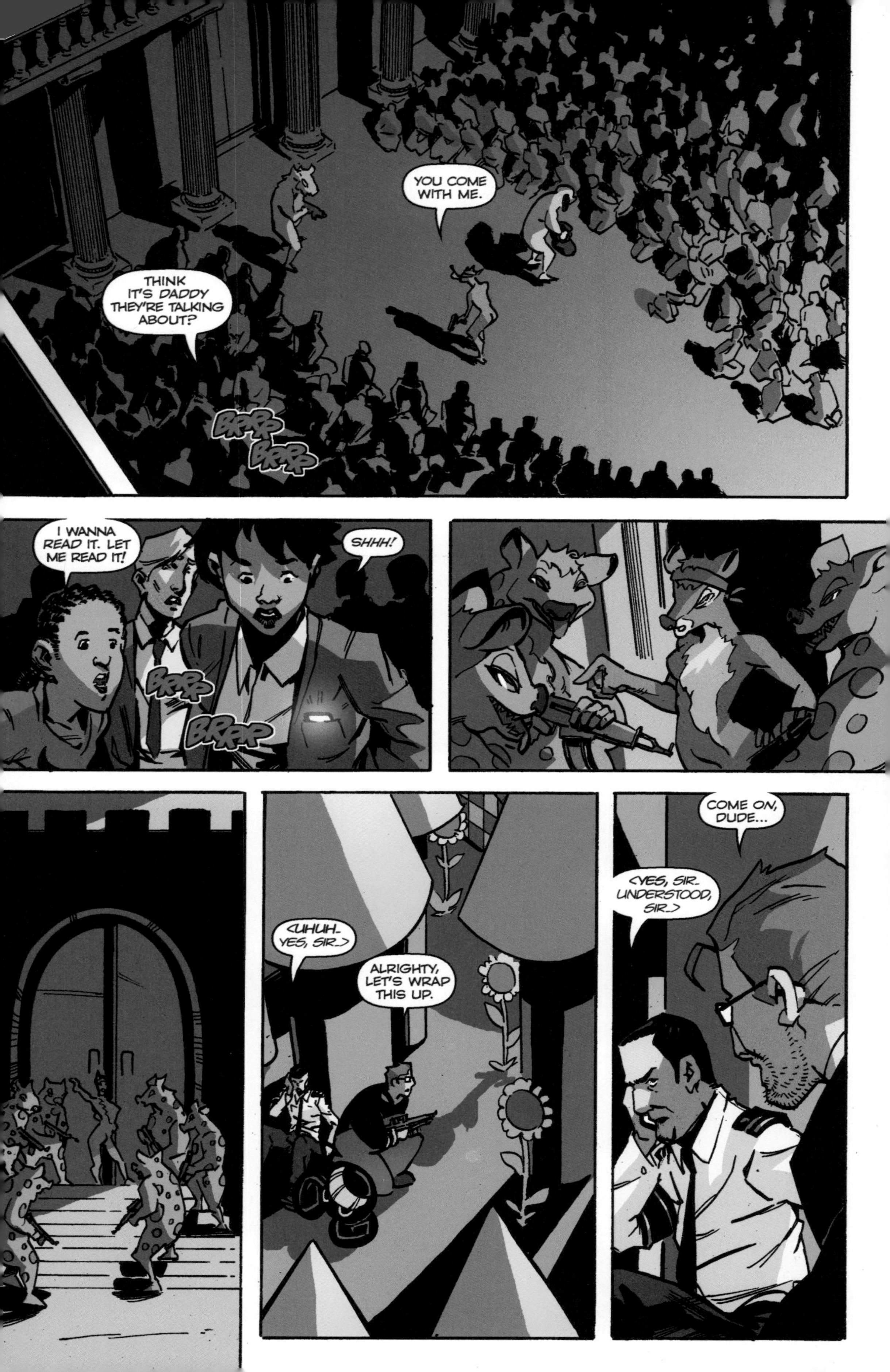

YOU COME WITH ME.
THINK IT'S *DADDY* THEY'RE TALKING ABOUT?
BRRR
BRRR
I WANNA READ IT. LET ME READ IT!
SHHH!
BRRR
BRRR
COME ON, DUDE...
<UHUH. YES, SIR.>
ALRIGHTY, LET'S WRAP THIS UP.
<YES, SIR. UNDERSTOOD, SIR.>

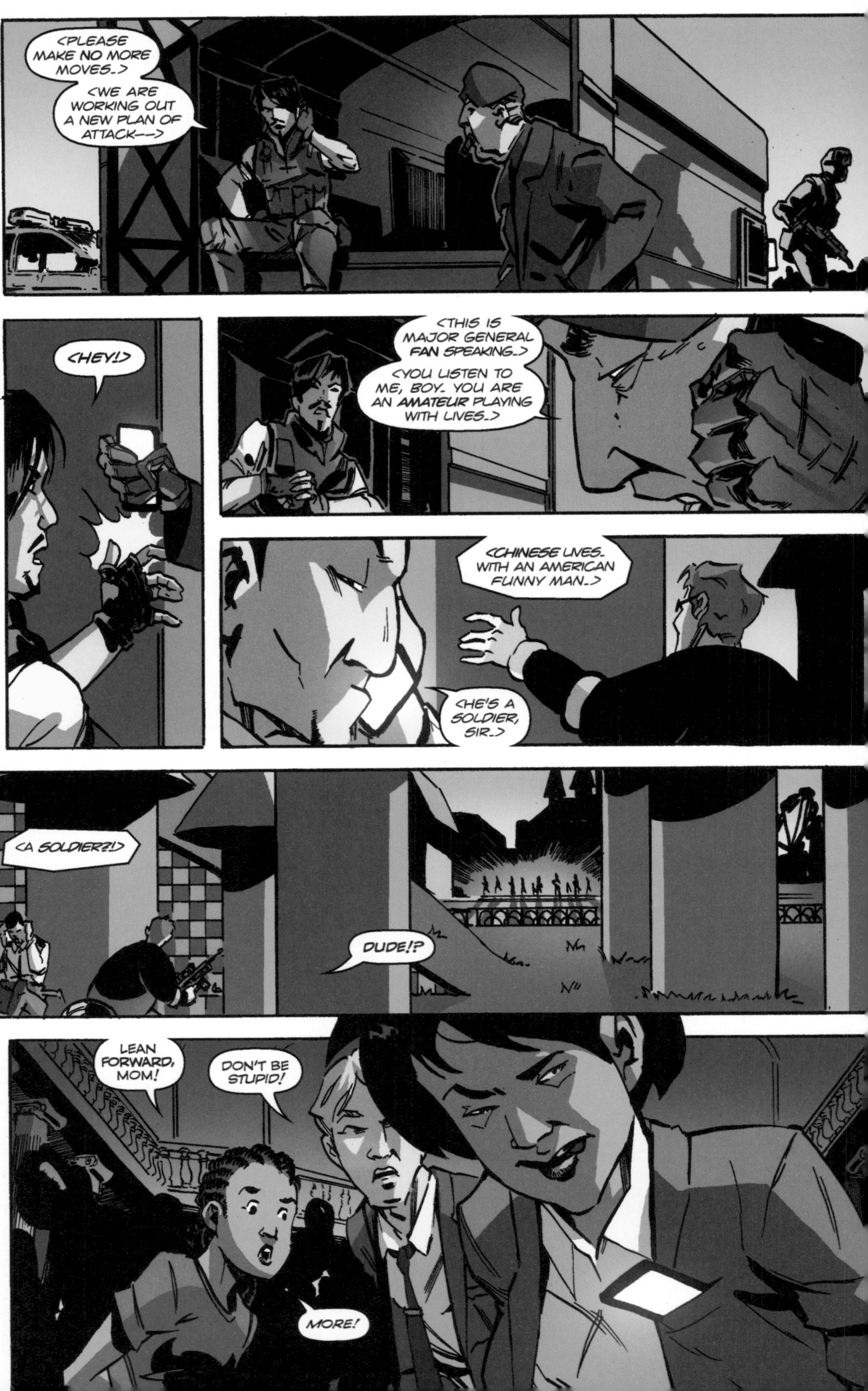
<PLEASE MAKE NO MORE MOVES.>
<WE ARE WORKING OUT A NEW PLAN OF ATTACK-->
<HEY!>
<THIS IS MAJOR GENERAL FAN SPEAKING.>
<YOU LISTEN TO ME, BOY. YOU ARE AN AMATEUR PLAYING WITH LIVES.>
<CHINESE LIVES. WITH AN AMERICAN FUNNY MAN.>
<HE'S A SOLDIER, SIR.>
<A SOLDIER?!>
DUDE!?
LEAN FORWARD, MOM!
DON'T BE STUPID!
MORE!

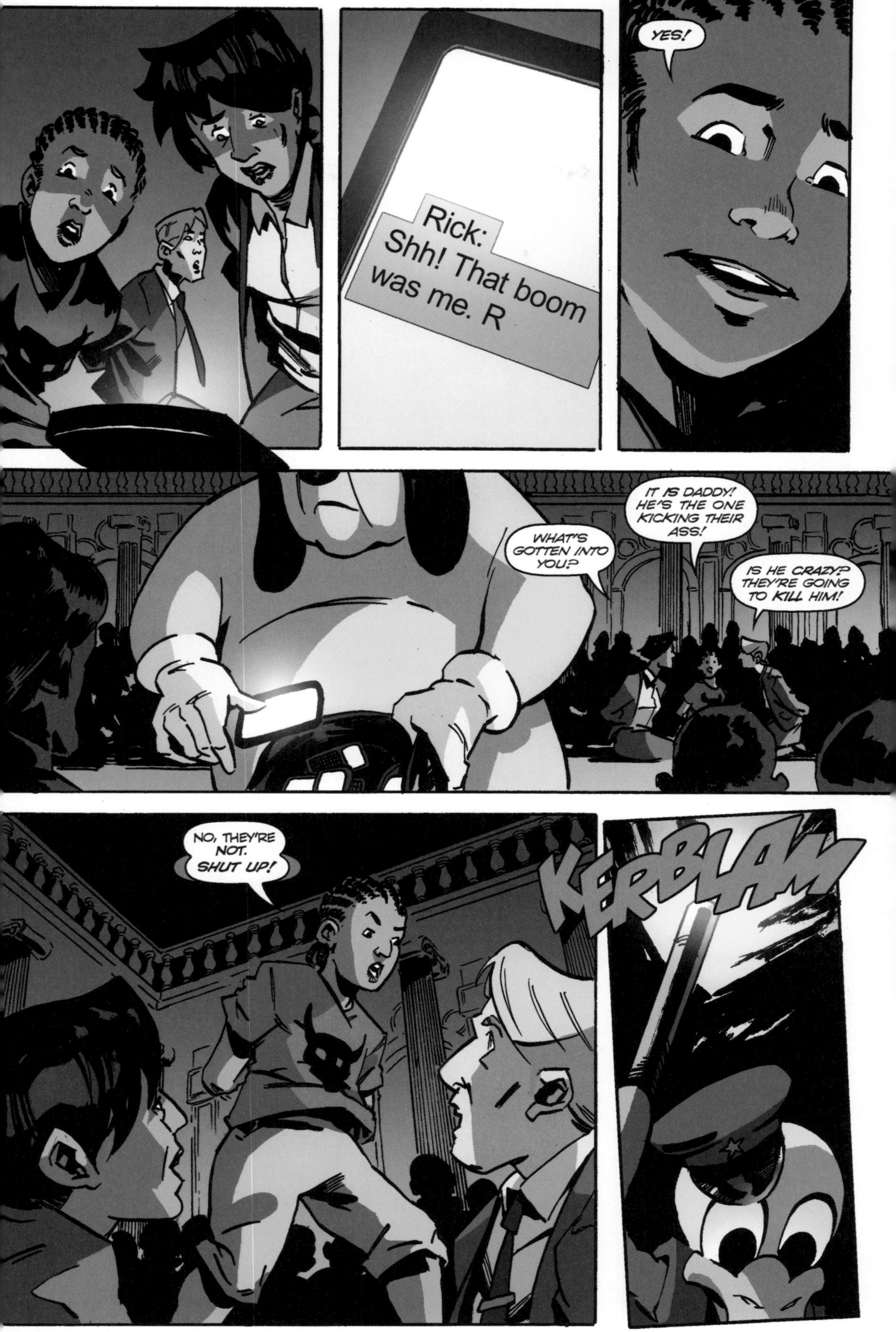
Rick:
Shh! That boom
was me. R
YES!
WHAT'S GOTTEN INTO YOU?
IT IS DADDY! HE'S THE ONE KICKING THEIR ASS!
IS HE CRAZY? THEY'RE GOING TO KILL HIM!
NO, THEY'RE NOT. SHUT UP!
KERBLAM

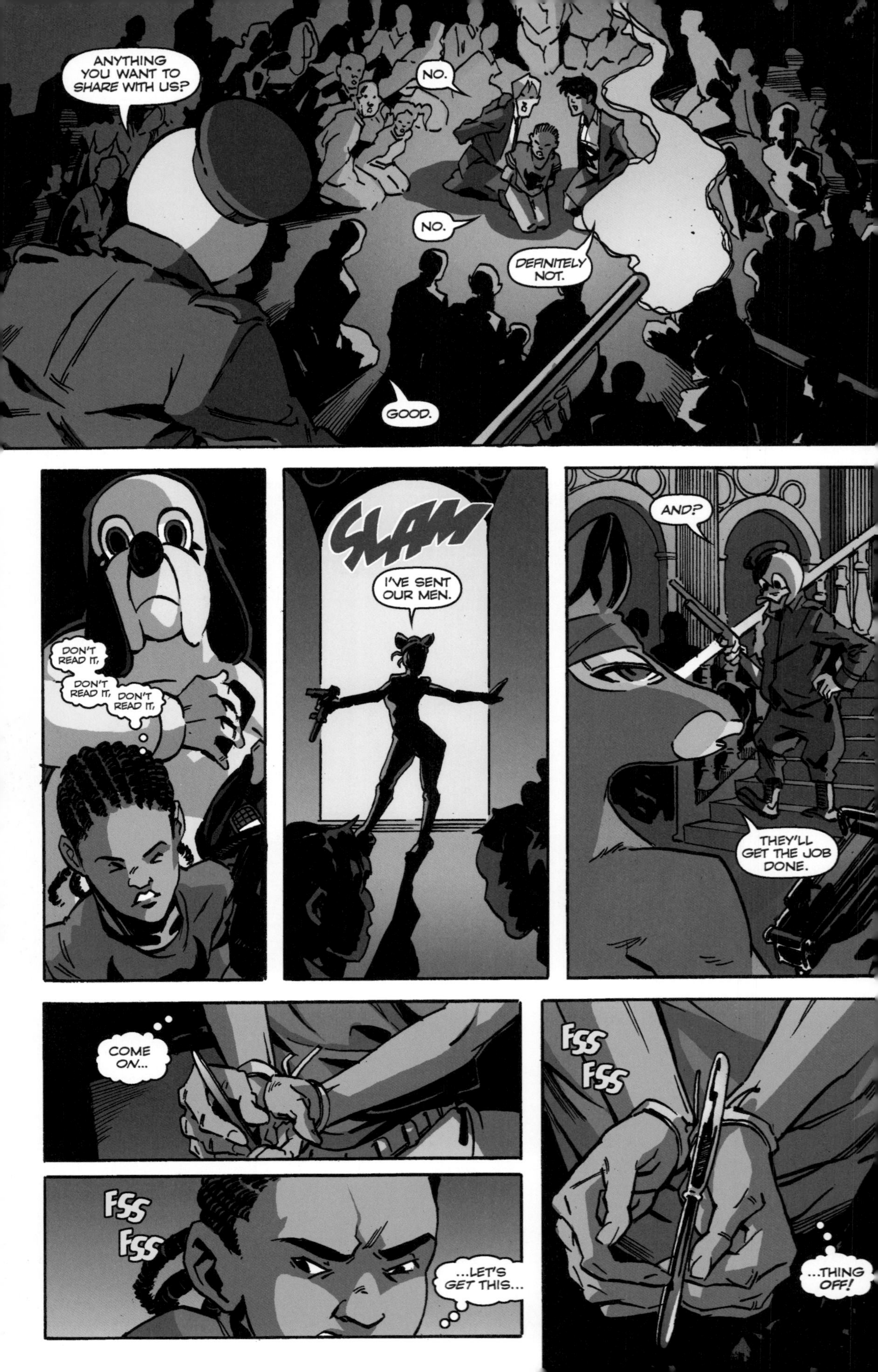
ANYTHING YOU WANT TO SHARE WITH US?
NO.
NO.
DEFINITELY NOT.
GOOD.
DON'T READ IT,
DON'T READ IT,
DON'T READ IT,
SLAM
I'VE SENT OUR MEN.
AND?
THEY'LL GET THE JOB DONE.
COME ON...
FSS
FSS
...LET'S GET THIS...
FSS
FSS
...THING OFF!

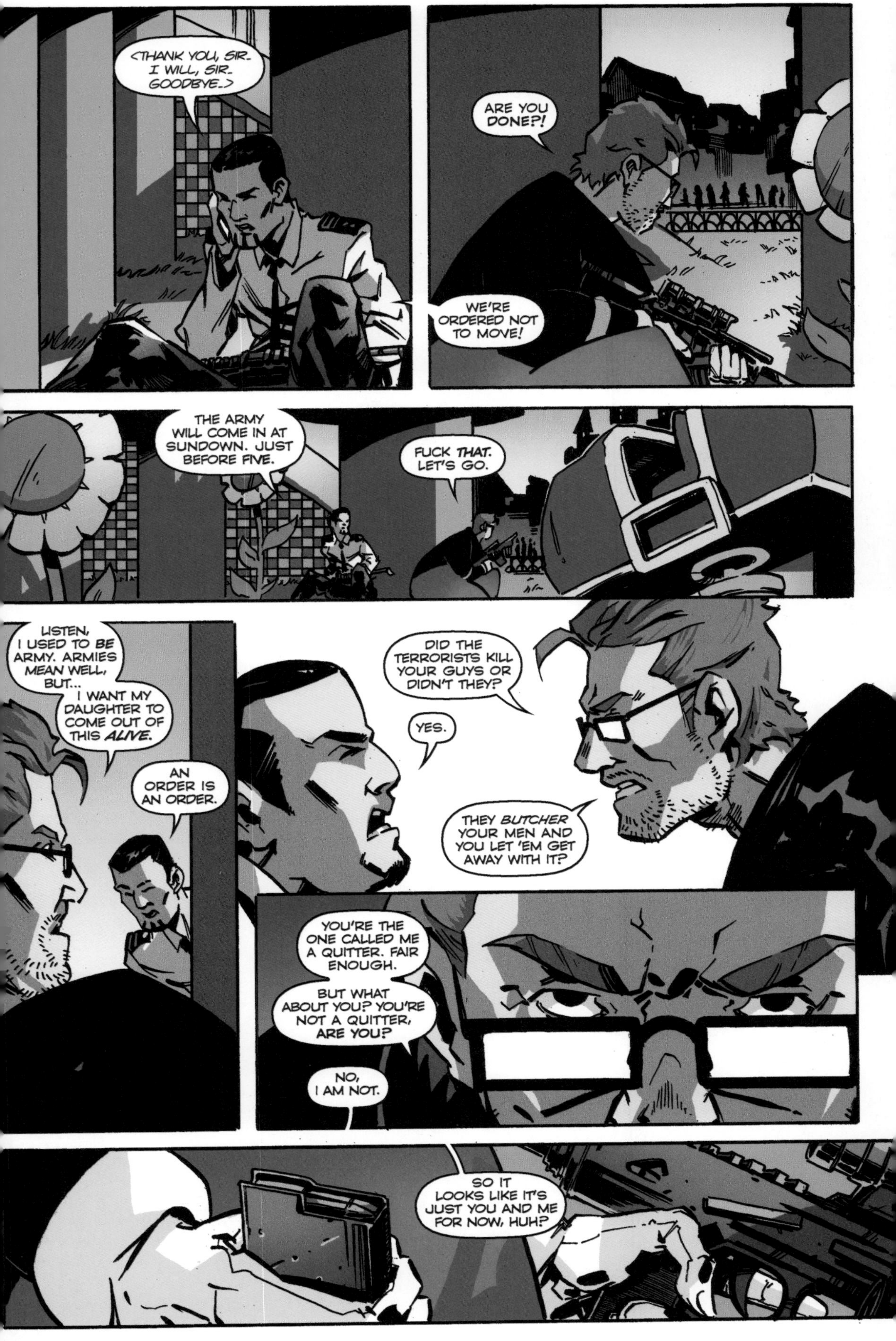
<THANK YOU, SIR. I WILL, SIR. GOODBYE.>
ARE YOU DONE?!
WE'RE ORDERED NOT TO MOVE!
THE ARMY WILL COME IN AT SUNDOWN. JUST BEFORE FIVE.
FUCK THAT. LET'S GO.
LISTEN, I USED TO BE ARMY. ARMIES MEAN WELL, BUT...
I WANT MY DAUGHTER TO COME OUT OF THIS ALIVE.
AN ORDER IS AN ORDER.
DID THE TERRORISTS KILL YOUR GUYS OR DIDN'T THEY?
YES.
THEY BUTCHER YOUR MEN AND YOU LET 'EM GET AWAY WITH IT?
YOU'RE THE ONE CALLED ME A QUITTER. FAIR ENOUGH.
BUT WHAT ABOUT YOU? YOU'RE NOT A QUITTER, ARE YOU?
NO, I AM NOT.
SO IT LOOKS LIKE IT'S JUST YOU AND ME FOR NOW, HUH?

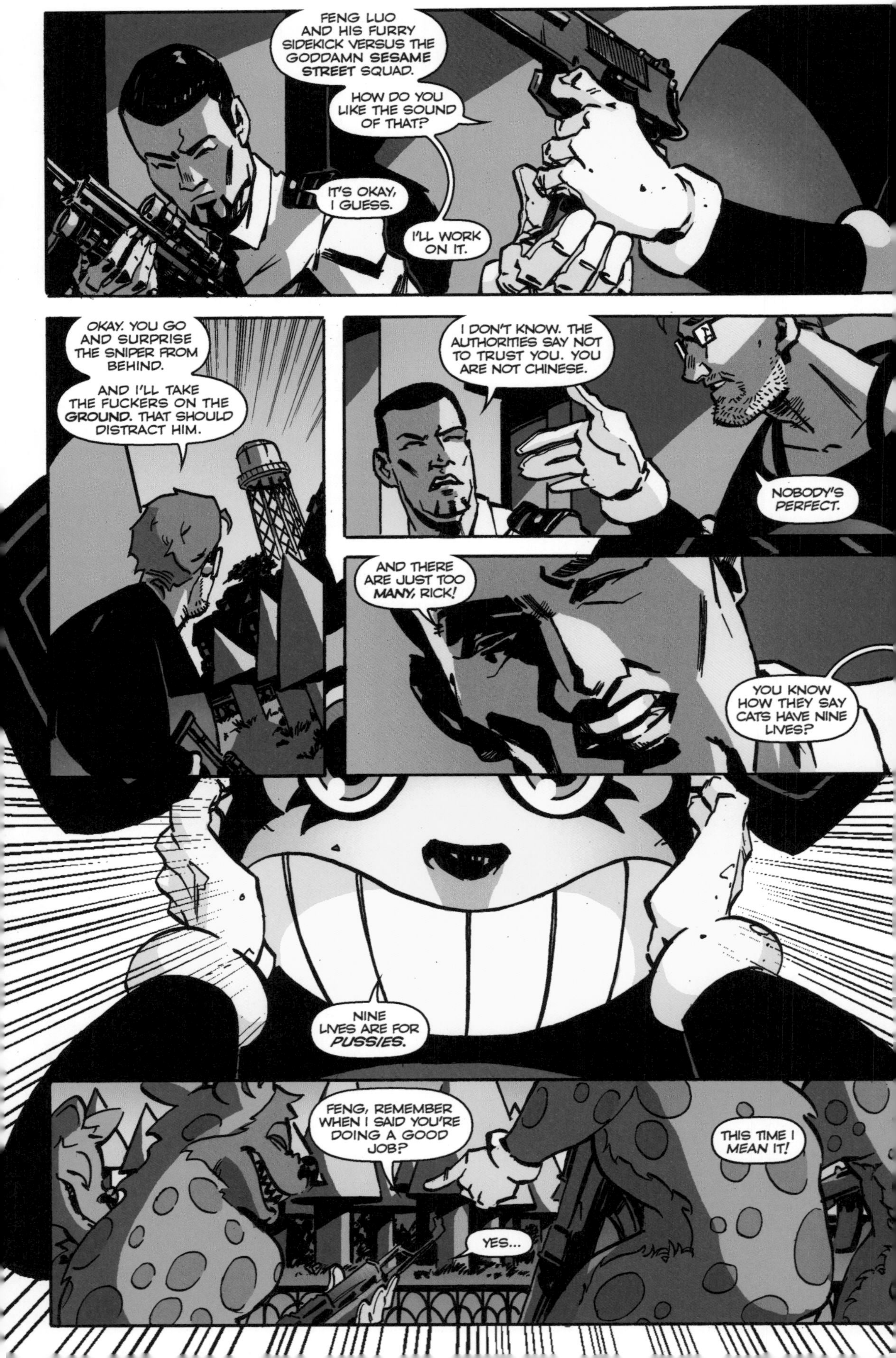
FENG LUO AND HIS FURRY SIDEKICK VERSUS THE GODDAMN SESAME STREET SQUAD.
HOW DO YOU LIKE THE SOUND OF THAT?
IT'S OKAY, I GUESS.
I'LL WORK ON IT.
OKAY. YOU GO AND SURPRISE THE SNIPER FROM BEHIND.
AND I'LL TAKE THE FUCKERS ON THE GROUND. THAT SHOULD DISTRACT HIM.
I DON'T KNOW. THE AUTHORITIES SAY NOT TO TRUST YOU. YOU ARE NOT CHINESE.
NOBODY'S PERFECT.
AND THERE ARE JUST TOO MANY, RICK!
YOU KNOW HOW THEY SAY CATS HAVE NINE LIVES?
NINE LIVES ARE FOR PUSSIES.
FENG, REMEMBER WHEN I SAID YOU'RE DOING A GOOD JOB?
YES...
THIS TIME I MEAN IT!

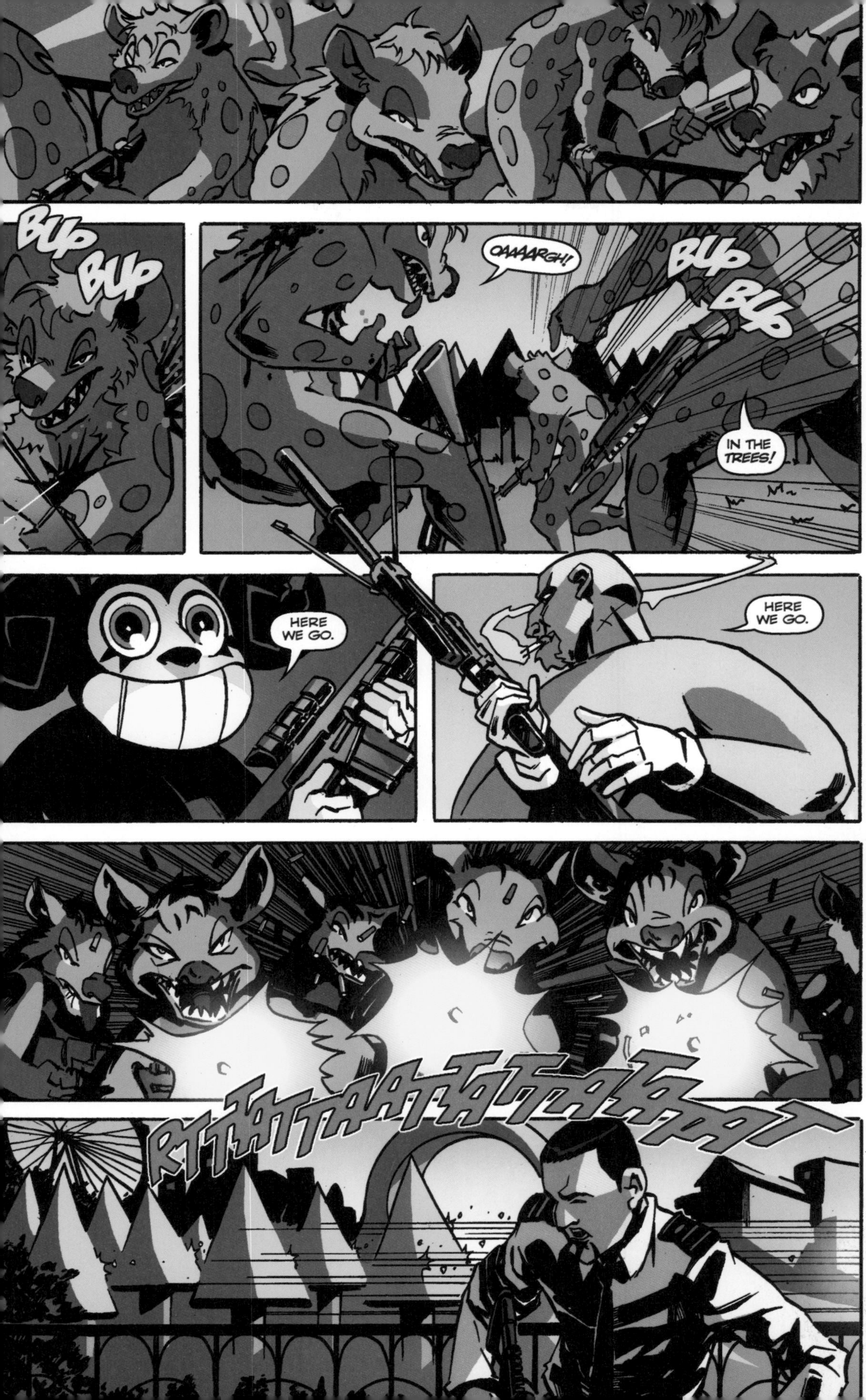
BUP
BUP
OAAAARGH!
BUP
BUP
IN THE TREES!
HERE WE GO.
HERE WE GO.
RTTTATTTAATATTATTATAPAAT

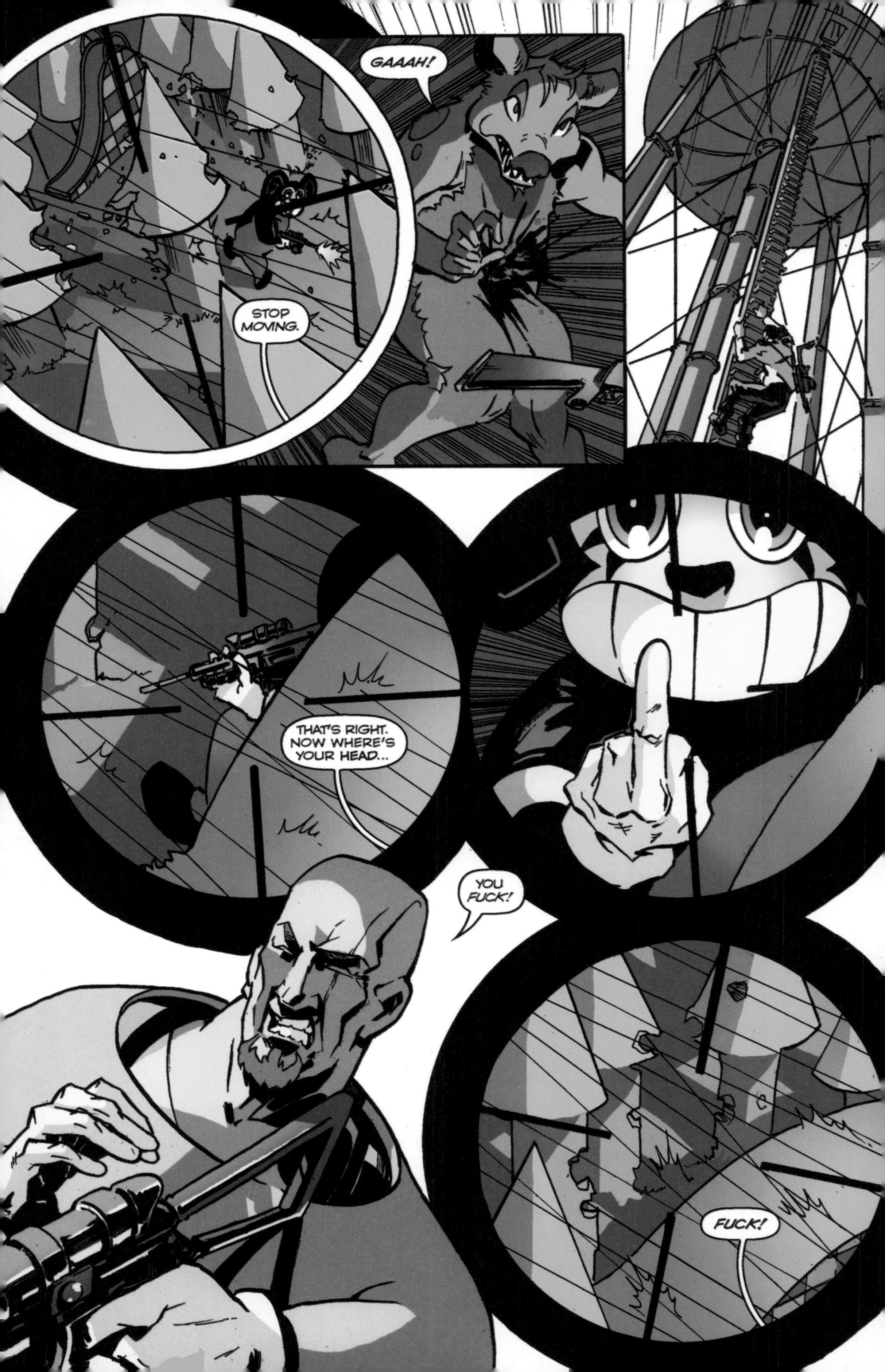
GAAAH!
STOP MOVING.
THAT'S RIGHT. NOW WHERE'S YOUR HEAD...
YOU FUCK!
FUCK!

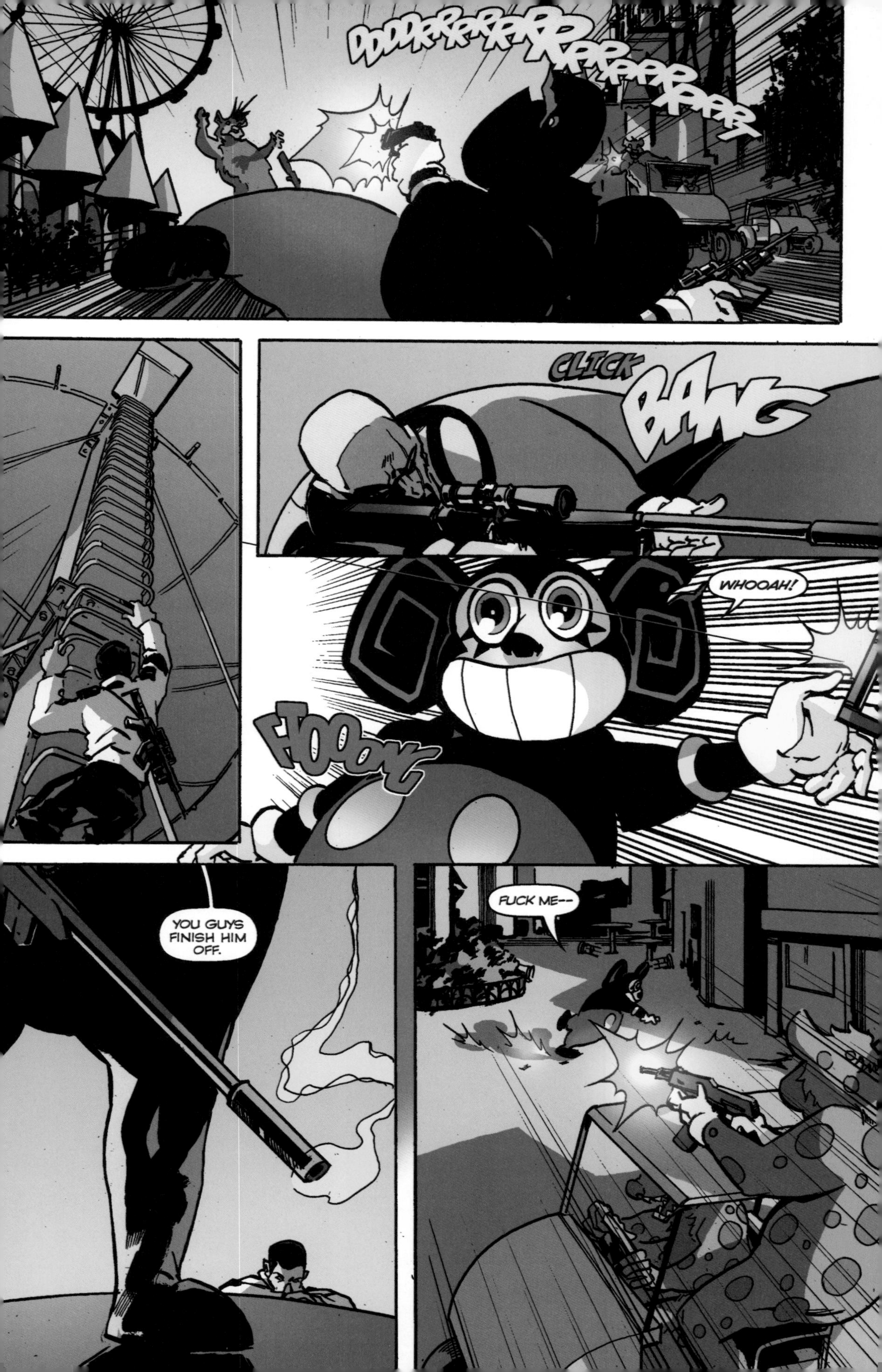
DDDDRRRRRRRRRRRRRRRRRRRRRRRRRRRT
CLICK
BANG
WHOOAH!
FTOOOM
YOU GUYS FINISH HIM OFF.
FUCK ME--

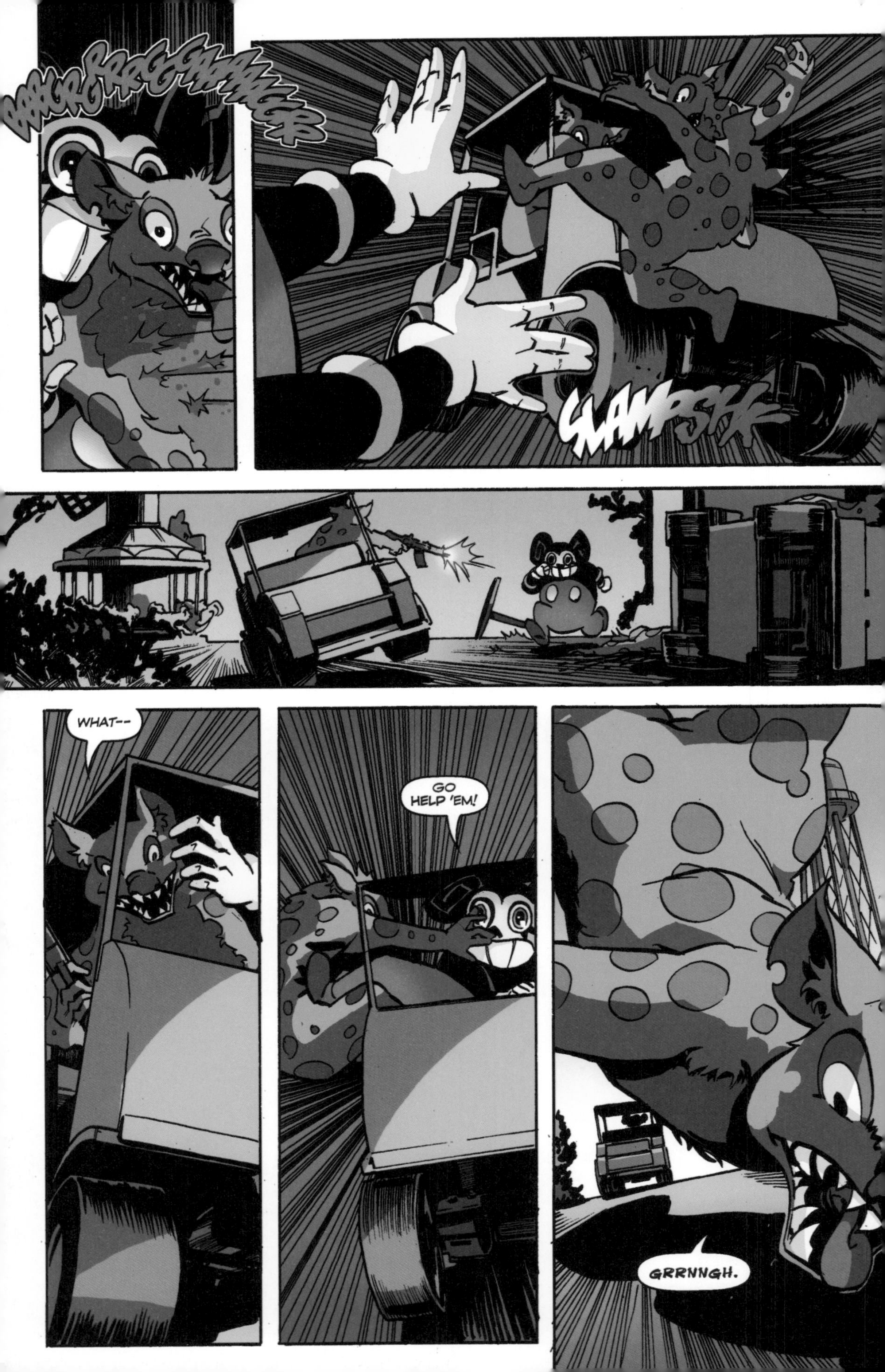
BRRRGRRRGGAAAAAGR
SLAMPSH
WHAT--
GO HELP 'EM!
GRRNNGH.

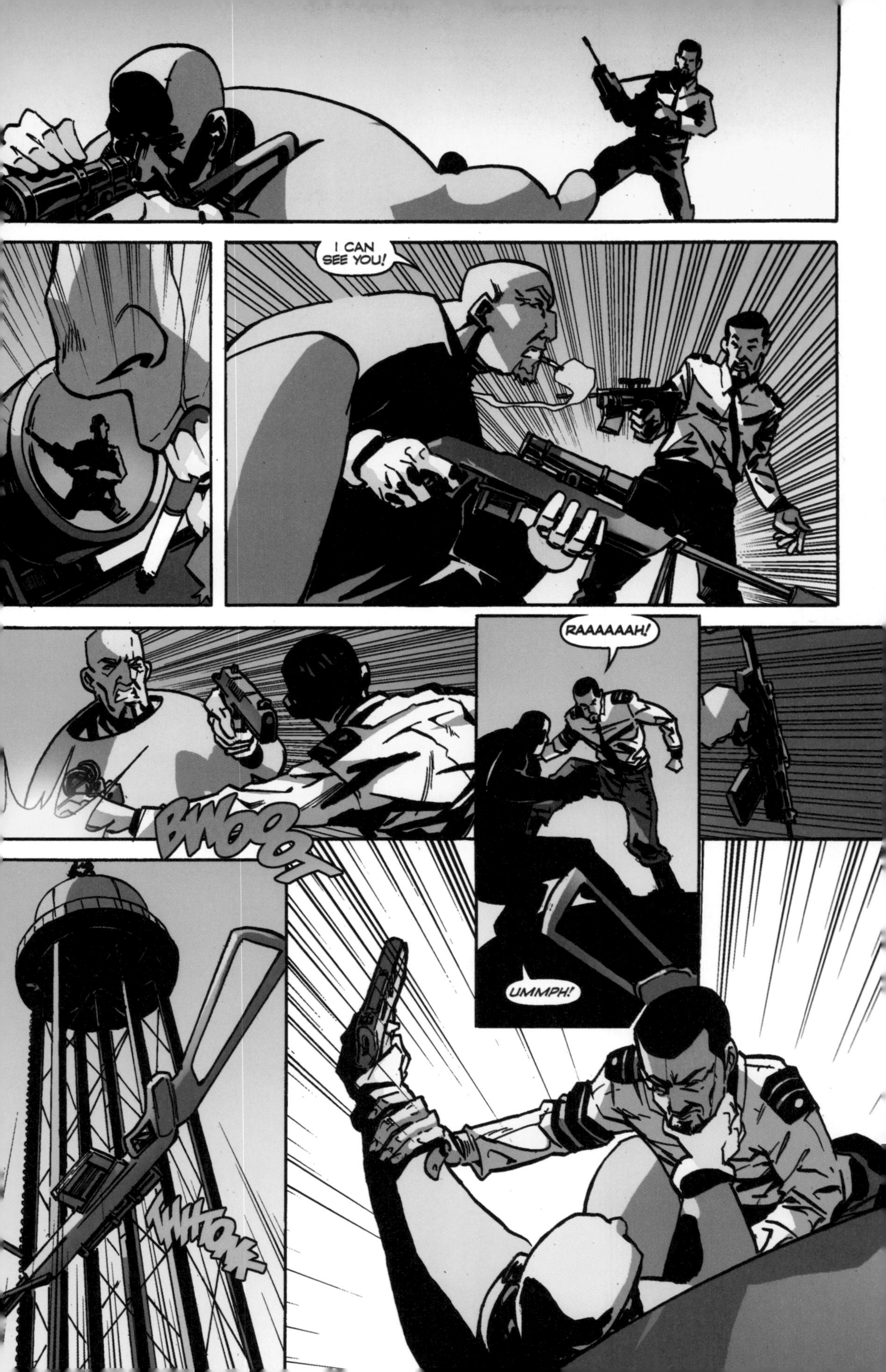
I CAN SEE YOU!
BWOOOT
RAAAAAAH!
UMMPH!
THHONK

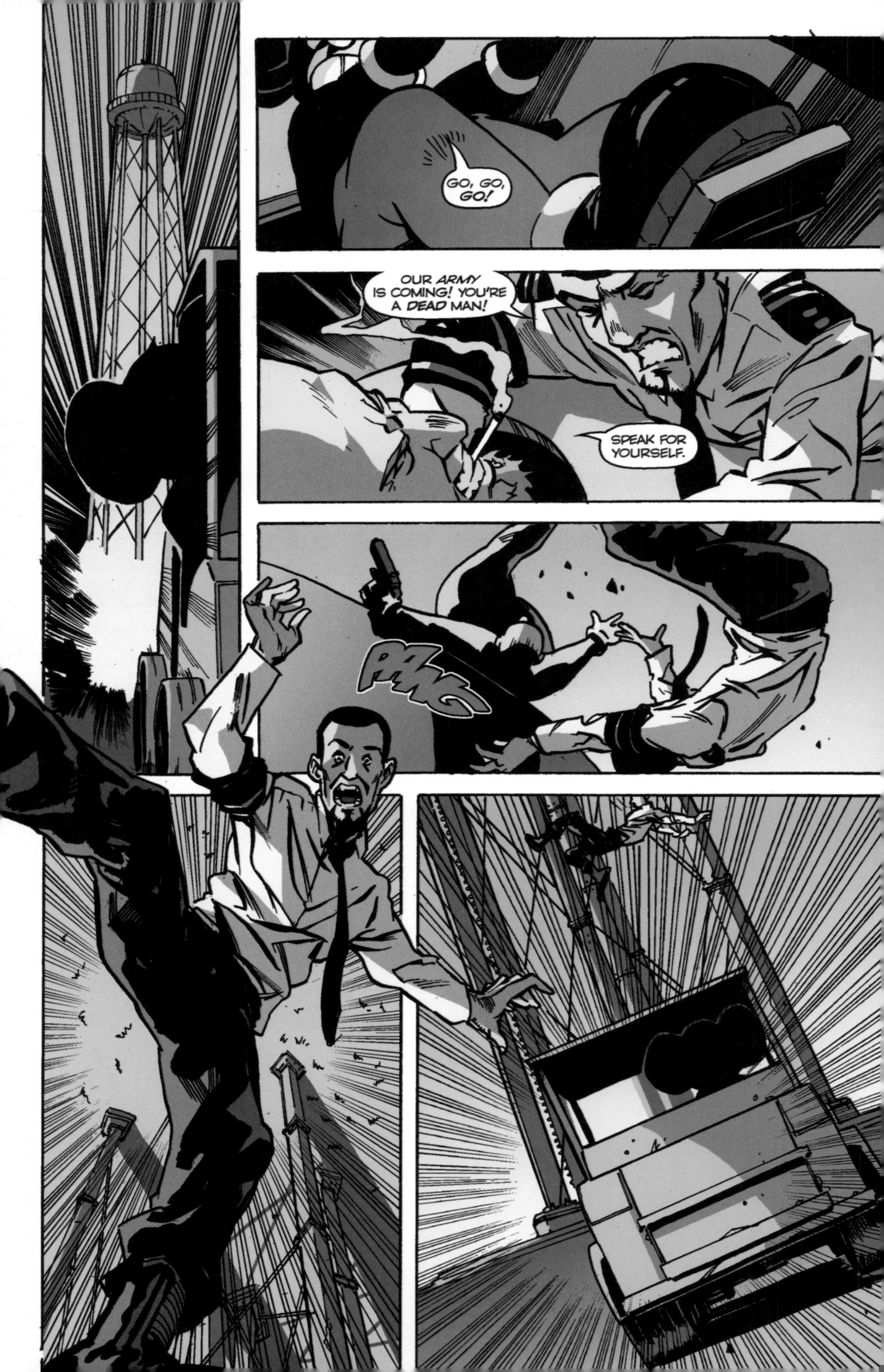
GO, GO, GO!
OUR ARMY IS COMING! YOU'RE A DEAD MAN!
SPEAK FOR YOURSELF.
PANG

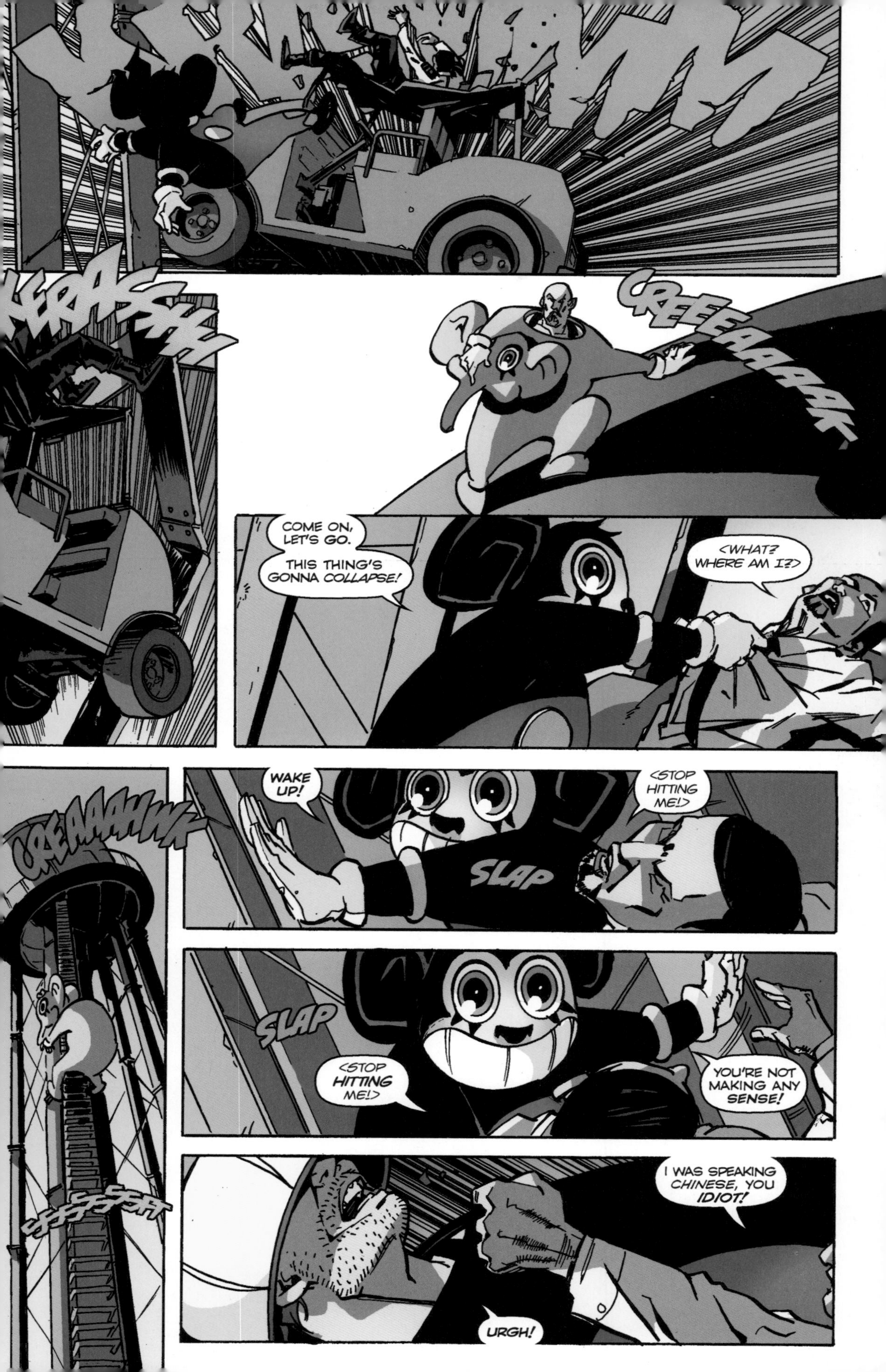
KERASSH
CREEEAAAAK
COME ON, LET'S GO.
THIS THING'S GONNA COLLAPSE!
<WHAT? WHERE AM I?>
CREAAAHNK
WAKE UP!
SLAP
<STOP HITTING ME!>
SLAP
<STOP HITTING ME!>
YOU'RE NOT MAKING ANY SENSE!
I WAS SPEAKING CHINESE, YOU IDIOT!
URGH!

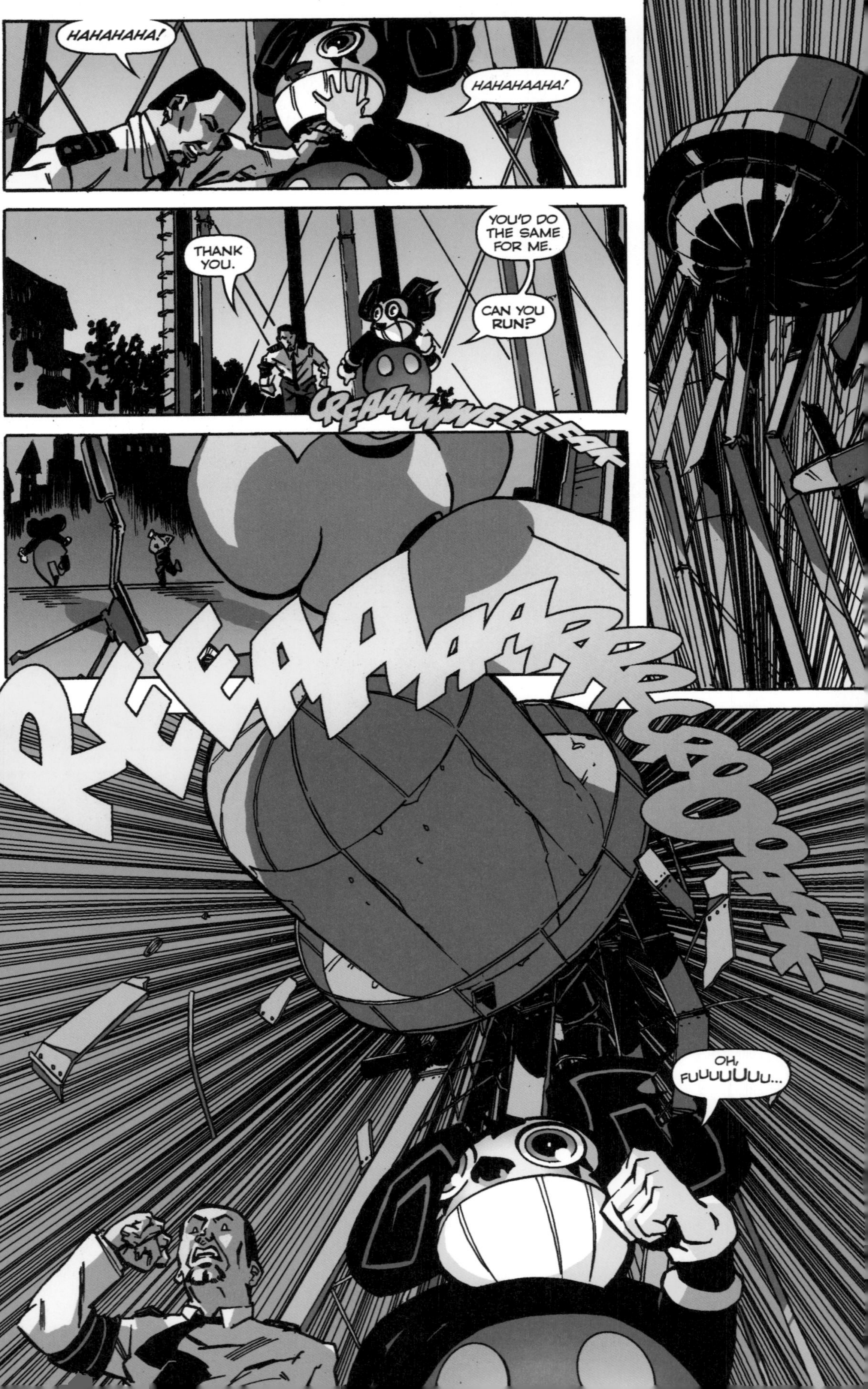
HAHAHAHA!
HAHAHAAHA!
THANK YOU.
YOU'D DO THE SAME FOR ME.
CAN YOU RUN?
CREAAWWWEEEEAK
REEAAAAARRRCROOOAAK
OH, FUUUUUUU...

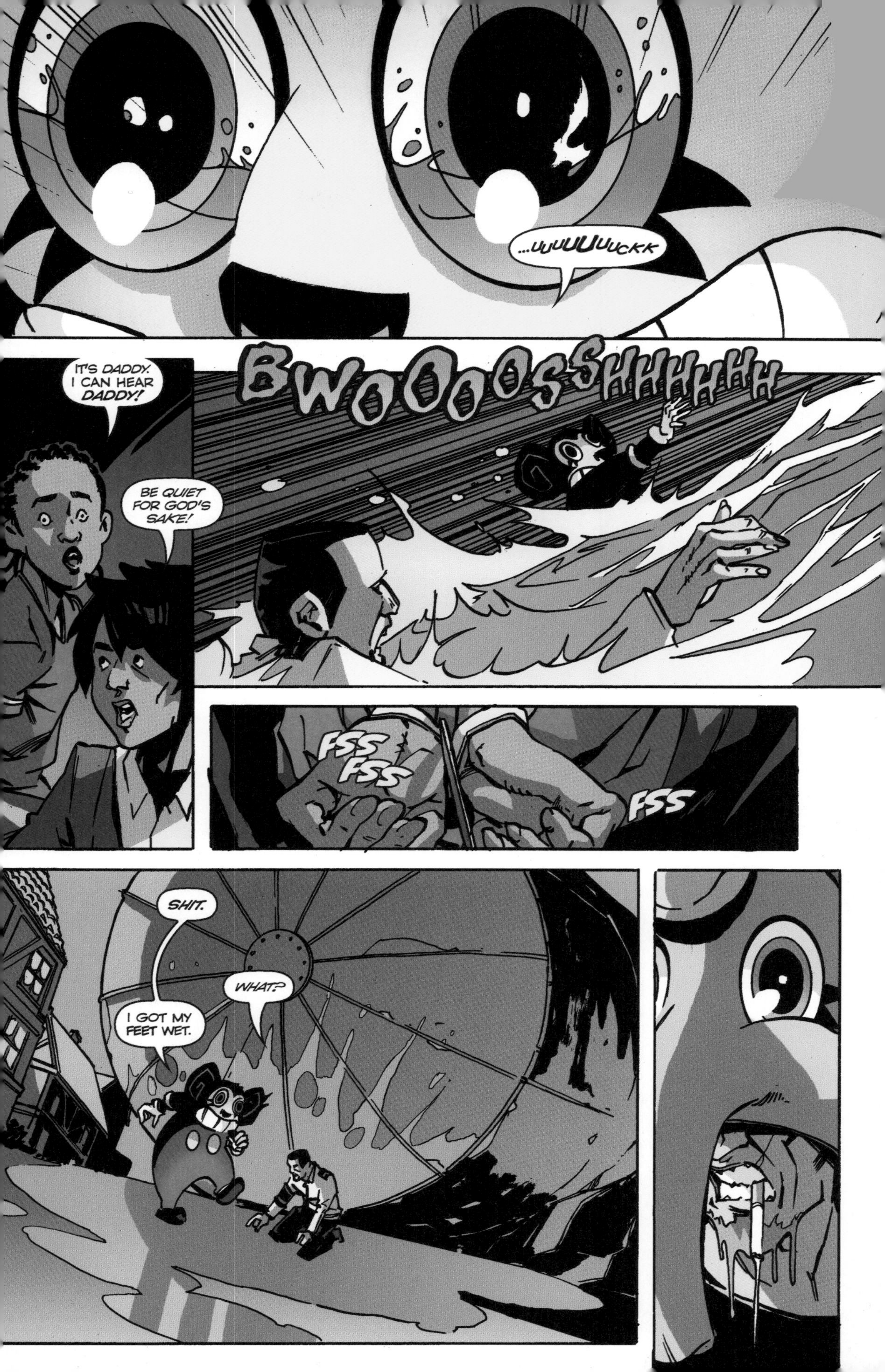
...UUUUUUUCKK
IT'S DADDY. I CAN HEAR DADDY!
BE QUIET FOR GOD'S SAKE!
BWOOOOOSSHHHHHH
FSS
FSS
FSS
SHIT.
WHAT?
I GOT MY FEET WET.

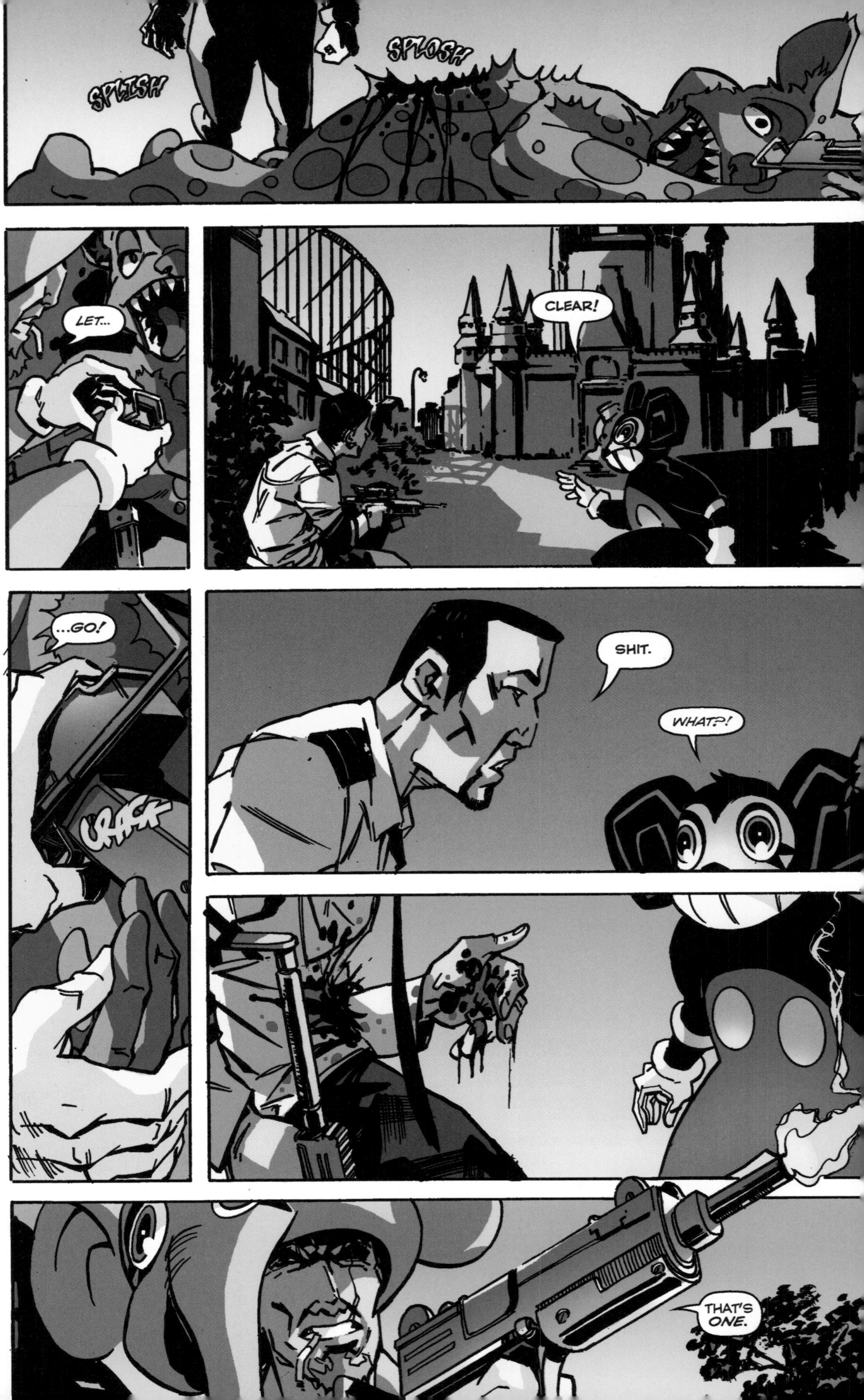
SPLISH
SPLOSH
LET...
CLEAR!
...GO!
CRACK
SHIT.
WHAT?!
THAT'S ONE.

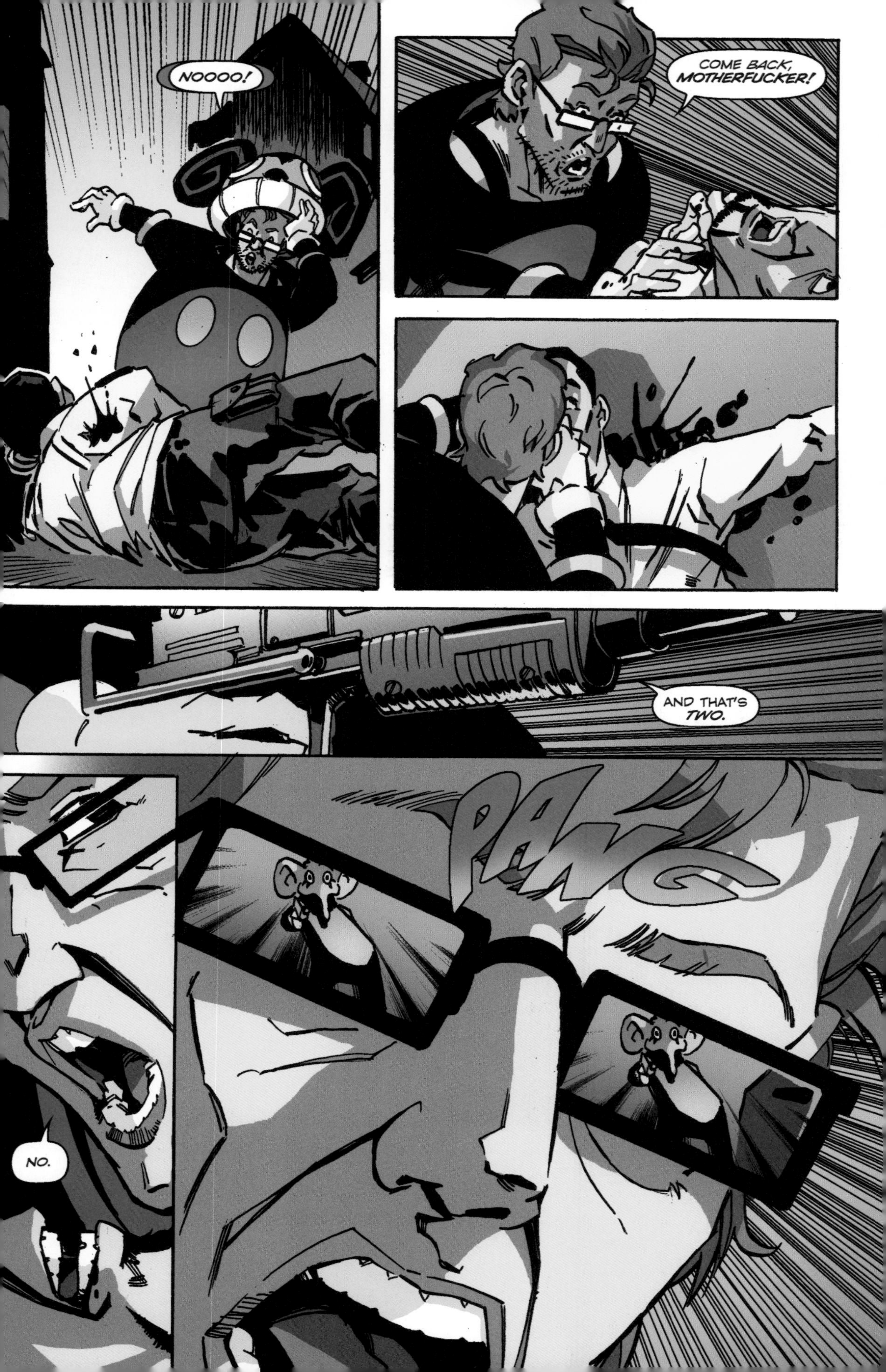
NOOOO!
COME BACK, MOTHERFUCKER!
AND THAT'S TWO.
PANG
NO.

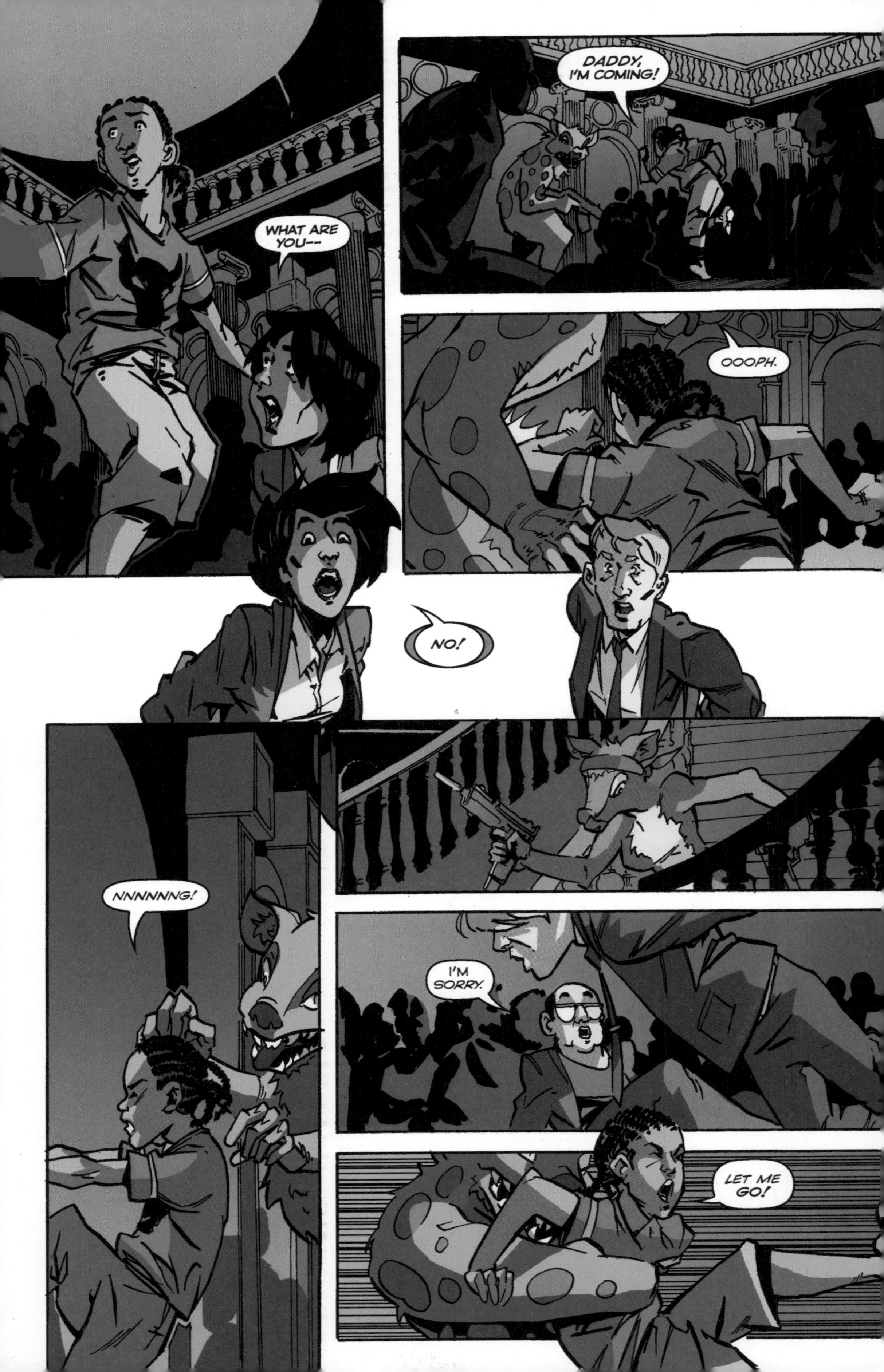
WHAT ARE YOU--
DADDY, I'M COMING!
OOOPH.
NO!
NNNNNNG!
I'M SORRY.
LET ME GO!

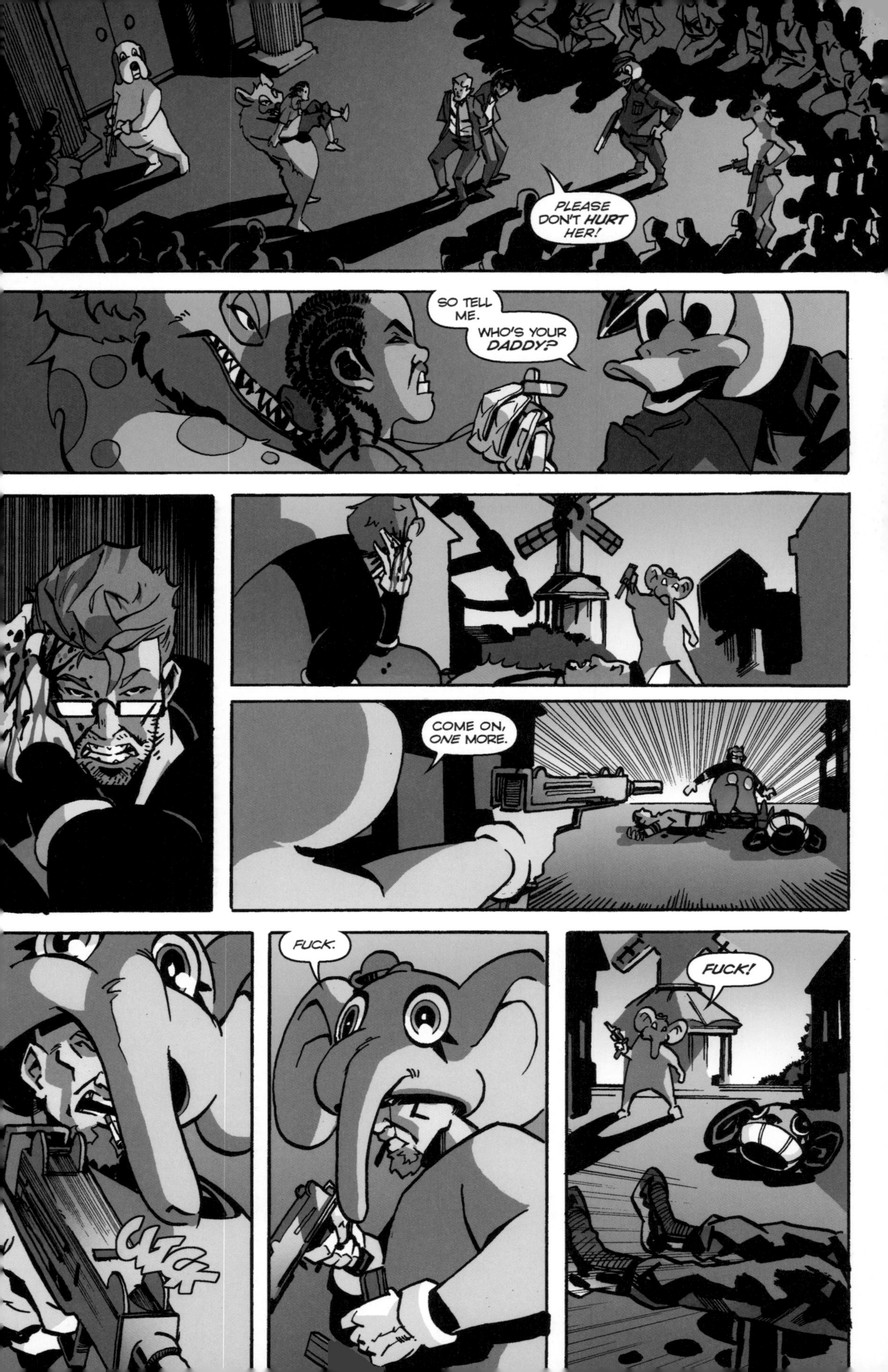
PLEASE DON'T HURT HER!
SO TELL ME.
WHO'S YOUR DADDY?
COME ON, ONE MORE.
FUCK.
FUCK!

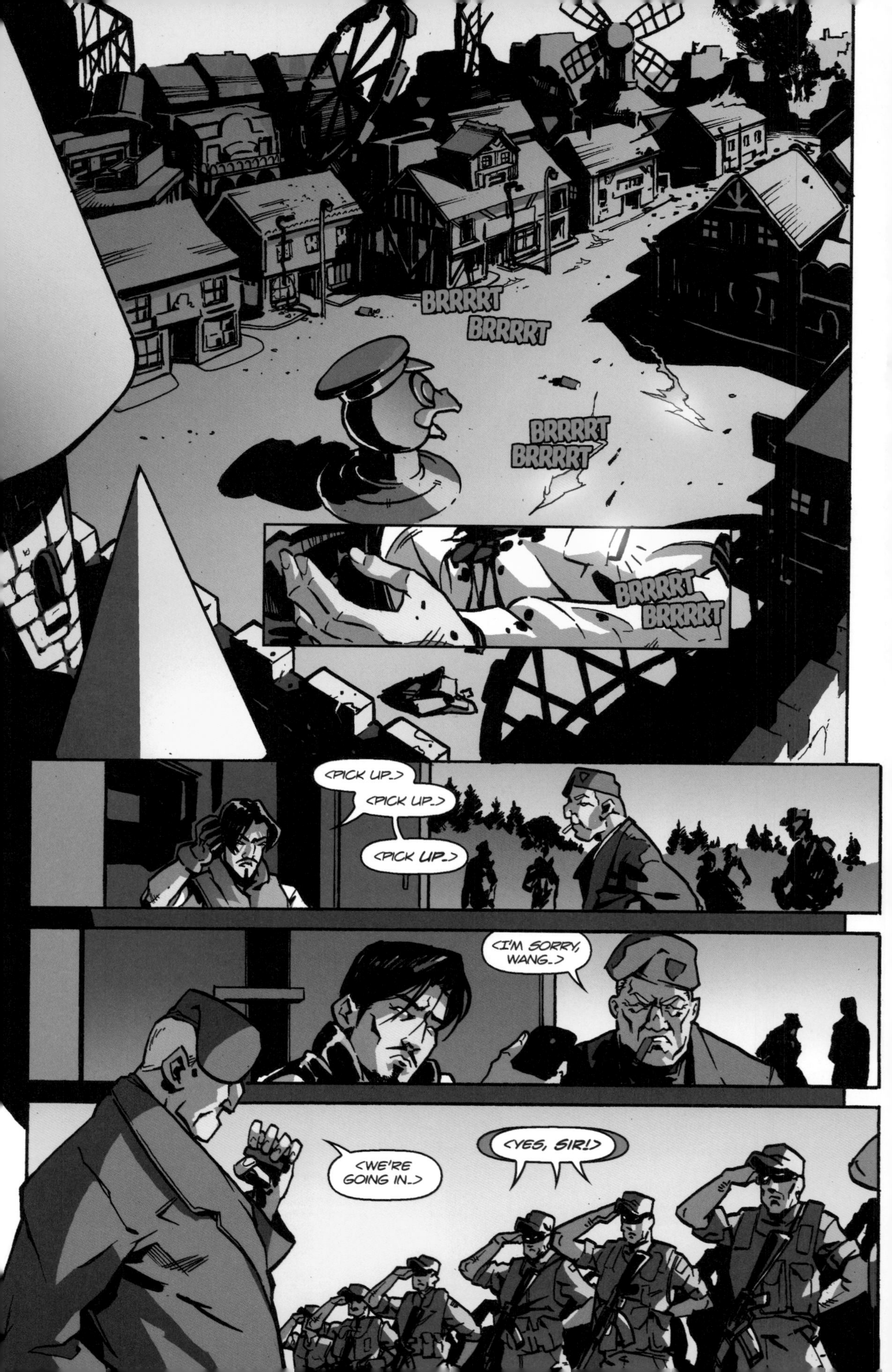
BRRRRT
BRRRRT
BRRRRT
BRRRRT
BRRRRT
BRRRRT
<PICK UP.>
<PICK UP.>
<PICK UP.>
<I'M SORRY, WANG.>
<WE'RE GOING IN.>
<YES, SIR!>

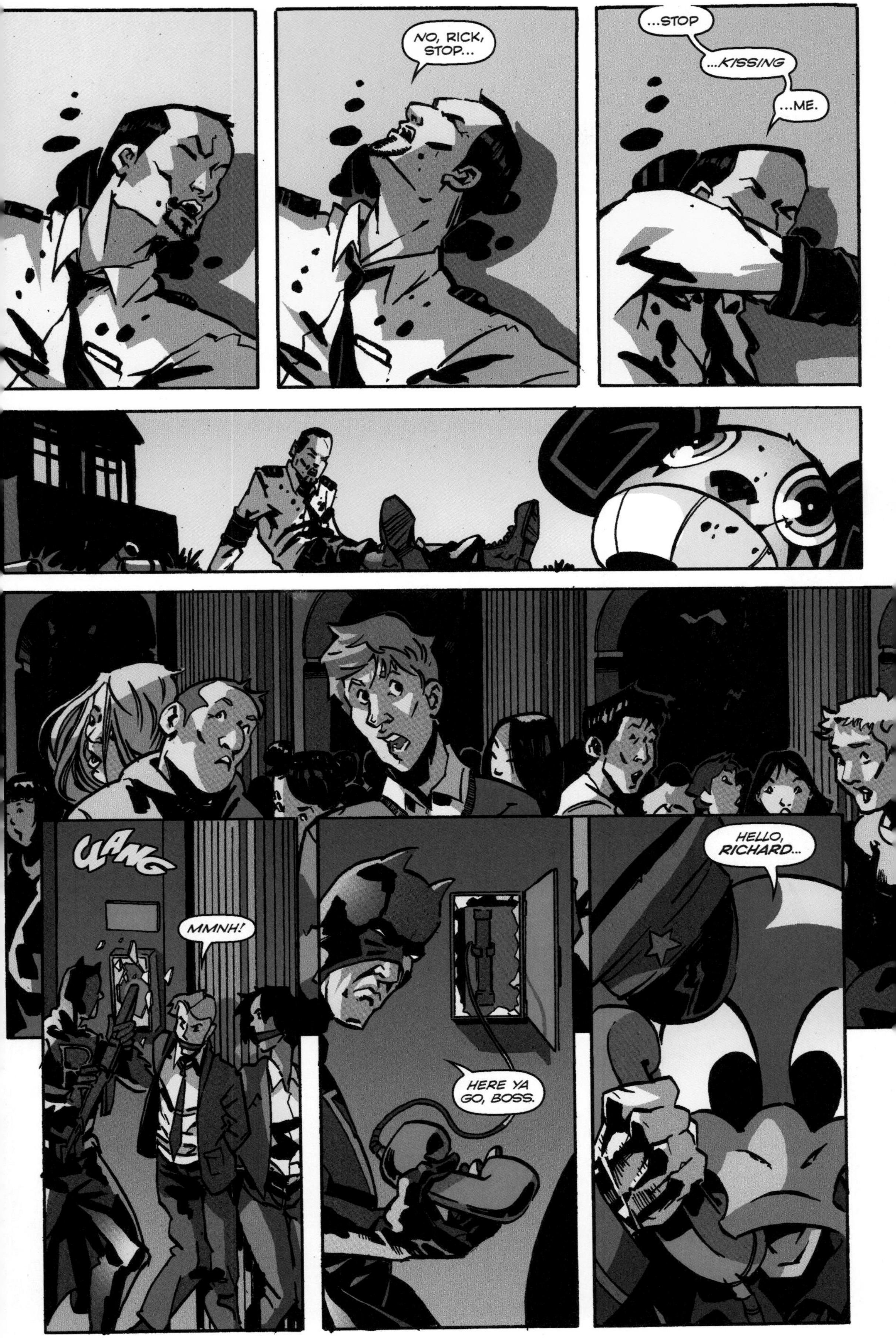
NO, RICK, STOP...
...STOP
...KISSING
...ME.
CLANG
MMNH!
HERE YA GO, BOSS.
HELLO, RICHARD...

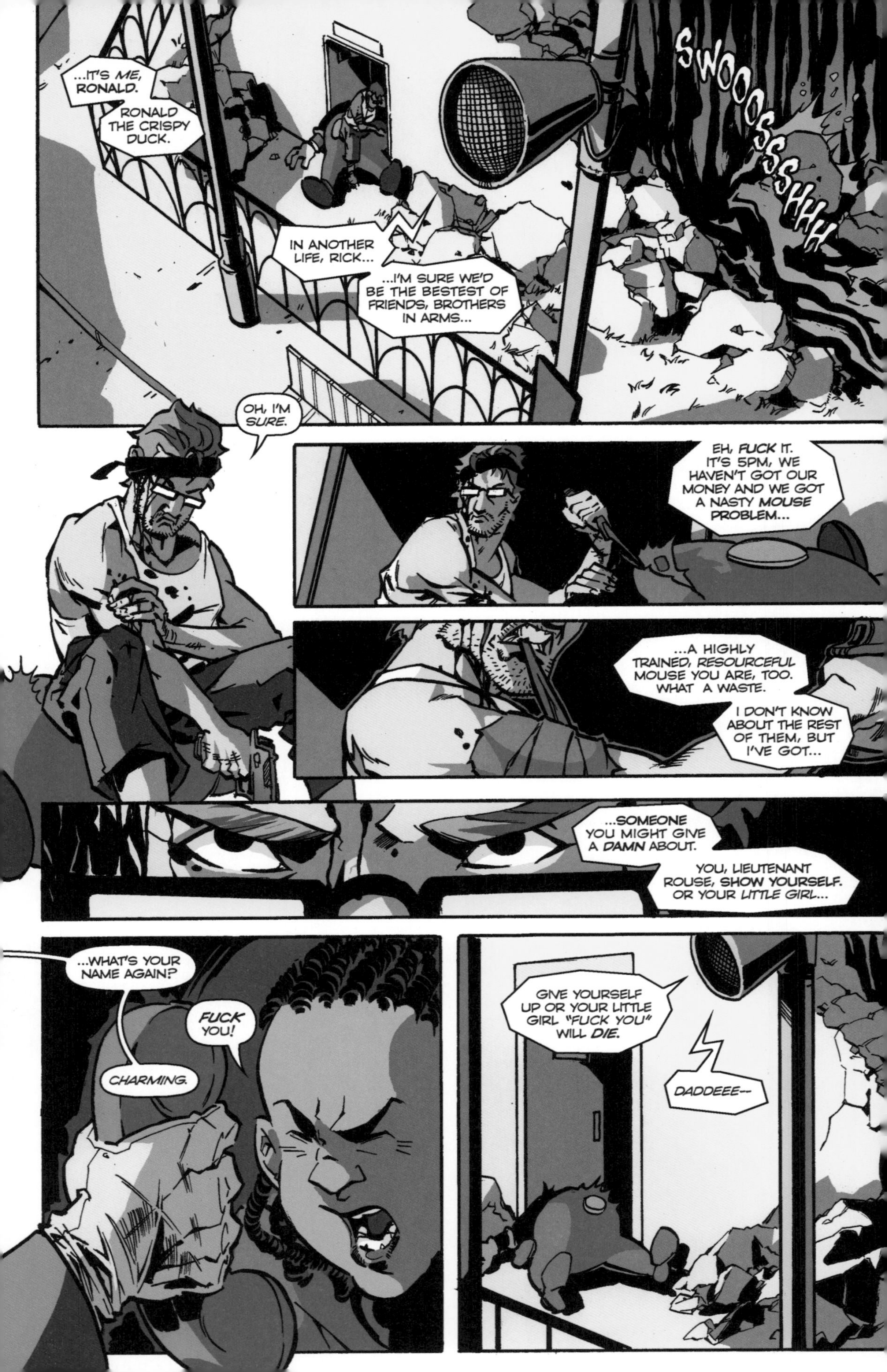
...IT'S ME, RONALD.
RONALD THE CRISPY DUCK.
SWOOOSSSHHH
IN ANOTHER LIFE, RICK...
...I'M SURE WE'D BE THE BESTEST OF FRIENDS, BROTHERS IN ARMS...
OH, I'M SURE.
EH, FUCK IT. IT'S 5PM, WE HAVEN'T GOT OUR MONEY AND WE GOT A NASTY MOUSE PROBLEM...
...A HIGHLY TRAINED, RESOURCEFUL MOUSE YOU ARE, TOO. WHAT A WASTE.
I DON'T KNOW ABOUT THE REST OF THEM, BUT I'VE GOT...
...SOMEONE YOU MIGHT GIVE A DAMN ABOUT.
YOU, LIEUTENANT ROUSE, SHOW YOURSELF. OR YOUR LITTLE GIRL...
...WHAT'S YOUR NAME AGAIN?
FUCK YOU!
CHARMING.
GIVE YOURSELF UP OR YOUR LITTLE GIRL "FUCK YOU" WILL DIE.
DADDEEE--

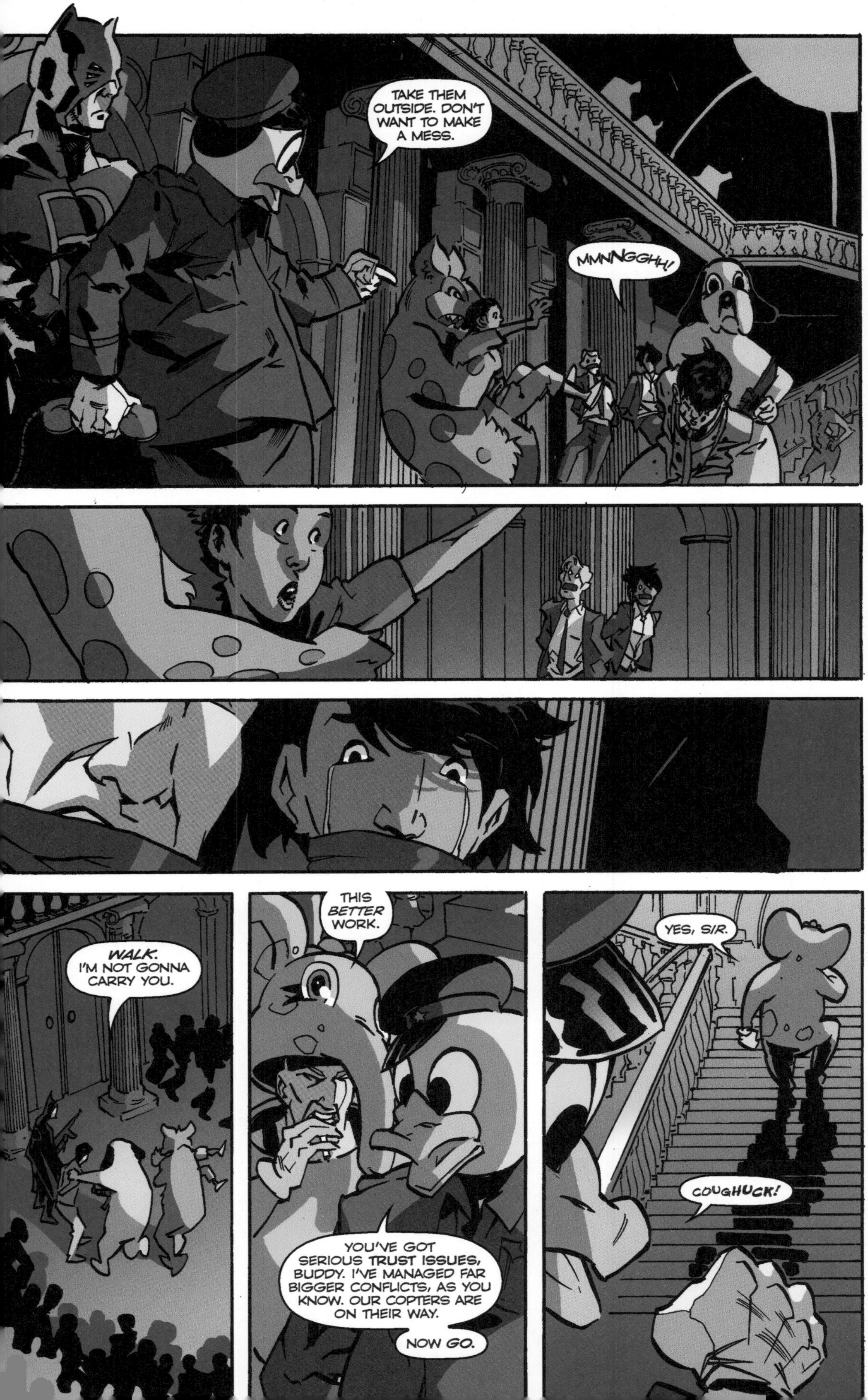
TAKE THEM OUTSIDE. DON'T WANT TO MAKE A MESS.
MMNNGGHH!
WALK. I'M NOT GONNA CARRY YOU.
THIS BETTER WORK.
YOU'VE GOT SERIOUS TRUST ISSUES, BUDDY. I'VE MANAGED FAR BIGGER CONFLICTS, AS YOU KNOW. OUR COPTERS ARE ON THEIR WAY.
NOW GO.
YES, SIR.
COUGHUCK!

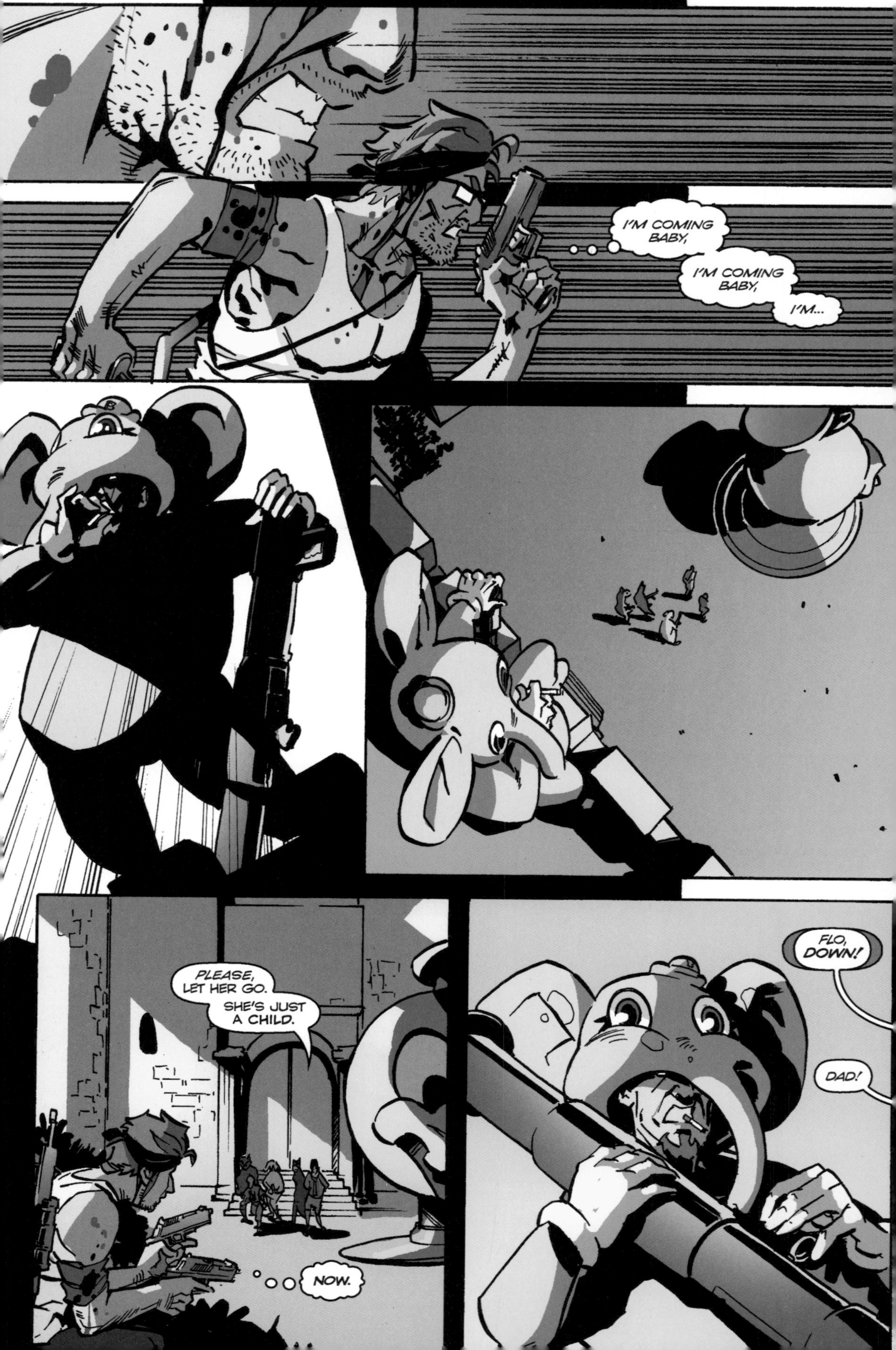
I'M COMING BABY,
I'M COMING BABY,
I'M...
PLEASE, LET HER GO.
SHE'S JUST A CHILD.
NOW.
FLO, DOWN!
DAD!

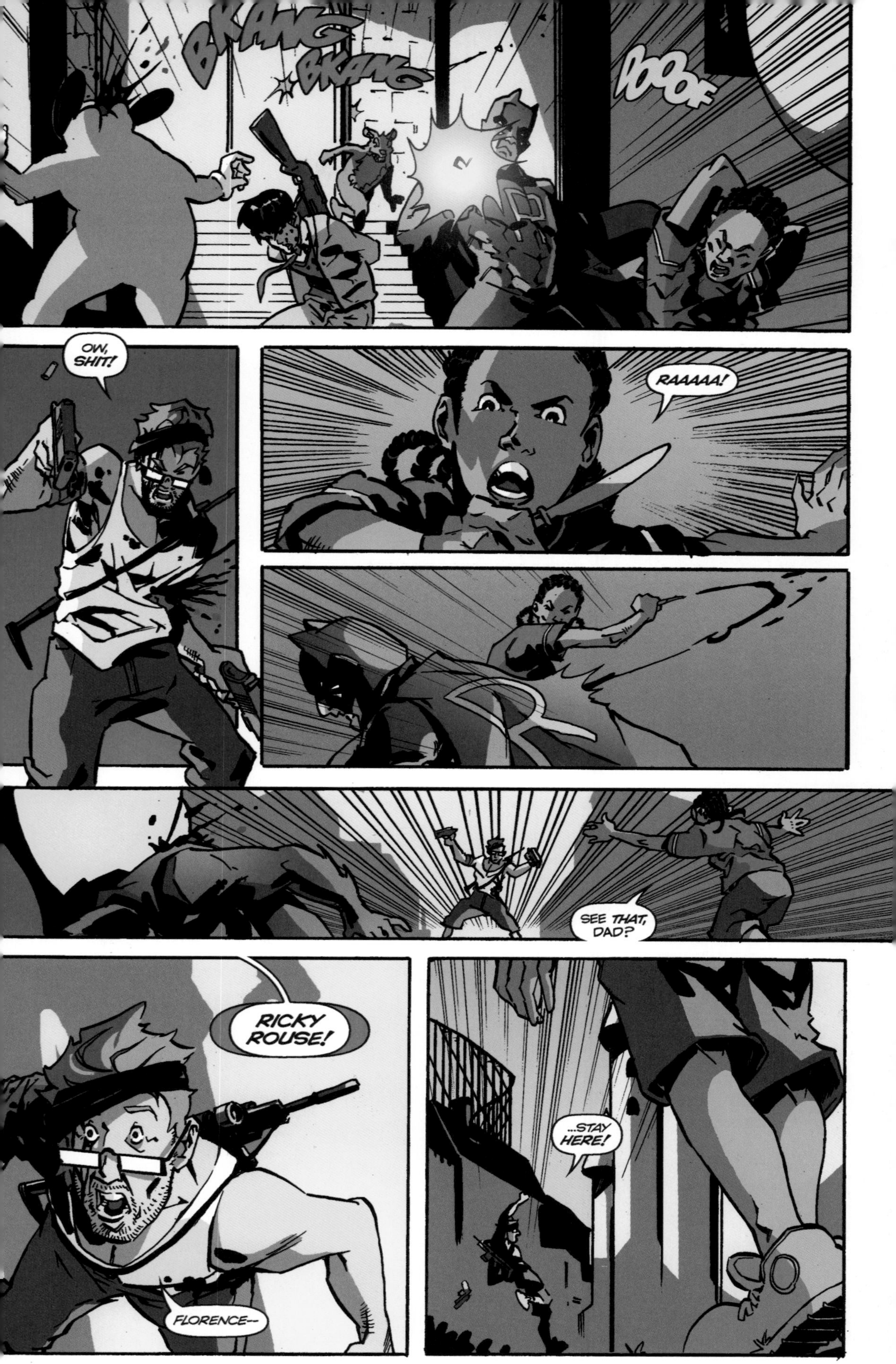
BKANG
BKANG
POOOF
OW, SHIT!
RAAAAA!
SEE THAT, DAD?
RICKY ROUSE!
FLORENCE--
...STAY HERE!

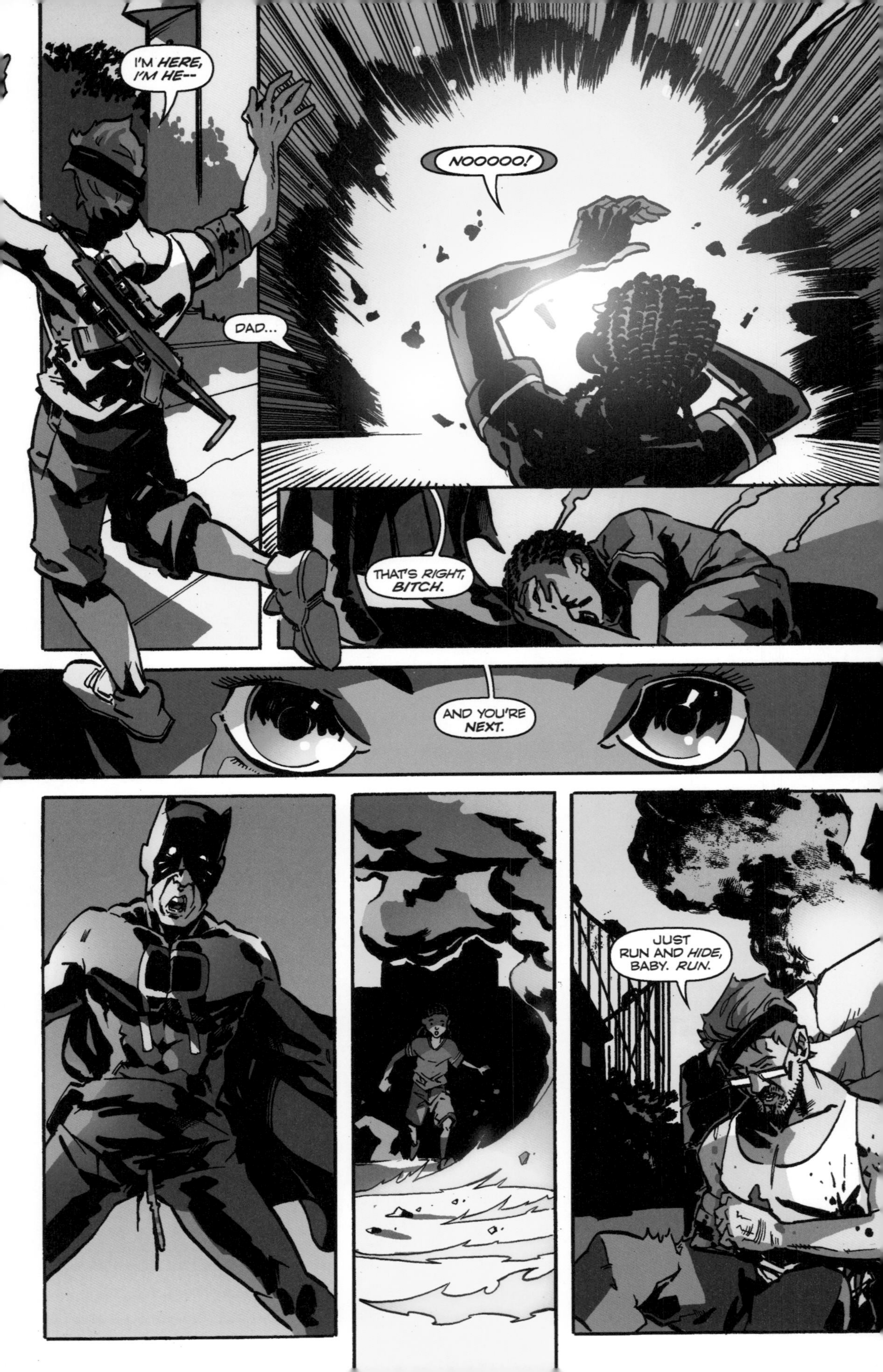
I'M HERE, I'M HE--
NOOOOO!
DAD...
THAT'S RIGHT, BITCH.
AND YOU'RE NEXT.
JUST RUN AND HIDE, BABY. RUN.

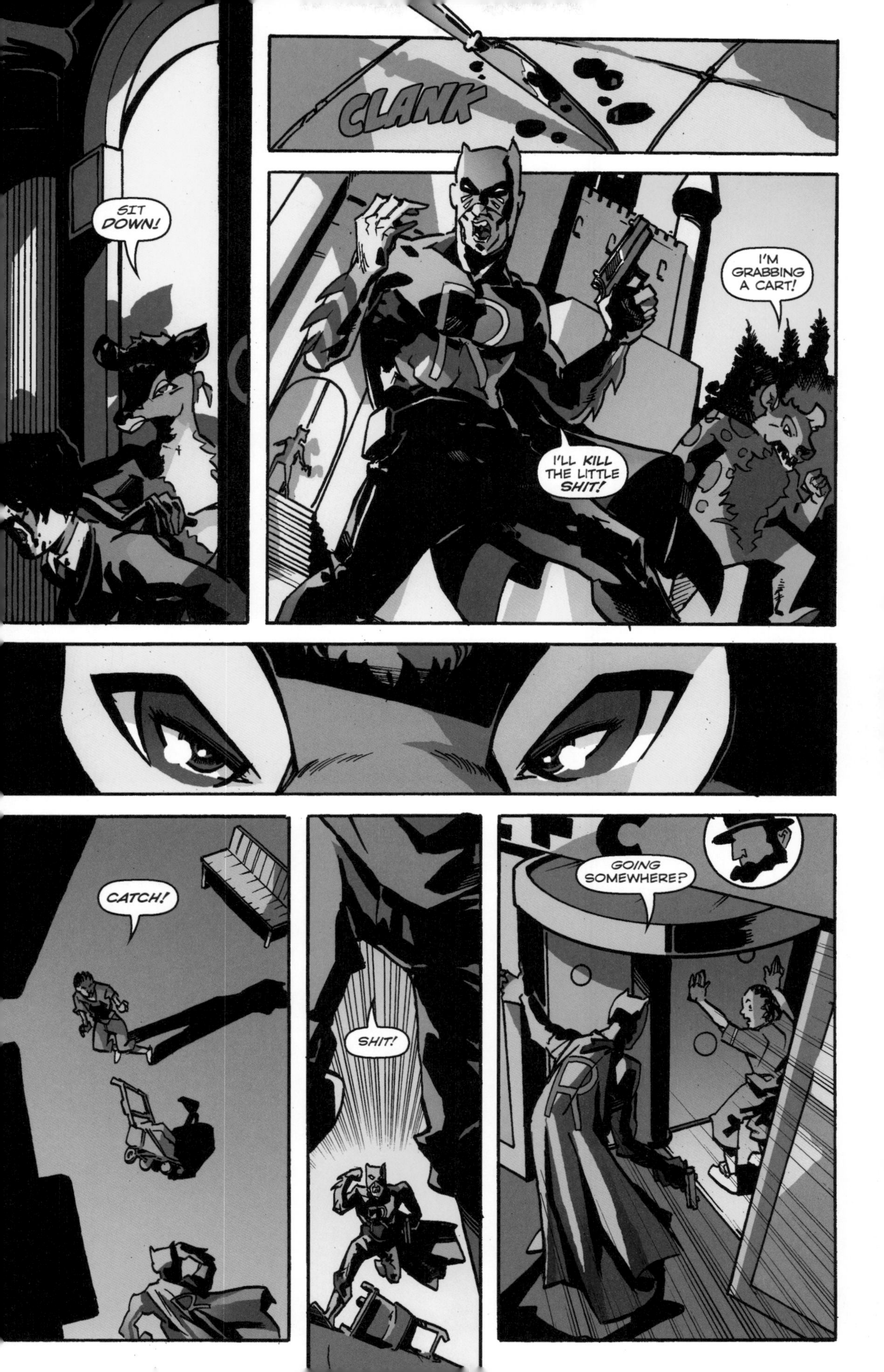
CLANK
SIT DOWN!
I'M GRABBING A CART!
I'LL KILL THE LITTLE SHIT!
CATCH!
SHIT!
GOING SOMEWHERE?

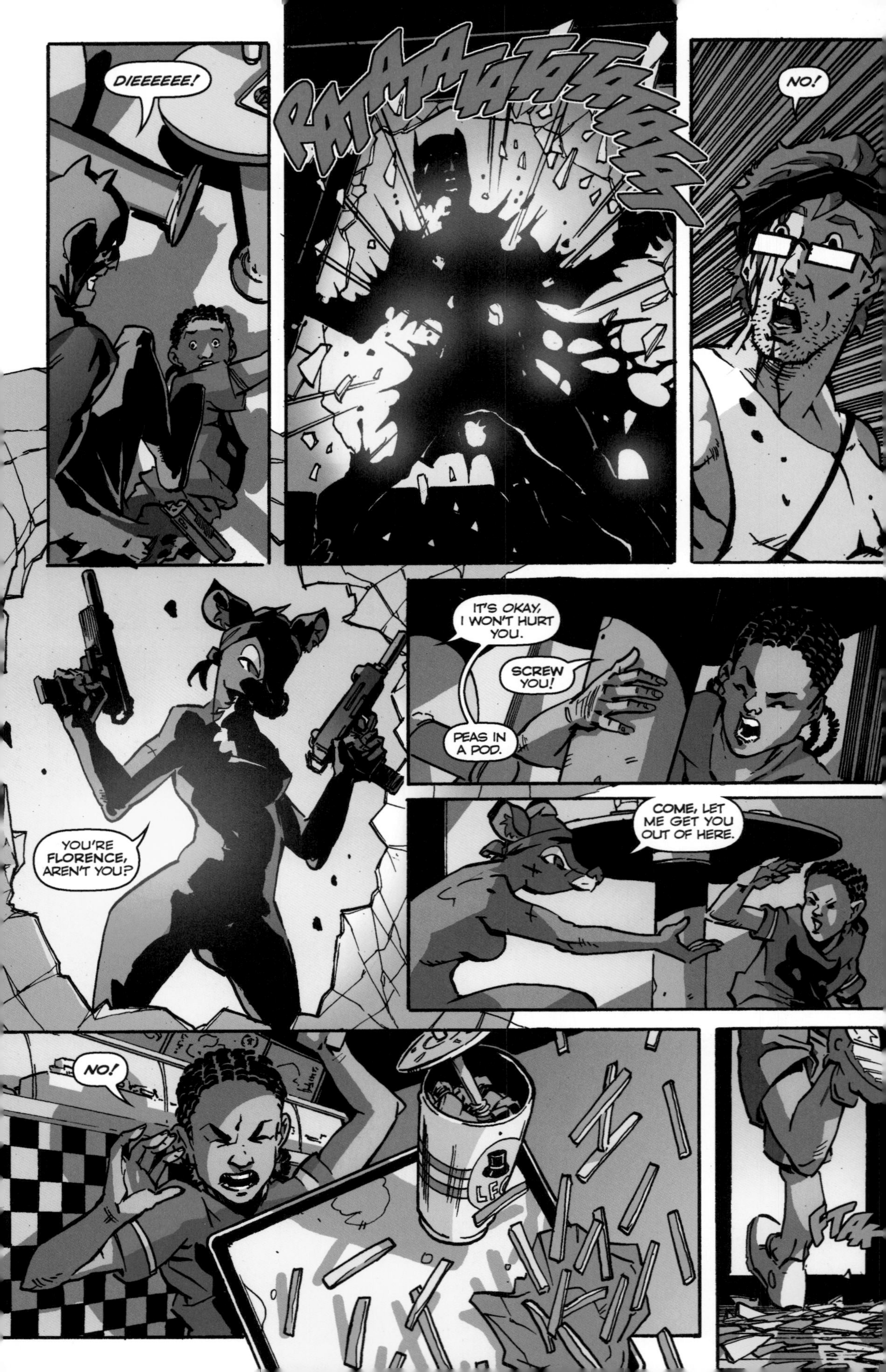
DIEEEEEE!
RATATATATATATATATAT
NO!
YOU'RE FLORENCE, AREN'T YOU?
IT'S OKAY, I WON'T HURT YOU.
SCREW YOU!
PEAS IN A POD.
COME, LET ME GET YOU OUT OF HERE.
NO!
FTAK

DADDY?

COME IN HERE.

NO!

WAIT, NO!

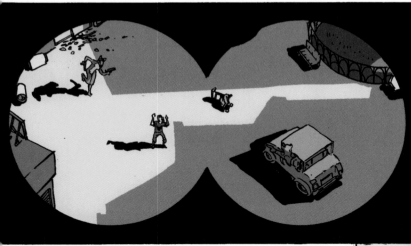

HMMM.

HEY! STOP!

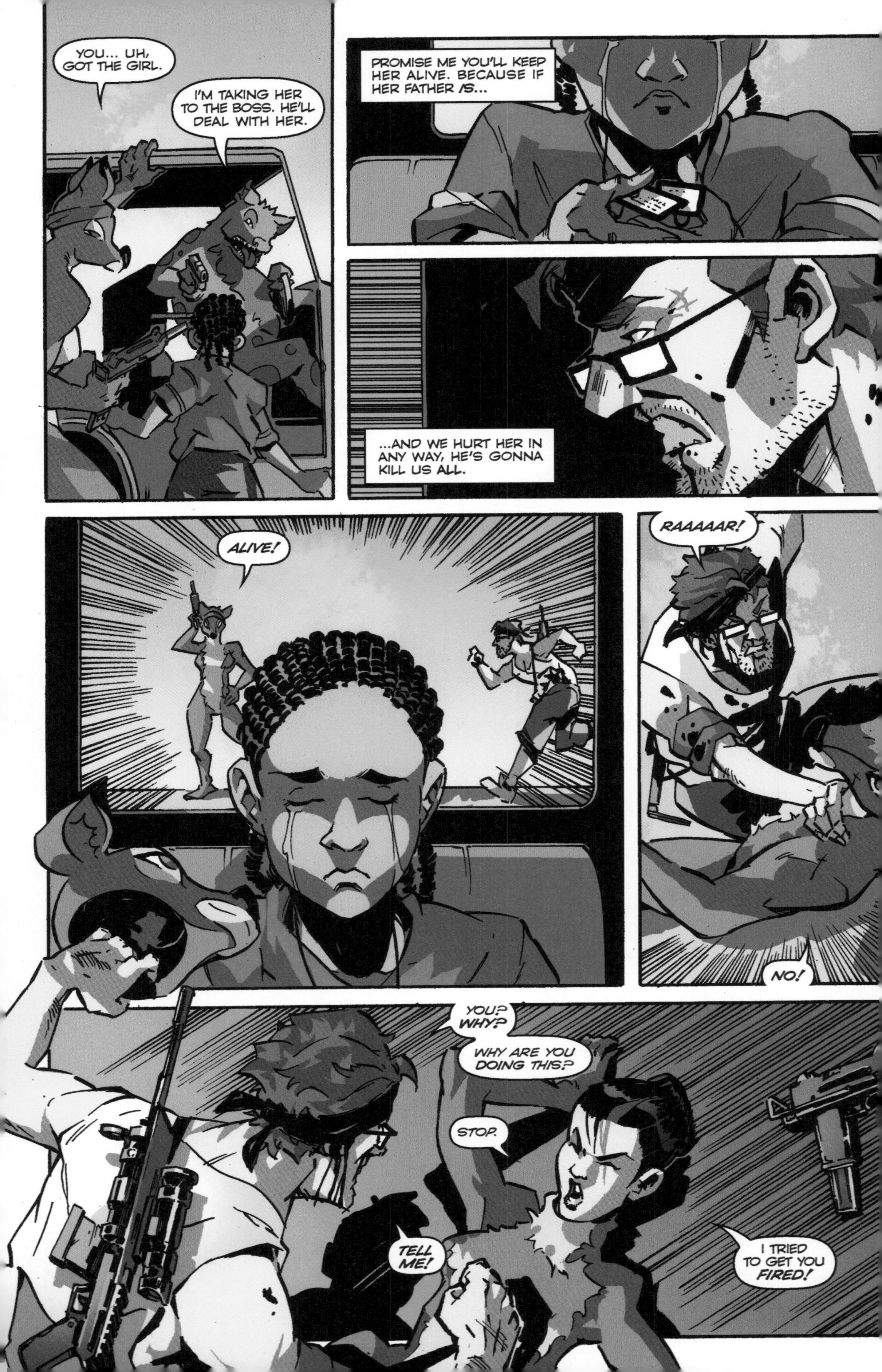
YOU... UH, GOT THE GIRL.
I'M TAKING HER TO THE BOSS. HE'LL DEAL WITH HER.
PROMISE ME YOU'LL KEEP HER ALIVE. BECAUSE IF HER FATHER IS...
...AND WE HURT HER IN ANY WAY, HE'S GONNA KILL US ALL.
ALIVE!
RAAAAAR!
NO!
YOU? WHY?
WHY ARE YOU DOING THIS?
STOP.
TELL ME!
I TRIED TO GET YOU FIRED!

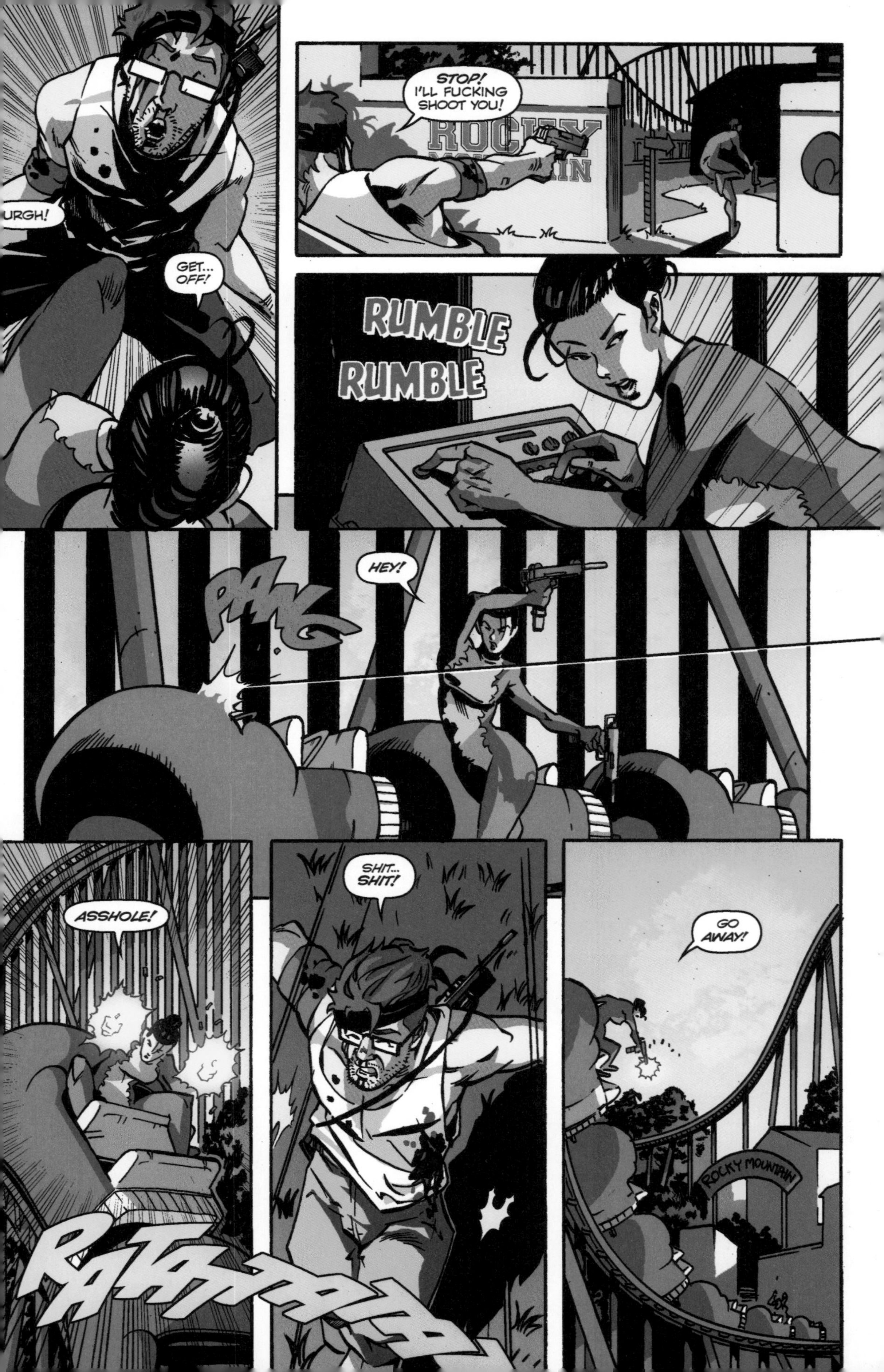
URGH!
GET... OFF!
STOP! I'LL FUCKING SHOOT YOU!
ROCKY
RUMBLE
RUMBLE
HEY!
PANG
ASSHOLE!
RATATATA
SHIT... SHIT!
GO AWAY!
ROCKY MOUNTAIN

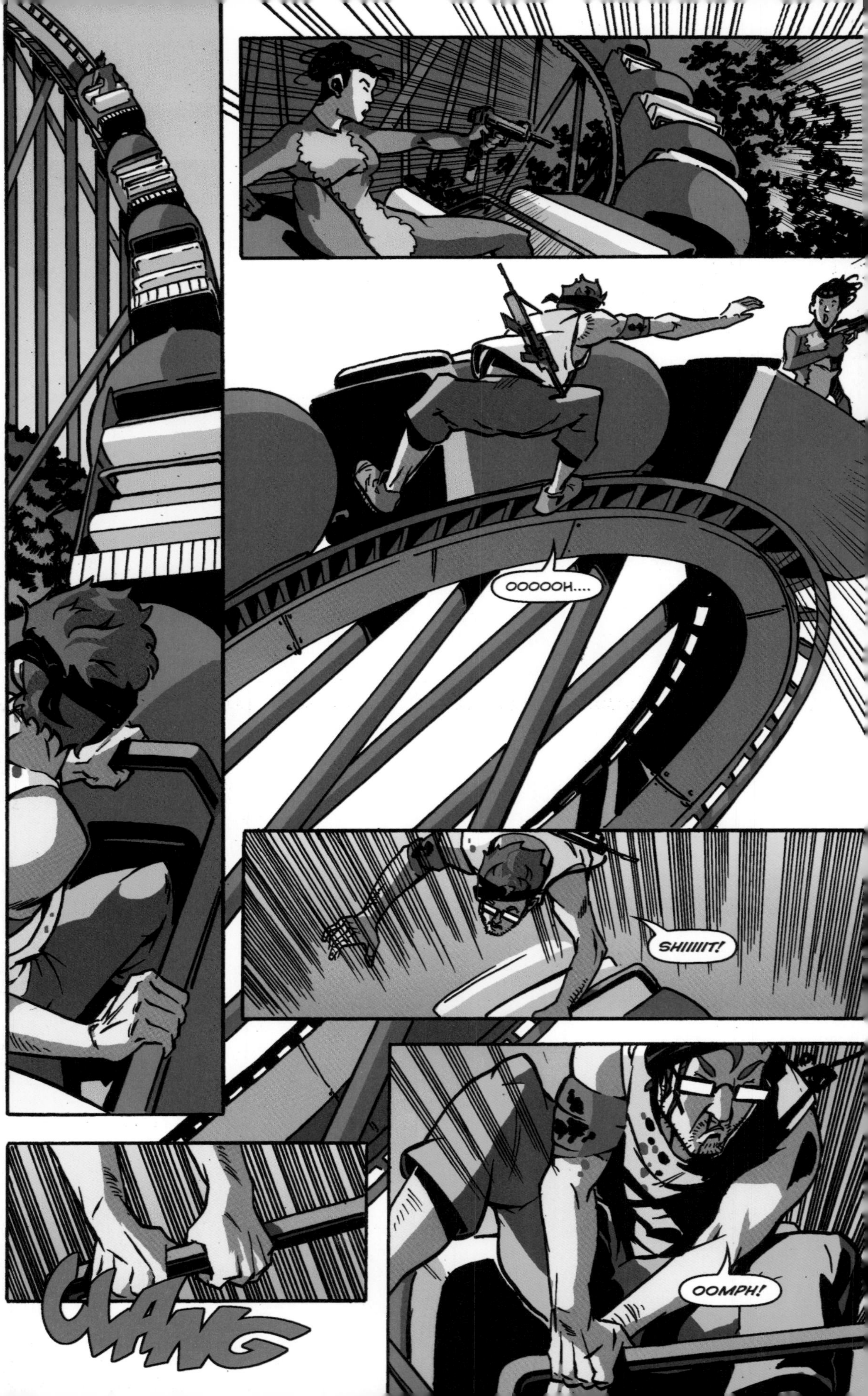
OOOOOH....
SHIIIIIT!
CLANG
OOMPH!

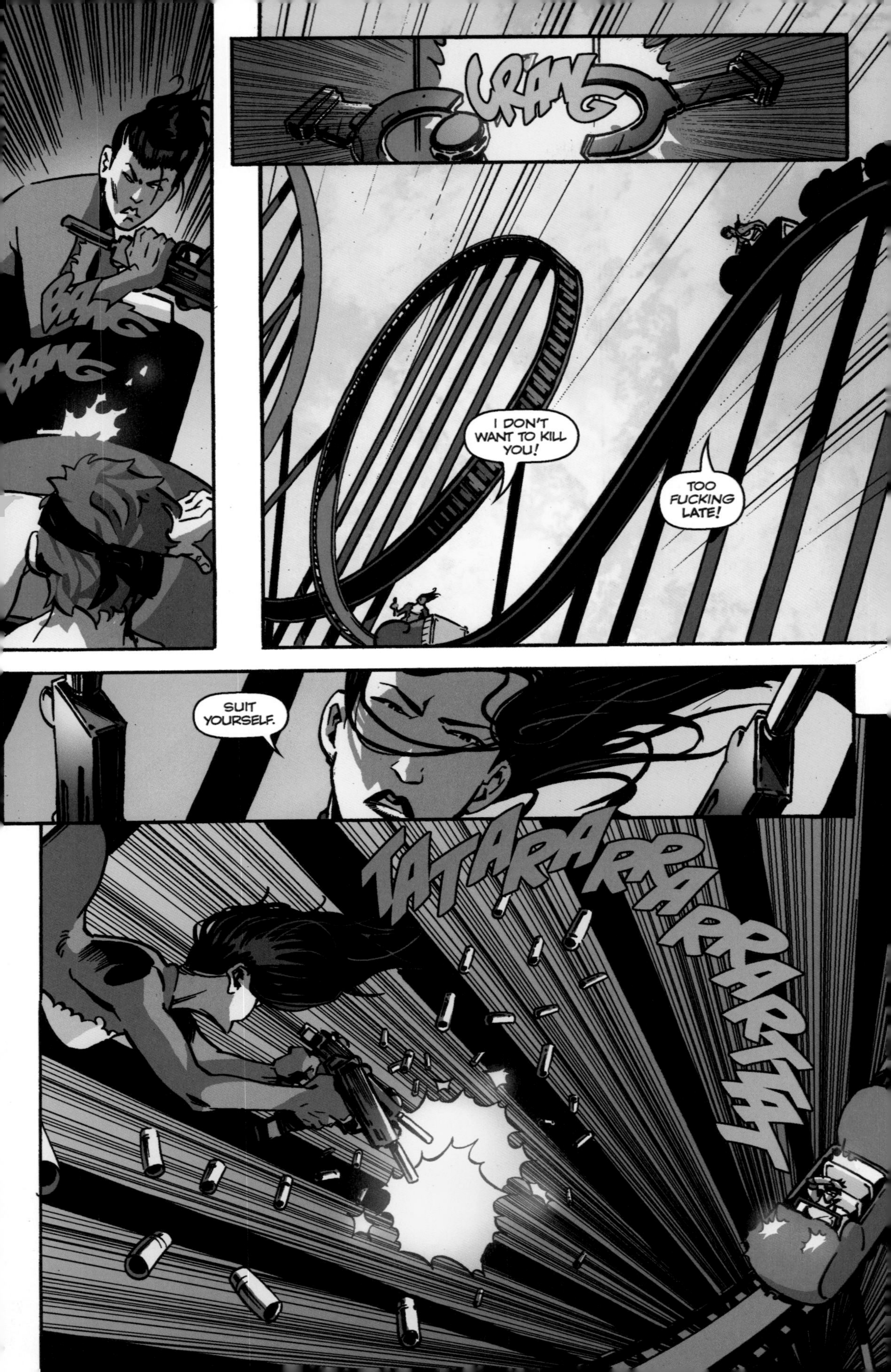
BANG
BANG
CRANG
I DON'T WANT TO KILL YOU!
TOO FUCKING LATE!
SUIT YOURSELF.
TATARARARARARTAT

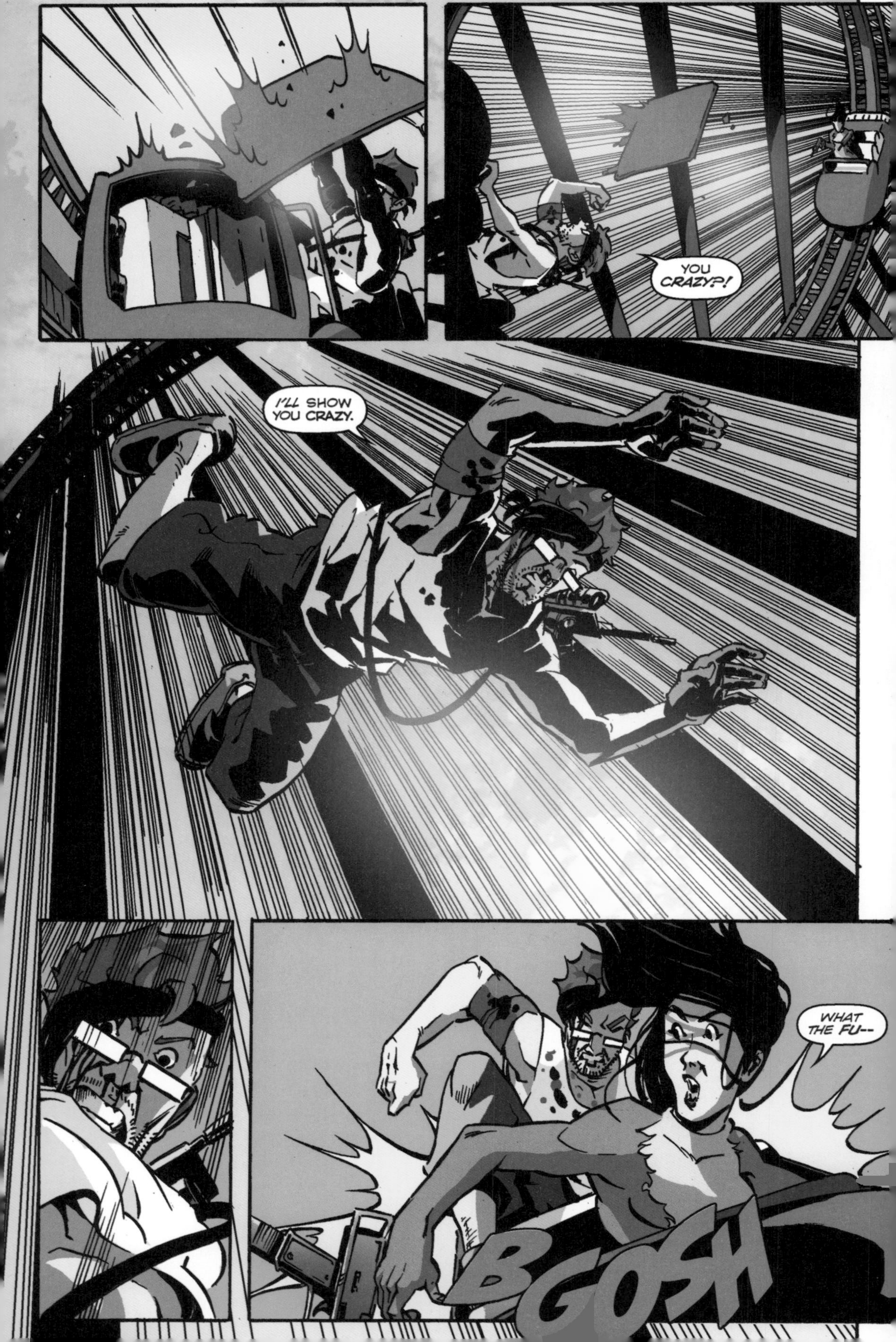
YOU CRAZY?!
I'LL SHOW YOU CRAZY.
WHAT THE FU--
BGOSH

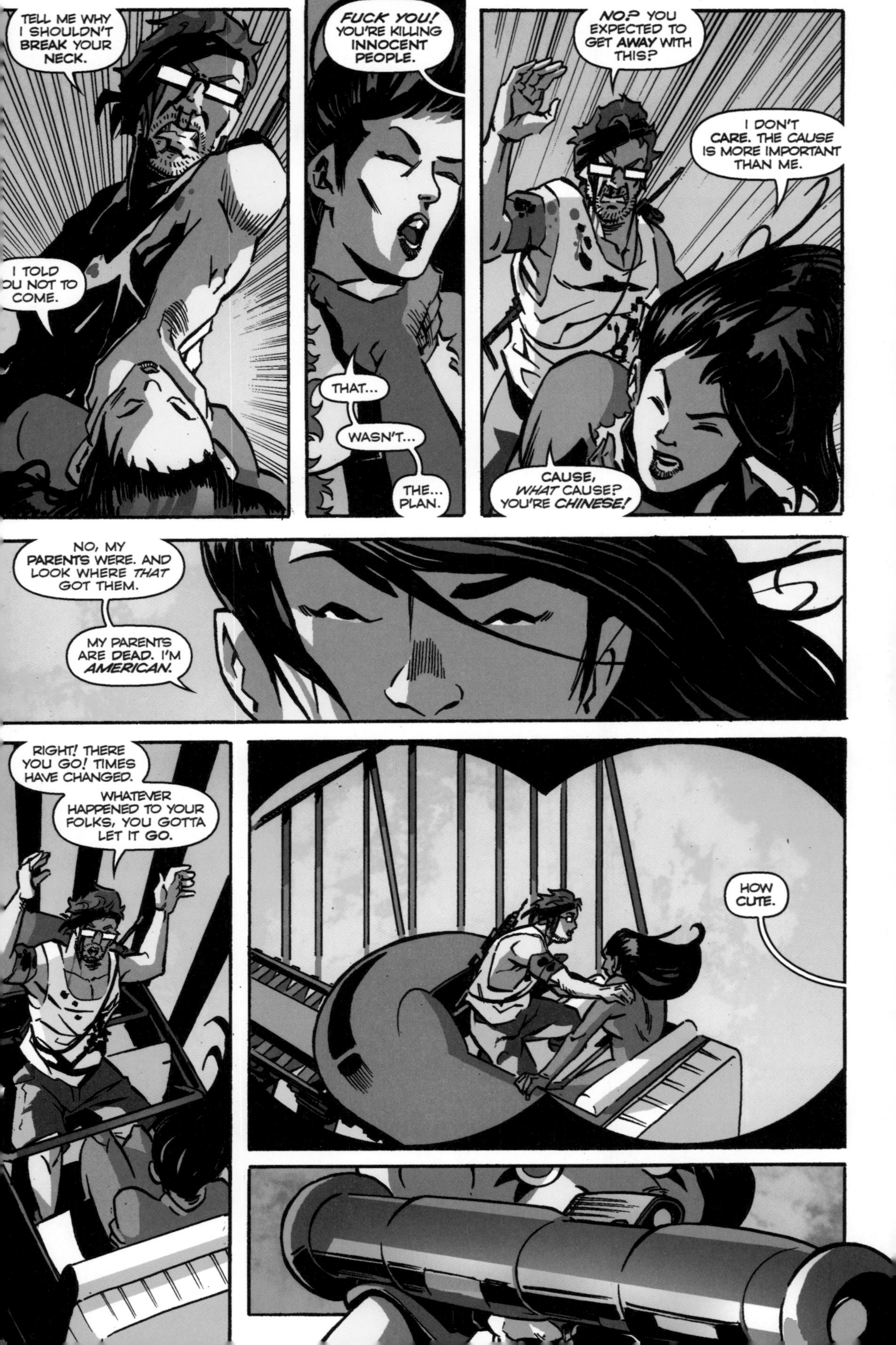
TELL ME WHY I SHOULDN'T BREAK YOUR NECK.
I TOLD OU NOT TO COME.
FUCK YOU! YOU'RE KILLING INNOCENT PEOPLE.
THAT...
WASN'T...
THE... PLAN.
NO? YOU EXPECTED TO GET AWAY WITH THIS?
I DON'T CARE. THE CAUSE IS MORE IMPORTANT THAN ME.
CAUSE, WHAT CAUSE? YOU'RE CHINESE!
NO, MY PARENTS WERE. AND LOOK WHERE THAT GOT THEM.
MY PARENTS ARE DEAD. I'M AMERICAN.
RIGHT! THERE YOU GO! TIMES HAVE CHANGED.
WHATEVER HAPPENED TO YOUR FOLKS, YOU GOTTA LET IT GO.
HOW CUTE.

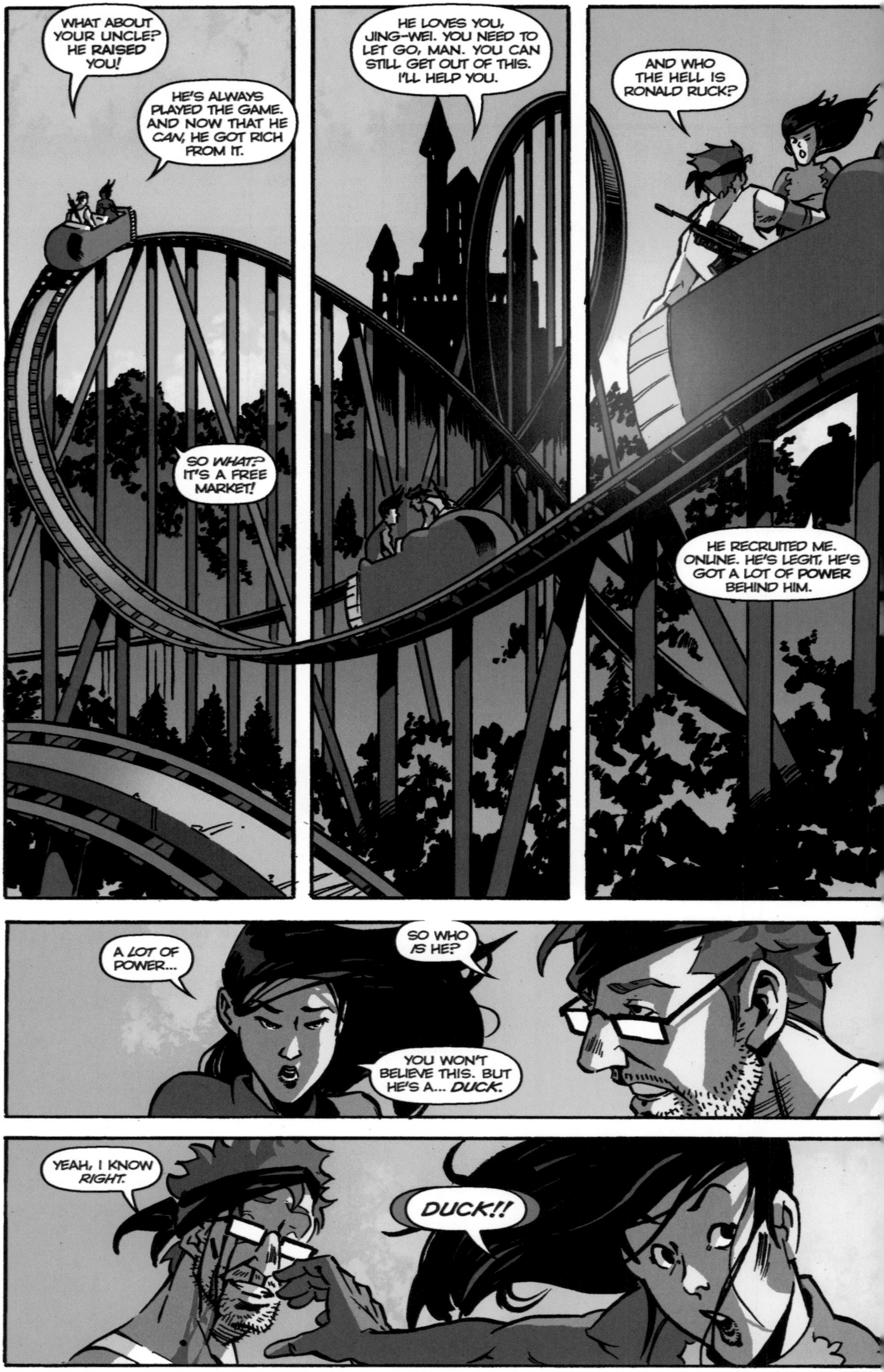
WHAT ABOUT YOUR UNCLE? HE RAISED YOU!
HE'S ALWAYS PLAYED THE GAME. AND NOW THAT HE CAN, HE GOT RICH FROM IT.
SO WHAT? IT'S A FREE MARKET!
HE LOVES YOU, JING-WEI. YOU NEED TO LET GO, MAN. YOU CAN STILL GET OUT OF THIS. I'LL HELP YOU.
AND WHO THE HELL IS RONALD RUCK?
HE RECRUITED ME. ONLINE. HE'S LEGIT, HE'S GOT A LOT OF POWER BEHIND HIM.
A LOT OF POWER...
SO WHO IS HE?
YOU WON'T BELIEVE THIS. BUT HE'S A... DUCK.
YEAH, I KNOW RIGHT.
DUCK!!

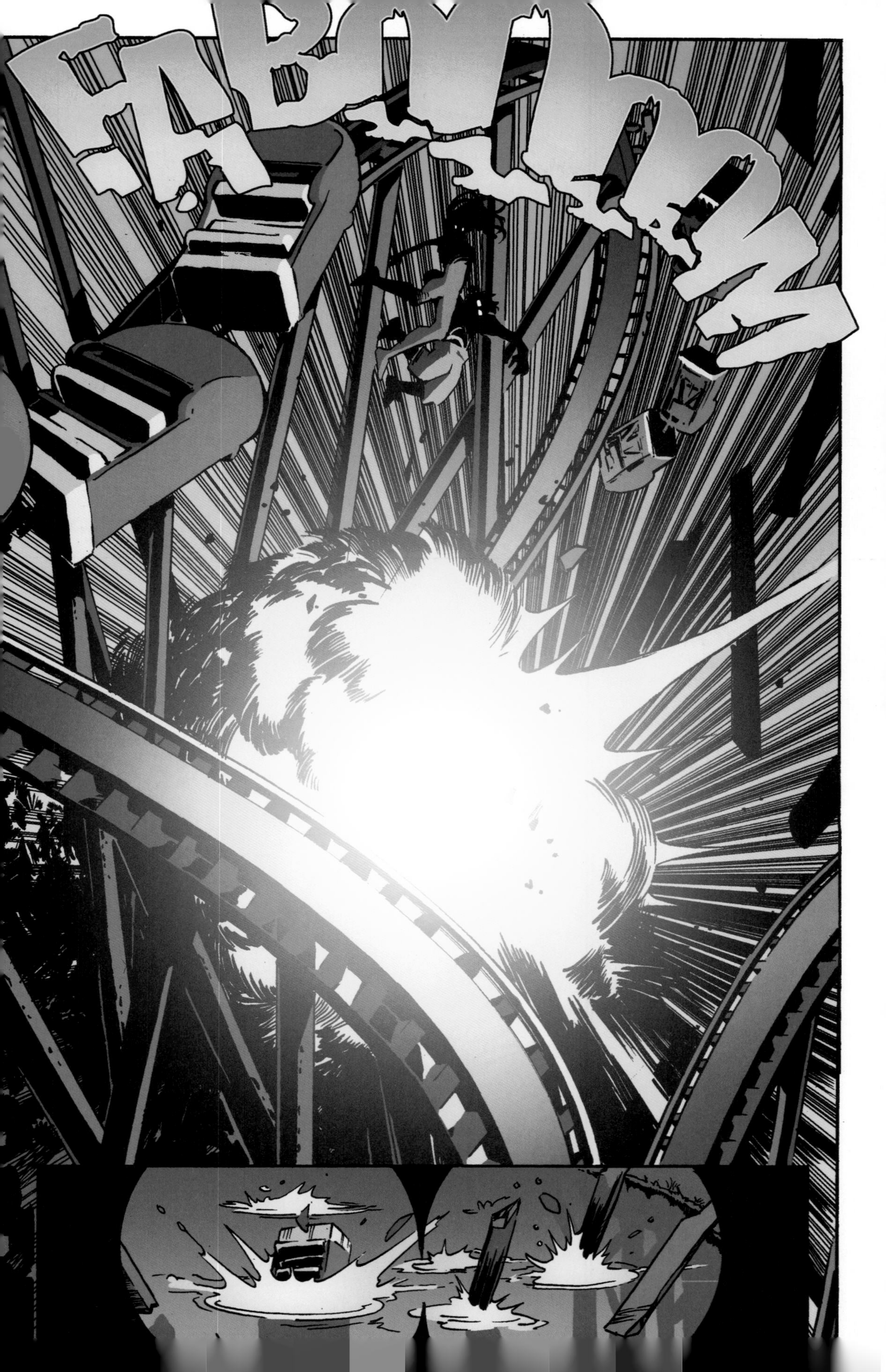
FABOOM

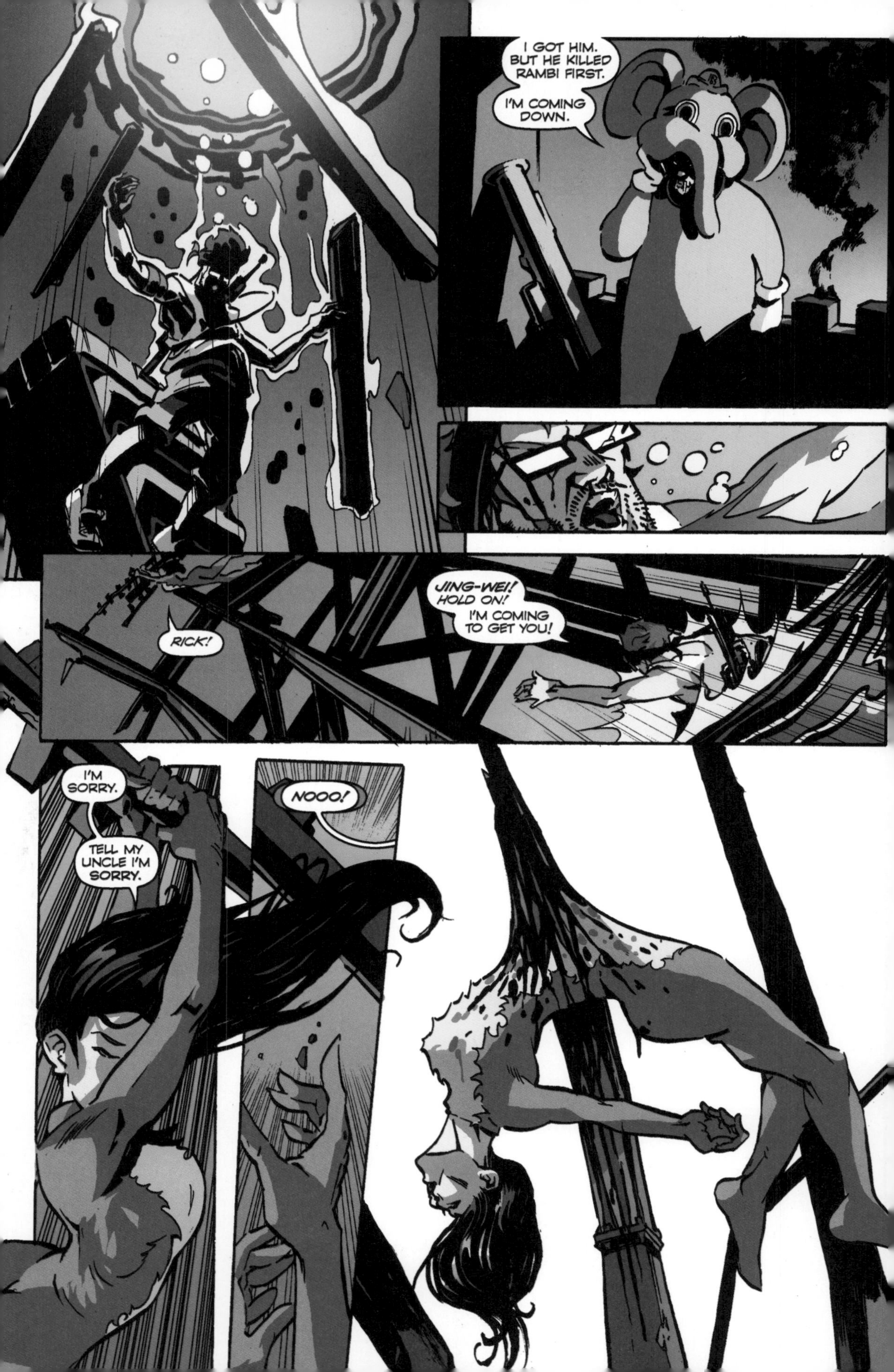
I GOT HIM. BUT HE KILLED RAMBI FIRST.
I'M COMING DOWN.
JING-WEI! HOLD ON!
I'M COMING TO GET YOU!
RICK!
I'M SORRY.
TELL MY UNCLE I'M SORRY.
NOOO!

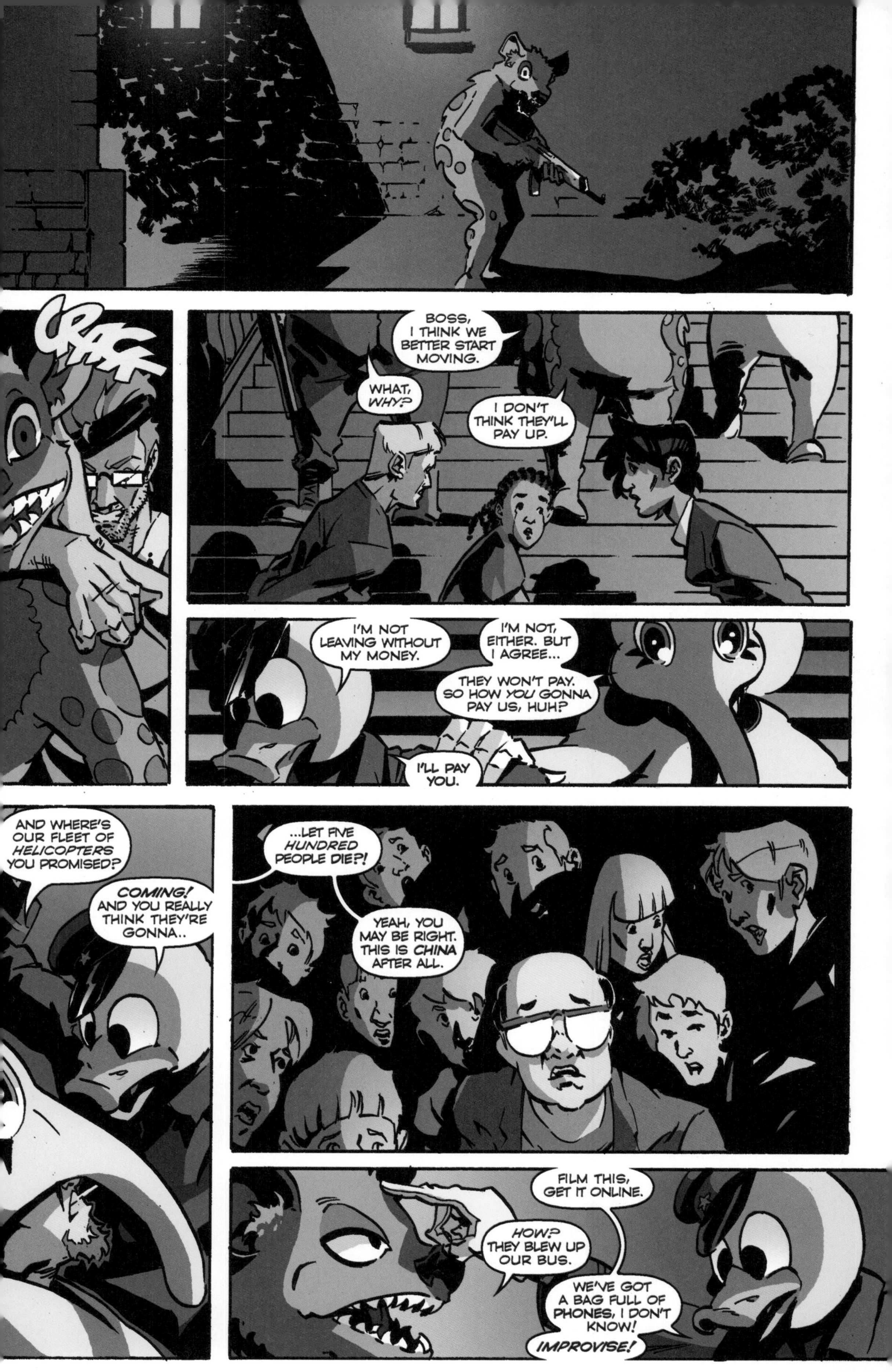
CRACK
BOSS, I THINK WE BETTER START MOVING.
WHAT, *WHY?*
I DON'T THINK THEY'LL PAY UP.
I'M NOT LEAVING WITHOUT MY MONEY.
I'M NOT, EITHER. BUT I AGREE...
THEY WON'T PAY. SO HOW *YOU* GONNA PAY US, HUH?
I'LL PAY YOU.
AND WHERE'S OUR FLEET OF *HELICOPTERS* YOU PROMISED?
COMING! AND YOU REALLY THINK THEY'RE GONNA..
...LET FIVE *HUNDRED* PEOPLE DIE?!
YEAH, YOU MAY BE RIGHT. THIS IS *CHINA* AFTER ALL.
FILM THIS, GET IT ONLINE.
HOW? THEY BLEW UP OUR BUS.
WE'VE GOT A BAG FULL OF PHONES, I DON'T KNOW! *IMPROVISE!*

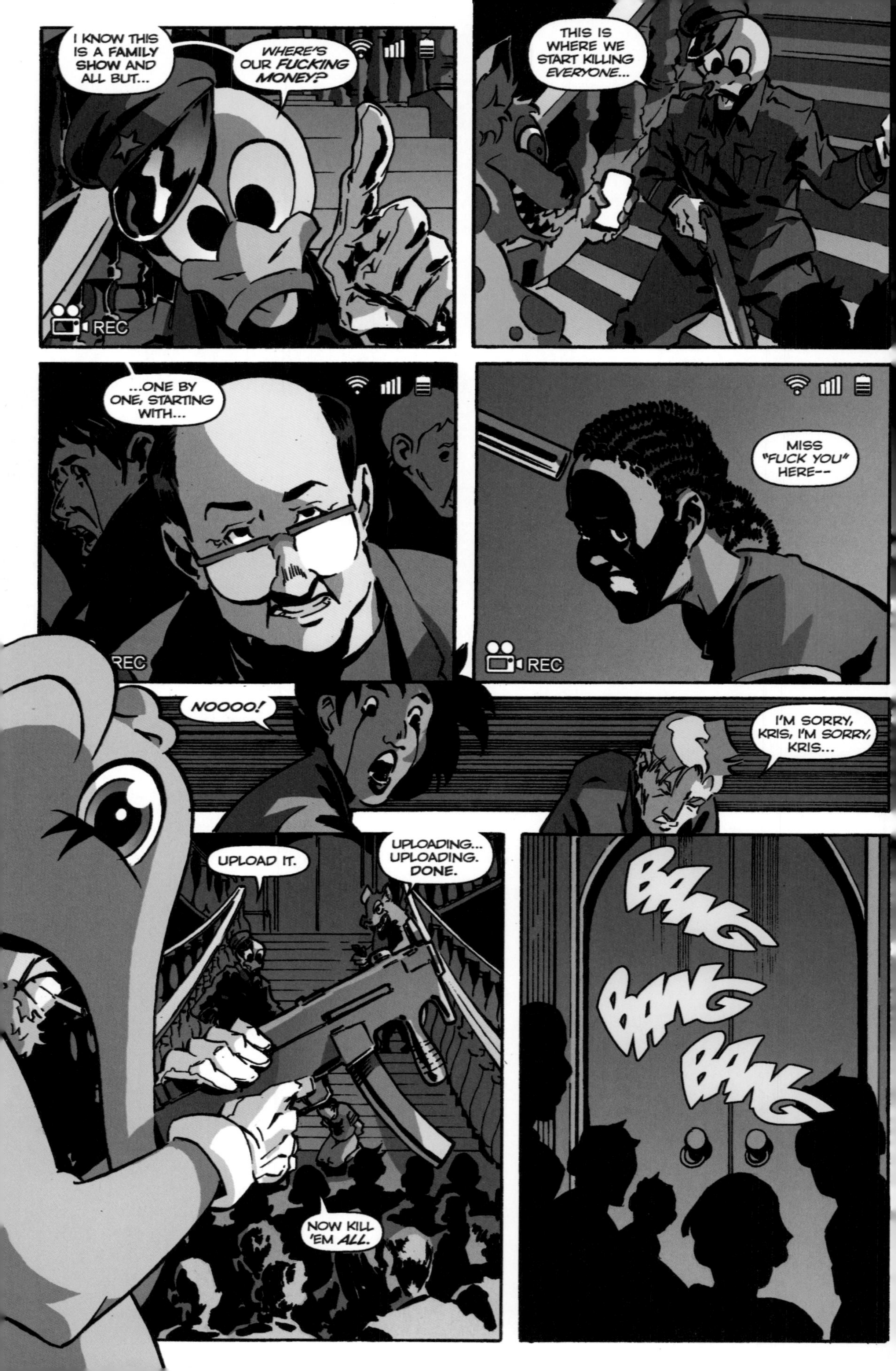
I KNOW THIS IS A FAMILY SHOW AND ALL BUT...
WHERE'S OUR *FUCKING* MONEY?
REC
THIS IS WHERE WE START KILLING *EVERYONE*...
...ONE BY ONE, STARTING WITH...
REC
MISS "FUCK YOU" HERE--
REC
NOOOO!
I'M SORRY, KRIS, I'M SORRY, KRIS...
UPLOAD IT.
UPLOADING... UPLOADING. DONE.
NOW KILL 'EM *ALL*.
BANG
BANG
BANG

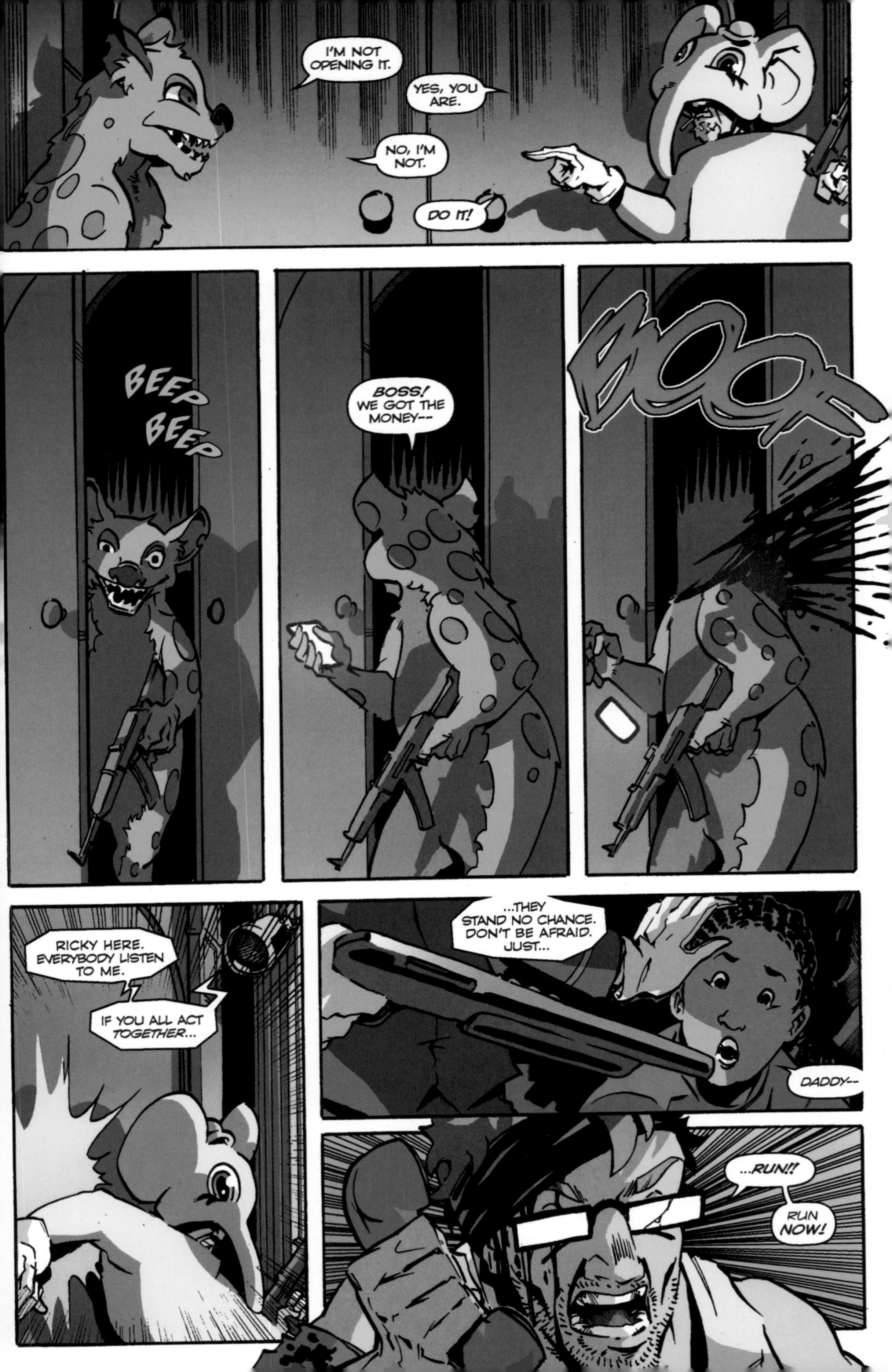
I'M NOT OPENING IT.
YES, YOU ARE.
NO, I'M NOT.
DO IT!
BEEP BEEP
BOSS! WE GOT THE MONEY--
BOOF
RICKY HERE. EVERYBODY LISTEN TO ME.
IF YOU ALL ACT TOGETHER...
...THEY STAND NO CHANCE. DON'T BE AFRAID. JUST...
DADDY--
...RUN!!
RUN NOW!

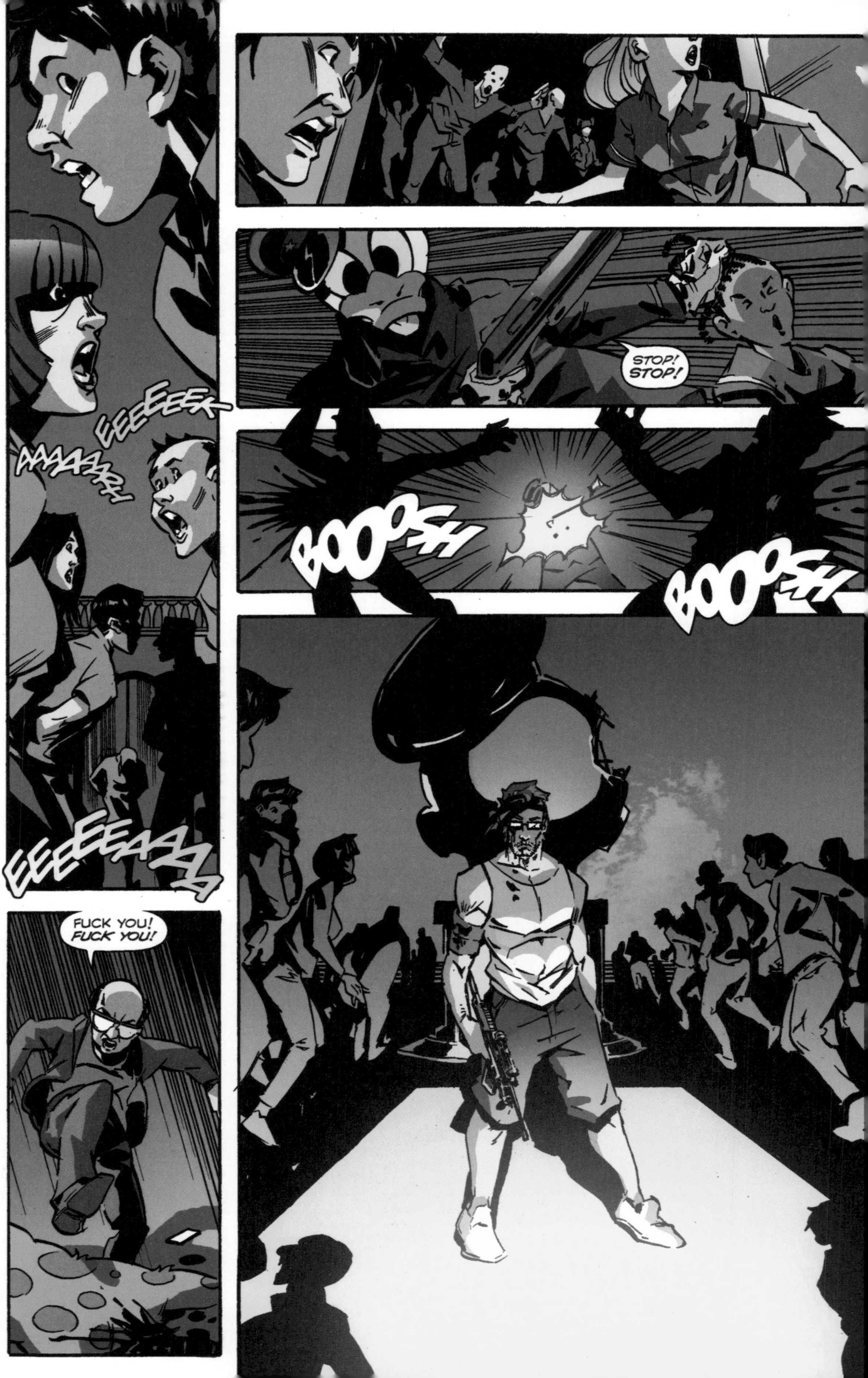
EEEEEEK
AAAAARGH
EEEEEAAAAA
STOP! STOP!
BOOOSH
BOOOSH
FUCK YOU! FUCK YOU!

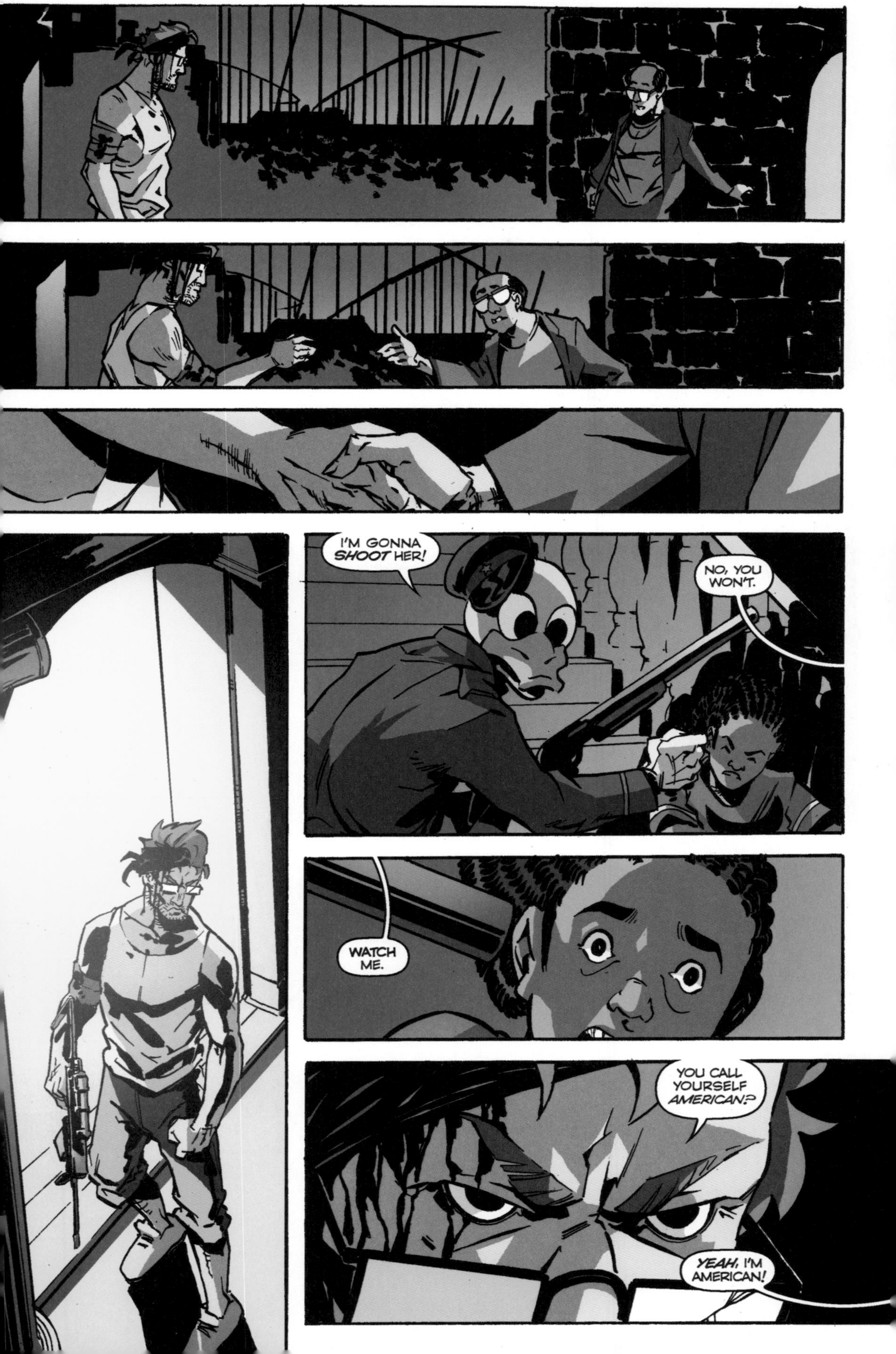
I'M GONNA SHOOT HER!
NO, YOU WON'T.
WATCH ME.
YOU CALL YOURSELF AMERICAN?
YEAH, I'M AMERICAN!

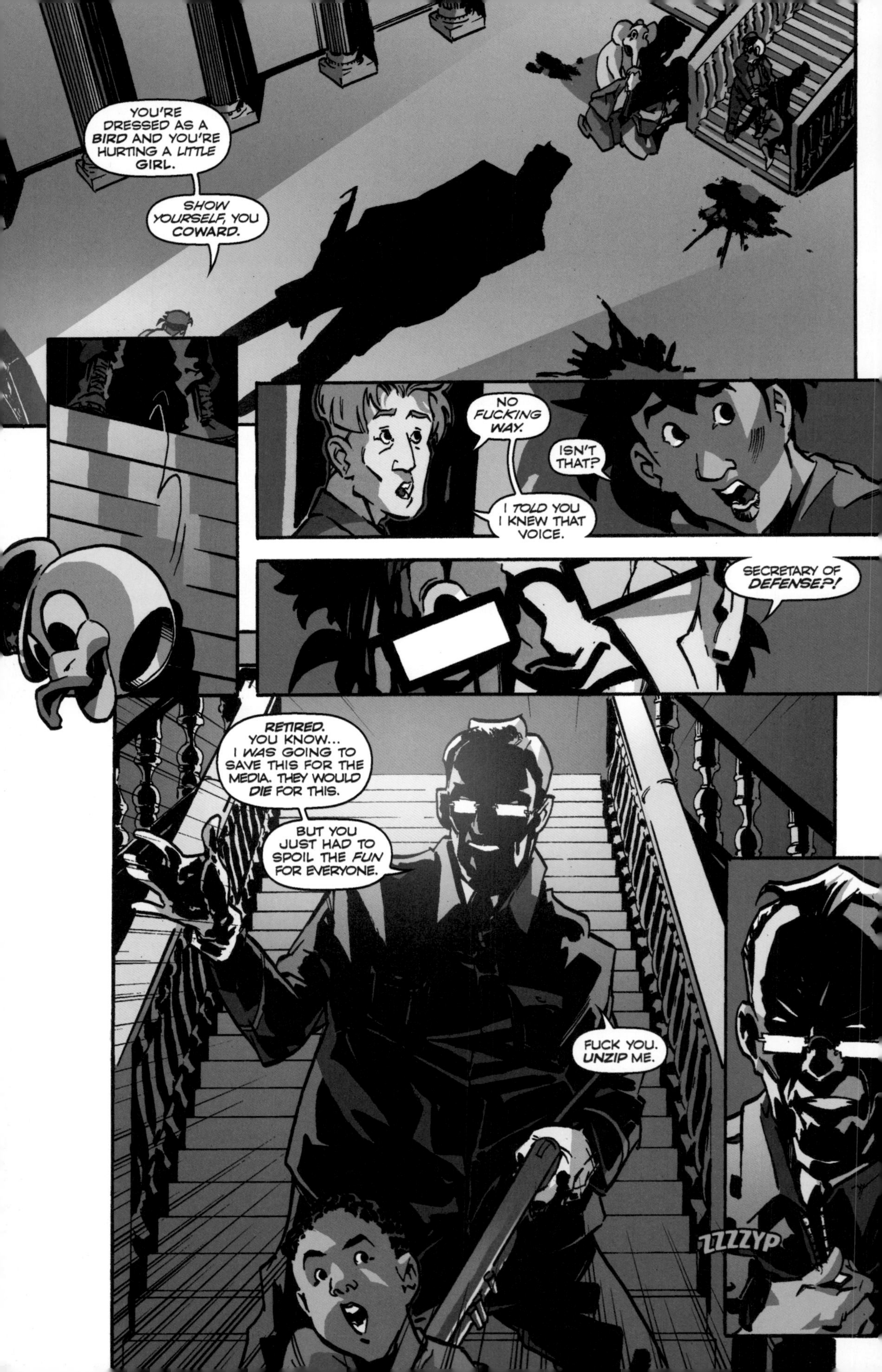
YOU'RE DRESSED AS A BIRD AND YOU'RE HURTING A LITTLE GIRL.
SHOW YOURSELF, YOU COWARD.
NO FUCKING WAY.
I TOLD YOU I KNEW THAT VOICE.
ISN'T THAT?
SECRETARY OF DEFENSE?!
RETIRED. YOU KNOW... I WAS GOING TO SAVE THIS FOR THE MEDIA. THEY WOULD DIE FOR THIS.
BUT YOU JUST HAD TO SPOIL THE FUN FOR EVERYONE.
FUCK YOU. UNZIP ME.
ZZZZYP

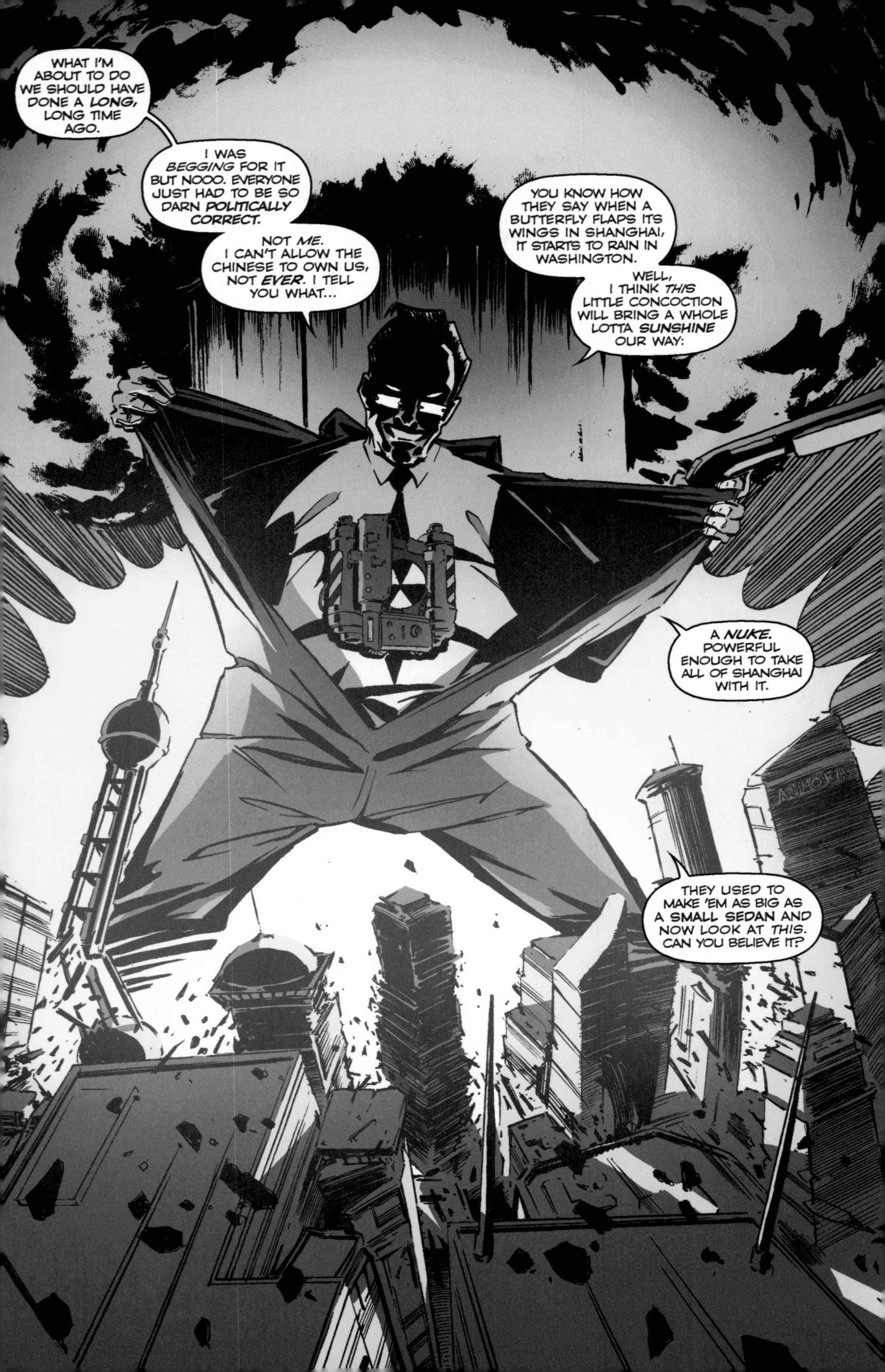
WHAT I'M ABOUT TO DO WE SHOULD HAVE DONE A *LONG*, LONG TIME AGO.
I WAS *BEGGING* FOR IT BUT NOOO. EVERYONE JUST HAD TO BE SO DARN ***POLITICALLY CORRECT.***
NOT *ME.* I CAN'T ALLOW THE CHINESE TO OWN US, NOT ***EVER***. I TELL YOU WHAT...
YOU KNOW HOW THEY SAY WHEN A BUTTERFLY FLAPS ITS WINGS IN SHANGHAI, IT STARTS TO RAIN IN WASHINGTON.
WELL, I THINK *THIS* LITTLE CONCOCTION WILL BRING A WHOLE LOTTA ***SUNSHINE*** OUR WAY:
A ***NUKE.*** POWERFUL ENOUGH TO TAKE ALL OF SHANGHAI WITH IT.
THEY USED TO MAKE 'EM AS BIG AS A **SMALL SEDAN** AND NOW LOOK AT *THIS.* CAN YOU BELIEVE IT?
AURORA

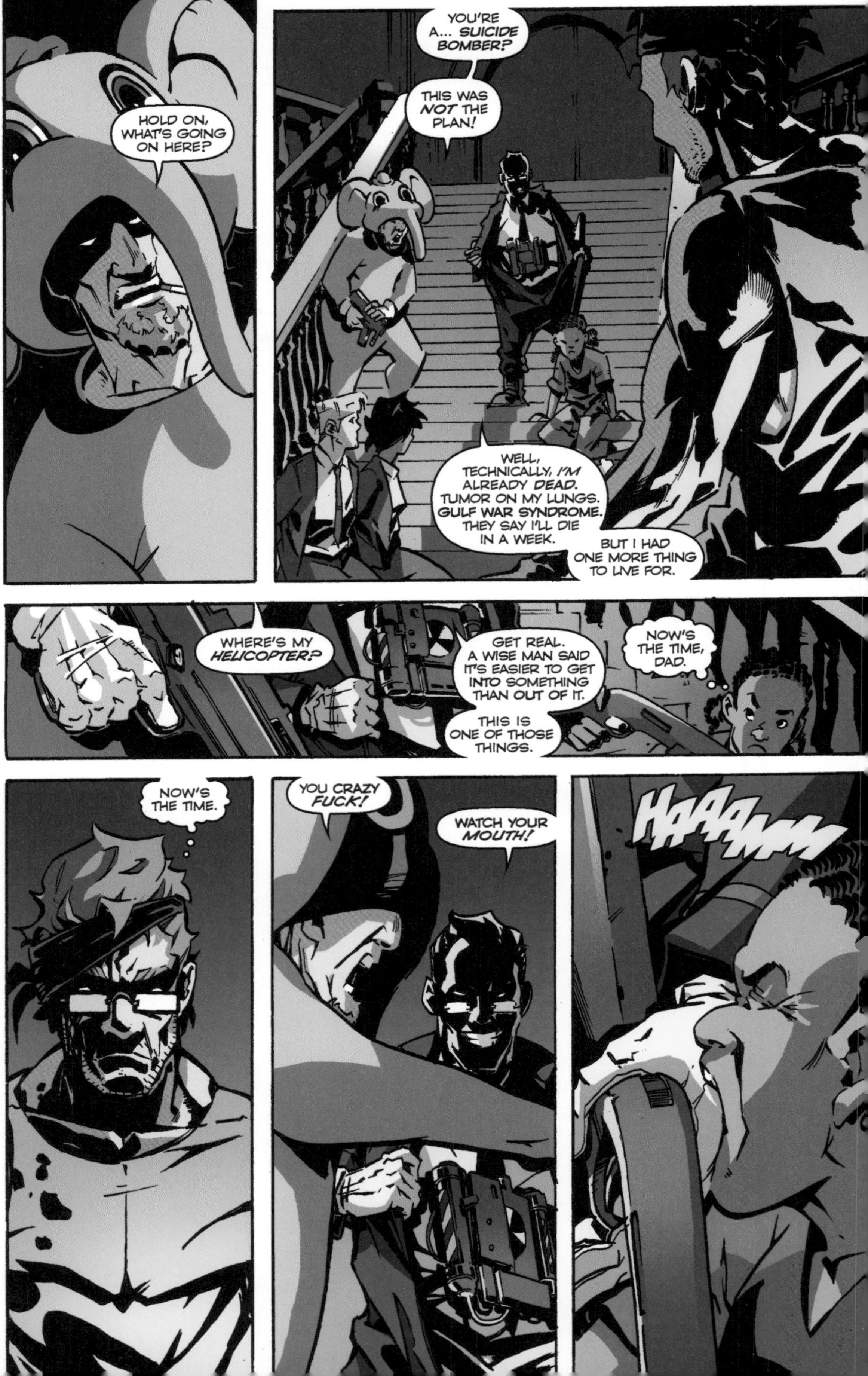
HOLD ON, WHAT'S GOING ON HERE?
YOU'RE A... SUICIDE BOMBER?
THIS WAS NOT THE PLAN!
WELL, TECHNICALLY, I'M ALREADY DEAD. TUMOR ON MY LUNGS. GULF WAR SYNDROME. THEY SAY I'LL DIE IN A WEEK.
BUT I HAD ONE MORE THING TO LIVE FOR.
WHERE'S MY HELICOPTER?
GET REAL. A WISE MAN SAID IT'S EASIER TO GET INTO SOMETHING THAN OUT OF IT.
THIS IS ONE OF THOSE THINGS.
NOW'S THE TIME, DAD.
NOW'S THE TIME.
YOU CRAZY FUCK!
WATCH YOUR MOUTH!
HAAAMM

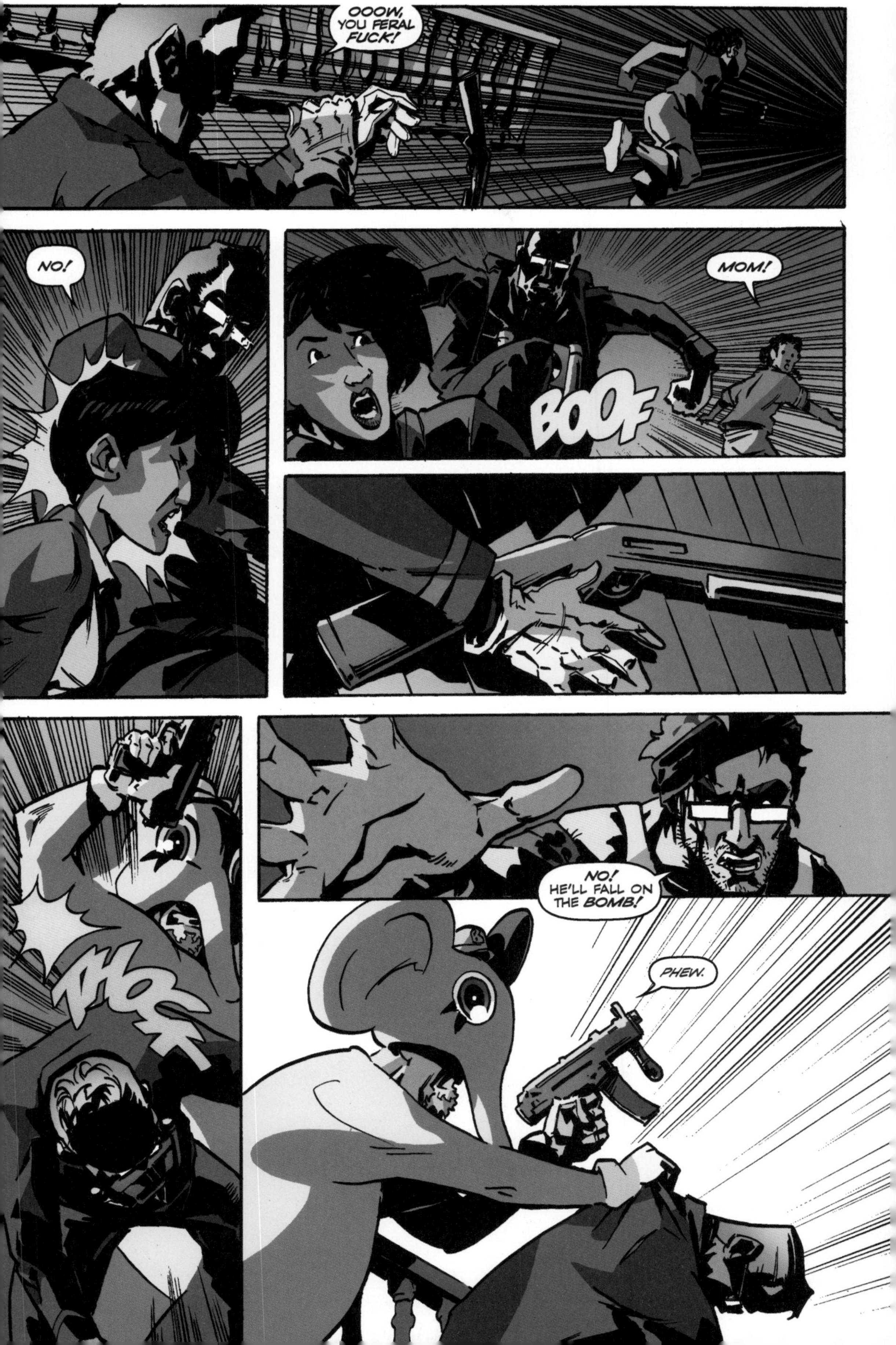
OOOW, YOU FERAL FUCK!
NO!
MOM!
BOOF
THOCK
NO! HE'LL FALL ON THE BOMB!
PHEW.

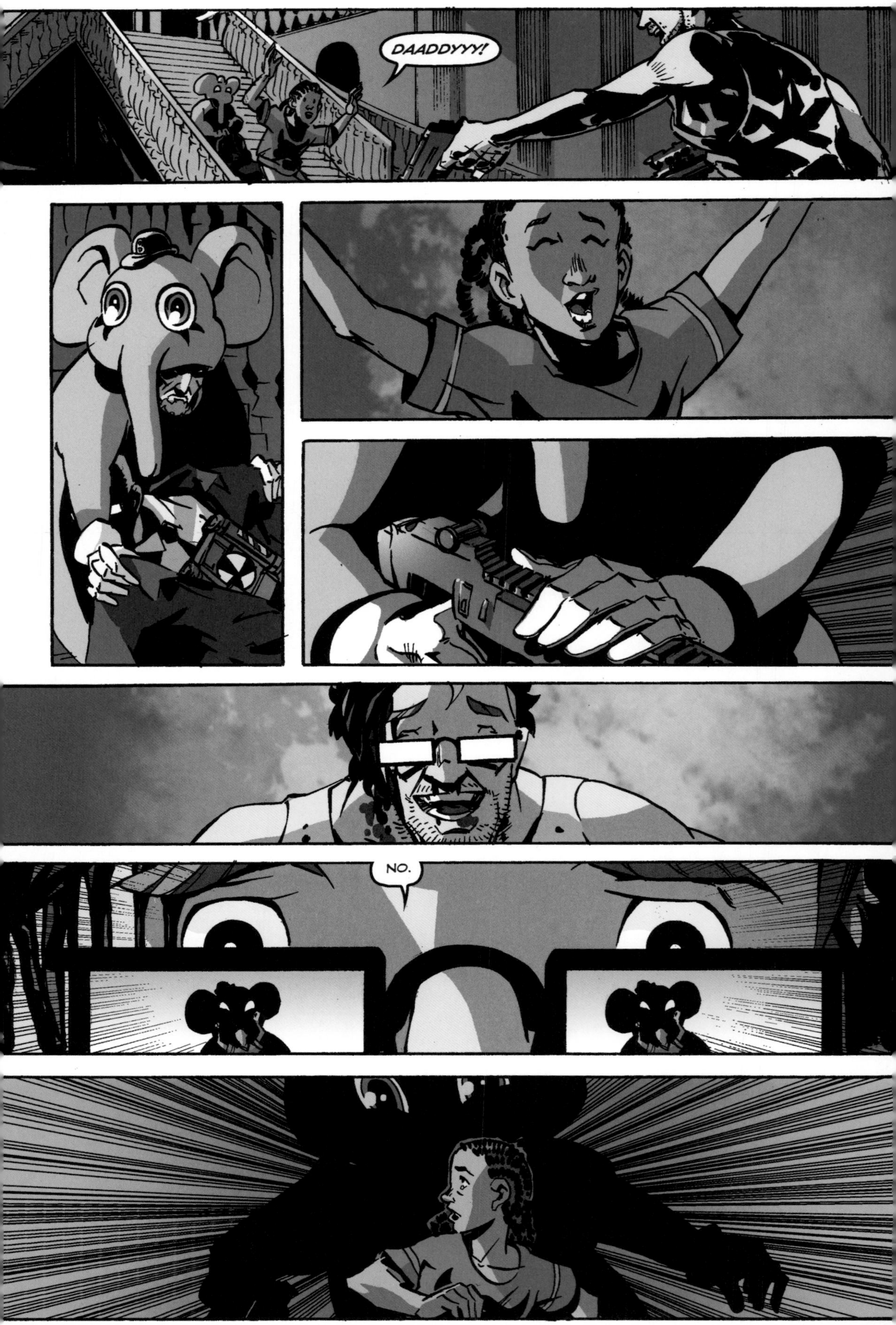
DAADDYYY!
NO.

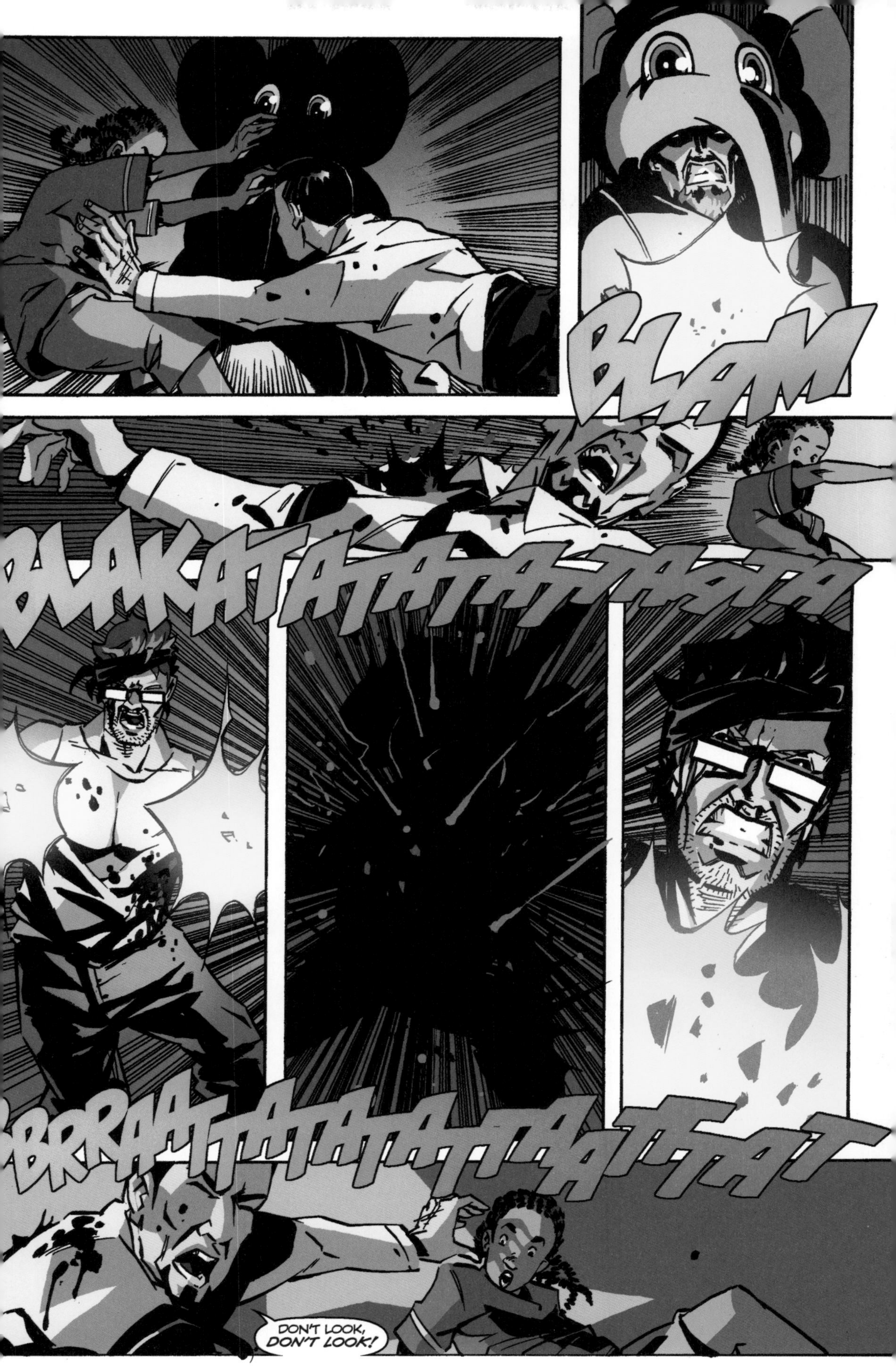
BLAM
BLAKATATATATATATA
BRRAATTATATATATATATTAT
DON'T LOOK,
DON'T LOOK!

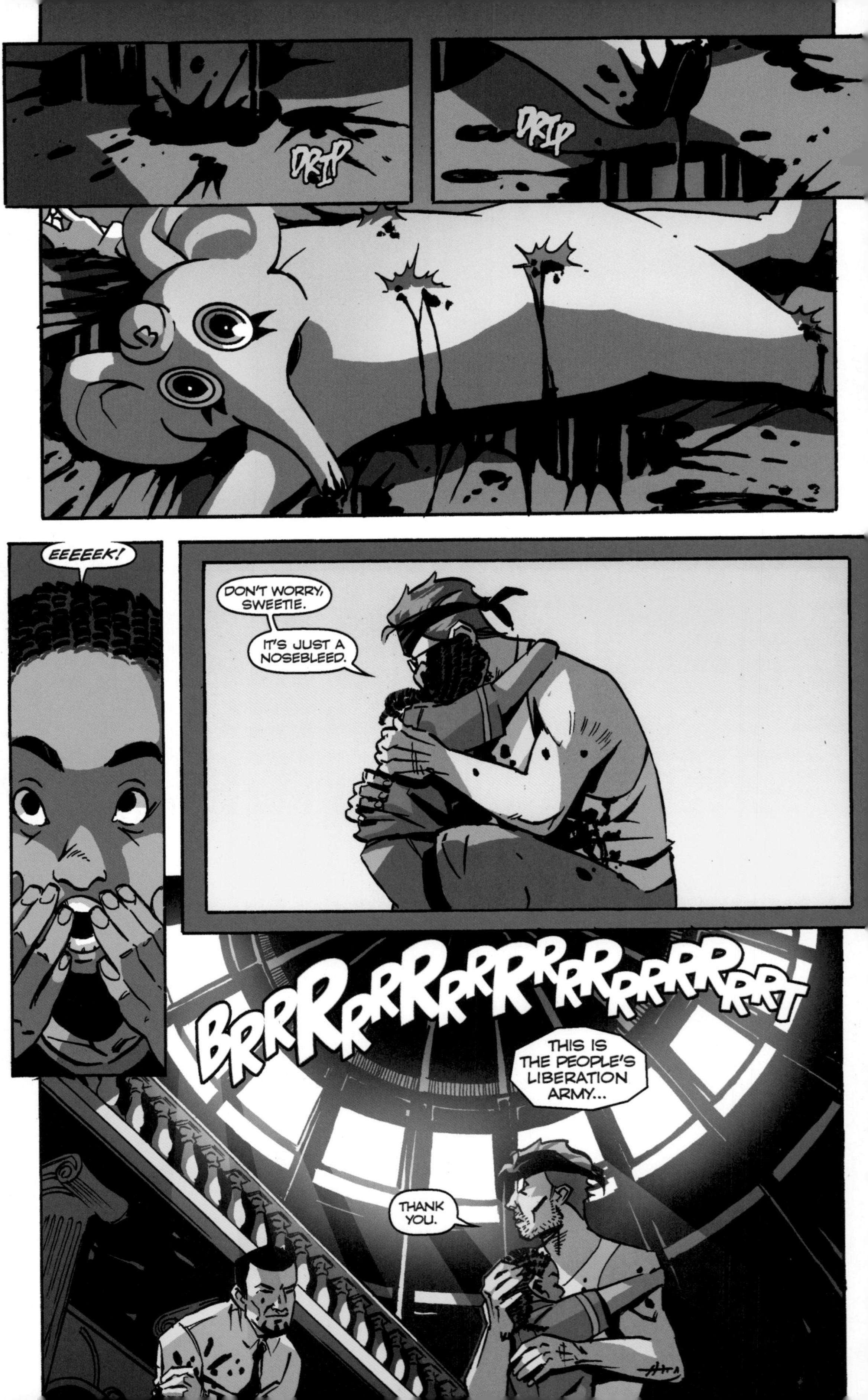
DRIP
DRIP
EEEEEK!
DON'T WORRY, SWEETIE.
IT'S JUST A NOSEBLEED.
BRRRRRRRRRRRRRRRRRT
THIS IS THE PEOPLE'S LIBERATION ARMY...
THANK YOU.

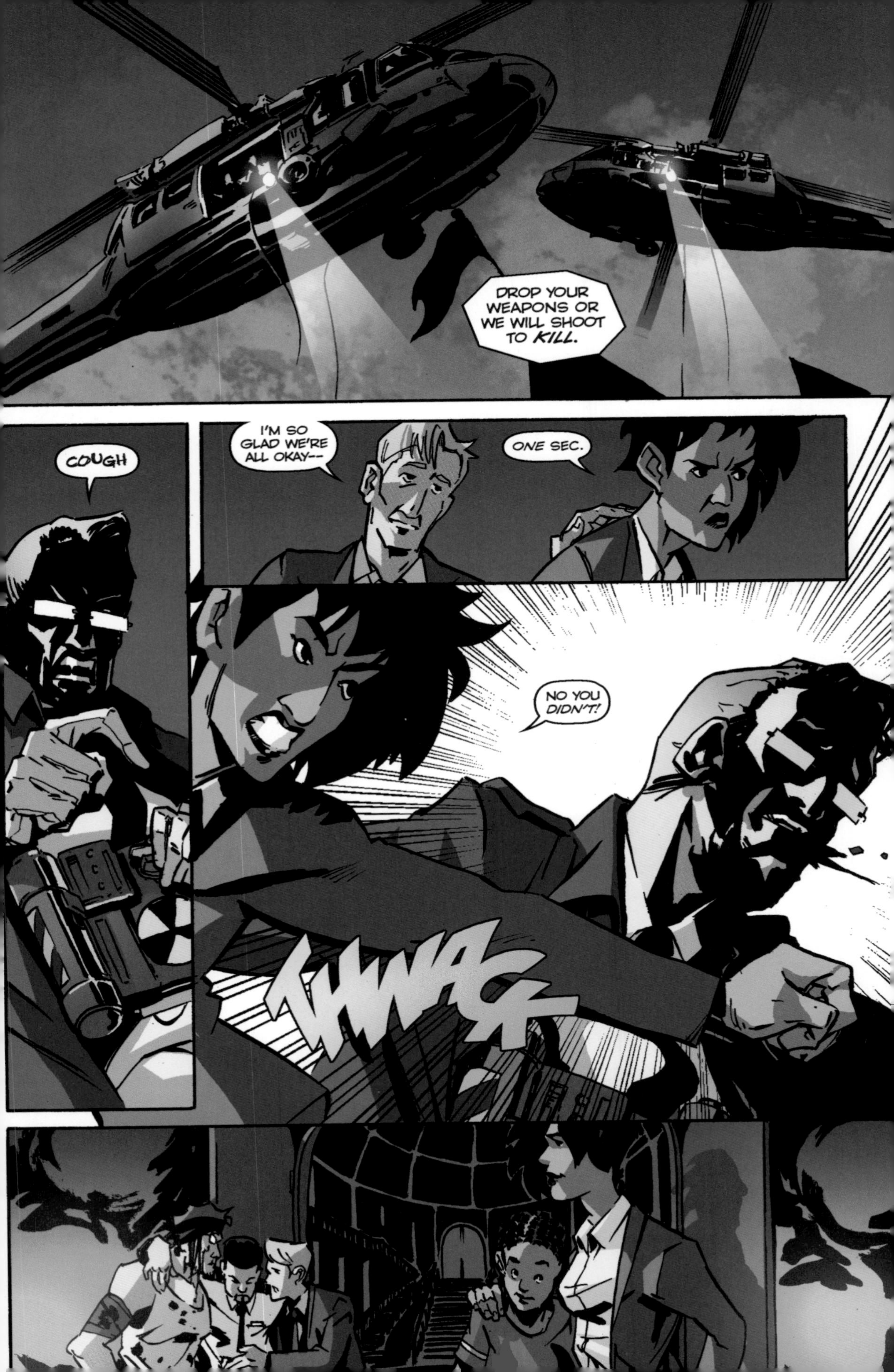
DROP YOUR WEAPONS OR WE WILL SHOOT TO KILL.
COUGH
I'M SO GLAD WE'RE ALL OKAY--
ONE SEC.
NO YOU DIDN'T!
THWACK

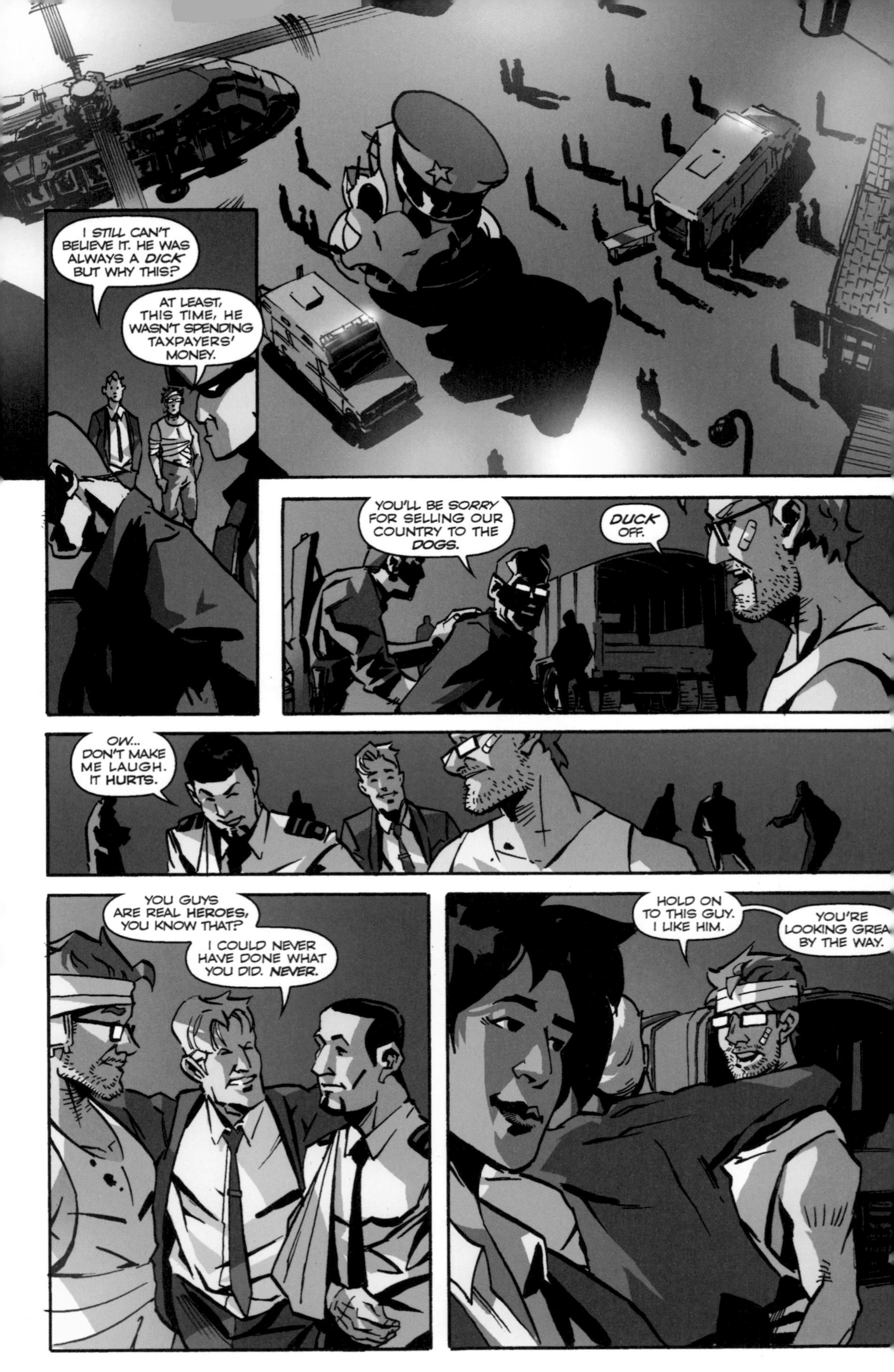
I STILL CAN'T BELIEVE IT. HE WAS ALWAYS A DICK BUT WHY THIS?
AT LEAST, THIS TIME, HE WASN'T SPENDING TAXPAYERS' MONEY.
YOU'LL BE SORRY FOR SELLING OUR COUNTRY TO THE DOGS.
DUCK OFF.
OW... DON'T MAKE ME LAUGH. IT HURTS.
YOU GUYS ARE REAL HEROES, YOU KNOW THAT?
I COULD NEVER HAVE DONE WHAT YOU DID. NEVER.
HOLD ON TO THIS GUY. I LIKE HIM.
YOU'RE LOOKING GREA
BY THE WAY.

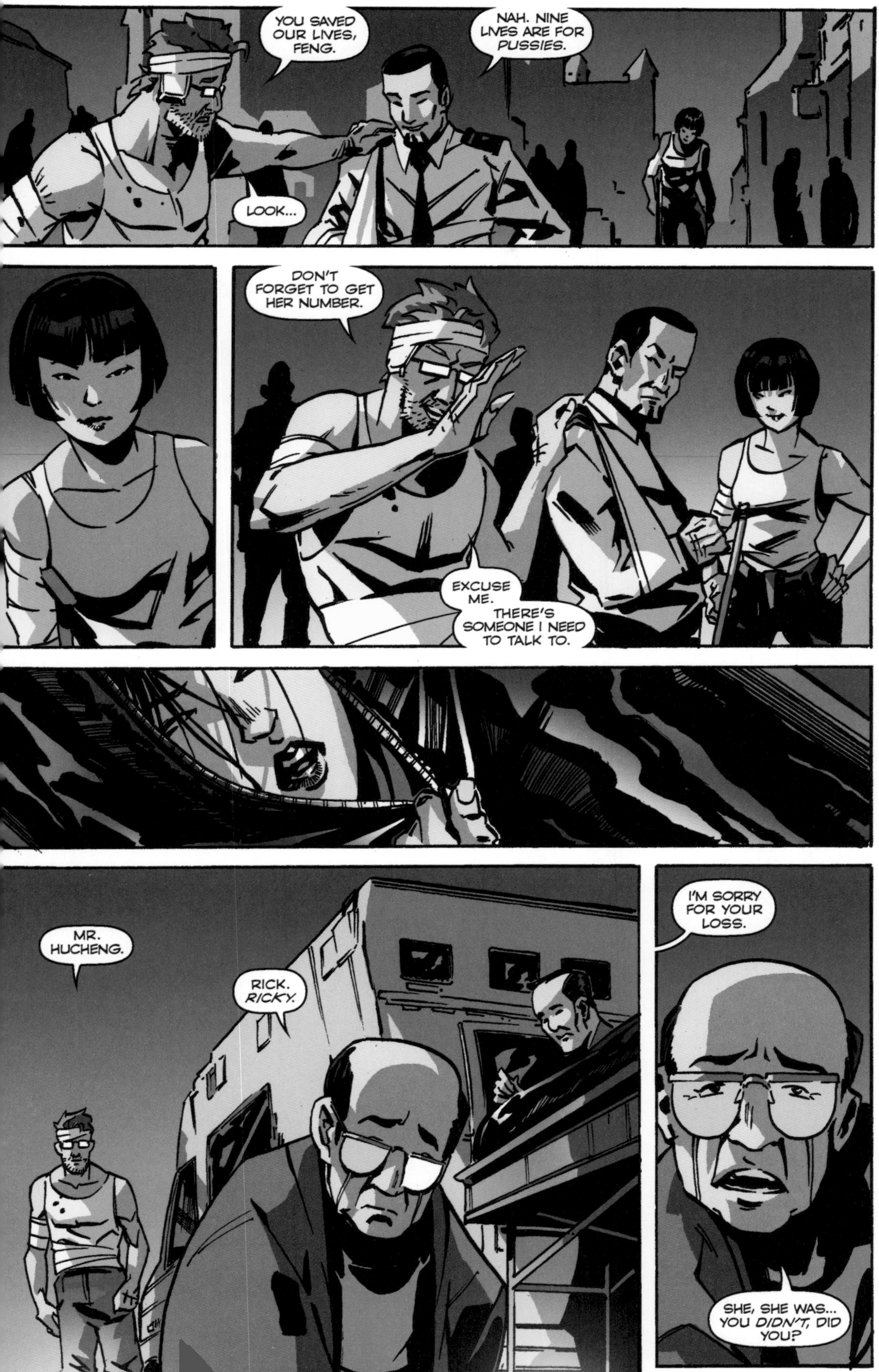
YOU SAVED OUR LIVES, FENG.
NAH. NINE LIVES ARE FOR *PUSSIES*.
LOOK...
DON'T FORGET TO GET HER NUMBER.
EXCUSE ME.
THERE'S SOMEONE I NEED TO TALK TO.
MR. HUCHENG.
RICK. *RICKY.*
I'M SORRY FOR YOUR LOSS.
SHE, SHE WAS... YOU *DIDN'T*, DID YOU?

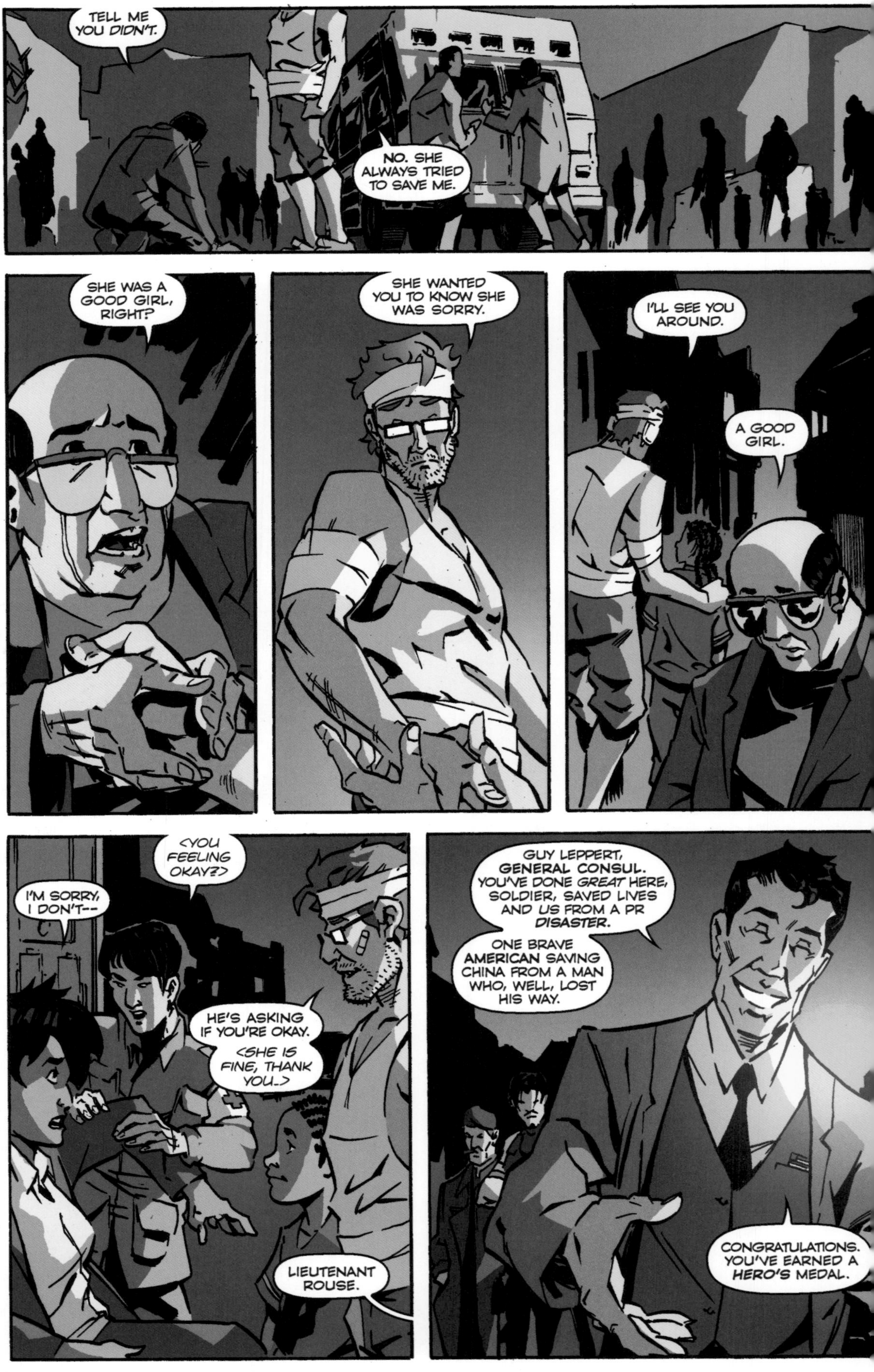
TELL ME YOU DIDN'T.
NO. SHE ALWAYS TRIED TO SAVE ME.
SHE WAS A GOOD GIRL, RIGHT?
SHE WANTED YOU TO KNOW SHE WAS SORRY.
I'LL SEE YOU AROUND.
A GOOD GIRL.
<YOU FEELING OKAY?>
I'M SORRY, I DON'T--
HE'S ASKING IF YOU'RE OKAY.
<SHE IS FINE, THANK YOU.>
LIEUTENANT ROUSE.
GUY LEPPERT, GENERAL CONSUL. YOU'VE DONE GREAT HERE, SOLDIER, SAVED LIVES AND US FROM A PR DISASTER.
ONE BRAVE AMERICAN SAVING CHINA FROM A MAN WHO, WELL, LOST HIS WAY.
CONGRATULATIONS. YOU'VE EARNED A HERO'S MEDAL.

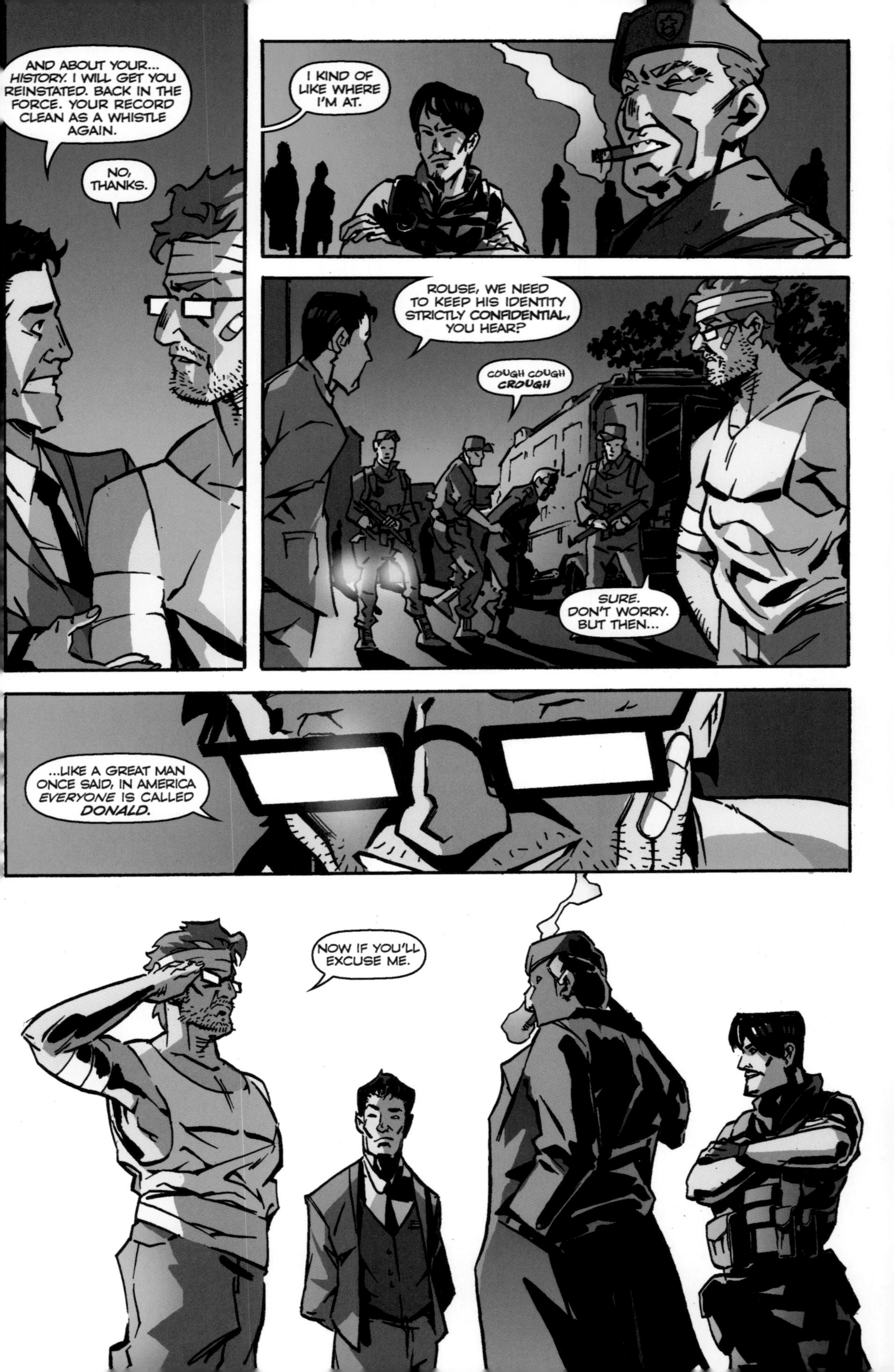
AND ABOUT YOUR... HISTORY. I WILL GET YOU REINSTATED. BACK IN THE FORCE. YOUR RECORD CLEAN AS A WHISTLE AGAIN.
NO, THANKS.
I KIND OF LIKE WHERE I'M AT.
ROUSE, WE NEED TO KEEP HIS IDENTITY STRICTLY CONFIDENTIAL, YOU HEAR?
COUGH COUGH CROUGH
SURE. DON'T WORRY. BUT THEN...
...LIKE A GREAT MAN ONCE SAID, IN AMERICA EVERYONE IS CALLED DONALD.
NOW IF YOU'LL EXCUSE ME.

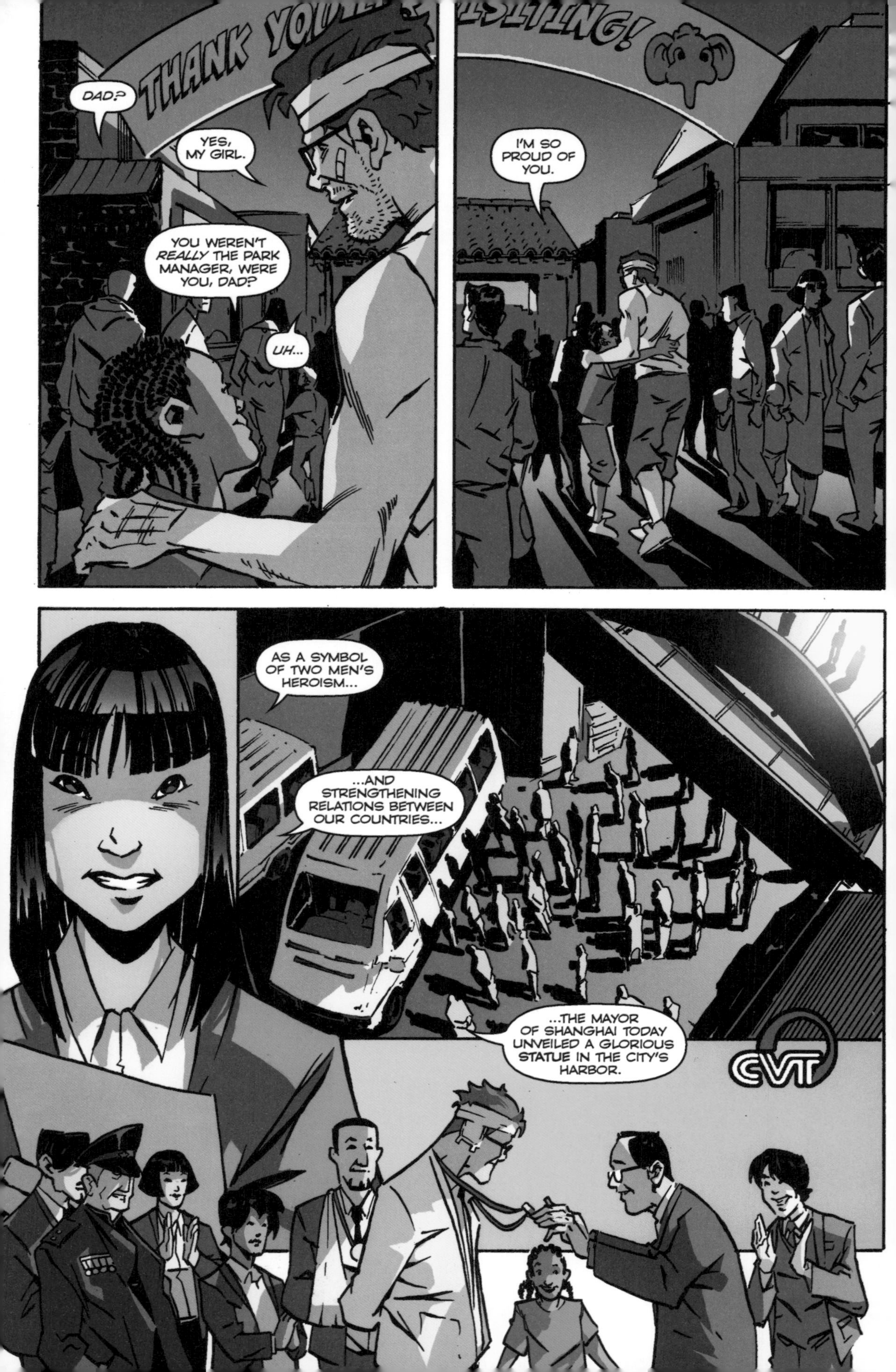
THANK YOU
DAD?
YES, MY GIRL.
YOU WEREN'T *REALLY* THE PARK MANAGER, WERE YOU, DAD?
UH...
I'M SO PROUD OF YOU.
AS A SYMBOL OF TWO MEN'S HEROISM...
...AND STRENGTHENING RELATIONS BETWEEN OUR COUNTRIES...
...THE MAYOR OF SHANGHAI TODAY UNVEILED A GLORIOUS STATUE IN THE CITY'S HARBOR.
CVT

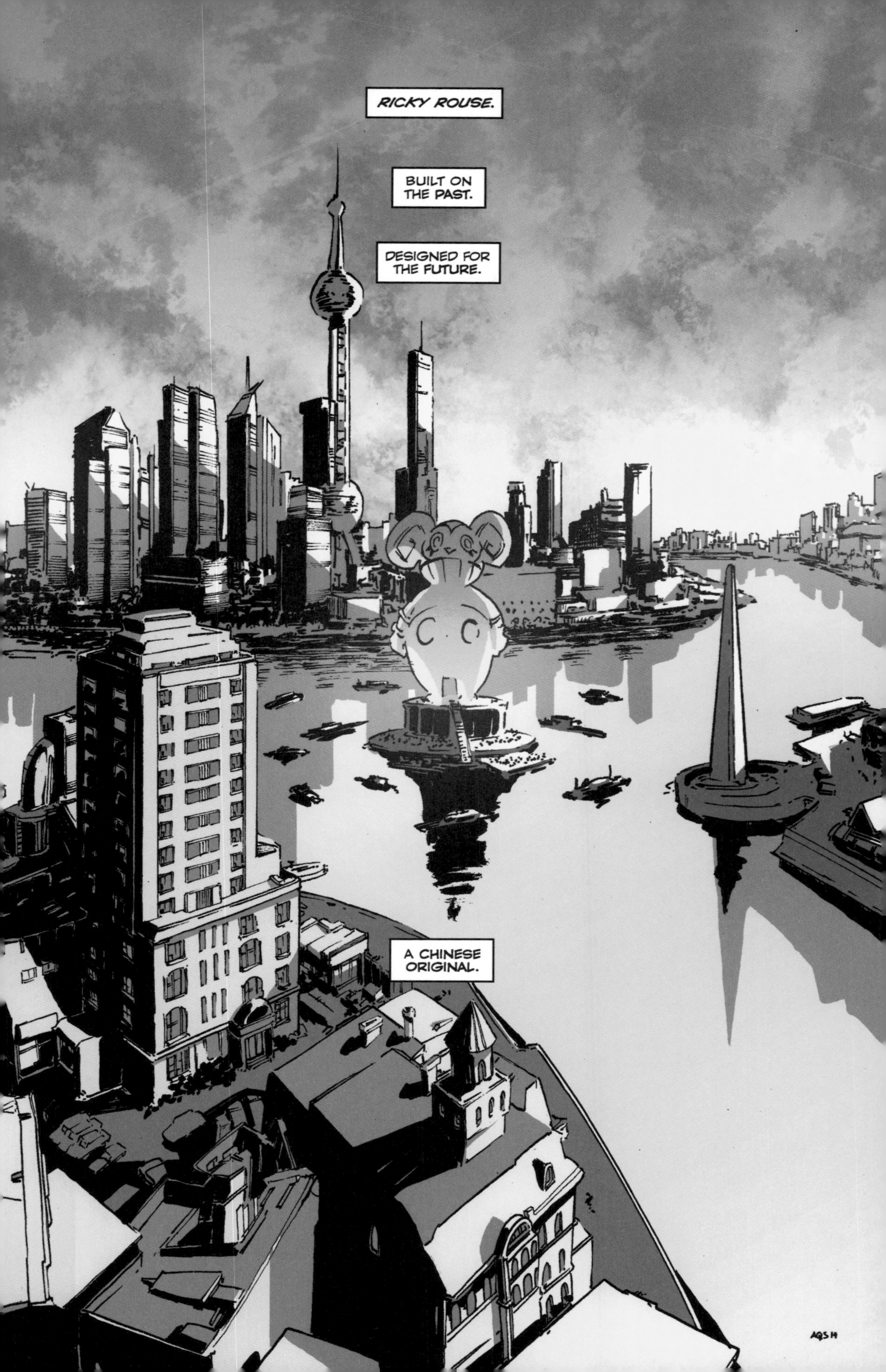

RICKY ROUSE.
BUILT ON THE PAST.
DESIGNED FOR THE FUTURE.
A CHINESE ORIGINAL.
AQS 14

ACKNOWLEDGEMENTS

I would like to thank...

John Aggs – Paul Duffield – Megan Elliott – Pauline Fowler – Danny Graydon – Linda Jaivin – Mark Jones – Allen Leitch, Dan Higgott and the whole SPOV gang – James Lavelle – Hugo Luczyc-Wyhowski – Matt Mason – Philip Munger – India Osborne – Tim Pilcher – Chris Sprigman – Lee Stone – Jamie White

...and everyone else who helped make this book a reality, especially Emma, Sam, Lizzie, Paul and Guillaume at SelfMadeHero. To them, I'd also like to apologise. For everything.

I'm dedicating this book to Alex, my tireless creative partner and the badass mother of our two children. Hopefully Olivia and Raphael will never feel the need to read this thing, or else how could they ever take me seriously?

Oh, and no real mascots were harmed in the making of this book. Only cheap knockoffs.

They deserved it.

– Jörg Tittel